2nd Edition

Technical Writing
for Success

Darlene Smith-Worthington

Sue Jefferson

THOMSON

SOUTH-WESTERN

Australia · Canada · Mexico · Singapore · Spain · United Kingdom · United States

THOMSON

SOUTH-WESTERN

Technical Writing for Success

Darlene Smith-Worthington and Sue Jefferson

VP/Editorial Director
Jack W. Calhoun

VP/Editor-in-Chief
Karen Schmohe

Executive Editor
Eve Lewis

Project Manager
Penny Shank

Consulting Editor
Anne Lynn Minick

VP/Director Educational Marketing
Carol Volz

Marketing Manager
Courtney Schulz

Marketing Coordinator
Linda Kuper

Production Editor
Darrell E. Frye

Production Manager
Patricia Matthews Boies

Manufacturing Coordinator
Kevin Kluck

Media Developmental Editor
Matthew McKinney

Art Director
Stacy Jenkins Shirley

Production House
New England Typographic Service (NETS)

Cover Designer
Joe Pagliaro Graphic Design

Cover Images
©PhotoDisc, Inc.

Internal Designer
Joe Pagliaro Graphic Design

Printer
Courier – Kendalville

For more information contact South-Western,
5191 Natorp Boulevard,
Mason, Ohio, 45040.
Or you can visit our Internet site at: http://www.swlearning.com

Page 4, "Rebuilding Your Engine" reprinted with permission of Summit Racing Equipment, Akron, Ohio.

Page 151, Figure 6.4, Graphic reprinted with permission of Susan Q. Nobles, Pitt Community College, Greenville, NC.

Your Communication Solution

PREFACE

Welcome to *Technical Writing for Success*! If developing skills for a successful future is important to you, this textbook was designed for you. We believe there is a need for a technical writing textbook that is lively and relevant for students and easy to use and effective for instructors.

Technical Writing for Success offers a usable, relevant, comprehensive, and appropriate text. This highly readable book will motivate you to use the thinking, listening, composing, revising, editing, and speaking skills employers demand in the workplace.

SKILLS FOR FUTURE SUCCESS

Technology is changing our world almost daily, and successful employees (and students) will be those who:

- Communicate effectively with others at all levels, both inside and outside the organization.

- Learn and change as the demands of the workplace change.

- Work in teams.

- Use technology to get the job done efficiently and economically.

- Think critically and solve problems.

- Make important decisions.

Success in the workplace begins in the classroom as students develop the skills they will need to compete in a global economy.

PHILOSOPHY

Technical Writing for Success supports these beliefs about the teaching of technical communication:

- Students learn more readily when they have a need for the knowledge or the skill being taught and when they perceive the learning as relevant.

- Technical communication complements, rather than conflicts with, traditional English and literature instruction.

- Students must take responsibility for their learning.

- Technical communication classrooms should be active and interactive places as students apply communication skills they are learning.

- Students develop critical thinking skills through discovery learning.

- Students benefit from collaborative learning activities.

- Students are especially motivated to improve communication skills when the topic relates to their area of career interest and when the skills are taught in that technical context.

- Effective teaching starts with the familiar and moves toward new concepts and skills.

TOOLS FOR DEVELOPING SKILLS

Technical Writing for Success was designed to encourage students to acquire many workplace skills through integrated and applied instruction. It features:

- an engaging writing style
- student and real-world models
- writing process instruction
- editing and revision checklists
- technical reading guidelines
- write-to-learn activities
- employment communications
- terms and definitions
- case studies
- collaborative activities

- technical writing style tips
- audience analysis instruction
- discovery learning opportunities
- primary and secondary research
- anecdotes and examples, including Focus on Ethics, Communication Update, See the Sites, Communication Dilemma, and Writing@Work

MESSAGE TO THE STUDENT

How important is technical communication for you? If you aren't certain, read advertisements for jobs or ask employers what skills are necessary. In the employment and academic world, you can be only as effective as your communication skills will allow you to be. No matter how proficient your technical skills, if you cannot communicate your ideas to others you cannot function successfully.

While technical communication skills are essential, gaining those skills should not be a painful process. In fact, one of the aims of this textbook is to be lively and connected to your interests. You may even be surprised that technical communication builds on your composition skills but is not like English or writing classes you have had before.

ABOUT THE AUTHORS

Darlene Smith-Worthington and Sue Jefferson are full-time teachers who are enthusiastic and earnest supporters of education that prepares people for the world of work. Darlene Smith-Worthington is a community college instructor who also has experience editing a weekly newspaper, directing public relations for a junior college, and managing small businesses, including a farming operation. Sue Jefferson has taught in private and public school systems (both middle and high school), and in a university. In addition to teaching, she has owned and managed a restaurant and a local weekly magazine. Currently, she chairs the English and Humanities Department at Pitt Community College.

Both authors have taught technical writing for more than 18 years. Using their business backgrounds and their combined 40 years' teaching experience, the authors present real-world-based reporting materials and sensible, useful teaching suggestions.

HOW TO USE THIS BOOK

The following features are included to enhance learning:

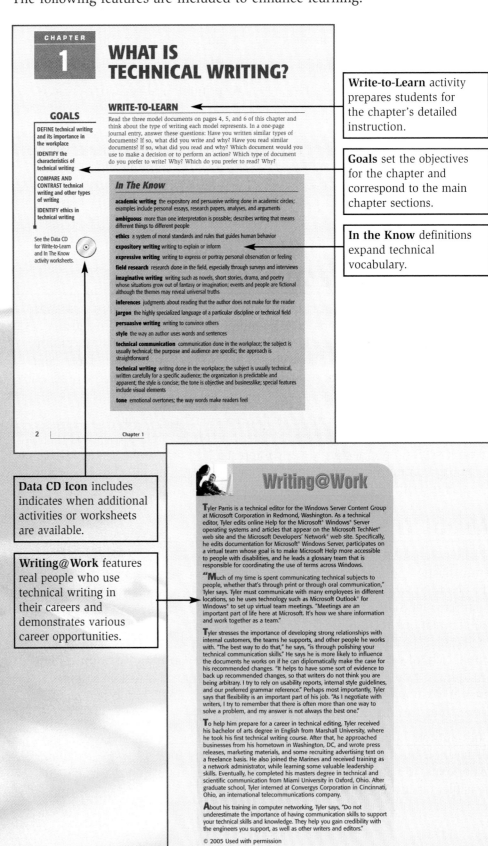

Write-to-Learn activity prepares students for the chapter's detailed instruction.

Goals set the objectives for the chapter and correspond to the main chapter sections.

In the Know definitions expand technical vocabulary.

Data CD Icon includes indicates when additional activities or worksheets are available.

Writing@Work features real people who use technical writing in their careers and demonstrates various career opportunities.

CHAPTER

1

WHAT IS TECHNICAL WRITING?

WRITE-TO-LEARN

Read the three model documents on pages 4, 5, and 6 of this chapter and think about the type of writing each model represents. In a one-page journal entry, answer these questions: Have you written similar types of documents? If so, what did you write and why? Have you read similar documents? If so, what did you read and why? Which document would you use to make a decision or to perform an action? Which type of document do you prefer to write? Why? Which do you prefer to read? Why?

GOALS

DEFINE technical writing and its importance in the workplace

IDENTIFY the characteristics of technical writing

COMPARE AND CONTRAST technical writing and other types of writing

IDENTIFY ethics in technical writing

See the Data CD for Write-to-Learn and In The Know activity worksheets.

In The Know

academic writing the expository and persuasive writing done in academic circles; examples include personal essays, research papers, analyses, and arguments

ambiguous more than one interpretation is possible; describes writing that means different things to different people

ethics a system of moral standards and rules that guides human behavior

expository writing writing to explain or inform

expressive writing writing to express or portray personal observation or feeling

field research research done in the field, especially through surveys and interviews

imaginative writing writing such as novels, short stories, drama, and poetry whose situations grow out of fantasy or imagination; events and people are fictional although the themes may reveal universal truths

inferences judgments about reading that the author does not make for the reader

jargon the highly specialized language of a particular discipline or technical field

persuasive writing writing to convince others

style the way an author uses words and sentences

technical communication communication done in the workplace; the subject is usually technical; the purpose and audience are specific; the approach is straightforward

technical writing writing done in the workplace; the subject is usually technical, written carefully for a specific audience; the organization is predictable and apparent; the style is concise; the tone is objective and businesslike; special features include visual elements

tone emotional overtones; the way words make readers feel

2 | Chapter 1

Writing@Work

Tyler Parris is a technical editor for the Windows Server Content Group at Microsoft Corporation in Redmond, Washington. As a technical editor, Tyler edits online Help for the Microsoft® Windows® Server operating systems and articles that appear on the Microsoft TechNet® web site and the Microsoft Developers' Network® web site. Specifically, he edits documentation for Microsoft® Windows Server, participates on a virtual team whose goal is to make Microsoft Help more accessible to people with disabilities, and he leads a glossary team that is responsible for coordinating the use of terms across Windows.

"Much of my time is spent communicating technical subjects to people, whether that's through print or through oral communication," Tyler says. Tyler must communicate with many employees in different locations, so he uses technology such as Microsoft Outlook® for Windows® to set up virtual team meetings. "Meetings are an important part of life here at Microsoft. It's how we share information and work together as a team."

Tyler stresses the importance of developing strong relationships with internal customers, the teams he supports, and other people he works with. "The best way to do that," he says, "is through polishing your technical communication skills." He says he is more likely to influence the documents he works on if he can diplomatically make the case for his recommended changes. "It helps to have some sort of evidence to back up recommended changes, so that writers do not think you are being arbitrary. I try to rely on usability reports, internal style guidelines, and our preferred grammar reference." Perhaps most importantly, Tyler says that flexibility is an important part of his job. "As I negotiate with writers, I try to remember that there is often more than one way to solve a problem, and my answer is not always the best one."

To help him prepare for a career in technical editing, Tyler received his bachelor of arts degree in English from Marshall University, where he took his first technical writing course. After that, he approached businesses from his hometown in Washington, DC, and wrote press releases, marketing materials, and some recruiting advertising text on a freelance basis. He also joined the Marines and received training as a network administrator, while learning some valuable leadership skills. Eventually, he completed his masters degree in technical and scientific communication from Miami University in Oxford, Ohio. After graduate school, Tyler interned at Convergys Corporation in Cincinnati, Ohio, an international telecommunications company.

About his training in computer networking, Tyler says, "Do not underestimate the importance of having communication skills to support your technical skills and knowledge. They help you gain credibility with the engineers you support, as well as other writers and editors."

© 2005 Used with permission

What Is Technical Writing? | 3

Rebuilding Your Engine

Excessive **smoking** or **knocking** could mean it's time to rebuild your engine. When it comes time to rebuild, consider Summit's 1) Engine Kits or 2) Re-Ring Kits.

Engine Kits
Engine kits can be purchased with one of the following combinations:

- premium forged TRW pistons and moly rings,
- premium cast TRW pistons with moly rings, or
- cast TRW pistons with regular rings.

The kits also come with TRW main, cam and rod bearings; a TRW high volume oil pump; top quality Fel-Pro Blue Perma Torque gaskets; a set of oil and freeze plugs; and Clevite assembly lube. See Table 1 for a cost breakdown.

Re-Ring Kits
If your present pistons are in good shape and you don't need main and cam bearings or an oil pump, Re-Rings Kits may work. They include regular or moly rings, rod bearings, and a Fel-Prol Blue Berma Torque gasket set. See Table 2 for. . . .

Table 1 Engine Kits			
Engine	Our Good Kit: Case Pistons Regular Rings	Our Better Kit: Cast Pistons Moly Rings	Our Best Kit: Forged Pistons Moly Rings
Chevy 327 '62-'66	$214.95	$219.95	$308.95
Chevy 350	$172.95	$184.95	$298.95

Reprinted wi
Figure 1.1 Tech

4

> **Opening real-world model** adds relevance to the chapter.

A PROCESS FOR TECHNICAL WRITING

So far you've learned why people write at work; how to plan for audience, purpose, scope, and medium; and how to conduct research. Now that you're ready to write, how do you begin? Where will the words come from to fill the pages of your document? They will come from you through a process of **planning, drafting, revising, copyediting,** and **publishing**—otherwise known as the **writing process.**

The writing process used by technical writers has much in common with the writing process used by any writer: the essayist, novelist, journalist, or songwriter. How consideration of au spend the early sta technical data requ graphics and page

Furthermore, tech software becomes writing process wi familiar with.

To learn about the Ashley makes as s educators. She is o of researching new

When Ashley first will be; she knows to improve instruc the process, from o

WARM UP

Think of the last writing assignment you completed. Maybe it was a letter or a report for class. What process did you follow? What did you do first? second? third? and so forth?

See the two Letters to Students on the nature of the writing process, which are located on the Data CD.

> **Warm Up** activity in every section focuses students on what they already know about the subject.

TONE

Tone describes the emotional flavor (the way the words make you feel) of a document. The tone of a document also gives the audience an idea of the kind of document they are reading.

The tone of the personal essay is casual. The tone of the research paper is objective. The tone in technical writing is best described as objective or businesslike.

The expressive nature of a personal essay can run a range of emotions—sadness, excitement, irony, humor. The aim of research papers or technical documents is not to convey emotion. In fact, emotion can get in the way of a technical document.

Readers of technical documents read for information, not for entertainment. They read to learn something or to take action. Some say technical writing is boring because of its lack of emotion. For the person needing or wanting that information, the topic is not boring.

Focus on Ethics

When you enter the workplace, you may be asked to sign a code of ethics, no matter what profession you pursue or where you work. Just as different careers generate different kinds of documents, different documents must follow a strict set of guidelines, laws, or principles outlined in the company's code of ethics.

Many companies have their code of ethics posted on the Internet for anyone to see. For example, large companies such as General Electric, Merrill Lynch, Kroger, and Eli Lilly post codes about a variety of concerns–from animal drug testing to diversity. Most likely, your school has a code of ethics that you follow.

Sometimes an individual's ethical code may conflict with others' behavior. If your personal ethics conflict with workplace practices, you can define yourself by how well you stand up for your own ethics. Doing so is not easy, however. If you discover that the company paying your salary is falsely advertising, you may find it can be difficult to criticize. If you believe that making fun of a person with a physical challenge is wrong, but you find yourself in a work group who is laughing at such a person, then your personal code conflicts with the group's. You need to be courageous to behave ethically, and such courage, although not always initially rewarded in the workplace, will help to establish yourself as an ethical employee, eventually.

Anderson, Paul V. *Technical Communication: A Reader-Centered Approach*
Harcourt Brace and Company, 1999.

> **Focus on Ethics** provides examples and scenarios of real-world ethical dilemmas for students to consider.

Stop and Think

Drawing from the activities in this section's Warm Up, write your own definition of technical writing. Make sure you incorporate concepts from this section, such as subject, organization, audience, style, tone, and special features.

> **Stop and Think** exercises conclude each section to check comprehension or to prepare students for the next section.

14   Chapter 1

Whichever technique you use will generate a collection of ideas you want to cover in the message or body. With all of the ideas before you, you can start to be critical. Cut the ones that are unnecessary and change those that do not communicate exactly what you want to say. Prewriting is also the time to rank ideas. Consider what you will place first, second, third, and so on.

PREWRITING E-MAILS

Prewriting for e-mail involves planning to communicate with readers who have diverse needs and expectations. First, remember that busy professionals may receive a great volume of e-mail. Thus, your SUBJECT line must be specific and descriptive; it should immediately show readers how the topic relates to them. If your SUBJECT line is poorly written, chances are the receiver will delete your message without reading it.

Second, consider the reader's expectations for formality and length. If you are sending an e-mail to people within your company or organization, you are likely to know the formality they expect by referring to other e-mails. For instance, the corporate climate may be formal, so readers might expect complete sentences, correct punctuation, and few or no abbreviations.

However, others with whom you communicate electronically may be more comfortable with informal e-mails—incomplete sentences; little punctuation; and the many abbreviations writers have developed to make online exchanges fast, such as *BTW* for *by the way* or *HAND* for *Have a nice day.*

In addition to level of formality, plan the length of your messages to meet readers' needs and expectations. Since people generally read e-mail from a computer screen rather than print hard copies, keep messages as brief as possible so that people can read the text without scrolling through several pages. Short messages also allow for easier response. If you have a long, involved message, send it as several different e-mails or create a document with a word processor and send the long document as an attachment.

Third, plan for diff[...]
such as bulleted lis[...]
the recipient's soft[...]

Fourth, clearly exp[...]
understand. For ex[...]
readers realize whi[...]

Finally, plan for ha[...]
harshly criticize ea[...]
angry. Wait until y[...]
Using all capital le[...]
when you intend t[...]
phrase with asteris[...]

Another way to co[...]
created on the key[...]
Yet writers must ca[...]
expressed in an e-[...]
misunderstood.

SEE THE SITES

To learn about writing processes for all types of correspondence, including business letters, e-mails, and memos, check out Colorado State's writing web site.

To view e-mail makeovers, articles about business writing, checklists to guide your writing, and more, log on to the E-write Online site. You can even take a quiz to test your e-mail know-how!

You can find the url for both sites in the web links on techwriting. swlearning.com.

See the Sites feature web sites that take students beyond the text and enhance communication concepts.

Communication Update contains information on cutting edge communication technologies.

Communication Update

Technical writers must be familiar with desktop publishing software to do their jobs. Using programs such as Microsoft® Word, Adobe® PageMaker®, or QuarkXPress™, they can apply special features to their documents, such as boldfacing, underlining, bulleted lists, tables, graphs, and diagrams. Most desktop publishing software even allows writers to make professional-looking newsletters, brochures, and books.

Use the Communication Update worksheet on the Data CD to practice applying special features.

In technical writing, the needs of the reader dictate every decision the writer makes. In the technical writing model, the writer worked hard to present the information the reader needs in a format that is easy to read. The headings, boldface type, special table, and no-frills language show that the writer is conscious of the reader.

ORGANIZATION

The personal essay and research paper make standard use of a topic sentence and transitional expressions, but you still need to read far into each document before the main point and the organization become apparent.

The technical writing model, however, uses headings to help you perceive the organization at a single glance before you read. The use of *1)* and *2)* in the first sentence helps draw your eye to the subject of this document before you read. Also, headings give readers an opportunity to read only what they want or need to read. When a customer who is interested in rebuilding an engine wants to price only the re-ring kits, the heading "Re-Ring Kits" allows his or her eye to travel quickly to the information needed.

SPECIAL FEATURES

The technical document is the only document of the three examples at the beginning of this chapter to use special features. Technical writers use special features such as bold, italics, capital letters, columns, underlining, and bulleted lists to draw attention to certain words and help important information stand out. Also, the use of graphics, such as tables, graphs, pictures, and diagrams, helps relay complex information quickly for the audience.

More than the research paper or personal essay, the technical document

---

Technical writers face a double challenge: not only must they write with clear, accurate, and specific words, but they also must design the document to look inviting and attractive. Technical writers, therefore, are production artists: writing with precision to locate the best word and sentence structure for the message *and* designing pages that combine a professional image with a user-friendly approach. To do so, technical writers use a tool of their trade: desktop publishing software that allows them to craft documents that meet their readers' needs.

STYLE

The **style** of a document usually gives an audience an idea of the type of document they are reading. For example, the personal essay is casual, almost conversational, and predictable for an essay. You are probably comfortable with this style, having written personal essays in school. The writer uses examples and some description. The style of the research paper is also predictable for a research paper.

The technical document uses a simple, concise, straightforward style that is easily understood. The long sentences are simply lists. The other sentences are short, and the sentence order is predictable. There are no surprises for the reader. The vocabulary is highly specialized, the **jargon** of the automotive technician.

Communication Dilemma

Isabel was recently assigned as the lead Technical Communicator on a team that is developing a high-profile software package known as SpeedQuest. She is responsible for coordinating communication between the programming team and the marketing team. For Isabel, this position means a likely promotion and career advancement. She knows a promotion would help her support her family, so she is eager to do a good job.

One evening Isabel overhears the lead computer programmer tell the project manager that SpeedQuest is not as advanced as advertised in the company's marketing materials. The programmer recommends delaying the launch date, but the project manager ignores the suggestion, deciding to issue a second release after the product is complete.

The next day in the meeting to discuss the marketing materials, Isabel struggles to decide whether she should list in the brochures SpeedQuest features that do not work yet. She knows the features would help sales of SpeedQuest. On the other hand, she knows that if she tells the truth and decides not to publish information about the features, she may not get the promotion she is counting on. What should Isabel do?

Communication Dilemma features provide real-world communication situations and questions to increase students' critical-thinking skills.

POINT YOUR
BROWSER
techwriting.swlearning.com

SUMMARY

1. Summaries and abstracts are condensed versions of longer documents. In a summary, the writer clearly and logically presents only main ideas. The length of the original and the writer's purpose determine the length of the summary. Abstracts are shorter than summaries and cover the main idea of the original.

2. A mechanism description describes the main parts of a device or mechanism and tells the purpose of the mechanism and overall design, what the various parts are, what they look like, and what their functions are.

3. Trip reports tell supervisors and coworkers what was gained from a business trip. The report includes only the most helpful details of the trip.

4. Incident reports, also called accident reports, describe an unusual incident or occurrence.

5. Progress reports describe the status of work on one particular project for a specified period.

6. Periodic reports describe the progress of all ongoing projects in an organization or an organization division during a specified time period.

7. Progress and periodic reports require writers to consider the interests of the audience and the schedule of the project or the organization.

Summary reviews the key concepts of the chapter.

Checklist ◄

Checklist encourages students to be responsible for their own success.

■ Have I designed, organized, and written the document with the audience in mind?

■ Have I analyzed my audiences and determined what readers need to know?

Build On What You Know

1. The statements listed in *a* through *j* will go into a progress report. Identify each statement as Work Completed, Work Scheduled, or Problems/Projections.

   a. We have purchased a site license from NetBright for our network.

   b. The CD-ROM, which was delivered last Friday, was damaged in shipping so that it is inoperable.

   c. We installed screensavers on all computers.

   d. If all work scheduled is completed as we expect, the network will be ready for the team orientation on September 23.

   e. This week the system director will order the serial cable we need.

   f. The hardware security system we requested was $300 over our budget.

   g. Each computer will be named so that users can easily identify it.

   h. A system administrator will have to be trained before we can operate fully.

   i. We connected the laser printer to the network and tested it.

   j. We forgot to order a surge protector for the computer attached to the LCD projection panel, so we cannot use this equipment until the order comes next week.

2. Some sentences below are vague, and some include the writer's personal opinions. Revise each sentence to make it specific and factual. Invent details as needed.

   a. The calibrator is several minutes off schedule.

   b. The phenomenal response to our new computer safety education program shows that this new program will benefit employees.

   c. To get to the

   d. The line wa
      on safety.

   e. We can asse
      fancy case c
      than we pla

3. Evaluate your
   build sound sy
   such as speake
   equipment you
   note the cards
   trade or buy. M
   with your clas

End-of-Chapter exercises and activities include practice exercises, case studies, and suggestions for writing to reinforce and assess learning.

Apply What You Learned

4. Write a long summary, a short summary, and an abstract on one of the following: a magazine article, a textbook chapter, a sporting event, a meeting, a TV show, a movie, a classroom lecture, or a speech.

5. List five to ten mechanisms you know well. These could be mechanisms you use at work, at home, or at school. Consider using VCRs, telephones, curling irons, stereo equipment, car equipment, telescopes, farm equipment, computers, exercise machines, cash registers, or tools. Write a mechanism description for one of the items. Include a diagram of the mechanism in your report.

6. Take a trip to gather information about something that interests you. Before you go, list questions to answer during the trip. You could visit a college, a business, a school's lab facilities or sporting event, a museum, or a historical site. Write a trip report to your instructor, your parent, or a real or fictional supervisor who answers the questions. Use memo format.

7. Think of a time something went wrong. You may have had a problem at school or work. Perhaps you observed someone else's problem. After identifying and analyzing a specific audience, write an incident report describing the incident and what you learned from it.

8. Consider any project you are working on at home, school, or work as a progress report topic. Your audience will be a person or group of people who have an interest in or make decisions about the project. Use the appropriate format and organization for the topic and audience.

9. If you are seeking a summer or part-time job or applying for admission to a school, write a progress report to your adviser or family about how you are accomplishing your goals.

10. Think of groups to which you belong: a family, a club, a neighborhood, a school. With one group and a particular time period in mind, plan and write a periodic report for a specific audience. Describe the ongoing activities for your group or your unit of the larger organization.

11. Write a periodic report using the following case study.

As the Drafting Club chair, you receive organization funds from the Student Government Association (SGA). You report to the SGA twice a semester to tell them what the club is doing. Your next report is due January 6, 20—. In this report, you will discuss Professional Pursuits, Service, and Membership. The club is more active than ever. Over the holidays, five members attended the American Institute of Building Design meeting in Las Vegas and brought back information to share with other members. The club began the school year with 21 members, and two students joined in the second semester. This year's service project is to plan the city's first Habitat for Humanity house. Club members have completed the exterior drawings and submitted them for approval. They will finish the interior drawings before school ends. All 23 members of the club have participated in this service project.

Work Is A Zoo!

You have decided to apply for an associate marketing position at the zoo. Even though you are already working at the zoo, you must go through the application process again. Because the job is important to you, you want to spend plenty of time getting the process right. You know that several other candidates are being considered, and you need to keep your options open in case the new position falls through.

In addition, you need to be prepared to discuss salary and job expectations if you are offered the position. Your Uncle Mark is a marketer with a publishing company in New York City, and you know he is respected in the field. But you aren't as familiar with career opportunities in the marketing field as you'd like to be. You decide to spend a little time getting familiar with the industry.

Do some research in the marketing field using publications, the Internet, and personal contacts. Do a web search for "marketing." Other key words might be "careers," "public relations," or "marketing salaries." Numerous publications provide business and industry information. For example, the Department of Labor publishes the Occupational Outlook Handbook. Another source might be the Occupational Outlook Quarterly, which includes up-to-date information about employment trends, new occupations, and employment outlook. Check your library and the Internet for these sources.

You updated your resume to include your current position at the zoo. You also added Anya as a reference. Now it is time to write the letter of application.

Remember, letters of application usually include comments about:

- The job you are applying for.
- Your familiarity with the type of job.
- Your attached resume.
- The best way to contact you.

Write a letter of application to the head of the zoo's marketing department, Nedra Kaplan. Remember to state why you are interested in the job and what you think you bring to the job. Is your current experience an asset? What has your current experience taught you?

From *Words@Work* 1st edition by VANDALAY GROUP © 2000. Reprinted with permission of South-Western, a division of Thomson Learning: www.thomsonrights.com. Fax 800 730-2215.

WORK IS A ZOO In addition to researching the marketing field, research jobs at a zoo to learn what specific knowledge and experience is required. If you can, talk to someone who works at a zoo to learn more. Use the worksheet on the Data CD to help you write your letter of application.

Work is a Zoo! case study at the end of each chapter allows students to apply technical writing concepts in a real-world, ongoing scenario.

The Inside Track
TECH WRITING TIPS

ORGANIZING WITH THE DIRECT APPROACH

The way you organize ideas in conversation and the way you organize for writing can be quite different. To understand the difference, think of a recent exciting event in your life. Imagine telling friends about this event in a casual conversation. Now write a one- or two-paragraph description as if you were speaking to friends. In your description, include a sentence containing the main idea. Compare the organization of the two messages. Where did you place the main idea?

In many technical reports and documents, the main idea should be placed first for the convenience of the reader. Use this strategy to organize good news and informative memos. This strategy calls for putting the most important idea, or the information the reader needs most, first and reserving explanatory and supplementary ideas for later in the memo. Figure 1 illustrates the direct approach to organizing a message.

MAIN IDEA

Background
Examples
Illustrations
Supplementary
Data

Figure 1 Model for Direct Approach to Organization

As Figure 1 shows, when you organize for your reader, you place the main idea first. Then you add other statements in order of most important to least important. As the writer, you must decide how much information your reader needs and how far to continue with background and explanation.

The Inside Track, which is located at the end of the book, contains 26 pages of suggestions and tips for improving technical writing style.

SUPPLEMENTS

The following supplements are available to accompany the textbook.

	Instructor's Resource CD (IRCD)	Student Data CD
Lesson Plans	✔	
Chapter Activities	✔	✔
Solutions to Chapter Activities	✔	
Sample Documents	✔	✔
Worksheets for the Work is a Zoo! Case Study	✔	✔
Teaching Masters	✔	
PowerPoint® Slides	✔	
Chapter Tests in PDF Format	✔	
Additional Chapter Activities	✔	

Student Resources. The student Data CD provided with *Technical Writing for Success* includes **enrichment activities** that provide additional opportunities for students to learn and apply the principles of effective technical writing. The Data CD also includes **sample documents** as well as additional worksheets to supplement the **Work is a Zoo! case study.**

The *Technical Writing for Success* **web site** can be accessed at www.techwriting.swlearning.com. The site contains additional **web links,** activities to complement the **See the Sights** feature, and **crossword puzzles.**

Instructor Resources. The resources available to instructors using *Technical Writing for Success* include the following items:

- **Instructor's Resource CD.** The instructor's resource CD (IRCD) contains **lesson plans** for each chapter, **chapter activities** and **solutions, sample documents,** and worksheets to accompany the **Work is a Zoo! case study.** In addition, over **100 teaching masters** are available on the IRCD to assist with the discussion of concepts. These teaching masters contain sample documents, checklists, and summaries of key concepts to support and supplement chapter material. **PowerPoint® slides** and **tests in PDF format** are available for each chapter. Many chapters contain **additional activities** you can also provide for students.

- **Electronic Test Bank.** The electronic test bank includes test questions for each chapter and gives you the ability to edit, add, delete, or randomly mix questions.

- **The *Technical Writing for Success* Web Site.** This site can be accessed at www.techwriting.swlearning.com and contains additional web links, activities to complement the See the Sights feature in the text, and crossword puzzles.

REVIEWERS

The authors appreciate the following educators who reviewed the manuscript and made suggestions for improvement:

Sara A. Baker
Fabens, Texas

Janet S.Cook
Hutchinson, Kansas

Ruth A. Goodwin
Albemarle, North Carolina

Rhonda Hatter
Reston, Virginia

Joan M. Heck
Longwood, Florida

Linda Hoff
Kewanna, Indiana

Becky Kammeyer
Gas City, Indiana

Tina McCloud
Mt. Vernon, Indiana

Karen McKay-Hanks
Jacksonville, Florida

Maryann Roeske
Three Lakes, Wisconsin

Linda S. Thompson
Kenosha, Wisconsin

Christopher S. Williams
San Diego, California

TABLE OF CONTENTS

Chapter 1 What is Technical Writing?   2

You Are a Technical Writer!   7
Characteristics of Technical Writing   11
How Technical Writing Compares to Other Writing   15
Ethics and Technical Writing   17
Chapter 1 Review   20

Chapter 2 Plan for Your Audience and Purpose   24

Meeting the Audience's Needs   27
Planning Your Document's Purpose, Scope, and Medium   37
Chapter 2 Review   42

Chapter 3 Technical Research   46

Researching at Work   49
Finding Secondary Data   51
Documenting Secondary Sources   56
Evaluating Sources   61
Taking Notes from Sources   64
Collecting Primary Data   68
Chapter 3 Review   76

Chapter 4 The Writing Process   80

A Process for Technical Writing   83
Planning   85
Drafting and Revising   90
Copyediting and Publishing   93
Writing Collaboratively   96
Chapter 4 Review   102

Chapter 5 Brief Correspondence   106

Introduction to E-mails, Memorandums, and Letters   111
Audience   114
Prewriting   116
Formatting   119
Composing the Message   126
Chapter 5 Review   138

Chapter 6 Document Design and Graphics — 142

Designing the Document — 145
Who Reads Graphics? — 148
Formatting Graphics to Make Them Easy to Understand — 150
Constructing Graphics for Audience and Purpose — 154
Chapter 6 Review — 166

Chapter 7 Instructions — 170

Getting Started on Instructions — 173
Organizing and Formatting Instructions — 175
Composing Instructions — 179
Writing Online Instructions — 186
Chapter 7 Review — 188

Chapter 8 Informative Reports — 192

Summary and Abstract — 196
Mechanism Description — 199
Trip Report — 201
Incident Report — 203
Progress and Periodic Reports — 205
Chapter 8 Review — 212

Chapter 9 News Releases and Science Lab Reports — 216

News Releases — 221
Science Lab Reports — 228
Chapter 9 Review — 234

Chapter 10 Employment Communication — 238

Who Reads Employment Communication? — 242
Getting Started on Employment Communication — 244
Formatting and Organizing Resumes — 246
Composing Resumes — 254
Composing Employment Letters — 258
Chapter 10 Review — 264

Chapter 11 Oral Presentations — 268

Planning — 271
Organizing and Composing — 273
Preparing — 276

Rehearsing 283
Presenting 285
Organizing a Group Presentation 287
Chapter 11 Review 290

Chapter 12 Recommendation Reports 294

What is a Recommendation Report? 300
Getting Started on Recommendation Reports 303
Formatting and Organizing Recommendation Reports 306
Composing Recommendation Reports 311
Chapter 12 Review 314

Chapter 13 Proposals 318

What is a Proposal? 335
Getting Started on Proposals 338
Composing Informal Proposals 340
Composing Formal Proposals 346
Chapter 13 Review 352

Chapter 14 Technical Reading 356

Technical Reading vs. Literary Reading 359
Strategies for Reading Technical Passages 361
Chapter 14 Review 374

Inside Track

Organizing with the Direct Approach 378
Tone 380
Parallelism 382
Economy 385
Using Numbers 389
Clarity 392
Active and Passive Voice 394
Gender Unbiased Language 397
You Attitude 399
Effective Transitions 401

Glossary 404
Index 411

WHAT IS TECHNICAL WRITING?

GOALS

DEFINE technical writing and its importance in the workplace

IDENTIFY the characteristics of technical writing

COMPARE AND CONTRAST technical writing and other types of writing

IDENTIFY ethics in technical writing

See the Data CD for Write-to-Learn and In The Know activity worksheets.

WRITE-TO-LEARN

Read the three model documents on pages 4, 5, and 6 of this chapter and think about the type of writing each model represents. In a one-page journal entry, answer these questions: Have you written similar types of documents? If so, what did you write and why? Have you read similar documents? If so, what did you read and why? Which document would you use to make a decision or to perform an action? Which type of document do you prefer to write? Why? Which do you prefer to read? Why?

In The Know

academic writing the expository and persuasive writing done in academic circles; examples include personal essays, research papers, analyses, and arguments

ambiguous more than one interpretation is possible; describes writing that means different things to different people

ethics a system of moral standards and rules that guides human behavior

expository writing writing to explain or inform

expressive writing writing to express or portray personal observation or feeling

field research research done in the field, especially through surveys and interviews

imaginative writing writing such as novels, short stories, drama, and poetry whose situations grow out of fantasy or imagination; events and people are fictional although the themes may reveal universal truths

inferences judgments about reading that the author does not make for the reader

jargon the highly specialized language of a particular discipline or technical field

persuasive writing writing to convince others

style the way an author uses words and sentences

technical communication communication done in the workplace; the subject is usually technical; the purpose and audience are specific; the approach is straightforward

technical writing writing done in the workplace; the subject is usually technical, written carefully for a specific audience; the organization is predictable and apparent; the style is concise; the tone is objective and businesslike; special features include visual elements

tone emotional overtones; the way words make readers feel

Writing@Work

Tyler Parris is a technical editor for the Windows Server Content Group at Microsoft Corporation in Redmond, Washington. As a technical editor, Tyler edits online Help for the Microsoft® Windows® Server operating systems and articles that appear on the Microsoft TechNet® web site and the Microsoft Developers' Network® web site. Specifically, he edits documentation for Microsoft® Windows Server, participates on a virtual team whose goal is to make Microsoft Help more accessible to people with disabilities, and he leads a glossary team that is responsible for coordinating the use of terms across Windows.

"Much of my time is spent communicating technical subjects to people, whether that's through print or through oral communication," Tyler says. Tyler must communicate with many employees in different locations, so he uses technology such as Microsoft Outlook® for Windows® to set up virtual team meetings. "Meetings are an important part of life here at Microsoft. It's how we share information and work together as a team."

Tyler stresses the importance of developing strong relationships with internal customers, the teams he supports, and other people he works with. "The best way to do that," he says, "is through polishing your technical communication skills." He says he is more likely to influence the documents he works on if he can diplomatically make the case for his recommended changes. "It helps to have some sort of evidence to back up recommended changes, so that writers do not think you are being arbitrary. I try to rely on usability reports, internal style guidelines, and our preferred grammar reference." Perhaps most importantly, Tyler says that flexibility is an important part of his job. "As I negotiate with writers, I try to remember that there is often more than one way to solve a problem, and my answer is not always the best one."

To help him prepare for a career in technical editing, Tyler received his bachelor of arts degree in English from Marshall University, where he took his first technical writing course. After that, he approached businesses from his hometown in Washington, DC, and wrote press releases, marketing materials, and some recruiting advertising text on a freelance basis. He also joined the Marines and received training as a network administrator, while learning some valuable leadership skills. Eventually, he completed his masters degree in technical and scientific communication from Miami University in Oxford, Ohio. After graduate school, Tyler interned at Convergys Corporation in Cincinnati, Ohio, an international telecommunications company.

About his training in computer networking, Tyler says, "Do not underestimate the importance of having communication skills to support your technical skills and knowledge. They help you gain credibility with the engineers you support, as well as other writers and editors."

Rebuilding Your Engine

Excessive **smoking** or **knocking** could mean it's time to rebuild your engine. When it comes time to rebuild, consider Summit's 1) Engine Kits or 2) Re-Ring Kits.

Engine Kits

Engine kits can be purchased with one of the following combinations:

- premium forged TRW pistons and moly rings,
- premium cast TRW pistons with moly rings, or
- cast TRW pistons with regular rings.

The kits also come with TRW main, cam and rod bearings; a TRW high volume oil pump; top quality Fel-Pro Blue Perma Torque gaskets; a set of oil and freeze plugs; and Clevite assembly lube. See Table 1 for a cost breakdown.

Re-Ring Kits

If your present pistons are in good shape and you don't need main and cam bearings or an oil pump, Re-Rings Kits may work. They include regular or moly rings, rod bearings, and a Fel-Prol Blue Berma Torque gasket set. See Table 2 for. . . .

Table 1 Engine Kits			
Engine	Our Good Kit: Case Pistons Regular Rings	Our Better Kit: Cast Pistons Moly Rings	Our Best Kit: Forged Pistons Moly Rings
Chevy 327 '62-'66	$214.95	$219.95	$308.95
Chevy 350 '67-'80	$172.95	$184.95	$298.95
Chevy 350 '81	$181.95	$189.95	$291.95

Reprinted with permission of Summit Racing Equipment, Akron, Ohio.

Figure 1.1 Technical Writing Excerpt

The First American Automobile Race

At 8:55 a.m. on November 28, 1895, six "motorcycles" left Chicago's Jackson Park for a 54-mile race to Evanston, Illinois and back through the snow. Number 5, piloted by inventor J. Frank Duryea, won the race in just over 10 hours at an average speed of about 7.3 miles per hour! The winner earned $2,000 and the enthusiast who named the horseless vehicles "motorcycles" won $500.

Only two years earlier in Springfield, Massachusetts, brothers Charles and J. Frank Duryea had built and driven what they claimed to be the first American gasoline-powered automobile. Yet, as if by spontaneous combustion, over 70 entries were filed for the *Times-Herald* race, a response so overwhelming that President Cleveland asked the War Department to oversee the event. Following their victory in the race, the Duryeas manufactured thirteen copies of the Chicago car, and J. Frank Duryea developed the "Stevens-Duryea," an expensive limousine, which remained in production into the 1920s.

There were American antecedents to the Duryeas' winning vehicle. As early as 1826, Samuel Morey filed a patent, bearing the signatures of John Quincy Adams and Henry Clay, for an internal combustion engine. George Brayton, Stephania Reese, Henry Nadig, and Wallis Harris all produced self-propelled machines.

Charles Black developed an 18 horsepower "chug buggy" in 1891—the same year John Lambert developed a three-wheel motor buggy. After seeing the 1895 *Times-Herald* race, Lambert produced four-wheel vehicles at his Buckeye Manufacturing plant.

The Stanley twins built a steam-powered vehicle in 1897. The "Stanley Steamer" achieved fame when brother F.E. Stanley did a mile in 2:11 on a dirt track with a 30 degree incline. George Eastman bought the rights to the Stanleys' earlier photographic patents, supplying the brothers with capital to manufacture 200 standing orders for the Steamer, which eventually became the "Locomobile." By the time Henry Ford incorporated the Ford Motor Company in 1903, the Stanleys' plant already employed 140 workers.

Like its predecessor horseracing, automobile racing provided the stiff competition, which helped to "refine the breed." When the Stanleys brought their 150 horsepower "T.E. (Thoroughly Educated) Wogglebug" to the 1906 winter races at Ormond Beach, Florida, driver Fred Marriott clocked 127.66 mph, becoming the first to move faster than 2 miles per minute.

In 1911 the Indianapolis 500 was born. This famous race fostered the development of innovations such as the rear view mirror. By the time Berna Eli "Barney" Oldfield sped to the top of Pike's Peak in 1915, motorcar production was booming and automobile racing a well-established sport.

Source: The Library of Congress, *Today in History;* online at http://memory.log.gov/ammem/today/nov28.html.

Figure 1.2 Research Paper Excerpt

Owning a Car

Owning a car is not all it is cracked up to be. A year ago, I wanted to buy a car, but I could not afford one on my own. I talked to my parents about my desire to own a car, and they offered to make the down payment on a used Ford Mustang. However, I was responsible for the monthly payments, half the insurance premium, and the cost of maintenance. I thought I could handle the payments by waiting tables at Schooner's. The job promised to cover all my expenses—that is, until the restaurant closed for repairs.

I tried to find a temporary job to cover my expenses in the meantime, but no place would hire me for just a couple of months. And then my "maintenance-free" Ford sprung a leak when the radiator rusted out. One problem after another occurred: oil changes, inspection stickers, a headlight out, a fuse blown—I began to wish I lived in a big city with public transportation. Better yet, I began to wish I lived in a very small town where I could ride my bike everywhere. If I rode my bike instead of driving a car, I could save money on gas and repairs and get exercise at the same time.

After just a few months of being broke with no job and a useless car that I could not even afford to put gas in, I traded the car for a bicycle. Now I ride my bike everywhere. I do not have to put gas in the bike; I just have to put air in the tires every now and then. The best part about owning a bicycle instead of a car, besides saving money, is the exercise I am getting. I enjoy riding my bike so much that I have entered several bicycle races. I finally won my first race—the Glendale Speed Race. I won first place out of 525 entries! What could be next . . . the Tour de France?

Figure 1.3 Personal Essay Excerpt

YOU ARE A TECHNICAL WRITER!

Have you given someone written directions or drawn a map to your home? Have you written quick instructions for using a fax machine at work? Have you told someone how to change the oil in a car or how to make french toast? If you answered *yes* to any of these questions or have had similar experiences, you have already engaged in technical writing or technical communication.

See the Writing Model worksheet on the Data CD for activities for Figures 1.1 to 1.3.

Brainstorm the types of technical writing you already know. Use the You are a Technical Writer worksheet on the Data CD to guide you.

© DIGITAL VISION

DEFINITION OF TECHNICAL WRITING

Candice, an award-winning saxophonist, began teaching saxophone lessons to sixth graders. For the first lesson, she drew an alto sax diagram and quickly developed a step-by-step guide explaining how to take the instrument apart and reassemble it. When she saw how easily students could follow her instructions, she was happy to know that her words were helping others learn to do something she enjoyed.

Candice might have been surprised to learn that she was using technical communication. She was giving practical information to a specific audience, information that would enable her audience to take action. When she referred to the diagram and explained the procedure aloud to her students, she was using **technical communication.** When she wrote the instructions to accompany her diagram, she was using **technical writing.**

Technical documents can range from a half-page memo announcing the winner of a DVD raffle to a research grant proposal requesting money to build an animal shelter. The term *technical writing* describes documents produced in areas such as business, science, social science, engineering, and education. Sales catalogs, business letters, financial reports, standard operating procedures, medical research studies, lab reports—all of these and more are examples of technical writing.

TECHNICAL WRITING IS ESSENTIAL IN THE WORKPLACE

Written communication is essential in the workplace for many reasons. Written communication allows readers to read and study at their own convenience, pass along information easily to others, and keep a permanent record for future reference.

An executive reserves the afternoon hours between meetings to review employment resumes. A financial report becomes part of an organization's financial history, which can be read by stockholders and against which later financial reports can be compared. Written communication allows writers to craft their message until it is complete and accurate and communicate the same information efficiently to readers in different locations.

A computer programmer rewrites the specifications for new software until they are accurate and complete. A news release announcing a merger of two publishing firms or the firing of a football coach is read by readers in different locations. A memo written to prepare employees for a plantwide shutdown is introduced one way to administrative assistants anticipating a few days off, another way to plant supervisors who must work through the shutdown, and yet another way to vendors who will be told to hold all shipping for a week. The basic information remains the same, but the implications for each of these readers are different.

Everywhere you look, information from every direction competes for your attention: television, radio, newspapers, magazines, books, e-mail, the Internet, CD-ROMs, DVDs. Because of information overload, you need to be able to read documents quickly and efficiently, you need to understand them the first time, and you need to know that the information is accurate. Up-to-date information provides companies with a competitive edge, speeding critical decision making and allowing job specialization.

Technical writers who help companies manage the information overload are vital resources. They understand that their readers must be able to skim text, skip text, and find important information quickly. Good writers understand that they will not always know who is reading their writing (especially with e-mail) or how it is used. As a professional in great demand, the technical writer faces a challenging, exciting, and rewarding future.

ALL PROFESSIONS REQUIRE TECHNICAL WRITING

Regardless of the career you choose, you will write in the workplace. Conservative estimates suggest that you will spend at least 20 percent of your time writing in a technical or business occupation. Professionals in engineering and technology careers spend as much as 40 percent of their time writing. In a series of interviews with business and technical managers at six major employers in the southeastern United States, these managers all agreed that clear and effective writing is a crucial skill needed to advance in the corporate world.

Different careers generate different kinds of reports: Nurses chart a patient's medical condition so that the nurses on the next shift can continue patient care. Police accident reports record facts for later use in court. Chemists and engineers document procedures to comply with government regulations; accountants prepare annual client reports. Sales representatives write sales proposals; professors write grant proposals; park rangers write safety precautions; insurance claims adjusters write incident reports; travel agents design brochures; and public relations officers write news releases, letters, and speeches.

When you write, you demonstrate your ability to analyze, solve problems, and understand technical processes. For example, Johann Buchner, personnel director for Osgood Textile Industries, impresses his supervisor and earns his colleagues' respect when his tax-deferred retirement plan proposal is approved. On the other hand, the drafting crew at Stillman Manufacturing is frustrated with Tetrianna Danielli's instructions for

installing wireless computing at the industrial site. The crew must redraft plans because Tetrianna's instructions are vague and incomplete. When writing is not clear, the thinking behind the writing may not be clear either.

All careers rely on technical communication to get the job done. Technical writing is the great connector—the written link—connecting technology to

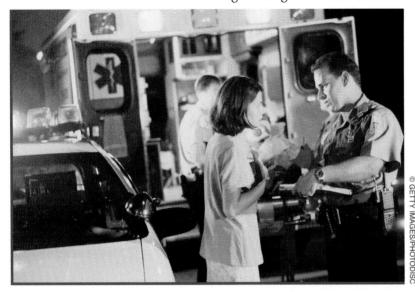

user, professional to client, colleague to colleague, supervisor to employee, and individual to community. No matter what career you choose, you can expect to read and compose e-mail, send accompanying attachments, give and receive phone messages, and explain procedures.

In addition to work-related writing, the responsibilities of being a community and family member require technical communication. Figure 1.4 shows how Sergeant Thomas Hardy of the Palmer City Police Department, father of two and concerned citizen, uses technical communication on the job and at home.

Colleagues: e-mail, collaborative incident reports

Boy Scout Den Parents: fund-raiser announcements, directions to jamboree, invitations to join troop

Victims: incident reports, investigative reports

Legislators: letter and e-mail in favor of clean-air regulations

Lawyers, Court Officials: depositions, testimonies, statements (may be televised)

State FBI Office: letter of application and resume for a position that would advance his career

Greenpeace Volunteers: journal of nature hike

Community Members: safety presentation at the high school

Supervisees: employee regulations, letters of reference, training procedures

Local Newspaper Editor: letter thanking community for help with jamboree; press release announcing purchase of state-of-the-art police car

Suspects: incident reports, interrogation results, procedures, recommendations for sentencing or early release

Children: letter while they are at summer camp

Figure 1.4 Sergeant Hardy's Technical Communication at Home and on the Job

 Stop and Think Discuss the importance of technical writing in the workplace. Why do you think writing affects your chances for advancement?

CHARACTERISTICS OF TECHNICAL WRITING

Technical writing shares many characteristics with other kinds of writing, but it is also significantly different. From the factual treatment of the subject to audience considerations, technical writing is unique. Subject, audience, organization, special features, style, and tone all contribute to the description of writing appropriate for the workplace.

SUBJECT

The subject of each model at the beginning of this chapter is cars, but the approach to this subject is different for each document. The personal essay expresses a young driver's frustration at the cost of owning an automobile, an experience with which you can probably identify. **Expressive writing** is created to convey personal observations and relies on personal experience for research.

© GETTY IMAGES/PHOTODISC

The research paper's purpose is not to relate personal experience, but to explain facts gained from library research. Writing to explain or inform is **expository writing.** While most academic research papers are factual papers written on topics interesting to the reader, the technical document (even a technical research document) is written to fulfill a need.

Often the need is to get information or to perform an action. Here someone with a vintage car may need to rebuild an engine; the technical document fulfills the special needs of a specific reader. The writer of this technical document also hopes to persuade the reader to buy the kits from the Summit catalog instead of somewhere else. Persuasive writing may require library research, scientific observation, or field research (use of surveys and interviews). Whether to inform or persuade, technical writing relies on data presented with precision and accuracy.

AUDIENCE

The writer of the personal essay expects some understanding from his or her readers as they share experiences; the writer also expresses his or her point of view. The writer of the research paper may be interested in the subject and hopes a reader will read the research paper for facts.

The technical writer, however, expects more from a very specific reader—one needing information about engine kits and possessing knowledge of the topic and its specialized vocabulary. The technical writer not only expects the reader to understand the writing, but also wants the reader to do something after reading—order an engine kit. When you want something specific from a reader, you must work hard as a writer to meet the reader's needs.

WARM UP

Review the three models on pages 4, 5, and 6 of this chapter. Describe the research required for each document. Why might someone read each document? What does each writer want from his or her audience? What has the writer done to consider the reader's needs? Use the Comparing Writing Environments worksheet on the Data CD.

In technical writing, the needs of the reader dictate every decision the writer makes. In the technical writing model, the writer worked hard to present the information the reader needs in a format that is easy to read. The headings, boldface type, special table, and no-frills language show that the writer is conscious of the reader.

ORGANIZATION

The personal essay and research paper make standard use of a topic sentence and transitional expressions, but you still need to read far into each document before the main point and the organization become apparent.

The technical writing model, however, uses headings to help you perceive the organization at a single glance before you read. The use of *1)* and *2)* in the first sentence helps draw your eye to the subject of this document before you read. Also, headings give readers an opportunity to read only what they want or need to read. When a customer who is interested in rebuilding an engine wants to price only the re-ring kits, the heading "Re-Ring Kits" allows his or her eye to travel quickly to the information needed.

SPECIAL FEATURES

The technical document is the only document of the three examples at the beginning of this chapter to use special features. Technical writers use special features such as bold, italics, capital letters, columns, underlining, and bulleted lists to draw attention to certain words and help important information stand out. Also, the use of graphics, such as tables, graphs, pictures, and diagrams, helps relay complex information quickly for the audience.

More than the research paper or personal essay, the technical document relies on special features. Technical documents require more visual effort to grab and hold the readers' attention. Writers use some of the following special features to make their documents more effective for the audience:

1. Columns—one, two or three?

2. Color—which ones and how much?

3. Letterhead and logo—how large? where to place? middle, upper left or right, or side?

4. Graphs—one-, two-, or three-dimensional? horizontal or vertical? with color?

5. Tables—how many columns? with or without color?

6. Photos—what subject? what style? black and white or color photos?

7. Sidebars—what information to highlight? where to place?

8. Clip art—to add humor, set a tone, or celebrate a season?

9. Font size and style—how many are appropriate? What size is readable for the audience?

Technical writers face a double challenge: not only must they write with clear, accurate, and specific words, but they also must design the document to look inviting and attractive. Technical writers, therefore, are production artists: writing with precision to locate the best word and sentence structure for the message *and* designing pages that combine a professional image with a user-friendly approach. To do so, technical writers use a tool of their trade: desktop publishing software that allows them to craft documents that meet their readers' needs.

STYLE

The **style** of a document usually gives an audience an idea of the type of document they are reading. For example, the personal essay is casual, almost conversational, and predictable for an essay. You are probably comfortable with this style, having written personal essays in school. The writer uses examples and some description. The style of the research paper is also predictable for a research paper.

The technical document uses a simple, concise, straightforward style that is easily understood. The long sentences are simply lists. The other sentences are short, and the sentence order is predictable. There are no surprises for the reader. The vocabulary is highly specialized, the **jargon** of the automotive technician.

Communication Dilemma

Isabel was recently assigned as the lead Technical Communicator on a team that is developing a high-profile sofware package known as SpeedQuest. She is responsible for coordinating communication between the programming team and the marketing team. For Isabel, this position means a likely promotion and career advancement. She knows a promotion would help her support her family, so she is eager to do a good job.

One evening Isabel overhears the lead computer programmer tell the project manager that SpeedQuest is not as advanced as advertised in the company's marketing materials. The programmer recommends delaying the launch date, but the project manager ignores the suggestion, deciding to issue a second release after the product is complete.

The next day in the meeting to discuss the marketing materials, Isabel struggles to decide whether she should list in the brochures SpeedQuest features that do not work yet. She knows the features would help sales of SpeedQuest. On the other hand, she knows that if she tells the truth and decides not to publish information about the features, she may not get the promotion she is counting on. What should Isabel do?

TONE

Tone describes the emotional flavor (the way the words make you feel) of a document. The tone of a document also gives the audience an idea of the kind of document they are reading.

The tone of the personal essay is casual. The tone of the research paper is objective. The tone in technical writing is best described as objective or businesslike.

The expressive nature of a personal essay can run a range of emotions—sadness, excitement, irony, humor. The aim of research papers or technical documents is not to convey emotion. In fact, emotion can get in the way of a technical document.

Readers of technical documents read for information, not for entertainment. They read to learn something or to take action. Some say technical writing is boring because of its lack of emotion. For the person needing or wanting that information, the topic is not boring.

Focus on Ethics

When you enter the workplace, you may be asked to sign a code of ethics, no matter what profession you pursue or where you work. Just as different careers generate different kinds of documents, different documents must follow a strict set of guidelines, laws, or principles outlined in the company's code of ethics.

Many companies have their code of ethics posted on the Internet for anyone to see. For example, large companies such as General Electric, Merrill Lynch, Kroger, and Eli Lilly post codes about a variety of concerns–from animal drug testing to diversity. Most likely, your school has a code of ethics that you follow.

Sometimes an individual's ethical code may conflict with others' behavior. If your personal ethics conflict with workplace practices, you can define yourself by how well you stand up for your own ethics. Doing so is not easy, however. If you discover that the company paying your salary is falsely advertising, you may find it can be difficult to criticize. If you believe that making fun of a person with a physical challenge is wrong, but you find yourself in a work group who is laughing at such a person, then your personal code conflicts with the group's. You need to be courageous to behave ethically, and such courage, although not always initially rewarded in the workplace, will help to establish yourself as an ethical employee, eventually.

Anderson, Paul V. *Technical Communication: A Reader-Centered Approach*
Harcourt Brace and Company, 1999.

Stop and Think Drawing from the activities in this section's Warm Up, write your own definition of technical writing. Make sure you incorporate concepts from this section, such as subject, organization, audience, style, tone, and special features.

HOW TECHNICAL WRITING COMPARES TO OTHER WRITING

Technical writing has much in common with the academic writing you have experienced in school. Technical writing also shares aspects of the literature you have read. The differences, however, set technical writing apart from other writing that is familiar to you.

© GETTY IMAGES/PHOTODISC

WARM UP

From your experience with writing, what characteristics does good writing share? In other words, how would you describe good writing?

TECHNICAL WRITING AND ACADEMIC WRITING

Academic writing, such as a personal essay or research paper, must be unified, coherent, and well organized. Technical writing must be unified, coherent, and well organized. Style and standard usage (the spoken and written English expected in business communication) are important in academic and technical writing. Both types rely on a process of thinking and writing that takes place over a few hours, a few days, or several weeks. The purpose is often the same: to inform or persuade.

The difference between the two is in the presentation, audience, and approach. Academic writing includes paragraphs—usually an introductory paragraph, paragraphs that develop a thesis (a statement of purpose), and a concluding paragraph. Academic writing is written for an academic audience—an instructor, your classmates, or a group of interested scholars. Its purpose is to expand on an idea or make observations about human experience. For example, Francis Bacon's essay entitled "On Reading" elaborates on the benefits of reading. Mark Twain in "Two Views of the Mississippi" observes that while a close study of the river is necessary to reveal its dangers, the study also takes away its mystery. Human experience is vast, open to interpretation according to the beliefs of the writer. As a result, the subject matter, style, and tone in academic writing are more varied than the subject matter, style, and tone in technical writing.

Check out the College View web site for information about the technical communication career, salaries, the job outlook, and more. Learn about a typical day in the life of a technical communicator.

Discover the technical communication field by going to the Society for Technical Communication web site. This site provides articles about the profession, ethical choices, employment news, resume tips, information about loans, and networking opportunities.

You can find the url for both sites in the web links on techwriting. swlearning.com. You will also find a worksheet for activities.

Technical writing also includes paragraphs. It, too, often begins with an introduction and closes with a conclusion. But technical writing (with its headings, itemized lists, boldface type, and graphics) looks different from academic writing. Technical writing is written for a specific audience. The subject is generally technical, business-related, or scientifically oriented. Generally, there is less flexibility in the subject matter, style, and tone.

TECHNICAL WRITING AND IMAGINATIVE WRITING

Imaginative writing also holds principles of unity, coherence, and standard usage. Imaginative writers also let their ideas emerge and develop over time. However, such writing is less academic and more artistic and creative than technical and academic writing.

Imaginative writing can be **ambiguous,** meaning different things to different people. Imaginative writing also requires the reader to draw inferences, to make judgments that the writer does not state.

Technical writing should be unambiguous and direct. A work of literature may be rich because it means different things to different readers. A reader might ponder the different meanings of the old man's voyage in Hemingway's *The Old Man and the Sea,* but W. Earl Britton says "that the primary, though not the sole, characteristic of technical and scientific writing lies in the effort of the author to convey one and only one meaning in what he says" (114).

The meaning of a sentence in technical writing must be clear. "Turn there," the man said, and the woman turned left when he meant for her to turn right. The word *there* can have different meanings for different people. However, "Turn right at the next paved road, called Nottingham Road" has only one meaning.

Imaginative writing requires you to make inferences. When Emily Dickinson writes: "Because I could not stop for Death—He kindly stopped for me—The Carriage held but just Ourselves—and Immortality," at first, you may have more questions than answers. Why is death being personified? Why does Dickinson capitalize *Death, Carriage, Ourselves,* and *Immortality?*

You expect to make inferences about poetry. You do not expect to make inferences about technical writing. If the poet's doctor gave the following instructions to a nurse, what would happen? *Because I could not remember the name of Ms. Dickinson's medication, would you kindly call the pharmacy and ask for the bottle that holds the blue and red pills?* Poor Ms. Dickinson. She'd find more comfort in the words of her poem than in the advice of her doctor.

Stop and Think

Write a paragraph comparing technical writing to academic and imaginative writing.

ETHICS AND TECHNICAL WRITING

WARM UP

As a member of your school's web site design team, you find a current story about two students to be misleading. What is the right thing to do in this situation?

Ethics is a system of moral standards and rules that guide human behavior. Ethical systems vary from one culture to another and from one individual to another, but their common intent is to work toward a fair and just treatment of human beings. Ethics (from the Greek word *ethos*, which means "character") determine what treatment is right or good. Ethics include a person's character, the inner strength and personal sense of integrity that allow him or her to behave in an acceptable and ethical manner. Ethical conduct is found wherever there is a spirit of mutual respect and the desire for responsible behavior.

© DIGITAL VISION

ETHICS IN THE WORKPLACE

Ethical conduct is important in the workplace—so important that ethical standards are protected by the legal system. Companies can be sued for such ethical misconduct as endangering the environment, selling a product that hurts customers, or failing to hire workers fairly. Tobacco companies have been sued for endangering an individual's health. Accident victims claim neglect on the part of car manufacturers. At any time, you can find examples such as these in news reports of companies whose ethics are questionable. Behind each ethical infraction is writing—memos, letters, advertising, meeting minutes—that helped to hide or expose the misconduct.

People have a choice. They can choose to act ethically or unethically. Even a choice not to act carries ethical implications. When top officials at Enron chose to misrepresent financial data, some employees remained silent. As a result, thousands of employees lost their retirement funds. Enron crashed, its stock plummeted, officials were indicted, and court trials began. When people lack the character to stand up for the ethical codes that define them, the consequences are far-reaching.

Use the Code of Ethics worksheet on the Data CD to see how Jeoffrey follows STC's code of ethics on his job.

ETHICS FOR TECHNICAL COMMUNICATORS

The Society for Technical Communicators (STC), an organization dedicated to advancing the technical communication profession, has adopted a code of ethics for its members. Read the code in Figure 1.5, written specifically for technical communicators. In the example that follows the figure, see how Jeoffrey Bolushi follows this code on the job.

Legality We observe the laws and regulations governing our profession. We meet the terms of contracts we undertake. We ensure that all terms are consistent with laws and regulations locally and globally, as applicable, and with STC ethical principles.

Honesty We seek to promote the public good in our activities. To the best of our ability, we provide truthful and accurate communications. We also dedicate ourselves to conciseness, clarity, coherence, and creativity, striving to meet the needs of those who use our products and services. We alert our clients and employers when we believe that material is ambiguous. Before using another person's work, we obtain permission. We attribute authorship of material and ideas only to those who make an original and substantive contribution. We do not perform work outside our job scope during hours compensated by clients or employers, except with their permission; nor do we use their facilities, equipment, or supplies without their approval. When we advertise our services, we do so truthfully.

Confidentiality We respect the confidentiality of our clients, employers, and professional organizations. We disclose business-sensitive information only with their consent or when legally required to do so. We obtain releases from clients and employers before including any business-sensitive materials in our portfolios or commercial demonstrations or before using such materials for another client or employer.

Quality We endeavor to produce excellence in our communication products. We negotiate realistic agreements with clients and employers on schedules, budgets, and deliverables during project planning. Then we strive to fulfill our obligations in a timely, responsible manner.

Fairness We respect cultural variety and other aspects of diversity in our clients, employers, development teams, and audiences. We serve the business interests of our clients and employers as long as they are consistent with the public good. Whenever possible, we avoid conflicts of interest in fulfilling our professional responsibilities and activities. If we discern a conflict of interest, we disclose it to those concerned and obtain their approval before proceeding.

Professionalism We evaluate communication products and services constructively and tactfully, and seek definitive assessments of our own professional performance. We advance technical communication through our integrity and excellence in performing each task we undertake. Additionally, we assist other persons in our profession through mentoring, networking, and instruction. We also pursue professional self-improvement, especially through courses and conferences.

Adopted by the STC Board of Directors, September 1998

Used with permission from the Society for Technical Communication, Arlington, Virginia.

Figure 1.5 Ethical Principles for Technical Communicators

Jeoffrey Bolushi is an English instructor with credentials in technical communication. He is a freelance writer for Fontaine Powerboat Company's sales catalog. Jeoffrey often faces ethical dilemmas, but if he follows the principles of the STC code, he will meet his legal obligations.

On the news, he hears that the fire extinguisher he described in last week's draft has been recalled. He calls the executives at Fontaine to make sure they know about the product recall and then honors suggestions not to include the extinguishers in the catalog until Fontaine resolves the matter. He will meet his deadlines and will make sure the products he describes, such as floatation devices, meet safety standards.

Jeoffrey describes products honestly. He writes and rewrites—even simple catalog descriptions—to be concise and accurate, double-checking measurements for marine batteries so the company does not misrepresent their size and strength. When a Fontaine yacht wins second place at a national boat show, Jeoffrey is careful to quote the exact wording of the award and does not attempt to cover up the second-place rating. He obtains written permission from the customer who agreed to be quoted in the catalog. He works on the catalog only at night or on weekends, careful not to spend time at school on this project. He uses his own computer and e-mail service for the catalog. After the catalog has gone to print, Jeoffrey discovers a pricing error and calls the printer to stop production until he can send the correction.

Jeoffrey keeps Fontaine's business practices confidential. He does not disclose the prices of products to his friends, even though he knows what the markup is for every item. As an incentive to get customers to look through the catalog, the company inserts trivia quizzes whose answers are found throughout the catalog. Correct answers carry discounts on products, but Jeoffrey does not tell his brother, a boating enthusiast, where the answers are. When Wan Lee Shirt Factory wants to hire Jeoffrey to write a similar catalog, Jeoffrey asks permission from Fontaine to show Wan Lee the catalog he wrote for Fontaine.

Because Jeoffrey helps the company produce a catalog with concise and accurate descriptions, the company exceeds sales quotas for the year. With the increase in sales comes a bonus for Jeoffrey and the satisfaction of knowing that folks are enjoying the waterways. When IRS auditors ask to see pricing records, the catalog is submitted as evidence of fair sales.

As you can see, Jeoffrey does more than simply describe boats, motors, lights, and flotation devices. He creates the link between customers and sales representatives, IRS auditors and company owners, corporate returns and public safety. In short, he is the guardian of a company's reputation: his catalog is the face the company wears for its mail-ordering public.

Stop and Think

What specific responsibilities do the "Ethical Principles" assign to a technical communicator?

■ *Chapter 1 Review*

POINT YOUR BROWSER

techwriting.swlearning.com

SUMMARY

1. You have probably already used technical writing if you've given someone directions, written a recipe, or explained closing procedures at work.

2. Readers use technical writing to get information, make a decision, or complete a task. Not every piece of technical communication is a written document; technical communication also can be an oral presentation.

3. Technical writing is critical in the workplace. Writing effectively improves your chances of being hired and promoted.

4. Technical writing is required in all professions.

5. Technical writing exhibits the following characteristics: subject— technical, factual; audience—carefully considered; organization— predictable, apparent; special features—visual elements; style—concise, direct, specialized vocabulary; tone—objective, businesslike.

6. Technical writing differs from traditional academic writing in its presentation, approach to subject matter, and audience. Technical writing differs from imaginative writing in its "one-meaning-and-one-meaning-only" presentation.

7. Ethics is a system of moral standards and rules that guide human behavior. Ethical conduct is important in the workplace—so important that ethical standards are protected by the legal system.

8. The Society for Technical Communication has adopted the Ethical Principles for Technical Communicators, a code of ethics to guide the behavior of its members. The principles address the communicator's responsibility to respect the law, promote public good, protect the confidentiality of clients, produce top-quality writing, keep business dealings fair, and improve skills.

Checklist

- Can I define technical writing?

- Can I list the characteristics of technical writing?

- Can I give examples of technical writing in the workplace?

- Can I list ways technical writing differs from academic and imaginative writing?

- Can I list ways technical writing is similar to academic writing?

- Can I define ethics?

- Can I explain why ethics is important in the workplace?

- Can I give an example of how ethics is used in the workplace?

- Can I explain the Ethical Principles for Technical Communicators adopted by the Society for Technical Communication?

Build On What You Know

1. What characteristics does technical writing share with other writing?

2. Which of these subjects would most likely be written about in a technical style? Which of these subjects would most likely be written about in an academic style?

   a sunset   homelessness   a first car

   electric circuits   graduation   a wedding

   a computer screen   a close friend   flowers

3. Which of the statements below would you expect to come from a technical writing document? Which would come from imaginative literature? How can you tell? What are your clues?

   a. My memory of her will never fade; she brought music into my life.

   b. There are two types of computer RAM (random access memory): static RAM and dynamic RAM.

   c. Most intriguing is the adaption of Corvette Z52 calipers to the car.

   d. The mist peeked over the marshland.

   e. Once upon a time, there was a princess who ruled a great country.

   f. The video output stage simply provides the voltage amplication and driving power for the cathode-ray tube and accepts the vertical and horizontal blanking signals.

4. Find a piece of technical writing (or any kind of writing) that you think is ineffective. Write a brief analysis of the writing, focusing on the characteristics that make it ineffective. Then analyze a piece of writing that you believe is effective. Compare the two pieces of writing for subject, audience, organization, style, tone, and special features.

5. In groups, discuss the ethical dilemma in the following situations.

   a. You are the owner of Fresh Air, an air-conditioner repair company. You have recently learned that your most requested air conditioner repairperson lets Freon® escape into the air (an illegal activity).

   b. You are making $60,000 a year at Weller Pharmaceuticals. You have just heard a rumor that an expensive anticancer drug produced by the company is ineffective; in fact, the drug weakened the immune system of patients who have used it. Your company has invested $2 million in developing the drug and must continue sales for another year just to recover the costs.

6. Juan is hoping to get a promotion and a raise next month. His manager asks him to report on Mark's efforts. Mark is Juan's coworker, who happened to apply for the same promotion as Juan. Even though Mark has handled projects well, Juan does not want him to look too good in the eyes of his manager. Juan tells his manager that Mark missed some deadlines and disappointed some clients. Did Juan act ethically? List possible consequences of Juan's behavior.

Apply What You Learned

7. Do you think you will make a good technical writer? Why or why not? What skills do you think you need to improve your technical writing? How do you think you can acquire those skills?

8. Conduct an Internet search for the keywords *technical writing, technical editing,* and *technical communication.* Write a summary of your findings and share your summary with the class.

9. Read an article in your favorite magazine or textbook. Choose three technical writing features. How do those features make the writing easy to read?

10. Write a short report describing the writing skills that are required in three of the following careers. You may need to research some of the job titles to learn the kinds of writing the jobs require. Or choose three careers that interest you and write a short report describing the writing skills those careers require.

Computer Software Engineer	Desktop Publisher	Physical Therapist
Database Administrator	Medical Assistant	Audiologist
Personal and Home Care Aide	Research Scientist	Veterinary Technologist
Reference Librarian	Accountant	Real Estate Agent
Acquisitions Editor	Electrical Technician	Interior Designer
Food Service Aide	Project Manager	Purchasing Agent

11. Find an example of technical writing written by someone who holds a job you might like to have someday. Ask a family member, friend, or employer for an example or search the Internet. Explain the purpose of the example and the way the author used technical writing characteristics to achieve the purpose.

12. Watch the local news and read your local newspaper to find a news story that reports a breach of ethics by a company, an employee, a sports figure, or a politician. Bring the story to class. In small groups, discuss the consequences to the company or the consequences to the individual under scrutiny.

13–14. Use the Apply What You Learned worksheet on the Data CD for examples of sample questions.

13. Interview a businessperson about his or her technical writing on the job. What types of documents does this person write most often? Ask if you may bring a sample of the writing to class.

14. Ask a technician or scientist about his or her technical writing on the job. Ask whether a mistake has ever been made as a result of imprecise reporting.

Use the Work Is A Zoo! activity checklist on the Data CD to help you start planning your assignments.

Work Is A Zoo!

Several months ago you were hired as a marketing and public relations assistant at the regional zoo. You enjoy the work, especially because it combines two of your life interests—wildlife conservation and marketing.

Your newest project is ZiPS (Zoo in Partnership with Science), an outreach program that targets science instructors. Soon ZiPS will kick off with a children's contest in which contestants draw and submit a logo for the petting zoo. Other parts of the program are still in the planning stages.

Anya Erhard heads the public relations division in the marketing department. Anya has helped orient you to working at the zoo. You also work with Tyrone Johnston, the other full-time public relations person.

When Anya was explaining her work, she said, "You'll never believe how much writing I do here!" She went on to tell you that she communicates with coworkers through e-mail, phone calls, and even informal conversations at lunch. Anya also writes letters, reports, and proposals to the zoo board and to local instructors.

She offered some advice: "A few weeks ago I wrote to some science instructors and told them that we use learning technologies in our programs. I was talking about computers and multimedia tools, but some of them thought I meant coming to the zoo to watch TV! Make sure you think out your message ahead of time—it is a big part of being a success here!"

It is now June, a busy time at the zoo. To keep track of all that is going on, you create a checklist of upcoming assignments for your new job.

PLAN FOR YOUR AUDIENCE AND PURPOSE

WRITE-TO-LEARN

Think of something you did recently that you told a lot of people about. Consider how your description of the incident changed depending on whom you talked to. Write a page telling how you described this incident to 1) authority figures (such as parents, instructors, or employers) and 2) close friends (who could include sisters and brothers). Did the purpose of your conversation change when you switched audiences? If so, how? How did each audience affect your tone, your body language, your choice of words, and the information you chose to include or leave out?

GOALS

DETERMINE how to meet the needs of a select and multiple audience

PLAN a document's purpose, scope, and medium

See the Data CD for Write-to-Learn and In The Know activity worksheets.

In The Know

accommodate to adjust; to change circumstances so that others will be more comfortable or more at ease

culture the special beliefs, customs, or values that are specific to a particular group of people or a particular region

format the details of a document's arrangement: the type of document, its length, the preferred style manual, and its organization

jargon the highly specialized language of a discipline or technical field

multiple audience an audience that includes readers whose points of view differ

primary the reader(s) you are responsible to first; the reader(s) who asked for or authorized the document

purpose a specific end or outcome to be obtained; what you want your reader to do after reading your document

role the function or job someone performs at work

scope the extent of treatment, activity, or influence; what is included and what is not included

secondary audience the reader(s) you are responsible to after you have met the needs of the primary audience

select audience a single person or group whose point of view is the same

medium a means by which information is conveyed, such as a newspaper article, a television commercial, or a speech before a live audience

Writing@Work

Kerry Broderick works as a copy director for an advertising agency in Cincinnati, Ohio. She writes short-form copy and longer documents for all types of advertising projects. Her responsibilities include assigning projects for her writers and managing budgets. She also gets to meet with and make presentations to clients.

Kerry realizes that advertising is sometimes seen as an unethical profession, and she believes that is unfortunate. "In my experience, it is only the very inexperienced marketer who would underestimate customers' intelligence by lying. Customers almost always know when they are being treated in a condescending manner." As for stereotypes, which may be perceived by some as natural in advertising, Kerry avoids them. "We avoid stereotypes simply by making sure we are communicating in a genuine fashion. If you have respect for your audience, you would never use stereotypes or sexist language. It is not good writing, and it is certainly not good business."

Advertising depends on writers who can write persuasively. Kerry goes about this type of writing by knowing her audience, listening carefully to them, and always offering them content and information that is worth their time. In advertising, a writer must really know his or her audience to be able to communicate effectively with them. Kerry says, "As with all good writing, knowing your audience is of utmost importance. We use a combination of research and trial and error to try to make sure what we offer readers fulfills a need."

Kerry believes that what really makes a good writer is "a person who always asks questions. A researcher, a thinker."

Before working as a copy director, Kerry worked as an editor in the pharmaceutical and criminal justice fields. Before that, she was a composition/freshman English professor at the university level. She has a bachelor's degree and a master's degree in English literature from the University of Cincinnati.

© 2005 Used with permission

Pet Travel Requirements

Dogs and cats must be at least 8 weeks old and must have been weaned before traveling by air. Kennels must meet minimum standards for size, strength, sanitation, and ventilation.

Size and Strength. Kennels must be enclosed and allow room for the animal to stand, sit, and lie in a natural position. They must be easy to open, strong enough to withstand the normal rigors of transportation, and free of objects that could injure the animal.

Sanitation. Kennels must have a solid, leak-proof floor that is covered with litter or absorbent lining. Wire or other ventilated subfloors are generally allowed; pegboard flooring is prohibited. These requirements provide the maximum cleanliness for the animal to travel.

Ventilation. Kennels must be well ventilated with openings that make up at least 14 percent of the total wall space. At least one-third of the openings must be located in the top half of the kennel. Kennels also must have rims to prevent ventilation openings from being blocked by other cargo. These rims, usually placed on the sides of the kennel, must provide at least three-quarters of an inch clearance.

Source: USDA, "Traveling with Your Pets," APHIS TRAVEL WEB HOME, updated Oct. 1998.
http://www.aphis.usda.gov/oa/pubs/petravel.html.

Figure 2.1 Sample Document Written for a Specific Audience

MEETING THE AUDIENCE'S NEEDS

WARM UP

Suppose your younger brother or sister did something that made you unhappy. How would you talk to your brother or sister about the problem? Now suppose the person who offended you was a coworker. How would your audience affect what you said?

Technical writing is written for an external audience. You may write a poem or short story without the intention of sharing it with anyone, but technical writing implies an audience, often a very specific audience.

In technical writing, the writer is transparent. A technical writer is like a member of a stage crew, a behind-the-scenes operator, whose primary obligation is to satisfy the audience's need for information. In a good play, the audience is barely aware of the crew at work, moving sets and producing sound on cue, but without them, the show would not go on. Similarly, good writers produce work without drawing attention to their role.

© GETTY IMAGES/PHOTODISC

Audience and *reader* are nearly interchangeable terms. As technical communication expands to include multimedia presentations, audience has a broader meaning. Sometimes the audience is not a reader, but a listener or an observer. In either case, technical writers must know who the members of their audience are, what they already know, and what they need or want to know.

The writer's relationship to the readers is also important. Are the readers customers or coworkers, managers, peers, or subordinates? Usually, your relationship to your readers will determines how you write your document —the tone you use, the formality of your document, and its medium.

In Figure 2.1, the passage tells specific readers (pet lovers planning air travel with their pets) information they need (how to make sure their pets are safe and comfortable). The writer does not bring attention to herself, but instead provides objective, helpful information. Notice the details the writer included—animals must be 8 weeks old, the ventilation must make up at least 14 percent of the total outside area—added to give readers all of the information they need.

Do you understand the message below? It is written in Morse code—letters as a series of dots and dashes. Many people have no need to know Morse code. They are not the targeted audience; therefore, the message fails to communicate.

-.-   -.   ---   .--

-   ....   -.--

.-   ..-   -..   ..   .   -.   -.-.   .

A Navy radio operator during World War I understood this code. The operator's audience shared a common mission: to receive important military messages over long distances. In short, the Navy radio operator used Morse code to meet the highly specific needs of a particular audience.

To communicate successfully, you must speak the "language" of your audience. Failure to speak in terms your reader expects creates a barrier that prevents communication, much as the Morse code keeps you from understanding its message. Whether your audience is a **select audience** (one person or one single-interest group) or a **multiple audience** (a variety of people representing different backgrounds and opinions), you must understand what your audience needs and wants. Understanding your audience's knowledge level, role, interests, cultural background, and personality is the first step to successful communication.

Attending to the needs and wants of your audience is much like attending to a special guest in your home. You are conscious of this person's presence and make every effort to make this person feel welcomed. For example, a Spanish-speaking exchange student from Argentina spoke English moderately well, enjoyed playing the guitar, and was accustomed to sweet rolls for breakfast. His American host family attended to his needs and wants by defining unfamiliar words, borrowing a guitar for him to play, and baking cinnamon rolls for breakfast. Just as the host family gave special consideration to the Argentine student, you should consider your audience as well, making every effort to **accommodate** your audience's needs and wants.

The relationship between the writer and the reader is supply and demand. When your manager needs to know the cost of hiring an administrative assistant, you provide cost. When the outside maintenance crew needs to know how to protect themselves from West Nile Virus, you research mosquitoes and tell them how to prevent mosquitoes from breeding and biting. When the plant director wants the information in a safety brochure, you design a brochure. When the crew wants the information in an e-mail, you write and send an e-mail. When the audience is unsure of its needs, the writer helps the audience think through the communication situation.

In technical writing, one rule dominates: *the needs and wants of your audience dictate every decision you make as a writer.* The writer uses a skill to provide a valuable service. Think of it this way: the writer is the server; the audience is the person ordering from the menu. If the person ordering requests mashed potatoes with peanut butter and bacon bits, then the server must oblige!

MEETING THE NEEDS OF A SELECT AUDIENCE

Sometimes your audience will be a specific person or a select group with a common interest. After you have identified the readers in a select audience, consider how their knowledge level, role(s), interest(s), cultural background, and personality may influence what you write and how you write it. Age, experience, attitude, organizational distance, income, and politics may affect the language you choose to communicate successfully. As Figure 2.2 illustrates, targeting the special needs of a select audience requires a writer to consider several factors at once.

Communication Update

Did you know that many software programs allow you to write the same document but tailor it to the needs of different audiences? For example, Microsoft® Word allows you to create links in a document for users to click when they want more information about a subject. The software also allows you to include nested documents for different audiences. In addition, for international audiences, you can write and edit documents using many different languages.

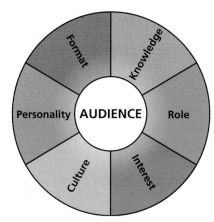

Figure 2.2 Targeting Your Audience's Needs

Knowledge Level What people know and how well they know it varies widely from one person to the next. As such, knowledge level can be high, low, or moderate. It can be technical or nontechnical. Ask yourself what your readers know or do not know about your subject. If you tell them what they already know, you risk wasting their time (not to mention yours); yet if you omit something they need to know, you have not done your job.

For example, the knowledge level of Christopher's parents prevented them from understanding a medical report. After falling down a flight of stairs, two-year-old Christopher was taken to the emergency room by his distraught parents. Christopher's emergency room report read as follows: "The child suffered from contusions and lacerations." *Contusions* and *lacerations* are familiar terms to doctors and nurses. For Christopher's parents, however, the medical **jargon** (specialized vocabulary) did not communicate as well as these everyday terms familiar to most parents: "The child suffered from cuts and bruises." The medical jargon was confusing and made Christopher's fall seem worse than it was.

Experience, age, and expertise can affect how much someone knows. Christopher's parents lacked the experience and background of a doctor or nurse. Because of his age, Christopher did not understand medical terms either. The technician who X-rayed Christopher's finger did not know which medication to prescribe for the child's pain; however, the doctor did. The X-ray technician had expert knowledge in one area; the doctor had expert knowledge in another.

Role Consider your reader's **role** or area of responsibility before writing. Not only does role or job title affect knowledge level, it also affects what your reader thinks is important.

Understand your reader's role and accommodate it. An accountant is concerned about the company's finances. If you write a memo to the accounting office about a planned purchase, you should accommodate the accountant's role by including information about cost. The technician who reads the same memo may be more interested in the equipment being purchased, having little concern about the cost. For the technician, you should include sufficient information about the technical aspects of the equipment.

Interest When you can grab your readers' interest, they read with greater enthusiasm. Where you find common interest, take advantage of it. Where there is none, create it. Some readers, however, will never have an interest in your subject. Accept those readers' lack of interest and focus on giving them the information they need.

Interest can be affected by age, experience, cultural background, and role. Your interests now are different from what they were ten years ago because you have a wider range of experiences. The camping and fishing trips you enjoyed as a child may have been replaced by long motor trips and concerts as a young adult. If everyone in your family enjoys eating black beans and rice, you may have a taste for these foods because of Your cultural background. Right now your role is to be a student. When you join the work force, your interests will be determined in part by your professional role.

Cultural Background **Culture,** the ideas, beliefs, customs, and values of a group of people, affects what an audience considers to be proper behavior. Many beliefs regarding human relations are affected by an individual's cultural background. By failing to consider someone's cultural background, you risk offending your reader and creating barriers in the communication process.

In the United States, regional cultural differences affect communication. In the South, many parents insist that their children say, "Yes, ma'am," "No, ma'am," "Yes, sir," and "No, sir" to their elders as a sign of respect and proper etiquette. Other regions of the country do not rely as heavily on these endearments. While "Yes, ma'am" or "Yes, sir" is expected as a polite gesture in one region, the expression may sound out of place in another region.

U.S. businesses are becoming increasingly global. American-based businesses have interests abroad, including countries such as Switzerland, Poland, Russia, and Germany. Many documents are read by audiences outside the United States whose cultural differences affect communication. Where American business personnel perceive directness as a sign of open and honest business dealings, other cultures consider this approach brash and insensitive. Where American business relies heavily on written agreements ("put it in writing" and "read the fine print"), other cultures trust oral communication. Understanding these differences is imperative to accommodating your audience's cultural background.

Personality Personality can be affected by culture, heredity, age, experience, and role. Also, someone's personality can shape individual work habits. A legal researcher who prefers to work alone may appreciate receiving instructions through e-mail and therefore enjoys reading her e-mail. Someone who prefers to work in a group may want to receive oral

Chapter 2

instructions in a meeting where he can share his reaction with others. To this person, e-mail may be a nuisance. When communicating, you do not always know your readers well enough to make judgments about their personality. If you do know your readers, you can tailor your language appropriately.

In the following example, notice how Parham adjusts to the different personalities at work:

Parham is a successful manager. Part of his success comes from analyzing his subordinates' and supervisor's personalities. He knows his supervisor likes to make decisions based on facts. When Parham talks to her, he is direct and presents only the facts. When Parham writes to her, his tone is objective and he includes ample statistical data. In fact, the company's new medical plan is the result of Parham's very detailed proposal. Parham's line manager, on the other hand, is laid-back and wants to know only the bottom line. Memos to him are short, infrequent, and friendly. The line manager is not interested in details, would prefer a visit to a memo, and would be hurt if the tone were too formal. Parham has a good working relationship with this line manager, who might otherwise be suspicious of a supervisor.

Before you begin to write any technical document, analyze your audience to determine their special needs. Use the questions in the middle column in Figure 2.3 on the next page to help you decide what is important to remember about your reader(s). When you've answered the questions, place an asterisk next to the three most important things to remember about your audience. Then follow the suggestions in the third column for adjusting to your audience's needs.

After looking at Figure 2.3 closely, complete the Accommodating Your Audience's Needs worksheet on the Data CD.

TO ACCOMMODATE	ASK THESE QUESTIONS	MAKE THESE ADJUSTMENTS
Knowledge Level	What does my reader already know about the topic? What does my reader need to know? What does my reader want to know?	Add particular knowledge your audience does not have. Leave out or quickly summarize knowledge your audience already has. Decide how much technical language to include. Use informal definitions or a glossary, if necessary. Present complex information visually.
Interests	How strong is my reader's interest in my topic? Are my reader's priorities different from mine or the same as mine?	Appeal to known interests; try to create interest where there is none.
Role	Is my reader's role to make decisions, make suggestions, or implement action? What is my reader's job? Is it administrative? technical? clerical? other? Is my communication going to management, to a peer, or to a subordinate?	Include knowledge that the role requires. Write different parts for different roles.
Cultural Background	What is my reader's cultural background? What are my reader's beliefs? Are my reader's beliefs different from mine or the same as mine?	Understand how culture affects someone's beliefs and decisions. Learn about the cultural background of your audience.
Personality	What kind of personality does my reader have?	Adjust tone and medium to personality.

Figure 2.3 Accommodating Your Audience's Needs

MEETING THE NEEDS OF A MULTIPLE AUDIENCE

Some literary critics argue that Shakespeare was the greatest writer who ever lived. Shakespeare's success depended on his wit, his knowledge of theater, and his understanding of audience. The businessperson in Shakespeare knew he had to please England's royal family as well as the peasants who came to see his plays. He had to appeal to young and old, to men and women, to the educated and the uneducated. In the sixteenth century, Shakespeare wrote successfully to a multiple audience, an audience made up of multiple interests, with members whose needs and wants sometimes conflicted with one another.

Today technical writers face a similar challenge writing to an audience that can include executives, managers, and administrative assistants. In his day, Shakespeare was clever—he wrote different parts of the same play for different people. Today his "different parts for different folks" strategy is used by technical writers too, but technical writers go one step further: they "label" the parts with headings, short titles preceding sections of the document to alert readers to the information written for them.

Another strategy for meeting the diverse needs of a multiple audience is to determine who comes first; in other words, whose needs are most important. To help you decide what data to focus on as you write, divide your audience into two groups: the primary audience and secondary audience. Think of the **primary audience** as readers or listeners you are responsible to first and the **secondary audience** as readers or listeners you are responsible to after you have met the needs of the primary audience. Both audiences are important, but as a writer, you must organize your tasks according to some kind of priority.

Walsh Plastics is contemplating building a factory in Thailand. Suppose you are the writer of the feasibility report analyzing the move for the entire company. The president of Walsh Plastics, the two vice presidents, and the company lawyer must decide whether to open a factory in a foreign country. They constitute the primary audience. The architect who will design the new plant, the sale representatives who will move, and the floor supervisors who will train new workers make up the secondary audience. How will you address each audience's needs and wants?

The criteria in Figure 2.4 may help you determine who the primary and secondary audiences are for other writing projects.

Primary Audience: Person(s) Who:	Secondary Audience: Person(s) Who:
Asked for or authorized the document.	Will be affected by the document or may use the information for future actions or decisions.
Will probably read the entire document.	Will probably read selected sections of the document.
Will make decisions based on the document.	Will implement decisions that are made.
Will request action based on the document.	Will take the action that is requested.

Figure 2.4 Primary and Secondary Audiences

Bella, a computer programmer, faced the challenging task of writing a proposal for the inventory management program of a local school system. The primary audience, the director, contracted services with Bella, specified what the program needed to do, and decided who would be trained to use it. The secondary audience included assistants who would key data, the new programmer who would modify the program, and the superintendent who would confirm that the programmer had fulfilled his or her contract terms.

Bella's audience ranged from readers with little knowledge of computer programming to readers with extensive knowledge of programming. To accommodate all of their needs, she wrote different parts of the report for different people:

Cover memo	written for the superintendent
Executive summary of the project	written for the director
Introduction to the manual	written for everyone
Procedures	written for the director and assistants
Appendix	written for the programmer

Figure 2.5 on the next page reveals the adjustments Bella had to make to accommodate the multiple audience's needs. Chapter 12 will cover long reports with different headings that are written to accommodate a multiple audience.

Sometimes, though, when a document is short, you can simply revise it for each audience and send it separately. For example, an e-mail from the director of information systems to the network administrators telling them

Focus on Ethics

As a writer, you must be aware of stereotypes in your writing to avoid biased language. Sometimes the stereotype is so engrained in the culture that you do not realize you are using biased language. You probably know that you should avoid sexist language in your writing (referring to men and women differently), but stereotypes can include more than men and women. People also can be stereotyped because of race, sexual orientation, age, physical disability, religion, ethnicity, and weight.

In your writing, strive to present everyone as equal human beings. There are several ways to do this. First, avoid sexist language by referring to men and women in the same way. For example, do not assume that all doctors are men and all nurses are women. Avoid using examples that reinforce stereotypes.

Do not mention a person's physical characteristics if they are not relevant. If you would not say, "Our new software developer is Max, a smart white man without disabilities," then do not say, "Our new software developer is Sandra, a smart white woman with physical disabilities."

Sometimes you are not aware of the biased language. If you are not sure whether you have used stereotypes in your writing, ask another person to look over the document.

Anderson, Paul V. *Technical Communication: A Reader-Centered Approach*
Harcourt Brace and Company, 1999.

READER'S ROLE	READER'S NEEDS	BELLA'S ADJUSTMENT TO READER
Superintendent *Approver*	To know whether the money spent on the programmer's services was responsibly invested; to know if the contract terms had been completed.	Writes a cover memo briefly summarizing the report, describing the program, and outlining advantages to the school system. Uses little or no technical language. Carefully defines any technical terms.
Director *Decision Maker* *Manager*	To gain an overview of the program; to see whether the specifications agreed upon had been met; to receive a demonstration of the product.	Writes the executive summary, which presents the most important information in the report. Includes some technical language. Gives a formal demonstration of the program.
All *Roles Varied*	To understand the purpose of the manual and which parts will help each reader.	Explains the purpose of the proposal and its organization in the Introduction. Uses little or no technical language.
Programmer *Technician*	To understand the program structure; to know how best to extend the functionality of the program.	Uses Microsoft Visual® C++ to write the application. Documents with UML diagrams to indicate program structure. Places information in the appendix. Invites the programmer to the training session for assistants.
Assistants *Users*	To understand how to key, manipulate, and find data.	Writes the procedures that tell how to use the program. Uses short commands with occasional explanations. Uses screen shots as graphic aids. Offers a training session on how to use the program.

Figure 2.5 Accommodating a Multiple Audience

to bring down the network on Friday afternoon for routine maintenance specified what the network staff should do. The director reminded the network administrators that users would be notified and told to log off by noon.

When the director sent out the e-mail to users, she revised the message. Instead of specifying the work to be done, she asked users to log off by noon, announced that the maintenance was routine, and thanked them for their cooperation and patience. The reminder of the network outage in the bimonthly newsletter was even briefer.

Writing to a multiple audience, then, requires careful analysis of each possible audience member followed by a workable plan. Writing "different parts for different folks," focusing on the needs of the primary audience, and rewriting short documents are all strategies available to the technical writer. Remember, too, that an audience that you did not intend could read your document, so you must anticipate every possible audience member and write accordingly.

Stop and Think

Think of a political, social, or moral issue you feel passionately about. Suppose you had to convince the entire student body to agree with you. What kinds of adjustments would you make to appeal to your multiple audiences?

PLANNING YOUR DOCUMENT'S PURPOSE, SCOPE, AND MEDIUM

Understanding who your audience is and what they need and want is an important part of your job as a writer; however, you have other decisions to make before you are ready to write. Early in the writing process, determine the **purpose** of your document, its **scope,** and the **medium** you will use.

WARM UP

Suppose a local newspaper reporter had interviewed you about the incident you wrote about in the Write-to-Learn activity. How does knowing that the story will appear in print for a wider audience affect what you say and do not say? Suppose you were being interviewed before a live television audience.

PURPOSE

In technical writing, the purpose is to inform or to persuade; quite often, the purpose is both. Because so much of technical writing is intended to persuade, you need to consider your writing from the reader's perspective. How will your readers take the information you provide? For them, is the information good or bad news? Whom or what are you competing with for the reader's attention? Is there a time limit for responding? Do your readers *have* to read your document? In other words, how hard must you work to get and keep your reader's attention? You should address these and other concerns as you think about the purpose of your document.

To determine the specific purpose of your writing assignment, ask yourself some basic questions:

- What do I want to inform my readers about?

- What do I want to persuade or convince them of?

- What do I—or the person asking me to write—want to happen as a result of this document?

Using the following questions can help you pinpoint the purpose of your writing:

What do you want your readers to ...

do?	make a decision about?	buy?	understand?
learn to do?	change their minds about?	donate money to?	believe?
stop doing?	care about?	give time to?	create?
continue to do?	send information about?	invest in?	know?

A statement of purpose may be to inform citizens of the latest employment trends or to convince the public to purchase smoke alarms. The persuasive purpose also implies providing information. Therefore, a purpose to persuade always becomes a purpose to inform. To convince banking customers to invest their money in money market accounts, you also must inform them about the advantages of such accounts. To convince the public to purchase smoke alarms requires providing evidence supporting smoke alarm use.

A statement of purpose on the same topic can vary for each audience. Consider the new employee-evaluation system at Fabre Perfume Industries. Everyone gets evaluated; therefore, the purpose of the new Employee Evaluation Manual is to describe the procedure so that all employees will understand how they will be evaluated.

Supervisors, however, need to conduct the evaluations, so they receive the new Employee Evaluation Manual *and* the Evaluation Procedures Manual, the purpose of which is to tell supervisors how to conduct the new procedure—how to download forms, where to file them, and what the deadlines are. The topic, new evaluations, is the same, but supervisors need additional information.

SCOPE

Once you have a clear, stated purpose, you must decide the following: How thorough will my coverage be? What information do I include and leave out? Here you use your audience analysis and statement of purpose to make decisions about the scope of your writing—what it will and will not cover.

Suppose you are writing instructions to car owners. You have settled on this statement of purpose: The user should be able to change a tire after reading my instructions. If you wonder whether to include information about how to select a good tire or how often to rotate tires, you could review your statement of purpose and say no, my purpose is to explain how to change

Communication Dilemma

Just out of college, you have landed a job as a project manager for a large telecommunications company. You are the youngest person in your group, and you are eager to please your manager, Sophia.

The first day on the job, Sophia asks you to have lunch with the rest of your group. As you are eating, you talk about the coworkers you have met, how excited you are to begin using the software that has been given to you, and how impressed you are with the efficiency of the company. You tell Sophia and the rest of your coworkers how pleased you are to be in their group and how eager you are to start contributing to the company's goals.

Sophia then says something you do not expect. "Do not worry," she says, "one year at this place and you'll want to quit working, have children, and let your spouse be the sole breadwinner." For the first time since you started working, you are not sure what to say.

How should you address Sophia's comment?

a tire, not to sell tires or inform users about proper tire maintenance. If you are wondering whether to tell your reader that changing a tire is not difficult and that it is an important survival skill, you can ask this question: Will this information help me achieve my purpose with this audience; in other words, will it help my drivers change a tire? The answer is yes; you want to include anything that motivates your reader to perform your process.

MEDIUM

Finally, you need to choose a medium for delivering your message. What kind of document will you produce? Will it be printed? What medium will accomplish your purpose and appeal to your audience?

Do you need detailed instructions or a quick reference sheet? PowerPoint® slides or a memo? Do you need to post your document on the Web or send it as an e-mail attachment? Do you pay to print 20 copies of an 85-page formal proposal and then mail it, or is it more cost-effective to send 20 CD-ROMs that include an interactive menu, a video of the president, and photographs and samples?

As you are making your decision, ask yourself three questions:

1. Is the medium appropriate for my audience, message, and purpose?

2. Is the time and money required to produce the medium worth the possible outcome?

3. What media are available to me?

Using the interactive CD complete with video for your 85-page proposal certainly takes advantage of the features made possible by technology, but is it appropriate for your audience? Such a presentation could generate more interest than the printed page. The CD is compact, is easy to produce and mail, provides a lot of options for retrieval, and may appeal to an audience's fascination with technology, much like an audience enjoys the special effects of a science fiction movie. Once the CD is loaded, users have more choices. They can print some of it or all of the content.

However, for someone who just wants to read a document, the CD may be overwhelming and seem too complicated. If the reader does not have the most current video player loaded, the video of the president will not matter. Producing the CD may take extra time and greater skill, perhaps requiring the help of colleagues. You must ask yourself whether the possible outcome of this project is worth the extra effort. The extra time and effort may be worthwhile if you are hoping to land a major account with a media display. But if your audience is not the financial player you need, perhaps you are better off with the 85 printed pages or carefully chosen excerpts.

To help you decide what medium is appropriate, find out what kind of media are typically used in your organization. Your local department of social services may be used to e-mail with important memos and short reports to be placed in interoffice mail, but the state agency may expect your reports sent as word processing attachments to e-mail. Work at the national level may best be presented on a web site from which PowerPoint® presentations and brochures can be downloaded and printed.

While many businesses have state-of-the-art computer equipment and fast Internet connections, some small businesses, such as Air Care's home-heating and air-conditioning business, may have only a computer, a printer, and a minimum amount of accounting and word processing software. You, like Ramon, the owner of Air Care, may find yourself in a field for which you are well prepared professionally but not as adept with desktop publishing. So CD-ROMs and web pages are not options yet. Perhaps well-designed sales proposals, invoices, or interoffice memos meet the needs of this environment.

The **format** of your medium deals with the details of the document's arrangement: the type of document, its length, the preferred style manual, and its organization. Just as your English instructor may prefer that your essays be written a particular way, your employer may prefer that your document be written a particular way. Your English instructor may require papers to be typed and double-spaced, with the MLA Handbook for Writers of Research Papers style sheet used as a reference. Your employer may require company letterhead (with the company logo, address, and slogan) and may have already developed a company style sheet (a suggested list of headings and the preferred way to present data) for you to follow. Sometimes audience determines the format. Outside the organization, correspondence usually requires letters; inside the organization, correspondence usually requires memos. Format and formality level may depend on the subject matter, the audience, and company standards.

Electronic formats consist of e-mail, CD-ROM, online help, and web-based information. E-mail is an informal and quick (although not always reliable) way to communicate and can be used for inside and outside correspondence. Forms and procedures can be posted on a company's intranet web server where templates set up for page layouts assure design consistency.

Complete the Purpose, Scope, and Medium worksheet on the Data CD.

Technical writers have many avenues with which to convey information. Figure 2.6 shows some of those choices for a medium once the purpose and scope have been determined.

Purpose	Scope		Medium
To convince reader(s) to...	Includes...	Does NOT include...	Possible Choices
Prepare for hurricane (residents of North Carolina)	Emergency supplies, hurricane routes, shelters, procedures	Routes/shelters for states other than North Carolina	Brochure, newspaper insert
Operate Brand X scanner (new user)	Information for scanning photos and texts	Information for any brand other than X; how to repair	Short user's manual, online help
Stop smoking with nicotine patch (smoker of 10 years)	Information about the nicotine patch	Information about other methods such as gum, will power, hypnosis	Pharmaceutical insert for nicotine patch
Eat nutritious meals (teens)	Simple, quick recipes to meet basic nutrition needs; foods teens typically like	Recipes for heart patients, diabetics, or an aging population	Spiral bound cookbook with CD-ROM
Book a vacation (mid-income families)	Vacation spots with group activities and fun parks; reduced rates	Vacation spots with long flights or honeymoon plans	Magazine article, brochure, web site
Seek information about financial aid (high school senior)	Information about parental income and college plans	Opinions about the fairness of financial aid	Letter

Figure 2.6 Determining Medium Based on Purpose and Scope

Stop and Think

Analyze an assignment that one of your instructors has given you. What are the purpose, scope, and medium of the assignment?

■ *Chapter 2 Review*

POINT YOUR
BROWSER

techwriting.swlearning.com

SUMMARY

1. The needs and wants of your audience should dictate every decision you make as a writer.

2. A select audience is a specific single reader or a specific group of readers with a common purpose. Knowledge level, roles, interests, cultural background, personality, and format affect communication with a select audience.

3. Multiple audiences are readers with different points of view. Analyzing knowledge level, roles, interests, cultural background, personality, and format are still important when communicating with a multiple audience. You can make adjustments by writing different parts of a report for different readers, focusing on the needs of the primary audience, and revising a short document for different readers.

4. Analyze your audience.

5. After you have analyzed your audience, decide how you will accommodate your readers' needs and wants.

6. Early in the writing process, determine the purpose (what you want your reader to do after reading the document), scope (what you will include and exclude), and medium (the method of delivering the message—report, e-mail, letter, or CD).

7. When selecting the medium, consider what is appropriate for the audience, message, and purpose; whether the cost (time and money) of producing the medium is worth the possible outcome; and what media are available.

Checklist

- Is my audience a select audience or multiple audience?

- Have I analyzed the knowledge level, roles, interests, cultural background, and personality of my audience?

- If I am dealing with a multiple audience, have I selected a strategy for accommodating the needs and wants of the audience?

- Have I put into words the purpose of my writing assignment?

- Have I determined the scope of my writing assignment by deciding what it should and should not include?

- Have I found an appropriate medium for the writing assignment?

- Did I match the audience to the medium?

- Have I weighed the costs and time of producing the medium?

- Have I considered other available media?

- Have I selected an appropriate format for the audience and purpose of the writing assignment?

- Have I checked for stereotypes in my writing?

Build On What You Know

1. To make you more aware of audience, answer the following questions: Who might be the target audience for these TV shows or networks? What groups of people might they appeal to? Why?

Home Shopping Network	Monday Night Football	CMT (Country Music Television)
60 Minutes	Jeopardy	Nick at Nite
MTV	Star Trek: Enterprise	The History Channel

2. Consider the following terms. If any are unfamiliar to you, look them up in a dictionary or ask your family and friends. Which audience(s) would understand these terms?

blitz	RAM	curl	saute
goalie	handle	dunk	arabesque
rap	compost	angioplasty	starboard

3. Divide into teams of three or four students. Use the following scenario to answer Questions a–b.

   Sam, Julio, and Susan have just started publishing *TV Highlights,* a weekly magazine. Sam sells the advertising. Julio, a graphic designer, is responsible for the artwork. Julio's uncle is the owner. He makes most of the decisions but often defers to Julio's opinions. Susan is the accountant.

   Think about the role each person performs in this small company. How do each person's responsibilities affect decisions? How does each one's role affect how he or she communicates with the other people in the company? Also, think about the readers *TV Highlights* will serve. Who is the target audience?

   a. Julio wants a four-color cover for the first issue because he thinks the first issue should look impressive, but Susan thinks a four-color cover is too expensive. Sam says the advertisers do not care how many colors are on the cover; they only want the local high school's blue and red colors to be represented. Susan decides to write a report to Julio's uncle recommending a two-color cover for the first few issue. Who is Susan's audience for the report? What should she remember about her audience? What kind of information might she include to convince Julio's uncle (and Julio)? Should she include information about Sam's concerns?

   b. Ulrike Bohm, a freelance writer, has written to Julio asking what topics interest the magazine's readers. The magazine is written for a rural audience in the southeastern part of the United States. The average reader is a middle-aged woman. What types of articles do you think *TV Highlights'* readers are interested in?

Apply What You Learned

4. Name some slang terms that are used by your friends or that are popular with your generation. Why do these terms appeal to your age group? Ask your parents or grandparents for slang terms popular when they were growing up. What do you think about their slang terms? Would you use them? Why or why not?

5. Look through the comic section of the Sunday newspaper. Which comic strips appeal to which audiences? How do you know? For each comic strip, list the target audience and features about the comic strip that help you identify the audience.

6. Bring several issues of your favorite magazine to class. Spend 15–20 minutes looking at the table of contents and browsing through the articles and advertisements. Then, answer the following questions:

   a. Who is the intended audience?

   b. What are four things the editors have done to appeal to you, the reader?

   c. Do you like what the editors have done to appeal to you?

   d. Do you have suggestions for improving their appeal? What are your suggestions?

   e. Do you notice stereotypes in the magazines, particularly in the advertisements?

7. Go to your nearest newsstand, grocery, or bookstore. Notice which magazines appeal to specific interests and which magazines appeal to a general audience. In particular, look for these targeted groups: women, teens, sports lovers, craft lovers, technicians, parents, children, and a general audience.

   a. For each of these targeted groups, list several magazines that are obviously written for the target group.

   b. For each group, select one of the magazines you identified and look through it more closely. List at least four adjustments the editors made to accommodate the needs of their readers and to appeal to the readers' needs and wants.

   c. Write several paragraphs analyzing your favorite magazine for audience and purpose.

8. Write a letter to your employer requesting time off for a special event, such as homecoming or a family vacation. Then switch roles. Write a letter from the employer denying the time off. How are your letters different? How are they alike?

9. Write a letter to the President of the United States about a particular policy you like (or do not like). Tell a friend what you like (or do not like) about the same policy. How does your language change from audience to audience?

See the Data CD for a table in which you can write and organize your ideas.

Work Is A Zoo!

You will be spending some time helping Anya and Tyrone develop a promotion plan for ZiPS to present to local science instructors. (In fact, you and Tyrone will be giving a presentation on some research.) Anya asks you to give her your thoughts about communicating with these science instructors. Try jotting your thoughts in table format.

As you plan your approach:

- Define your purpose. Why do you want to communicate with science instructors? What is your goal? Try writing one sentence that defines your purpose for communicating.

- Analyze your audience. What do they know about the zoo programs? Do they see the connection between the zoo and their classroom activities? How might you convince them of the importance of a partnership? Perhaps some of these questions will help:

  - How many people are in the audience?

  - How old are they?

  - What do they already know?

  - What new information do they need?

  - What is their educational and cultural background?

  - What do I want them to do with the message?

- Collect information. What other information will help you appeal to the science instructors? Would it be helpful to interview science instructors who have used the zoo programs before? You will probably need to research the topic, make phone calls, talk to coworkers, determine ways to back up your ideas or arguments, and so on.

GOALS

DISTINGUISH the differences between researching at school and at work

IDENTIFY and locate secondary sources

DOCUMENT secondary sources

EVALUATE and **TAKE** notes from sources

COLLECT primary data

 See the Data CD for Write-to-Learn and In The Know activity worksheets.

WRITE-TO-LEARN

Think about a time when you researched a topic. What was the reason for your research? What did researching the topic involve? In other words, how did you conduct the research? Did your research include a survey, an experiment, or an interview? What did you learn from your research activities?

In The Know

archives collections or repositories of documents

citations written indications of the sources for borrowed materials

close-ended questions questions that restrict the number of possible answers

direct quotation the use of borrowed ideas, words, phrases, and sentences exactly as they appear in the original source

documentation a system of giving credit for borrowed ideas and words

open-ended questions questions that encourage the respondent to provide any answer he or she likes; the questions give no suggested answers

paraphrase presenting someone else's ideas in your own words, phrases, and sentence structure

periodicals materials published at specified intervals of time, such as magazines, journals, newsletters, and newspapers

plagiarism the act of using another person's words and/or ideas without properly documenting or giving credit

population the group from whom you want to gather data

primary sources direct or firsthand reports of facts or observations, such as an eyewitness account or a diary

reliable data provides results that can be duplicated under similar circumstances

respondents people chosen to answer questions

sample a subgroup with the same characteristics as the entire population

secondary sources indirect or secondhand reports of information, such as the description of an event the writer or speaker did not witness

summarize to condense longer material, keeping essential or main ideas and omitting unnecessary parts, such as examples and illustrations

valid data provides an accurate measurement of what you intend to measure

Writing@Work

Selam Daniel is a product research engineer at Procter & Gamble in Cincinnati, Ohio. In her position as product research engineer, she acts as the link between the consumer and the technology.

Selam's research is focused on understanding more about what consumers want, need, and believe. Her job is to link what she learns about consumers to Procter & Gamble's technical capabilities so that P&G can better meet the needs of its consumers. As a result of Selam's research, Procter & Gamble should be better able to understand its consumers and therefore develop products to meet consumers' needs, resulting in more sales than the competition.

In her position, Selam must write many documents for claims support. In its marketing communications, P&G makes claims to consumers about product benefits. All claims must be backed by consumer and technical data. Consumer data determines whether the claim is meaningful to the consumer. Technical data must prove that products can technically deliver what they claim to deliver. These documents must be able to answer any challenges raised by competitors.

Selam's documents must be well written and contain solid information. At times, a competitor's challenge may be taken to court. In these instances, it is imperative that Selam's research be thorough and her reports be well written and understandable. If Selam's reports are not solid and her information not properly documented, Procter & Gamble may lose the challenge. A lot rides on the depth of her research, but also on her ability to accurately communicate that research in her reports. P&G relies on Selam to be able to communicate effectively through her writing and to appropriately report the sources of her information.

Selam has a bachelor's degree in chemical engineering and a bachelor's degree in marketing, both from Massachusetts Institute of Technology. "In my engineering degree I learned the science, but my marketing degree was where I learned to make the data meaningful to the consumer and other nontechnical audiences," Selam explains.

Working Bibliography

Alika, Rachel, and Andrew M. Dalton. "Bacteria: The Good, the Bad, and the Uncertain." *Raleigh News and Observer* 23 Oct. 1980, east. ed.: A1 +

Berlin, Robert E., and Catherine C. Stanton. *Radioactive Waste Management.* New York: Wiley, 1989.

Kapsner, Jake. "Researchers Develop Munching Bacteria." *The Minnesota Daily Online* 21 Oct. 1998. 26 June 2003
< http://www.mndaily.com/daily/1998/10/21/news/ >

Schrempf, Rosalind. "World's Toughest Bacterium Has a Taste for Waste." *Energy Research News* Aug. 1998. 12 June 2003
< http://www.pln.gov/08_98?art2.htm >

"Witches' Brew of Weird Bugs." *Frontiers: The Electronic Newsletter of the National Science Foundation* Oct. 1996: 7 June 2003
< http://www.nsf.gov/od/lpa/news/publicat/frontier/ >

Yarrow, Houston. "Re: Questions on Medical Waste Management, Radiation." E-mail to the author. 24 May 2003
< http://www.nsf.gov/od/lpa/news/publicat/frontier/ >

Figure 3.1 Working Bibliography Model

RESEARCHING AT WORK

Employees rely on information they collect to solve problems, make decisions, answer questions, and perform many other work functions. On the job, research is usually involved in all of these situations (and more):

- Developing a new product
- Handling a production problem
- Purchasing equipment or services
- Establishing safety procedures
- Selecting employee benefits
- Planning an advertising campaign
- Expanding a market area

Unlike writing for school, writing on the job provides information to help the business operate effectively, not to show the writer's knowledge of the topic.

For example, if a nurse writes a fact sheet explaining how patients should manage their diabetes, the nurse is not writing to show how much he knows about the subject, but to teach patients how to stay healthy. If a chef creates standard operating procedures, the chef does not write the document to impress readers with how much she learned in school, but rather to ensure food safety. All of the information writers and researchers gather and present is used for effective job performance.

Before you can write at work, you often need to conduct research. In fact, many decisions and actions at work require more information than you have at hand. You probably begin by determining what you already know. Then, considering your audience, purpose, and scope, you gather and evaluate new information and probably form conclusions about the material you read. Before you conduct the research, you must make sure you know who,

WARM UP

Recall research tasks you may have done in a work setting. For each task, what was the purpose of the research? How was the workplace research different from research you have done for pleasure or at school? For example, how is researching the best solution for a Japanese beetle infestation in a lawn you are managing for a client different from finding more information about your favorite entertainer?

what, where, when, why, and how. For example, who is involved and who will use your research? What do they need to know? Where will you search for information, within or outside your organization? Why are you researching this topic? How will you collect information, and how will it be used? You also need a strategy for:

- Finding and evaluating the right material and the best sources.

- Conducting the research and reading efficiently.

- Carefully and accurately recording the information you find so you do not accidentally violate the owner's copyright.

- Documenting where you found the information so you or someone else can find it again.

Researchers may find some data easily, as in production figures that are readily available on the corporate network. Sometimes, though, they must search extensively for information.

Employees have two basic sources of information: secondary sources and primary sources. **Secondary sources** are reports or accounts of what someone else sees, hears, or thinks. When a newspaper reporter describes what executives of a closing textile plant said, that description is a secondary source. **Primary sources,** on the other hand, are direct or firsthand presentations of facts or observations. The writer or speaker is the one who witnessed the event or developed the idea.

For example, a diary is a firsthand account of the writer's experiences and is, therefore, a primary source. However, if you use ideas from another person's diary in a report on healthy lifestyles, the borrowed ideas become secondary data in your report because you did not experience or observe them yourself.

Likewise, hearing the company president, rather than the reporter, give reasons for the plant's closing is primary information.

Researchers generally start with secondary sources because they often give general overviews and offer good background information. Secondary sources are usually easier and less expensive to consult than primary sources. The overviews these sources can give help researchers understand what is already known about the topic. A problem solver may even learn that someone has already discovered a solution.

Stop and Think

How is researching at work different from researching at school? Why do professionals conduct research?

FINDING SECONDARY DATA

To solve most problems, your first step is to explore the available secondary data. After all, you do not want to reinvent the wheel. If the answer already exists, you do not need to spend time, effort, and money to rediscover it.

For work-related research, you will probably use one or more of the following sources of secondary data: your organization's correspondence and report **archives,** a library catalog, periodicals, and general reference materials. While these secondary data sources may be available in print or hard copy, most will be available in print and electronically.

WARM UP

As a new sales representative, you are going to Japan to meet your first prospective customer. If you know little about Japanese people and customs, where can you go to find out whether you should take the customer a gift and what is a good choice if you do take a gift? List several things you need to know and where you think you can find the information.

© GETTY IMAGES/PHOTODISC

CORRESPONDENCE AND REPORT ARCHIVES

A logical place to begin looking for an answer to a problem is in the organization where the problem occurs. Most organizations keep archives of all correspondence and reports. Especially in large organizations, archives are generally maintained in an electronic format, such as on computer disks or CDs.

On the other hand, some highly regulated organizations, such as pharmaceutical companies, may be required to keep print as well as electronic copies of essential information. Employees may use archived documents to learn about the history of the problem or topic. They may find letters, memos, or reports explaining when problems were first noted; what kind of investigation was conducted; and whether the solution was successful.

When the research topic does not have a history, relevant facts and statistics may be found in a variety of sources within the organization's records.

LIBRARY CATALOG

The researcher's next stop is either the company's library or a public or school library. Some large businesses have an in-house library that contains specialized materials relating to the business it serves. In addition to company-produced reports such as production figures, accident reports, and personnel information, these internal libraries typically hold materials employees need to stay current in the field in which they work. A software company's library probably contains books and journals specializing in software development and marketing. Since these company libraries focus specifically on the needs of employees, they do not compete with public or other libraries by carrying all types of reading and research materials. They often contain more electronic than paper resources. If no in-house library is available to the problem solvers, they must go to a school, municipal, or regional library.

Whether in an internal or public library, employees looking for secondary data find materials through the library catalog. The library catalog will help you find books, pamphlets, periodicals, audiovisual materials, and other holdings. Most libraries have computerized catalogs that are searchable by subject, title, author, and sometimes other categories, such as date or keyword.

After the user types the author's name, a title, or a subject, the online catalog displays a list of sources and their locations. Since materials are usually cataloged using authorized subject headings from *The Library of Congress Subject Headings,* using keywords found in this reference can make a search more effective. If a search yields one book with useful information, a new search using the keywords found in that book's entry will likely produce other useful sources. Most catalog systems also print requested entries. Generally, libraries have integrated systems so the online catalog can tell where a book is located and whether it is checked out.

If a researcher finds that a particular book is not in the library, the researcher may request that the book be ordered from another library through interlibrary loan. The book also may be found online through a service such as NetLibrary, which offers scanned electronic books.

Most online catalogs are user-friendly, but you should not hesitate to ask a librarian for help. Librarians can explain how to use the equipment, what the standard subject headings are, and how to search so you find what you need quickly and efficiently. Remember that the catalog will lead you to sources for background and in-depth information. For more recent data, use periodicals or Internet sources.

PERIODICALS

Magazines, journals, newsletters, and newspapers are called **periodicals** because they are published at specified intervals of time. (Journals are magazines that are published for a scholarly or academic audience.) When you need current information, periodicals, whether online or in print, are one type of source you should seek. All periodicals are more current than books, but newspapers, especially daily papers, provide even more current information than periodicals. In addition, many periodicals, such as *Newsweek* and *The New York Times,* are now published on the Internet and in print.

The next question is how to find the articles you need in the periodicals. Library catalogs will tell you what print periodicals the library holds in different subject areas, but to find specific articles, you need to search an index or a database.

In the past, indexes, printed on paper and bound as books or magazines, were time-consuming to use. Today most periodical searches are conducted electronically. Many web-based databases, available to libraries by subscription, index periodicals. SIRS, Gale, EbscoHost, ProQuest, and Elsevier are some of the best-known database providers. Some of the databases, such as Lexis-Nexis and Academic Universe (the academic version of Lexis-Nexis), are general; others are type-specific, such as SIRS, which includes publications dealing with the social sciences. In addition, some databases, such as Wall Street Journal Index and New York Times Index, specialize in newspapers.

You can access other indexes through a service provider such as OCLC (Online Computer Library Center, Inc.). For example, World Cat is an OCLC index of physical holdings (recordings, tapes, books, papers, and dissertations).

GENERAL REFERENCE MATERIALS

General reference materials such as encyclopedias, dictionaries, handbooks, almanacs, and fact books are quick ways to get information. Many users rely on easy access to general reference sources for background information. They may first check those available online, such as Grolier Online Encyclopedia or Merriam-Webster Online.

Some web sites even offer access to reference tools. For example, the Encyclopedia Britannica web site provides an encyclopedia, a dictionary, and an atlas. Also, the Bartleby Books site gives users access to several reference tools, including dictionaries, thesauruses, fact books, and books of quotations. Some materials are available on CD-ROM, such as Encarta, another encyclopedia.

Reference materials come in general interest versions. Some examples include *World Book Encyclopedia, Encyclopedia Britannica,* and *Webster's Dictionary.* Others are special interest versions, such as *Encyclopedia of Space Science and Technology (2003)* and *The American Heritage Stedman's Medical Dictionary (2002).* In addition, *The Encyclopedia of Educational Technology,* a web site created and maintained by San Diego State University, covers performance, training, and instructional design and technology.

ELECTRONIC RESOURCES

In addition to periodical databases, indexes, and online general reference materials such as encyclopedias and dictionaries, computers provide a wealth of information on countless topics. Because the Internet (also known as the World Wide Web, or simply the Web) is a worldwide collection of computer networks, it is an information highway connecting

Communication Update

When you go to the library, you may have access not only to that physical library, but also to thousands of other libraries throughout the world. World Cat, an Online Computer Library Center, Inc. (OCLC) service provider, links you through your library to the collections of more than 24,000 member libraries of OCLC. With this service you have access to more than 36 million records for books, manuscript collections, audiovisual materials, and countless computer files in a variety of languages.

government, military, educational, and commercial organizations and private citizens to a range of services and resources. Therefore, you can get information from a huge variety of sources over the Internet.

Users with access to local area networks (LAN) or to the Web may participate in bulletin boards, e-mail, listservs, and other means of exchanging information. If, for example, someone had problems with a particular car and was not able to resolve the issue with the car dealer, the car owner could retrieve consumer information from the manufacturer, advocacy groups, legal professionals, and other consumers online.

Finding Electronic Information How does a researcher get to the tremendous amount of information on the Internet? You can search the Web using a search engine such as Yahoo, Google, AltaVista, HotBot, Excite, and MetaCrawler in much the same way you search a database, using keywords and topics.

However, search engines do not look through all of the information on the Web. Each engine searches through only a portion of all of the sites. Even the metasearch engines, such as Momma and Metacrawler, do not cover the entire Web.

Even though search engines cover only a portion of the Web, the concern often is how to filter through so much information to find what is useful. Search engines use "spiders" to go out periodically and view web pages and links within sites; an "index" that catalogs words, Internet addresses, and other information about the pages the spider finds; and software to filter through all of the pages in the index to find matches when a search is requested. Since the "spider" goes out every few days or weeks, it detects changes made in web pages. However, until the information has been indexed, it is not available for researchers.

Because each search engine visits and indexes different sites and is updated at different times, you should routinely use at least three search engines. Then compare the results of your searches to determine which search engines are most effective.

Searching with Keywords Choose specific, precise keywords; then consider using the advanced or custom (terms may vary with search engines) search procedures to refine your search. The guidelines within the custom search or the Help section of the search engine should explain how to use logic or keyword connectors to limit or expand your search. The connectors listed below are typical.

TO LIMIT A SEARCH:

When you connect keywords with ...	the search yields sites containing ...
AND or +	both keywords
Example: juvenile AND diabetes	Sites that deal with juvenile diabetes
NOT or –	the first keyword, not the second
Example: diabetes-juvenile diabetes except juvenile	sites that deal with any type of
"keyword keyword" beside each other	the same keywords in the same order
Example: "capital punishment"	the same phrase

TO EXPAND A SEARCH:

OR	either keyword
Example: diabetes OR juvenile	diabetes and/or juvenile as the topic
Key* (wildcard)	the base or root within a word
Example: biblio* bibliophile, bibliotheca	bibliography, bibliographer,

Remember that you can get the same data in many different ways. One researcher may find an article by skimming a journal from the library shelf. Another researcher may do an online search in the library or on a home or office computer. Another may find a link to an online journal in a discussion group. Explore the many tools available to you for research.

Stop and Think Using the list you drafted in the Warm Up, underline the information that would come from secondary sources. For those underlined items, add any other sources or methods you can think of for accessing information.

DOCUMENTING SECONDARY SOURCES

Documentation is a way of giving credit to another person (writer or speaker) for his or her work; it is using a citation system to note whose ideas or words the writer is using and where he or she found them. Responsible writers document ideas and materials they borrow or use.

© GETTY IMAGES/PHOTODISC

Plagiarism is the term used at school for the act of using another person's words and ideas without giving credit. While plagiarism is a serious academic offense, sometimes causing students to fail a course or to be expelled from school, it is even more serious in the workplace. Theft of another's work often results in lost jobs, lawsuits, and ruined reputations.

In the musical version of plagiarism, members of the singing group Milli Vanilli actually were lip-syncing, rather than singing, their songs. When the public discovered the singers' deception, their careers were over.

Likewise, Doris Kearns Goodwin, a respected historian who won the Pulitzer Prize for History in 1995, taught and served on the Board of Overseers at Harvard, assisted President Lyndon Johnson with his memoirs, and won many awards, admitted to plagiarism in a book she wrote in 1987.

Despite a long career with many achievements and honors, this admission caused Goodwin to be ridiculed in public, scorned by her peers, and subjected to significant financial loss. The University of Delaware withdrew its invitation to her to make a graduation speech; PBS placed her on indefinite leave from the Jim Lehrer news show; she had to defend the credibility of all of her other books; and her publisher had to pay Lynn McTaggert, the author of the book from which Goodwin had extensively plagiarized. As you can see, plagiarism, intentional or accidental, can be damaging.

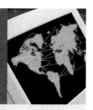

Communication Dilemma

You and your good friend Armando work for a desktop publishing company that creates marketing materials for bands giving concerts in your area. Your job is to contact the bands, design the posters and other marketing materials, and publish and distribute the materials. You have recently learned that you and Armando know the band members who are coming to your town to give a concert. In fact, you know the band members so well that you have copies of some of their unpublished songs they have written that they shared with you before they became famous.

Armando is in charge of creating the marketing materials for the band. When you look over the finished products, you notice he included parts of the unpublished songs as a way to lure fans to the concert. You feel uneasy about publishing these, but you know that you cannot reach the band members to ask permission because they are in Europe touring for a month before coming to town.

1. If you and Armando publish the songs, are you breaking copyright laws?
2. How can you find out?

You may ask, "What exactly do I document?" You document anything you use from another person's work. Remember, if you do not document, you are no longer borrowing; you are stealing and will be treated as an intellectual property thief. Therefore, to keep your credibility, reputation, or job, document borrowed phrases, sentences, or ideas in the form of summaries, paraphrases, and direct quotations. For instance, if you reported on the environmental impact of a new soy ink for your company's publications division, you would document researched facts, contradictory statements, and unique ideas.

On the other hand, you do not need to document common knowledge or information your audience typically knows. Yet common knowledge may differ for each audience, particularly expert audiences. For instance, the fact that Bill Gates is chief executive officer of Microsoft Corporation is common knowledge for an audience of computer engineers. Gates's management philosophy might be common knowledge for business school graduates. If information is common knowledge for your target audience, you do not need to document it. The same information directed to a different audience may not be common knowledge and, therefore, would need to be documented.

The writer's field determines the documentation format. For example, Modern Language Association (MLA) format, most likely taught in your English class, is the documentation system used in the humanities. Other documentation systems include the American Psychological Association (APA) system for social sciences and the Council of Biology Editors (CBE) system for biological sciences.

© DIGITAL VISION

In addition, most fields have a style manual. A style manual is a book of rules for developing a document, including formatting and documentation. *The Chicago Manual of Style*, the stylebook of The University of Chicago Press, is the preferred style manual for many technical fields.

Since each documentation system has a particular format, consult your instructor (or employer) for the appropriate style manual. For example, if, as a human resources officer, you investigate the effectiveness of a test used to screen job applicants (a psychology-related topic), you will probably use American Psychological Association (APA) style. However, a report outlining the water quality of a prospective site for a trout farm (a biology-related topic) may require that you use Council of Biology Editors (CBE) style guidelines.

All documentation systems explain how to identify each source. However, the emphasis, order, and punctuation may be different. The APA and CBE, for instance, emphasize publication dates in citations because dates are critical in the sciences. The MLA emphasizes the author and location in the text. This book uses the MLA system.

Documentation comes in two parts: 1) the Works Cited (or Bibliography), or list of sources at the end of the document and 2) the internal citations. The documentation process begins with a working bibliography.

BIBLIOGRAPHY AND WORKS CITED

A bibliography (also called Works Cited in MLA) is a list of sources that you used. While collecting data, researchers develop a working bibliography. They continue to locate and add new sources to the list during the research process. Sometimes they delete a source from the list when they find a more recent or reliable one.

SEE THE SITES

Although the University of Chicago Press online edition does not replace the book edition of the *Chicago Manual of Style,* you can still get information on how to cite books, electronic resources, journals, and newspapers.

The Modern Language Association (MLA) web site gives the history of MLA along with many book titles about the English language. You also can listen to archives of MLA radio programs.

You can find the url for both sites in the web links on techwriting. swlearning.com.

When the research is finished, writers use the list's final form to prepare a bibliography. A bibliography accomplishes three purposes: 1) it establishes credibility by showing readers what sources you consulted; 2) it allows others to find your information path so they can continue or evaluate the study; and 3) it gives credit to other people's thoughts, words, and sentences that you used.

As you look at secondary sources, you develop a paper or an electronic working bibliography. You can enter publication information for each source on a 3″3 5″ index card. Cards allow you to arrange entries easily for the final source list. However, many writers prefer to maintain bibliographic data electronically. Like the cards, computers allow you to easily add, delete, or move sources. In addition, software that automatically puts source information into MLA form is available. Hypertext programs show images of cards where users key bibliographic information.

After you complete the research and draft the document, you remove the sources you did not use. You place sources you did use in order. For MLA, use alphabetical order by the first author's last name or by the word that appears at the beginning of the entry, often a title if the author is not given. Other systems arrange sources differently. You will use the arranged cards to compose the Works Cited page, as shown in Figure 3.1. This page goes at the end of the document or report.

Focus on Ethics

Another aspect of borrowing or using others' words and ideas involves copyright. Copyright legally protects the rights of writers and gives them a way to control how their work is used. Copyright applies only to tangible and original expression, not to oral presentations.

Using copyrighted work requires special considerations. If the way you plan to use someone's words or ideas fits the definition of fair use, then you may use the work without payment or permission. Yet you still must give credit to the creator. Fair use guidelines are special exceptions that allow others to use a portion of a writer's work in a limited way. Fair use evaluates the purpose and nature of the new use, the character of the copyrighted work, the percentage of the work being used, and the effect of the use on the original's marketability. Ultimately, fair use requires that the new user not damage the original or profit from its use.

When you are uncertain about whether to request copyright permission or to document a source, consult other writers, your supervisor or mentor at work, or others with experience in the field. If you are still in doubt, it is better to request permission and to document. No writer or professional has ruined a reputation or career for overdocumenting, but many have for lack of documentation.

INTERNAL CITATIONS

People will assume ideas are yours unless they see a citation in the text. **Citations** are written indications of the source of borrowed materials. Enter internal documentation immediately after each summary, paraphrase, and direct quotation to tell your reader where you found the information. Internal citations in MLA consist of the author's last name (or a shortened form of the title if no author is named) and the page number. If the author's name is mentioned in the introductory sentence, only the page numbers appear in the citation. Readers then use the author's name or the title to find the full bibliographic entry in the alphabetical listings of works cited. At the end of the sentence (or group of sentences) containing the source material in your document, place the citation. Enclose the citation in parentheses and place the period after the ending parenthesis, as shown in Figure 3.2.

Excerpt from Research Document

A bacterium that can break down toxic waste and survive heavy doses of radiation, suggests one report, could help the United States speedily and inexpensively deal with its estimated 3,000 dump sites (Kapsner). This bacterium, according to an article in a National Science Foundation newsletter, is named *Deinococcus radiodurans*, which means "strange berry that withstands radiation," for its red color and its ability to live through 3,000 times more radiation than it would take to kill a person ("Witches Brew"). Not only can this bacterium survive, it even grows when constantly exposed to normally lethal doses of radiation. Perhaps the key is in the structure of the DNA repair systems, says one recent report (Spake 67).

Excerpt from Works Cited

Works Cited

Kapsner, Jake. "Researchers Develop Munching Bacteria." *The Minnesota Daily On-line*

21 Oct. 1998. 26 June 2003

<http://www.mndaily.com/daily/1998/10/21/news/>

Spake, Amanda. "Conan's Little Secret." *U.S. News & World Report* 20 Jan. 2003: 67.

"Witches' Brew of Weird Bugs." *Frontiers: The Electronic Newsletter of the National*

Science Foundation Oct. 1996: 7 June 2003

<http://www.nsf.gov/od/lpa/news/publicat/frontier/>

Figure 3.2 Internal Citation and Works Cited

 What happens when writers incorrectly or incompletely cite sources? What are the costs to businesses? to professionals?

EVALUATING SOURCES

As you have discovered, not everything that appears in print (or on your computer, radio, or TV) is true. In fact, many mistakes, untruths, and half-truths that you would not want to repeat are published. A financial planner who uses an unreliable source's information to make faulty investments for clients, for instance, will not stay in business. So, when you research, choose your data sources critically and carefully.

These guidelines for evaluating sources will help you get started.

PUBLICATION DATE

When you want to know the most recent discoveries and happenings in a particular area, you need up-to-date information. Therefore, you must check publication dates. Data in a book may be even older than the copyright date indicates, since some books take two or more years to be published. Likewise, web sites without dates may not have been checked or revised in years.

AUTHOR'S CREDENTIALS

Often the preface or introduction in a book outlines the education and experience of the writers or editors. Likewise, magazine and journal articles sometimes include brief biographies. Check web sites, particularly the beginning and ending pages, for an author's biography and credentials. If the publication gives no information about the author or editor, consider factors such as the reputation of the journal, publisher, or associated business or organization.

You also can check an author's reputation in reference sources such as *Who's Who in America, Contemporary Authors, Who's Who in Science,* and *Who's Who in Small Business and Entrepreneurship Worldwide.* Some of these references, such as *Contemporary Authors,* are found online.

Based on what you learn about the author's credentials, determine whether he or she qualifies as an expert in the field. If you have two sources on the same topic, you might find one author to be more credible than the other.

Check the author's methods and resources Usually, in the introduction of a book or in the opening paragraphs of an article, the author or editor will explain the methods used to reach the conclusions. If you believe those methods are flawed, the book or article loses credibility as a potential source. Likewise, you may evaluate a potential source by the resources its author uses. Resources may be mentioned in the text and listed in a works cited section or bibliography.

These guidelines will help with many sources, but the increasing availability of electronic materials means that researchers are spending more time and effort searching online. Therefore, you should give special consideration to evaluating electronic sources. Since its materials are not screened in any way, the Internet contains more trash than treasure. Remember that anyone, from the bored 10-year-old next door to the busy physics professor, can post a web site.

The following guidelines are especially useful in evaluating electronic information:

Is an author or sponsoring group listed? Are credentials or experiences noted to show that the author is an expert on the subject covered? Is the author or sponsor mentioned in other sources? If no author or sponsor were given, a critical reader would wonder why. For instance, an animal rights supporter could maintain an anonymous site emphasizing abusive aspects of corporate farming methods.

Electronic address The abbreviation in the web address should show that the source originates from:

Educational institution	.edu
Government organization	.gov
Military	.mil
Nonprofit organization	.org
For-profit or commercial organization	.com

Sites sponsored by schools are usually academic and objective, providing reliable information. Government-sponsored sites—whether local, state, national, or international—typically present reliable information, such as U.S. census data. However, these sites may be biased. For example, the President controls the press secretary's message and focus of a given story.

Likewise, many nonprofit organizations, such as the American Lung Association, maintain trustworthy sites, but some will be biased by the organization's agenda. For example, the National Rifle Association site is unlikely to provide statistics on the number of children killed by guns in their homes, but is more likely to show how many burglaries are stopped by homeowners with guns. However, commercial sites will almost always be biased. After all, readers cannot expect a web page sponsored by Gerber to tell parents why they should not feed Gerber baby food to their children.

References and/or links Does the web site include a list of sources used in preparing the page that readers can check? Are links to other reputable, reliable sites included? Are the links to scholarly sites or to commercial or obviously biased sites?

Balance and purpose Does the site present the subject fairly? Does it include opposing viewpoints? Is the design clear and careful to aid the reader's understanding, or does the design encourage strong reactions or confusion? Offensive images and cluttered, irrelevant information may be intended to create a particular response from users. For instance, viewers are more likely to have an emotional reaction than a logical response to an image of caged animals in a medical research facility. Understanding a site's purpose—to sell ideas, products, or services; to share knowledge; or to incite strong reactions—can help determine how reliable the information is.

 Stop and Think Read this case and consider possible outcomes: Colleen received time and money to study the effects of a particular veterinary medicine on humans. Her report requesting permission for this project was based primarily on one study published in an animal science journal. Over the last year, this study was largely discredited in animal and human medical journals.

WARM UP

Examine the notes you take during class. Approximately what percentage of the notes are written exactly in the instructor's or speaker's words? Approximately what percentage are written in your own words, your interpretation of the instructor's or speaker's comments? How many notes are your ideas or perhaps conclusions you came to as a result of something someone else said?

TAKING NOTES FROM SOURCES

Employees doing research note information they collect, just as you do when writing a paper in school. When you discover data you believe will be helpful, write complete and careful notes. Some researchers prefer to use 4″ × 6″ note cards because they are easy to arrange and carry. At the same time, laptop and handheld computers encourage most researchers to take notes electronically. The computer user can then transfer notes into the first draft of the report without having to retype them. Researchers reading a document online can copy and paste material they want to quote directly into the draft document.

© GETTY IMAGES/PHOTODISC

Before making notes, read the source material carefully. Understanding your sources thoroughly is an important part of being a successful researcher.

Read the excerpt in Figure 3.3 below from an article describing potential uses of the bacterium *Deinococcus radiodurans.* Jake Kapsner wrote the article, "Researchers Develop Munching Bacteria," for the *The Minnesota Daily Online.* You will find the complete bibliographic entry at the beginning of this chapter. This passage will be used to discuss note taking.

> Although the Cold War ended years ago, genetic researchers at the University are still fighting a $200 billion legacy of contaminated nuclear waste sites.
>
> A toxic-waste-munching bacterium that stands up to even the toughest radioactive environments could make cleaning up the approximate 3,000 nuclear waste sites in the United States quicker and cheaper. "The bug survives radiation . . . while diminishing liquid organic toxic waste," said Cleston Lange, a research co-author who finished his doctoral work in microbial biochemistry at the University. "Millions of gallons of toxic waste were amassed during the past 50 years of nuclear proliferation, primarily at U.S. Department of Energy sites where solvents were used to purify uranium," Lange said.

Figure 3.3 Excerpt from a Research Article

On each card or with the note-taking software you use, include 1) the information you want to use—only one idea per card, 2) the topic, and 3) the source and page number(s) from which you took the data. Figure 3.4 illustrates the way some researchers use note cards.

> Use for Deinococcus rad.   Kapsner
>
> According to a researcher at the University of Minnesota, the bacterium Deinococcus radiodurans could help the United States clean up around 3,000 nuclear waste dumps left over from the Cold War.

Figure 3.4 Model Note Card (Paraphrase)

You can use borrowed information in your notes in these three ways:
1) summary, 2) paraphrase, and 3) direct quotation.

SUMMARY

To **summarize** is to condense longer material, keeping the essential or main ideas and omitting nonessentials, such as the examples and illustrations. Be consistent with the source's idea, but use your words. When doing job-related research, you might summarize a journal article or chapter of a book that is helpful supporting evidence in a report. The original material you summarize might be an entire book, but your summary might be a few paragraphs or one sentence. The note in Figure 3.5 summarizes the original material you read in the article about bacterium.

> Bacterium to clean up nuclear waste dumps   Kapsner
>
> During the Cold War's 50 years of increasing nuclear arsenals, the United States developed a $200 billion problem in approximately 3,000 locations where toxic waste remained after liquids were used to purify uranium. A bacterium able to survive extreme radiation and to "eat" or break down pollutants may be a solution, reports an expert in microbial biochemistry at the University of Minnesota.

Figure 3.5 Summary Note Card

PARAPHRASE

To **paraphrase** is to borrow or use someone else's idea and to present it in your own words, phrases, and sentence structure. While a summary should be shorter than the original material, a paraphrase generally is about the same length or even a bit longer than the original. A writer paraphrases when the material supports a point but is not unique or dramatic enough to be quoted. Most of the materials writers use from other sources are paraphrased. Paraphrasing allows writers to include the thinking of many others while putting the borrowed ideas into the writer's own words and sentences. As you practice paraphrasing, you may find this process helpful:

1. Read the original carefully.

2. Put it aside.

3. Write the idea in your own way.

4. Compare your version with the original.

5. Be certain you have used your own words and sentence structure and have accurately conveyed the author's idea.

Figure 3.6 contains a paraphrase of the first sentence from the excerpt on bacterium. Notice that the wording and sentence structure is significantly different. Changing or moving a word or two is not effective paraphrasing. Avoid plagiarism by stating the borrowed idea in your own way, choosing words and sentence structure you would normally use, and properly crediting the author of the source.

Benefits of Deinococcus rad.	Kapsner
Bacteria that can break down toxic waste and survive heavy doses of radiation, suggests one report, could help the United States speedily and inexpensively deal with its estimated 3,000 nuclear waste sites.	

Figure 3.6 Paraphrase Note Card

DIRECT QUOTATION

Direct quotation is the third way writers incorporate borrowed material into their documents. When quoting, a writer uses ideas, words, phrases, and sentences exactly as they appear in the original. However, be careful not to overuse quotations; avoid a cut-and-paste patchwork style by making less than 20 percent of your document direct quotations. Copy phrases and sentences directly only when you cannot present the idea as well in your own words. For instance, if the original writer or speaker chose unusual words or composed unique or dramatic sentences, you may want your reader to get the flavor of the original by quoting directly. Another reason for using direct quotation is to enhance your credibility by using the words of a well-known authority. Figure 3.7 is a model of a notecard using direct quotation.

Damage Remaining after Cold War	Kapsner
While the age of nuclear proliferation has ended, according to one source, the United States is "still fighting a $200 billion legacy of contaminated nuclear waste sites."	

Figure 3.7 Direct Quotation Note Card

Introduce quotations Writers introduce quotations to make the writing smooth. Do not let quoted sentences stand alone. You can integrate quotations into your text with words such as "according to one expert" and "Greg Markham claims" or with complete sentences such as:

Benjamin Franklin gave this advice in *Poor Richard's Almanac:* "Early to bed, early to rise, makes a man healthy, wealthy, and wise."

Indicate added or omitted material When you need to add to or edit a direct quotation for clarity or conciseness, use brackets to set your changes apart from the quoted words, as in the sentences below.

Original: "After the board meeting in which a 2 percent fine was approved, she signed her resignation letter."

Addition for clarity: "After the board meeting in which a 2 percent fine was approved, [Margaret Fletcher] signed her resignation letter."

You may need to quote only part of a sentence. In this case, use an ellipsis, three spaced dots, to show where you omitted words from the original. However, if you include a paraphrase of the idea (rather than omit it), you will not need an ellipsis. If the reason for Fletcher's resignation is not important to your work, you might quote the source this way:

Omission: "After the board meeting [..., Margaret Fletcher] signed her resignation letter."

The ellipsis shows that the clause "in which a 2 percent fine was approved" was left out of the quotation.

Stop and Think When should a writer use direct quotation? Would you use an ellipsis or brackets to indicate that you left out part of a quoted sentence?

What could you do in the following situation?

You stained your new sweater with a chemical from the chemistry lab. You do not know the name of the chemical, but you remember the experiment and probably would recognize the bottle containing the chemical. You want to have the sweater cleaned, but you are afraid to do so without knowing which chemical caused the spot.

COLLECTING PRIMARY DATA

Many job-related problems or questions are too unique or too current for secondary sources to answer. A commercial fisher may learn more about a new net's effectiveness by asking other users and by experimenting than by reading the literature on nets. To solve work-related concerns, primary data may be more help. Primary data is gathered through field research: surveys, interviews, observation, and experimentation. Some field research is conducted in person, some by telephone, and some online.

© GETTY IMAGES/PHOTODISC

SURVEYS

Surveys gather facts, beliefs, attitudes, and opinions from people. Many businesses rely on surveys to collect information for decision making. One example is a questionnaire accompanying a product registration form for small appliances such as hair dryers. The manufacturer uses the data to determine who is buying the product, how the buyer learned of the product (what advertising method worked), and how satisfied the buyer is.

A survey works only when you know what you want to learn before you begin. Once you decide what you want to learn, you should 1) carefully select your audience or **respondents**, 2) decide how you will administer your survey, and 3) carefully plan your questions.

When you choose an audience, you must select a sample broad enough to represent that audience. **Population** is the target group from which you want to gather data. A garden center owner who wants to know whether customers will use a repotting service would have a population of all of the business's customers. If the owner cannot question all customers due to expense, time, or distance, she may choose a sample to provide representative answers. A **sample** is a subgroup that represents (has the same characteristics as) the entire group. Keep in mind that the sample must be small enough for you to be able to tabulate and analyze the results but large enough to provide meaningful results. In some situations, companies hire specially trained people to design and conduct surveys.

Once you know your audience, the next step is to decide how to administer the survey. You can administer questionnaires in person, by mail, by telephone, or by e-mail; many businesses survey by e-mail now. This decision is based on the kind of data you seek, how much time you have, and your budget. If you are asking personal or controversial questions, use a confidential mailed survey to ensure a higher return rate. And although many people believe their e-mail is private, it is far from secure. In fact, in the workplace, employers have the right to access information on company computers, so your e-mail there is subject to scrutiny. If time is a concern, telephone, e-mail, and in-person surveys offer faster responses than mail surveys. Also, remember that all survey methods can be costly.

Consider these suggestions as you prepare surveys:

Explain why you need the information and how it will be used Because you are asking respondents to share data, they have the right to know what you plan to do with the information. In a cover letter or an opening paragraph, explain what prompted the survey. Then describe the benefits. Estimate the time required to complete the survey. Many surveys also offer to send respondents results of the study.

Convince your audience to participate After all, you are asking for their time and thoughts. They may wonder what you are giving them in return. You might consider offering an incentive, such as coupons, free merchandise or services, improved or additional services, or discounts.

Logically order questions, beginning with easy-to-answer items If respondents have difficulty with the first questions, they are not likely to continue. The initial questions should ask for information that is easy to recall and not too personal. Also, arrange questions in logical groupings to aid respondents' memory.

Ask only necessary questions If you do not need the answer, do not ask the question. For example, do not ask about income if income is not relevant to the data you seek. People will not respond if they believe you are wasting their time.

Write clear and nonleading questions For responses to be useful, questions must be clear and precise. Compare the following two questions:

■ Do you shop by mail often?

■ Do you shop by mail once a month?

With the first question, the respondent will answer based on his or her definition of *often*. Such an answer may not be useful. Likewise, questions should not lead respondents to particular answers. Consider the following questions as an illustration:

■ Don't you believe that the cost of class rings is outrageous?

■ Why don't you buy your lunch in the school cafeteria?

The wording suggests a particular answer. Consider changing to:

- Do you believe the cost of class rings is reasonable or unreasonable?

- Is cost a factor in your decision to purchase lunch in the school cafeteria?

Make the question's purpose clear If the survey is to learn about consumers' reaction to your newspaper's new type style, do not ask such general questions as "Why did you purchase this newspaper?" Answers to this general question may vary tremendously, from "It was the cheapest one on the newsstand" to "This is the one my father reads." Such responses will not help you find what you want to know—whether people like the new type style.

Prefer facts to opinions When designing questions, seek facts whenever possible. Facts provide stronger, more credible evidence. For example, ask "Do you purchase from a mail-order catalog once a month or more?" rather than "Do you like mail-order shopping?"

Stick to one topic per question While you might be tempted to include several issues in one question, the answers will be useless if you do not know to which topic the person is responding. Suppose respondents say yes to the question "Are you ever concerned for your safety as you walk through the parking deck and up the stairs into the Whitley Building at night?" You do not know what concerns them—the deck, the stairs, the building, or the darkness.

Plan for tabulation Remember that once responses come in, you need to evaluate and interpret them. Your job will be easier if you design questions whose answers are stated as numbers. When you already know the range of possible answers, **close-ended questions**, such as these two, allow for a limited number of responses and are easy to tabulate.

Do you live within five miles of one of our stores?

Yes_____   No_____

Please indicate your level of satisfaction with your purchase.

1. Extremely Satisfied < >

2. Satisfied < >

3. Somewhat Satisfied < >

4. Somewhat Dissatisfied < >

5. Dissatisfied < >

6. Extremely Dissatisfied < >

Although more difficult to tabulate, **open-ended questions** are sometimes necessary to discover respondents' thoughts and feelings; unexpected attitudes or information may be uncovered this way.

Open-ended questions ask respondents to supply words, sentences, or short essays, as shown in the example on the next page:

How do you think RFG's board should respond to the new regulations?
What could Apgard Limited do to improve service to you and your organization?

Leave adequate space for answers when asking open-ended questions. Figure 3.8 gives examples of different types of questions.

Phi Rho

"Working Together to Serve"

Residents of Glenhaven:

We are considering your Glenhaven Retirement Community for our annual service project. With your help, we would like to learn more about your interests. We would like to contribute something worthwhile and lasting to your neighborhood. | **States the reason for the survey and how the results will be used.**

Please take about five minutes now to answer these questions and then place the completed form in the box marked "PHI RHO" in the Recreation Center by August 25. In case you'd like to know the outcome, we will post a copy of the results in the same location in August 30. | **Tells how much time the survey will take to complete; explains how to return the survey.**

1. Your age is ___45 or younger ___46-55 ___56-65 ___66-75 ___76-85 ___86 or older | **Single answer/ multiple choice**

2. Do you live alone? ___yes ___no | **Dual Alternative**

3. Indicate your preferences for our service project by ranking the items below from 1 to 7, 1 being most important and 7 being least important.
___nature trail ___picnic area ___flagpole ___shuffleboard game ___square-foot garden sites ___exercise path ___croquet lawn | **Rank order question**

4. Check the item which best reflects your opinion for completing the following sentences. If a new outdoor area is installed in the community, I am. . .
___willing to spend two hours per month on maintenance. ___willing to pay $5 or less a year to hire a maintenance service. ___not willing to maintain the area. | **Single answer/ multiple choice question**

5. Mark your level of satisfaction with the outdoor facilities now available at Glenhaven.
Very Satisfied < > Somewhat Satisfied < > Satisfied < > Somewhat Dissatisfied < > Dissatisfied < > Very Dissatisfied < > | **Close-ended question**

6. What outdoor activity (or activities) do you most enjoy?
_____
_____ | **Open-ended question**

Thank you for your participation!

Figure 3.8 A Mailed Survey

INTERVIEWS

Interviews, like surveys, are an excellent source of primary data. Interviews give you access to experts' facts, opinions, and attitudes that you might not find any other way. However, interviewing can be time-consuming and costly. To make the process as successful as possible, use the following guidelines:

© GETTY IMAGES/PHOTODISC

Define your purpose Know exactly what information you want from each interviewee. Write down the purpose and review it before talking to the interviewee.

Make an appointment Telephone, write, or e-mail the respondent to describe the topic and to request an interview. Whether you will be interviewing someone by telephone, by mail, via e-mail, or in person, ask the respondent in advance for a convenient time to conduct the interview. If the interview will be in person, offer to visit the respondent or to arrange a suitable place to conduct the interview. If the interview will be via mail or e-mail, agree on a time frame for sending questions and receiving answers. For interviews by instant messaging, set an appointed time. Make certain that the respondent understands the topic and that you have allowed reasonable preparation time. Moreover, be professional in your appearance, writing, and speaking.

Do your homework Do not expect the respondent to make all of the effort. Know as much as possible about the topic before you conduct the interview.

Plan and write your questions Prepare questions to bring out specific, detailed information. Avoid vague questions such as "How do you feel about responding to emergency calls involving hazardous materials?" Instead, ask clear, specific ones, such as "What training experiences have you had to prepare you for emergency situations involving toxic gases?" Also, avoid questions that require a yes or no response; they do not encourage the speaker to elaborate. In addition, avoid questions that reflect an opinion or bias, such as "Isn't it true that management overemphasizes shop safety?" Instead, ask for the respondent's views: "In regard to shop safety, does management underemphasize, overemphasize, or adequately emphasize?"

Many interviewers develop questions on a laptop or handheld computer. This lets them read the questions from the machine and record answers on it as the interview takes place. Some interviewers write questions on one sheet of paper and record answers on another. Others prefer to write each question along with its answer on a note card. A tape recorder may be helpful, but ask permission to record the interview before you begin. Choose the system that works best for you.

Conduct the interview in a competent and courteous manner Remember, you are in control and the success of the session depends on you, not the respondent. Make sure you do the following:

Be on time.	Dress appropriately.
Introduce yourself.	Speak in a clear, distinct voice.
Explain the purpose of the interview.	Be assertive, but not arrogant.
Keep on track; stick to the topic.	Avoid small talk.
Take notes, but not excessively.	Thank the respondent for his or her time.
Listen attentively.	Offer a handshake as you leave.
Ask for clarification or more details, if needed.	Add to your notes with a more complete summary as soon as you leave.

OBSERVATION

In addition to surveying and interviewing, observing is another method of collecting primary data. Professionals frequently rely on observation to solve problems in their jobs. Medical professionals observe patients to diagnose illnesses. Crop scientists observe the numbers and types of weeds and insects in a field to decide whether the crop should be sprayed. Highway departments count vehicles to decide where to place traffic signals. However, be careful when gathering data by observation; observers may be biased, or subjects may act differently if they know they are being studied. To collect credible data by observation, use these guidelines:

Train observers in what to look for, what to record, and how to record If you wanted to know about traffic at a certain intersection, you would train people to count vehicles; in addition, you would need to tell the observers the rules. For example, how would they count mopeds? If one observer counted mopeds with passenger vehicles, another observer counted mopeds with commercial vehicles, and the third did not count them at all, the data would be flawed. Also, be sure all observers are using terms the same way. For example, what is a peak period? If you tell observers that peak period is from 11 A.M. until 2:30 P.M., their traffic counts for peak period will be useful data because each observer counted during the same period.

Make systematic observations For instance, if the observers counting vehicles work only from 7–9 A.M. and 4–6 P.M., will you get an accurate picture? Since people are commuting to work and school during these times, you are likely to get inflated numbers.

Observe only external actions You cannot project internal actions or reasoning. For example, you may observe that 24 percent more people displayed flags this Independence Day than last, but you cannot say that more people are flying flags because they feel more patriotic. Report only actions you can see.

Quantify findings whenever possible Being able to assign statistics adds credibility, showing that an action or event was consistent.

Support your observations If you cannot quantify, support generalizations with details, examples, and illustrations. You might even make drawings or take photographs.

While observation can be a valuable source of primary data, consider the time, equipment, and cost. For instance, hiring and training people to count vehicles can be time-consuming and expensive. Even if you decide to place a mechanical device across the highway to count vehicles, it must be paid for and it will not describe the vehicles.

EXPERIMENTATION

Experimentation is causing an event so that an observer can test an assumption or a hypothesis (a statement of what the tester believes will happen). Experiments test whether a change in one factor will cause

© GETTY IMAGES/PHOTODISC

another factor to change. For example, if the owner of a car-cleaning business wants to know whether his current car wax or a new product gives the longest-lasting shine, the owner might polish half a car with the current wax and the other half with the new wax. He then would check the car periodically for shine.

Employees frequently use experiments in the workplace. Manufacturers often test new products in limited markets to see whether they will be successful. Managers may compare a current operating plan in one plant with a new one in another plant. Researchers may gather samples of air, water, soil, food, medicines, body tissues, or even construction materials for testing.

As with observation, experimenters must be careful to avoid elements that will make the experiment and its results invalid. Sometimes other factors or variables can affect the results of an experiment. For instance, using different cleaners on the two halves of the car would affect the results of the wax study. Using adults for conducting clinical trials of a drug meant for children would not provide meaningful information about how the drug will work on pediatric patients. Therefore, when you design an experiment, try to eliminate as many outside factors as you can.

Surveys, interviews, observation, and experimentation all serve as useful tools for getting information, and many researchers use a combination of these methods. Remember the stain on the wool sweater in the Warm Up? Even such an everyday problem as how best to clean a favorite garment may require you to interview, observe, and experiment to find a solution.

VALIDITY AND RELIABILITY

To maintain credibility, primary researchers look for valid and reliable data. You have **valid data** when you have accurately measured what you intended to measure.

For example, a clothing store owner wanted to know whether his business would attract as many customers if it were open on Sunday as it did on weekdays. He devised a test to collect data. The Sunday he chose was during a weekend when two big football games were being played in town and visitors filled the area hotels. Comparing the number of customers on that Sunday with the number of weekday customers would not generate valid data. The large number of visitors in town on that particular Sunday would influence the results.

Reliable data means that, under similar circumstances, the results can be duplicated. If you explain that mixing two liquid chemicals will create a solid, then others could try the same test. If they follow your procedures, the mixed liquids should solidify. Being able to repeat the test with the same results represents reliable data.

Stop and Think

What are three methods of collecting primary data? Why should you plan observations?

■ *Chapter 3 Review*

SUMMARY

1. Researching at work involves finding information to help people solve problems, make informed decisions, answer questions, and perform many other functions.

2. Secondary data, reports of information from someone other than the witness or the person directly involved, are usually found in a business, school, or public library through print or electronic means.

3. Writers must give credit for borrowed material by documenting the source. Failure to credit others for their words and ideas means risking reputation, employment, legal action, and financial reward.

4. Writers should evaluate sources by checking publication dates, the author's credentials, and the author's methods and resources.

5. As researchers find useful material, they take notes using one method or a combination of three methods—summary, paraphrase, and direct quotation—on note cards or a computer disk.

6. Primary data, information direct from the person involved, may be collected by surveys, interviews, observation, and experimentation.

Checklist

- Have I defined the problem or need for information?

- Have I considered what information I already have?

- Have I reviewed information available in my organization's archives relating to my problem or need?

- Have I viewed the library catalog, online when accessible or in the library when not accessible online?

- Have I searched periodical indexes and databases for more recent secondary sources?

- Have I relied on general reference materials, electronic or in print, for quick background information and for references to other sources?

- Have I searched the Web using strategies to filter for useful information, and have I found the most up-to-the-minute information?

- Have I given credit, using an appropriate style system, for borrowed words and ideas, unless the information is considered common knowledge or material in the public domain?

- Have I critically evaluated all sources of information before using the data?

- Have I developed notes using summary, paraphrase, and direct quotation?

- Have I considered collecting primary data using surveys, interviews, observations, and/or experimentation to find information not available through other sources? Have I planned for validity and reliability?

Build On What You Know

1. Compose a note card for each item below.

   a. On page 14 of *Farm Review*, Edwin F. Roberson's and Julius Schwartz' article, "Hog Farmers and Homeowners: Zoning Solutions," notes that municipal and regional governments are "legislating distance" between the farms' waste lagoons and residential areas. The article appears in the November 2003 issue of the magazine.

   b. In her 2004 book *Swine Herd Disease Management*, Dr. April P. Nuez writes, "Careful record keeping and close observation are the key to disease management." The book is 463 pages long, and this statement appears on page 259. The book was published by Delmar, a publisher located in New York.

2. Paraphrase each of the items below.

   a. The Center for Marine Conservation reported that volunteers scouring ocean beaches and inland shorelines cleaned up more than 7 million pieces of trash, including cigarette butts, bottles, cans, lightbulbs, syringes, and plastic bags.

   b. Yesterday, the Highway Department reported approval of a plan to open an 8.5-mile corridor between Henderson and Mount Clemmons. However, the new road may be a little bumpy because two sections of experimental asphalt, one designed to combat hydroplaning and the other made of crumbled tire rubber, are being used.

3. Choose a technical or scientific topic (for example, taxation of Internet sales, irradiation of food supply, or cosmetic use of botox). Find five sources, print and electronic, about the topic. Develop a working bibliography with each source listed in correct MLA bibliographic form.

4. You are calling Sanford Weiss to set up an interview about a new type of home security system he invented. What arrangements should you discuss with him? List at least three things you should cover in the phone call to set up the interview.

5. In small groups, locate and evaluate a web site. Consider purpose, types of information and graphics, evidence and references, factual or emotional information, design, completeness, and balance. Write several paragraphs describing the effectiveness (or lack of effectiveness) of the site based on your evaluation.

6. Identify a company where you might like to work and gather information that would help you apply for a job there. For instance, learn about products, services, or activities. Find out about the way the company is organized, the business philosophy it uses, and its niche in the marketplace. Write a report that would be helpful to other students who also might be interested in seeking employment with the company.

Apply What You Learned

7. Think of a subject or hobby that you know a lot about. In a brief essay, describe how you acquired your knowledge.

8. Find three specialized reference sources, such as a medical dictionary or an aerospace encyclopedia, relating to your future career field or a topic of interest. At least one of these reference sources should be online. List the reference sources and a description of what each one offers.

9. Collect questionnaires for class analysis. Determine effective techniques as well as weaknesses in the surveys' strategies.

10. Watch a televised or videotaped interview. Note the strategies the interviewer uses to make the interview effective.

11. Using the same keyword, use three different Internet search engines. Bring to class the first ten listings shown by each search and compare the results.

12. Go to the help section of any Internet search engine. Learn how this particular system works. Share what you learn with your classmates.

13. Using a full-text database available in your school or community library, find and print an article relating to your career field or term project. Write a summary of the article and bring the summary and the article to class.

14. Choose a topic relating to your career field. Search for secondary information to provide basic background information. Write an essay summarizing your findings and prepare a bibliography.

15. Prepare questions and interview someone in your field of interest. From that person, collect information about a particular research project he or she undertook. Ask about methods, difficulties, and the outcome of the research. Record your findings on your sheet of prepared questions.

16. In a small group, identify an issue at your school.

    a. Develop a survey to collect facts and opinions about the issue.

    b. Establish your audience and administer the survey in person.

    c. Tabulate the survey results.

17. Identify a problem at school, in your community, or at work.

    a. Decide what information you need to solve the problem.

    b. Determine how and where to find the information.

    c. Conduct the necessary research.

18. Choose a product to compare with a similar product or a product whose effectiveness for a particular use might be questioned. With that product in mind, design an experiment to test the question. Write a report on the experiment design, the findings of the experiment, or both. Be sure you collect valid and reliable data.

Use the Work Is A Zoo! worksheet on the Data CD to help you create the survey.

Work Is A Zoo!

ZiPS will only succeed if science instructors and their students use it! And to find out how to make it successful, you need to go to the instructors themselves.

You and Anya are developing a survey for instructors to find out how often they come to the zoo, what they like and dislike about coming, how the zoo can help them meet their classroom goals, what obstacles they foresee, and what suggestions they have.

You also are interested in learning the best age of students to target. Who is more likely to come? Is there a way to target all ages? Would it be good to talk to some students directly?

Develop a survey form for science instructors, keeping in mind your overall purpose. Think about some of these questions as you design your survey:

- How often do the instructors come to the zoo with their classes?
- What do they like about the zoo?
- What do they dislike?
- How can the zoo help them meet their classroom goals?
- What obstacles are there in a program like ZiPS?
- What other suggestions do they have?

Instructors do not have a lot of extra time, so be sure that the survey:

- Is easy to read and fill out.
- Asks only for necessary information.
- Is customized for the audience and purpose.

Remember to leave enough room for the user to fill out the form. Provide instructions for returning the survey.

THE WRITING PROCESS

GOALS

IDENTIFY a writing process that suits your writing style

PLAN your document

DRAFT and REVISE your document

EDIT your document

COLLABORATE constructively with others

See the Data CD for Write-to-Learn and In The Know activity worksheets.

WRITE-TO-LEARN

Think of a process you are familiar with that involves several steps and some time to complete. It could be an artistic, mechanical, construction, or athletic process—anything from making a craft or troubleshooting a computer to painting a room or learning a football play. In one page, answer these questions about your process: What steps do you follow? Do you ever need to retrace your steps? Are some steps more important or enjoyable than others? How did you learn this process? Does the process get easier for you the more you do it? Explain.

In The Know

collaborative writing writing with others in a group

copyediting proofreading a document for correctness in spelling, grammar, and mechanics and publishing a document in the appropriate format

draft an early version of a document that is subject to change

drafting the stage after planning when the writer actually writes a first, second, or third (or more) version of the document

freewriting writing freely to discover an idea; can be open (no topic yet), focused (on a topic), or looping (stopping, summarizing, and continuing)

groupthink the tendency of group members to conform to the wishes of the group without thinking through an issue individually

planning the first stage of the writing process during which a writer thinks of an idea and plans how to develop and research it

publishing sending a document to the person who requested it

recursive a circular or back-and-forth motion; describes the movement of the writing process back and forth along predictable stages

revising reading a document and making changes in content, organization, and word choice

shaping a step early in the writing process during which a writer narrows a topic, determines a direction for a topic, generates subtopics, and organizes the subtopics

tentative outline an informal, changeable plan for organizing topics and subtopics

writing process the stages a writer goes through to write a document; includes planning (prewriting, shaping, researching), drafting and revising, and copyediting (proofreading and publishing)

Writing@Work

Dave Borcherding spent seven years as an editor for Writer's Digest Books in Cincinnati, Ohio. In this job, Dave worked with authors to create how-to reference books for writers at all levels of their careers.

Dave's duties included everything from making sure the writer stayed focused, according to the book proposal, to carefully reading the book to make sure it flowed and that the manuscript was delivering everything a reader would expect it to deliver. He also copyedited for grammar, spelling, and punctuation. Throughout this process, Dave was constantly contacting the author, suggesting changes or asking for clarification of information. Discussions with authors can be tricky, as Dave notes. "Even if you think you're editing just another book on grammar, to the writer, it's a work of art. It's his or her baby. An indelicate critique of a writer's prose is like telling a new mother her baby has an ugly nose. You're not critiquing just the words on the page, after all; you're also criticizing the author's ability to write." When critiquing a writer's work, Dave offers these suggestions: Use a positive tone; be generous with praise; include yourself in your notes (for example, "Can we find a different example here?"); and offer choices instead of demanding specifics. It is extremely important to keep the writer's feelings in mind when you construct the critique.

Working in publishing, you must be able to get along with others. In addition to the close work with the authors, Dave worked with other Writer's Digest editors, sometimes sharing duties on a manuscript. While one editor may have worked with the author to develop the book, another may have been responsible for the content edit, and another for the copy edit. "Writer's Digest Books was a team effort. You didn't have one editor hoarding his authors; everyone shared," says Dave.

Although collaboration is important in publishing, some writers may take it to an unethical level by actually "borrowing" another writer's work. Such action is not collaborating and it is not borrowing: it is stealing. Any way you look at it, plagiarism is wrong. You are not only doing a disservice to the writer you plagiarize, you are also doing a disservice to yourself. You are wrong not to give credit to a writer whose ideas you may use in your writing, and you are also wrong not to give yourself the chance to create and develop as a writer. By plagiarizing, you are likely to slow or even stop your growth as a writer.

Dave has a bachelor's degree in English literature and has always had jobs where he can be around books or book lovers.

How the Brain Processes Information

Our brains begin as a single cell shortly after conception and then begin dividing in a process called *meiosis*. From this process comes a brain that has much in common with other human brains but is also different. Some brains are able to think visually. Others provide musical or linguistic talent. Still others posess athletic ability.

There is still much we do not know about the brain, but scientists are learning more about it all the time. The brain has more than a trillion nerve cells of two types. The adult human brain is a wet, fragile, pink mass; it feels like Play-Doh®. It can seem to stop time by recapturing a memory. It has enough energy to power a light bulb. It weighs a little over 3 pounds, is shaped like a walnut, and fits into the palm of your hand. It works constantly. It represents 2 percent of your body weight and consumes 20 percent of your calories and 25 percent of your oxygen. When it "thinks" harder, it uses more fuel. It changes physically as it adapts to its environment. It has connections between cells. It forms dendrites between neurons. It needs oxygen, glucose, and water to operate. The basic structure of the brain is common knowledge. It is divided into three parts: the forebrain, the midbrain, and the hindbrain.

Figure 4.1 First Draft of an Introduction in a Report

A PROCESS FOR TECHNICAL WRITING

WARM UP

Think of the last writing assignment you completed. Maybe it was a letter or a report for class. What process did you follow? What did you do first? second? third? and so forth?

So far you've learned why people write at work; how to plan for audience, purpose, scope, and medium; and how to conduct research. Now that you're ready to write, how do you begin? Where will the words come from to fill the pages of your document? They will come from you through a process of **planning, drafting, revising, copyediting,** and **publishing**—otherwise known as the **writing process.**

See the two Letters to Students on the nature of the writing process, which are located on the Data CD.

© GETTY IMAGES/PHOTODISC

The writing process used by technical writers has much in common with the writing process used by any writer: the essayist, novelist, journalist, or songwriter. However, each genre brings its own challenges. With the consideration of audience, purpose, and medium, technical writers must spend the early stages carefully planning their writing. Working with technical data requires thinking not only about words, but also about graphics and page design.

Furthermore, technical writers often work collaboratively. Sophisticated software becomes an integral part of the process, too. The technical writing process will build on the writing process you are already familiar with.

To learn about the technical writing process, you will follow the decisions Ashley makes as she participates in a collaborative writing project for educators. She is on a team of educators who have been given the task of researching new teaching methods for high school instructors.

When Ashley first meets with the team, she has no idea what her role will be; she knows only that she wants to offer practical ways for teachers to improve instruction. This chapter follows Ashley through each stage of the process, from coming up with her idea (How the Brain Processes

Information) in the planning stage to polishing the final paper in the publishing stage. The opening model in this chapter shows an early draft of her introduction. Other models in the chapter illustrate changes Ashley made in this draft as she worked through her writing process.

To manage the stages of the technical writing process effectively, you should understand three features of the process: it moves back and forth among predictable stages, it requires sufficient time to complete, and it varies from one person to the next. If you understand how the process works, you can customize each stage to fit your personality and thinking style.

WRITING IS RECURSIVE

Since writing is creative, it does not move forward smoothly from one step to the next. Although the overall process does progress logically from planning to writing the finished product, it is a backward and forward process—**recursive,** or circular, in nature.

For example, you may plan an article on new city bus routes and begin to write. Then you discover that you overlooked the route into your own neighborhood. You go back to the research stage and gather more information. Next, you hear that some citizens are upset about the proposed routes. You circle back and change your purpose to reflect their discontent. After interviewing a few concerned citizens, you revise again.

Documents change depending on which stage they are in. In some stages, writers expand documents, generating ideas and words without judging their usefulness. During other stages, writers make judgments, cutting some words and keeping others in the document.

WRITING TAKES TIME

Most writers need a certain amount of time to let ideas "cook" in their heads. The process can be compared to baking bread. You gather ingredients, mix them, knead the dough, and place the dough in a warm spot to rise. However, you can't make the dough rise; it rises in its own time because you set in motion the process for baking bread. Writing is like baking bread: the ideas need time to rise and develop.

WRITING IS DIFFERENT FOR EVERYONE

While the writing process does have stages, what people do in each stage differs from one person to the next. How people feel about the stages differs, too. Some people enjoy the prewriting and planning and dislike the revising. Others enjoy the revising but are frustrated by the planning. Some people let the ideas grow in their heads and write slowly with little revision. Others write lots of words quickly, using many drafts.

Stop and Think

Explain the recursive nature of the writing process. Why does the process take time? Why do you think the process is different for everyone?

PLANNING

Like other tasks, writing is easier when you have a plan. First, you must choose a topic. Second, you must decide how to shape and organize that topic. Once you organize your topic, you need to conduct research to get more information.

© GETTY IMAGES/PHOTODISC

CHOOSING A TOPIC

Your first task is to choose a topic. Sometimes your employer or instructor will give you a topic, and you can build on that idea. For example, if you are a trainer in the home office of the Pajoli's Pizza franchise, you might be asked to write an operating procedures manual for the entire chain. The manual includes the home office specifications: how to open the restaurant, how to close the restaurant, how to order, how to make each dish, and how to calculate food costs. Therefore, your research plan is straightforward: interview managers, observe them in action, and write the procedures step by step.

When you are building on someone else's idea, learn as much about the assignment as you can. Ask about audience, purpose, scope, and medium. Note any gaps in the analysis, ask questions, and make changes based on new information. For example, as the writer for Pajoli's manual, you note that some restaurant owners are Hispanic. Based on this new information, you provide a Spanish translation.

Building on someone else's idea can simplify the planning stage. Sometimes, however, your writing assignment will not be so specific; your employer or instructor may give you general guidelines and expect you to come up with ideas and a plan.

Freewriting, mapping, and journaling are all strategies that can help you choose a topic. For example, your assignment could be like Ashley's. When Ashley's team first met, no one had a direction or a topic for the project. Therefore, Ashley used freewriting and journaling to choose a topic.

Freewriting With **freewriting,** write what comes to mind without judging what you have written or worrying about grammar or sentence structure. Three variations of freewriting are open freewriting, focused freewriting, and looping.

With **open freewriting,** write about anything and see where your writing takes you. Ashley's open freewriting finally brings her to a possible topic in the last few sentences in Figure 4.2 below.

> What am I interested in? Today, not much today. Let's see. Okay, let's find a topic for the research. Could write about problem solving. Hmmmm. Also saw on Discovery Channel a segment on the brain and learning disabilities. Hmmm. I have a learning disability. Maybe I could research that. Yeah—why do I have a learning disability, and what instruction works best for me? That would help instructors in the classroom.

Figure 4.2 Ashley's Open Freewriting

With **focused freewriting,** choose a topic and freely associate ideas with that topic. This exercise, too, helps Ashley discover an idea.

> TOPIC: Learning: How do students learn best—with good instructors, when they are motivated? What makes a good instructor? One who has enthusiasm, one who knows the subject, one who knows how students learn, knows students' learning styles. Who was my best instructor? Mrs. Keel, but what made her good? Why do students not learn? What happens in the brain when someone learns? Do we know that? Maybe if we knew how the brain learns, instructors could do something to enhance that process.

Figure 4.3 Ashley's Focused Freewriting

With the **looping** technique, write for five minutes, stop, and summarize in a sentence what you have written. Staying focused on the summary sentence, write again for five minutes, stop, and summarize. Repeat the process until ideas appear, as they do here:

> First Loop (write for 5 minutes): Class, tired, sleepy, head hurts, had a hard time paying attention to the stock market seminar—too much math. I wish I had gone to the counseling workshop—that's more my style. My sister would love this though; she has an easy time with math—math whiz. Why is that? Why do some people learn some things more easily than others? (Stop and wait a few minutes.)
>
> Second Loop (write for 5 minutes): Why do some people learn some things more easily than others? Who else? Renee is really good at karate; Josh is good with cars but dislikes English. Why? Was Einstein's brain different from everybody else's? If I knew, would it help me and others learn math? What would help me with my learning problems in math? (Stop and wait a few minutes.)
>
> Third Loop: Ashley could take the last idea and loop around again.

Figure 4.4 Ashley's Looping Technique

Journaling Another way to find an idea is to write in a journal regularly. Here's a journaling entry Ashley wrote one morning:

 View Ashley's Cluster Map found in the sample documents on the Data CD.

> You know I had this strange dream last night—that I was late to class. Everyone was taking the exam and I had only 10 minutes to finish. I panicked but then saw three students get up and act out one of the problems. In the corner, I saw more students writing on the board. In the back, I saw students talking in a group. Suddenly the class became three classes—you know how weird dreams are. Somehow I knew all of these students were learning. What does that mean? Maybe that people have different ways of learning. Must be some kind of brain research on it.

Figure 4.5 Ashley's Writing Journal

Ashley notes that in several of her entries, she has come back to the question of what happens in the brain when people learn. Since she does not know much about brain research, she decides she would like to know more. At this point, she selects brain-based teaching as a possible topic.

SHAPING AN IDEA

After you choose a topic, you must **shape** and direct it. You must answer several questions in this stage: Is the idea narrowed or focused enough? How can I develop this idea? What are the subtopics or parts of the idea? How can I organize these subtopics?

Questioning, reading, mapping, and outlining will help you focus your idea and figure out subtopics.

Questioning Ashley uses questioning to shape her idea. Who will benefit from this topic? What do they need to know? When and where can they use this information? Why does learning take place? How can instructors improve learning in the classroom? After asking these questions, Ashley decided that the "why" and "how" answers were important for shaping her idea.

Reading Ashley also found some direction from the reading journal she kept as she read on her topic. She tagged some pages with sticky notes when she found something to help shape her topic.

> *Time* magazine article: talks about how windows of opportunity for learning open and close in the growing brain. Example: The neurons for learning language are active until about age 10. After that, neurons not used die out.
>
> *How the Brain Learns* by Sousa. Sousa stresses how the brain constantly adjusts to its environment. Gives lots of teaching suggestions for the classroom.

Figure 4.6 Additional Research Notes from Ashley's Writing Journal

Mapping Ashley uses cluster mapping to shape her ideas. She began with her topic in the middle and allowed ideas to radiate from the center, drawing lines to connect related topics. As she listed topics, her list grew into other clusters and generated more ideas for topics.

View the Formal and Informal Outline sample documents on the Data CD.

After looking closely at the cluster, Ashley knew she had to narrow her choices and decide which subtopics to include and which to leave out. All of the ideas were not relevant to her purpose, that is, to facilitate learning in a high school classroom. She decided not to include learning disabilities, since there was a strong disabilities support staff at her school where readers could get information on that topic. She also decided not to include left- and right-brain specialization, since her colleagues had already been trained in that area. She decided to leave out early brain development since this information would not apply to her young adult readers.

Outlining From the cluster map, Ashley outlined her topics in a **tentative** outline that will change as the writing process moves forward. Notice that this outline is not a formal one, yet it gives Ashley's paper a focus for her topics and subtopics.

Introduction—some interesting facts about the brain—to get students' attention

-Basic Brain Anatomy—explain basic parts of the brain and what each part does

-How neurons work—how a neuron fires and passes information from one to another

-Relate basic brain anatomy and neurons' firing to how the brain learns
(Show the actual changes in brain anatomy)

-Retention—what factors affect retention?

+Amount of sleep

+Timing of information presented

+Rehearsal

-Type of rehearsal

-Length of rehearsal

Figure 4.7 Ashley's Tentative Outline

As you outline topics, consider how to organize them. The document type may dictate the organizational pattern. You can use these organizational patterns to suit the document's purposes. Consider the following:

- Chronological order for things that must progress from first to last, such as a presentation

- Spatial order for arranging items in space, such as a description of an office, a factory, a landscape design, or a home

- Cause to effect order (or effect to cause) when you are writing about reasons for an event or the consequences of action

- Comparing and contrasting when you are recommending one product or action over another

- Classifying or breaking something down into parts when you are analyzing venture feasibility or product usefulness

- Problem and solution when you are proposing to define a problem and offer a solution

Other ways to organize data include strategies that meet your readers' needs. These strategies include:

- General to specific (or specific to general), depending on whether your audience needs the big picture or the details first

- Background before new information if your audience needs to know how something happens or happened before they accept new information

- Familiar to least familiar when you are giving the reader new knowledge

- Simplest to most complex (or most complex to simplest), depending on whether your audience already understands the complex ideas or needs to be led logically to them

- Most important to least important (or least important to most important), depending on whether your audience would benefit from reading the most important idea first or last

- A combination of methods for longer documents for which the audience requires different organization in different sections of the paper

Ashley decides to use a combination of methods for her document:

- Background before new information—Ashley thinks instructors need to understand the newest research about the brain before she presents the teaching strategies based on that research.

- Familiar to least familiar—Ashley thinks instructors will understand the new research better if she starts with information with which they are familiar, the structure of the brain.

- Simplest to most complex—Because instructors are busy, Ashley plans to introduce simpler ideas first, which can be incorporated quickly into lesson plans, before moving on to strategies that require more time to implement.

Consider what headings (short titles in your document that identify a topic) you will use and what the final document will look like. A heading is appropriate when you have several paragraphs that relate to a single topic and that will likely come from the outline you wrote. The document type—a report, a resume, a brochure—also will dictate your headings. After reviewing her tentative outline, Ashley converts her topics into a parallel structure and plans to use the following headings:

How the Brain Is Structured (first-level heading)

How Neurons Create Memories (first-level heading)

How Brain Structure and Activity Affect Learning (first-level heading)

How to Aid Retention (first-level heading)

      Amount of Sleep (second-level heading)

      Timing of Information Presented (second-level heading)

      Amount and Type of Rehearsal (second-level heading)

 Stop and Think   What strategies for freewriting and shaping have you used in the past? Which ones work best for you? Does this chapter present some methods you have not tried?

DRAFTING AND REVISING

You now have a plan and information about your topic, so you are ready to write. This part of the writing process is called the drafting and revising stage. Now is a good time to review your audience analysis and purpose for writing. Keep your audience and purpose in the back of your mind as you draft and revise.

© GETTY IMAGES/PHOTODISC

DRAFTING

When you begin to write, you are writing a **draft**—a paper that will change. Do not put off writing because you are waiting for that perfect first sentence to come to mind; just begin writing. The order you write in does not matter; what matters is the order in which the reader reads. Force a few words until they start to flow. Drafting is like trying new paint: you do not know whether you like the color until you roll it on the wall.

The Introduction The introduction is the first part your readers will see. It sets the tone and determines how receptive your readers are to the information you present. Use the introduction to:

- Relate to your readers (discuss a situation you and your readers have in common)

- Hold their attention (give startling statistics or an eye-opening quotation)

- Forecast what you will cover

- Identify questions that are answered in the document (list the questions)

- Identify the problem to be solved (define the problem)

- Give the background of the situation (give events that lead to the need for the document or research)

- Give a research overview (give the major headings; explain where/how the research was conducted).

The Subtopics As you write, you decide how to support your subtopics. As you think about ways to elaborate, explain, or prove your points, ask yourself what your readers need. Do they need:

- Long or short examples (of other customers who have used your product, of situations in which a solution did not work, or of jobs your company successfully completed)?

- Testimonials (of customers who are pleased with your product, from workers who had difficulty using equipment, or from references who will vouch for your character)?

- Quotations (from your software users, from a famous person or credible source willing to endorse your product, or from a stock market analyst)?

- Statistics (from a financial report showing your company is a good risk, from the *Statistical Abstract of the United States* showing the growing number of technical writers, or from a trade magazine estimating how many people will need plumbing services in the next year)?

- Historical facts (concerning war with Iraq and its effects on American consumers, the development of the personal computer, or CO_2 emissions from automobiles)?

- Financial facts or estimates (how much will the Clean Air Act cost American business, how will a 10 percent discount affect the purchase of 3,000 new books for the library, or how much will it cost to upgrade 12 computers compared to purchasing 12 new computers)?

The Conclusion Use your conclusion to do whatever the document type requires. Proposals may need a reminder of the solution; sales letters may need a call to action; a recommendation may need a summary of key points and a possible decision; a research paper may answer questions posed earlier in the document.

REVISING

When you finish drafting, you must revise your document. In this part of the process, you read your document and make changes to content, organization, and word choice.

Use your audience analysis and purpose statement to guide you as you read. Because the content affects the other revision strategies, begin with the general content first and then move to the details.

After you print a first draft, put it aside and wait. Come back to the draft later and read it to judge what does and does not work. Make notes in the draft. Draw arrows as you see that paragraph 3 really should be next to paragraph 6, and the example in paragraph 2 should be in paragraph 5— well, half of paragraph 5 really should be in the introduction and the other half should be deleted.

Writing can be an untidy process, as you can see in Ashley's second draft of her introduction in Figure 4.8.

View Ashley's third revision in the sample documents on the Data CD.

How the Brain Processes Information

Focus is off. Need to show how amazing the brain is. Need positive tone

Our brains begin as a single cell shortly after conception, and then begin dividing in a process we call meiosis. From this process comes a brain that has much in common with other human brains, but is also different. Some brains are able to think visually. Others' have musical or linguistic talent. And others' have athletic ability.

Their is still much we do not know about the brain, but scientists are learning more about it all the time. The brain has over a trillion nerve cells of two types: glial and nerve cells. The adult human brain is a wet, fragile, pink mass—feels like play dough. It can seem to stop time by recapturing a memory. It has enough energy to power a light bulb. It weighs a little over three pounds, is shaped like a walnut, and fits into the palm of your hand. It works constantly. Represents 2% of body weight and consumes 20% of our calories and 25% of our oxygen. It works unceasingly. When it "thinks" harder, it uses more fuel. It physically changes as it adapts to its enviroment. It has more connections, between cells. It forms more dendrites, between the neurons. It needs oxygen, glucose, and water to operate. The basic structure of the brain is pretty common knowledge. It is divided into 3 parts, the forebrain, the midbrain, and hindbrain.

Observations: some problem with P 2–not sure what it is; choppy sentences–fix later; several errors–fix later; REMEMBER: one thing at the time!

Figure 4.8 Ashley's Second Draft of the Introduction

Figure 4.9 provides a hierarchy of questions to ask yourself as you revise. Notice that they start with the general content and move to the details.

CONTENT QUESTIONS FOR REVISION

Do I have enough or too much information for my reader? Do I need to conduct more research or remove something?

Is my information clear? Do I need to revise for clarity?

Is my introduction effective? Do I need to revise to attract my readers' attention?

Is my purpose clear? Do I need to add a sentence that explains the purpose?

Do my details logically support my purpose?

ORGANIZATIONAL QUESTIONS FOR REVISION

Is the information in the best logical order for my reader? Do I need to move paragraphs or sections? Are my paragraphs and sections unified? Do I need to remove sentences that don't fit the purpose?

Do sections and paragraphs have topic sentences? Do I need to add topic sentences?

Are transitions clear between sections and paragraphs? Do I need to add transition sentences or phrases?

Does my conclusion logically end the document?

READABILITY QUESTIONS FOR ANALYSIS

Does my writing flow from one sentence and paragraph to the next?

Are sentences varied by length and type? Would my sentences be more interesting if I combined them?

Have I selected the best words? Do I need to replace overused words? Do I need to define words?

Figure 4.9 Hierarchy of Questions for Revision

Stop and Think

What did you find to be the three most helpful pieces of advice in this section? Why do you find them helpful?

COPYEDITING AND PUBLISHING

How important is an error-free document? In business, a professional image indicates a professional, responsible institution behind the image. In the absence of a person, the document represents a company; the document becomes the face of the company. If the face contains smudges and errors, the impression is negative. If the face is clean and attractive, the impression is positive. Therefore, after you have planned, drafted, and revised, you must put on the finishing touches by copyediting and publishing your writing. Copyediting means proofreading for spelling, grammar, and consistency. Publishing means sending your document to the person who requested it.

WARM UP

What is your impression when you find errors in a newspaper or textbook?

 Complete the Surgical Center Letter with Errors worksheet on the Data CD.

© DIGITAL VISION

COPYEDITING

After you have revised for content, organization, and word choice, it is time for copyediting, one of the final stages of the writing process. Your writing still needs final proofing and, in general, polishing.

Figure 4.10 lists copyediting questions to ask as you correct a document.

Do I have any sentence problems: fragments, run-ons, comma splices?

Is the punctuation correct?

Are my words used correctly? Have I double-checked frequently misused words?

Are words spelled correctly?

Is the documentation of sources accurate?

Does the document look professional?

Is the page design balanced and attractive?

Is the formatting consistent?

Figure 4.10 Copyediting Questions for Analysis

SEE THE SITES

At the Merriam-Webster online dictionary, you can quickly look up words and get definitions, parts of speech, and correct spelling. The web site also has a thesaurus that helps you find synonyms.

The encyclopedia.com web site, created by eLibrary, gives information about hundreds of research subjects. It offers daily fun facts, information about current and past events, and links to numerous other research tools.

You can find the url for both sites in the web links on techwriting. swlearning.com.

Sometimes the brain corrects errors as you read so that you don't notice them on the page. Reading aloud can help you catch fragments and awkward sentences. Reading each sentence aloud starting at the end of the paper and moving toward the beginning also can help. In addition, if you know a good grammarian and speller, ask that person to help you copyedit. You may be surprised at what you do not catch yourself!

Today, you can use electronic aids for copyediting. Most word processing programs will underline misspelled words as you type, alerting you to an error. You can check the spelling then and correct it, or you can wait until you finish the document to run the spell checker. The checker will locate misspelled words, flag places to correct, and ask which correction is appropriate.

However, the spell checker does not select the best word for you. For example, it will not flag an improper use of *their* or *there* if the word is spelled correctly but used incorrectly. In addition, technology creates new uses for existing words that spell checkers are not aware of.

The grammar checker operates the same way. It will flag sentences that might have problems, but you must understand grammar to know whether to change the wording. You can look up questions about grammar and mechanics in a current English handbook.

Other electronic aids include a dictionary (if you need to review a part of speech or a meaning of a word) and a thesaurus. A thesaurus is handy when you know a better word than the one you have used exists or when you have overused a word and need a synonym. However, words have subtle differences in meaning. *Roget's Thesaurus* lists *steal* as a synonym for *borrow*, but you cannot use the two words interchangeably. When using a word from a thesaurus, look up its use in a dictionary; otherwise, your use may be awkward, inaccurate, or comical.

PUBLISHING

When you have finished copyediting your document, you are ready to publish. In this final stage, make sure the document is professional, is ready on time, is presented in the form your reader needs, and uses sources correctly.

© GETTY IMAGES/PHOTODISC

The document should be printed on good paper, using a high-quality printer and print cartridge or toner. To make your deadline, have the document ready several days ahead of time to allow for mishaps—the printer not working, the cartridge running out of ink, or the power going out. If you are sending a document to a print shop, know how much time the printer needs. Include any accompanying letters and make sure appropriate people receive copies.

Document your sources using the appropriate style manual for the discipline. Do not risk plagiarizing your document. If in doubt, check a source.

Figure 4.11 shows the final draft of Ashley's introduction. Compare this version to the first draft at the beginning of the chapter to see the changes she made throughout the writing process.

How the Brain Processes Information

Three to five weeks after the sperm and egg unite, one of the cell layers of the embryo thickens and develops into a flat neural plate. From this plate comes a thinking mechanism that has much in common with other human brains but that also differs in remarkable ways. Some brains are wired to envision and build bridges, skyscrapers, and superhighways. Others create the songs of our youth, the art we hang on our walls, and the motion pictures that define our age. Still others manage the linguistic marvels of a best-selling novel or the complex motor skills of the ice skater.

Despite its obvious importance to our lives, there is still much we do not know about the brain. What we do know, however, is fascinating. We know it can reverse time by reliving a memory. We know it has enough energy to power a lightbulb. A wet, fragile, pink mass, the brain is shaped like a walnut and can fit in the palm of your hand. Weighing a little over 3 pounds, it comprises only 2 percent of your body weight but consumes 20 percent of your calories and oxygen. When it "thinks" harder, it actually uses more fuel.

Working around the clock, the brain constantly reshapes itself as a result of experience. It physically changes as it adapts to its environment, most noticeably in the number of connections, called dendrites, it forms between its cells, called neurons. So when learning takes place, the brain is physically altered forever. Since the brain is where learning begins and ends, an understanding of this process can help us become better instructors and learners.

Figure 4.11 Ashley's Final Draft of the Introduction

Stop and Think

What kinds of mistakes do you tend to miss when you copyedit your writing? Make a list of those mistakes and practice looking for them in a draft.

Describe an experience when you worked with others in a group or on a team. What role did you and others play? What was the final outcome? Could you have accomplished the final outcome by yourself?

Explain.

WRITING COLLABORATIVELY

Many writing projects are done collaboratively—newsletters, proposals, research projects, brochures, and web pages. The more complex and longer your project, the more likely you will work with others. Often writing produced collaboratively is greater than anything anyone could have written individually. Interdependence is necessary in today's work environment. You are stronger when you use others' strengths along with your own.

© GETTY IMAGES/PHOTODISC

The topic of your writing project may require input of people from several disciplines. Each person brings a special area of expertise to the project—whether it is medical, technical, socio-economic, business, political, design, or writing. Applying for a grant to aid a hospital in a rural community might involve the following people:

Chief Surgeon Dr. Edie Coltrain	to address medical needs and equipment
Hospital administrator Ray Guevara	to address hospital and equipment costs
Two members of the hospital's board of trustees (an educator and a prominent business leader)	to represent community concerns
City council member Julia McNeil	to represent local business concerns
Senator Colin Elks	to foster political support
Architect Holden Wacamau	to design the hospital trauma center requested in the grant
Professional grant writer Paula Solinski	to gather data from different areas to write, revise, edit, and publish the grant

A collaborative effort may be required not only for a long document, but also for a short piece of writing. A monthly departmental newsletter, for example, may include short articles from different employees with one editor putting the newsletter together, much the way a newspaper editor collects articles from reporters.

Complete the Observe a Group worksheet on the Data CD.

ADVANTAGES OF COLLABORATION

Employees pool their resources because collaboration works. Why? Collaboration:

- Brings together different knowledge. In this age of specialization, no one person has all of the answers. The more knowledge you can tap, the more credible your final project will be.

- Brings together different talents. Some people can depict information graphically; others are better at interviewing for information; others write well. Members can offer the team what they do best.

- Allows different perspectives and viewpoints. If all viewpoints in the group are conservative, the final project may be one-sided. Different perspectives offer wisdom and balance.

- Improves work relationships. During a work project, people form friendships, empathize with each other's work problems, and may be able to help with solutions.

- Is enjoyable. People who get along in a group have fun working with each other.

- Keeps one person from being responsible for the entire project. Often the work seems less stressful because the responsibility is shared.

DISADVANTAGES OF COLLABORATION

The rewards of collaboration are numerous, but not all group work produces good results. Working in a group can have pitfalls. For instance, collaboration:

- Can be a dreaded event. While most people enjoy working in a group, someone who does not get along with a group member may dread the experience. Some people prefer to work by themselves, and group interaction is frustrating for them.

- Can include conflict. However, some disagreements over content or procedure can be productive because they encourage more talking and thinking to reach the best outcome. Groups that learn to manage conflicts can work through them without creating ill will.

- Can take longer than working alone. Group communication requires more time. More time is needed to talk over solutions in a group, to collect data from different people, to read drafts, and to work through conflict.

- Can take away personal motivation. If someone has only a small interest in the group project, he or she may not care about the outcome and hence will not be productive.

- Can encourage groupthink. **Groupthink** happens when members of the group are too willing to go along with everyone else's wishes or with an authority figure without expressing their disagreement. The danger of groupthink is that members may be lulled into believing they are producing a superior product when, in reality, their unwillingness to confront tough issues produces a mediocre product. Groupthink results when people do not care enough about the project to risk confrontation or when people do not know how to manage conflict and therefore avoid it.

- Can lead to unequal workloads. Some task-oriented personalities will jump in to get the job done. Illness may keep someone else from working on the project. Sometimes members know more about an area of the project and assume more responsibility because of their specialized knowledge. In some instances, members just do not pull their weight. Inequity in workloads may lead to resentment.

- Can produce fragmented writing. If different parts are written by different people with little agreement on how the writing should be organized or without a designated editor, coherence and readability may suffer.

Despite the pitfalls, collaboration is necessary in the workplace. People who learn to work collaboratively show their managers and teammates that they know how to accomplish a task with others. Many job descriptions ask for individuals with people skills, and job interviews include questions about the applicant's ability to work with others. Being a team player is one of the most important skills you can have at work.

Focus on Ethics

Trust within a group is one of the most important factors in its success. Work to create trust by following these ethical guidelines:

Be responsible Keep your word; do what you say you are going to do.

Be loyal Avoid talking about others in the group to other group members or to people outside the group.

Be honest Make sure that any research you bring to the group is properly documented. If you do not provide a source, your entire group could get into trouble for plagiarism.

Be respectful Keep an open mind when individuals express opinions diferent from yours. Practice common courtesy. Show concern for others, say *please* and *thank you*, and apologize when necessary.

Be fair Do a reasonable share of work. Do not expect someone else to do more than a fair and reasonable share, and do not take credit for another group member's work.

ORGANIZING COLLABORATIVE PROJECTS

How do five or six people write one document? A **collaborative writing** project can be organized in one or more of the following ways.

Different people write different parts and then have one editor. Ashley's team eventually selected topics for a research paper required by the grant that funded the project. Each person wrote 15–20 pages on the following topics:

Communication Update

Since many companies hire employees from all over the globe, groupware tools are available for collaborating when employees are in different physical locations. Microsoft® Windows® includes an application called NetMeeting®, which allows users to hold videoconferencing sessions via the Internet, complete with a shared wipeboard for group brainstorming and discussions. Other groupware tools include WebEx™ and Lotus® Sametime.

Brian	Methodology and evaluation
Ashley	Brain research
Ray	Multiple intelligences
Mercedes	Teaching and learning styles
Sudomo	Technology in the classroom
Ashley	Final editor

Ashley agreed to be the final editor, so team members sent her their sections in a Microsoft® Word document. Ashley cut and pasted their work into a longer document and made changes to promote consistency in tone, documentation, and formatting. She sent segments back to members asking them to rewrite a section or to clarify their data. She received responses and incorporated them into the single document. Then she sent the final version to everyone so they could make last-minute changes. This system works well when topics can be distributed and when people agree ahead of time on matters of style, length, purpose, scope, and medium.

Different people submit data to a central person who compiles the information. For example, the grant writer for the rural hospital could collect information from notes, charts, spreadsheets, interview results, and rough drafts. She might need a letter written by the grant committee chair, but she would write most of the draft. After writing the final draft, she would send it to committee members for their feedback.

This system works well when the writing is specialized, such as grant writing. As a specialist in the grant-writing field, Paula is a paid consultant who knows the parameters of this grant, has experience pulling usable data from different sources, and understands how politics affect grant awards.

Different people write different stages. Writer 1 brainstorms ideas, organizes subtopics, and determines research questions. Writer 1 then passes this information to Writer 2, who collects the research. Writer 2 passes the plans for the document to Writer 3, who writes the first draft. Writer 3 passes the draft to Writer 4, who revises it. Writer 4 then gives the draft to Writer 5 for final editing and publishing.

A textbook chapter could be written this way, with the editor suggesting topics, a research assistant collecting data, the author writing the chapter,

Complete the Active Listening worksheet on the Data CD.

and the editor copyediting and publishing. This system works well with a team whose members are in the same field, who get along well, and who understand the writing process.

Groups divide research tasks and come together to write. For example, a committee of four team members divided research investigating an institution's compliance with financial regulations. They brought their research to one employee's office and composed their report aloud as a group. One team member suggested a sentence and another changed a word in that sentence while yet another team member typed the sentence. Everyone gave suggestions, including the person typing the information. In two hours, their report was written and sent to a copy editor. This system works well for people with outgoing personalities who have a format to follow and do not waste time haggling over word choice.

When writing a longer document, a group may need to meet regularly. To organize tasks for a longer document, use the first meeting (or the first several meetings) to:

Create a vision	Set meeting times/place
Clarify the group's purpose	Decide research plan
Analyze audience	Set up goals and tasks
Determine scope	Assign responsibilities
Select media and style guide	Set timeline for work

Communication Dilemma

Brian is a new instructor in Ashley's research group. Since the group has been holding meetings to discuss the project, Ashley has noticed that Brian doesn't seem interested in the project. Brian has not been doing his share of the work when the other members ask him to make phone calls or look up information. He is not prepared for the meetings; in fact, when other people talk, he doodles on his paper or stares out the window. Sometimes he skips meetings altogether without telling anyone beforehand. His comments, when he gives them, are negative.

Ashley thinks Brian's poor attitude is getting in the way of progress. She also believes he is frustrating the other team members, who are working hard to make the project a success. She has already overheard some of the members talking about what a poor team player Brian is.

Ashley does not want Brian's work habits to affect the final outcome of the team. What should Ashley do?

A leader or chair can set the meeting agendas, write minutes, keep the group on task, and act as a spokesperson. A good leader will make sure that everyone has a say as to what the goals should be and how the meetings should be run. When people help make decisions, they are more likely to support those decisions.

Complete the Teamwork worksheet on the Data CD.

USING POSITIVE WORK HABITS

Once meetings get under way, your leader and your teammates will count on your participation. To be a productive group member, you need good work habits and communication skills to show others they can count on you. To apply good work habits and contribute to the group effort, you must:

- Do your share of the work. This may include making phone calls, taking notes, looking up information, or making a diagram.

- Come prepared to each meeting. Look over the agenda and come with suggestions, a notebook, a pen, or a laptop to show that you have done your homework and know what will happen at the meeting.

- Be interested in the project. Give positive feedback. Show that you care about the final outcome.

- Be on time to meetings. If you cannot be on time, let your leader or a group member know. If you are habitually late to meetings, your group members might think you do not care about the project.

- Do not take criticism personally. Remember that your goal is to produce a good product. When someone questions your suggestions, see the questions as a way to improve the final outcome, not as a criticism of you. If you show you can handle constructive criticism, you will have an easier time offering it.

Good work habits are important to building group relationships, but communication skills are important, too. Your teammates cannot read your mind, but they can hear words and read body language.

The number one requirement for a group to work well together is trust. The second requirement is shared group vision and enthusiasm for the outcome. Being a responsible group member and a good communicator will help build trust between you and your group members.

Now that you understand the writing process, adaptations for collaborative writing, and some of the strategies for effective collaboration, you are ready to work on any writing project individually or with others.

Stop and Think

Using the suggestions for good work habits, take a personal inventory of your own work habits. Which ones do you practice regularly? Which ones need improvement?

■ *Chapter 4 Review*

POINT YOUR BROWSER

techwriting.swlearning.com

SUMMARY

1. The writing process is a creative act that moves back and forth among predictable stages, requires sufficient time to complete, and varies from one person to the next.

2. The first stage of the writing process, planning, begins with freewriting to generate ideas and moves to shaping to narrow a topic and organize those ideas.

3. Freewriting strategies include open freewriting (writing freely about anything), focused freewriting (writing freely on a specific topic), and looping (writing for five minutes, stopping to summarize in a sentence, and using the sentence to begin the process again).

4. Shaping strategies include questioning, reading, mapping, and outlining.

5. The second stage of the writing process is drafting and revising. The process involves writing a draft, analyzing its strengths and weaknesses, and revising the draft. The drafting and revising stage may be repeated two, three, four, or more times.

6. Drafts are revised in a hierarchy from big to little to make changes that affect the content and organization first before making changes that affect sentences, words, spelling, and grammar.

7. Copyediting includes reading for and correcting errors and publishing the final version.

8. Documents should be error-free and look professional to project a positive image for you or the company you represent.

9. In today's workplace, many writing projects are done collaboratively.

Checklist

- Do I understand the writing process?

- Have I considered how to adjust the writing process to meet my own personality and thinking style?

- Have I identified the planning strategies that work for me?

- Have I used shaping strategies to narrow my topic, generate subtopics, and organize them?

- Have I read and analyzed the first draft according to the hierarchy of "big to little"—from content, organization, and sentences to words and mechanics?

- Have I revised my first draft?

- Have I written as many drafts as I need to create a well-written document that meets the needs and wants of my audience?

- Have I copyedited my document to find all errors?

- Have I published my document in a form that is error-free and professional?

Build On What You Know

1. How is writing like one of these processes: climbing a mountain, growing a plant, training a dog, learning a song, or another process you can think of?

2. Combine the following sentences to make them more concise and to add variety to the sentence structure.

   a. Luis has been offered two jobs. One job is at the movie theater. The other job is at the golf course.

   b. He might take the job at the move theater. He would work at the concession stand. He would sell popcorn, drinks, and candy.

   c. He could take the job at the golf course. He would work at the golf pro shop. He would sell golf balls, tees, and other golfing supplies.

   d. One job pays more per hour. The golf course pays more per hour. The golf course is 10 miles from Luis's home.

   e. The job at the movie theater pays $.50 less per hour. It is a block from Luis's house.

3. Now put the revised sentences in exercise 2 into a paragraph. Add a topic sentence, a concluding sentence, and appropriate transitions.

4. Try to think of as many synonyms as you can for the following words. When you are finished coming up with synonyms on your own, consult a thesaurus for additional synonyms.

circumstance	run	shirt	end
excellence	communicate	a document	building
describe	repeat	fuel	employment

5. Use one of these techniques to practice thinking of a topic: open freewriting, focused freewriting, or looping.

6. Practice focused freewriting on one of these topics: environment, sports, music, or health.

7. Map your own writing process. Compare your process to your neighbor's, instructor's, or a family member's.

8. Keep a writing journal each day for five days. Write in it for 15 minutes at a time. At the end of five days, underline topics you might consider writing about. Choose one topic and practice mapping to come up with subtopics.

9. Interview a writer in your area (a newspaper reporter, a television reporter, or someone who writes at work). Ask this person about his or her writing process. Ask whether writing assignments have direction or if writers must come up with ideas themselves. Share your information with your classmates.

Apply What You Learned

10. Answer these questions about your writing process:

    a. Where do you prefer to write?

    b. Does the computer help or hinder your writing process? Explain your answer.

    c. Do you write with greater ease in the morning, in the afternoon, or at night?

    d. How do you prepare to write? Consider things such as playing music, gathering materials, making a sandwich, getting a beverage, or organizing your desk.

    e. What is the best piece you ever wrote? Describe your process. How did you know the writing was good?

    f. How do you know you have finished revising and copyediting and are ready to publish a document?

11. Write two paragraphs: one telling what you like about writing and one telling what you do not like about writing. Write one by hand on notebook paper and the other using a word processor. How does your writing process change?

12. Write a paragraph describing your favorite place by dictating your words to someone else. How does speaking aloud affect your writing process?

13. Listed below are the writing process steps. Rank them from easiest to the most difficult for you, with 1 being easiest and 8 being most difficult. Rank them again for the time each takes, with 1 being the least amount and 8 being the most. Which stage do you think is the most important? Why?

Prewriting	Drafting
Shaping	Revising 1
Researching	Revising 2
Publishing	Copyediting

14. Write an essay or a paragraph on a topic of your choice. After you complete one draft, trade your paper with at least two other students. Ask them to make comments using the list of questions for copyediting in this chapter.

15. Select one of the following topics to write a one-page essay: why people should exercise regularly, why people should stay informed of news events, or why people should recycle. Then practice writing collaboratively by dividing the topic into stages. Writer 1 will prewrite and organize three subtopics and pass the prewriting to Writer 2. Writer 2 will write the first draft and pass the draft to Writer 3. Writer 3 will revise and pass the revision to Writer 4, who will edit the revision, make changes, and turn in the final draft.

See the Data CD for the writing activity worksheet, which includes a table for you to use as a starting point.

Work Is A Zoo!

Tyrone is presenting some ideas for promoting ZiPS, and you are helping with the presentation.

As the two of you consider this presentation to the zoo personnel, you are also thinking about how to sell ZiPS to local science instructors. In the past, the zoo offered one-time events such as "Animals from the Plains" and "Major Marine Mammals" for science classes. However, attendance was low.

You think science instructors may consider it a hassle to bring classes to the zoo: coordinating permission slips, transportation, lunches, other classroom activities, and so on. Maybe they do not see the long-term educational value in the visits. Maybe they have not thought about the differences between studying science at the zoo and at school.

Compare and contrast the kind of science education that happens in the classroom versus science at the zoo.

Remember your goal is to show that science at the zoo *enhances* classroom science. It helps instructors do a *better* job!

Start by thinking about how science is the same in the classroom and at the zoo. Then think about how it is different. Organizing your ideas in a table may be a good place to begin. In addition, start thinking about ways to help instructors overcome some of the obstacles. Can the zoo provide lunches? What about a one-time permission slip?

BRIEF CORRESPONDENCE

GOALS

IDENTIFY brief correspondence

ANALYZE the audience for brief correspondence

PREPARE for and **DETERMINE** how to format e-mails, memorandums, and letters

UNDERSTAND and **USE** strategies for composing good news, bad news, and persuasive messages

See the Data CD for Write-to-Learn and In The Know activity worksheets.

WRITE-TO-LEARN

Consider the information you need to share with others in any work situation, whether it is a collaborative paper or a project for class, a task you manage at home, or a job you do for a wage. With one task or job in mind, write a few paragraphs about the information you need to give or receive from others and how you communicate. For example, if you are doing a team project, you might need to schedule a meeting or set a deadline. Is time a factor in the method of communication? Is a record of your communication an important factor? Is your communication usually face-to-face, over the telephone, in notes or letters, by e-mail, or through other means? What advantages and disadvantages have you found with the types of communication you use? In addition to the paragraphs, list in two columns advantages and disadvantages of each form of communication you use.

In The Know

block style the letter style that aligns the return address, dateline, and closing flush with the left margin

buffer something positive written to soften bad news to come

external audience a receiver outside the sender's organization

format the layout of a publication; standard elements of a document's presentation

goodwill the feeling of friendship; the value of doing things that create mutual admiration and respect

hooks attention-getters; words or sentences designed to engage the reader or to create interest in an idea

internal audience a receiver inside the sender's organization

Maslow's Hierarchy of Needs the division of human needs into basic needs (physiological, safety, and belonging) and higher-order needs (esteem and self-actualization)

memos/memorandums brief written internal communication

modified block style the letter style that begins the return address, dateline, and closing at the center of the page

sociological influences social factors such as culture, family, and class that cause buyers to purchase certain goods and services

testimonials personal stories or people's statements (often famous people) endorsing a product or service

Writing@Work

Brian Minick serves as senior technology lead for General Electric Aircraft Engines. He is responsible for coordinating technology efforts between different areas of the business.

As senior technology lead, Brian must correspond with people in other countries. The majority of his communication is through e-mail. In situations where Brian is communicating with people of different nationalities, he may have a question about the gender of the person he is corresponding with. Luckily, GEAE has a system in place to handle potentially embarrassing situations. For every project, Brian participates in team-building exercises to help him get to know the people he will be working with. One exercise consists of filling out a questionnaire. Some questions are personal, while others focus on what each team member will be able to bring to the project. When the questionnaires are complete, each team member is responsible for introducing someone else to the rest of the colleagues. This thorough communication ensures that team members will know something about each other and that they will feel more comfortable working together.

With a company like GEAE, much information sent via e-mail will be proprietary. GEAE addresses this sensitive issue with a standard footer that must be included at the end of each e-mail. This footer labels the information in the e-mail as proprietary and instructs the addressee not to distribute, copy, or publish the information. When Brian sends proprietary information to another company, he must ensure that the company agrees not to duplicate it.

As most companies do, GEAE has a policy regarding employees using e-mail for personal correspondence. GEAE's policy is reasonable—if the e-mail is helpful, such as employees' verifying doctors' appointments or arranging for child care, then it is OK. As long as employees are not abusing their e-mail privileges, then everything is fine. However, employees can be terminated on the spot for sending e-mails with inappropriate content.

Brian has a bachelor's of applied science degree in systems analysis from Miami University in Oxford, Ohio. He has worked at GEAE for four years.

© 2005 Used with permission

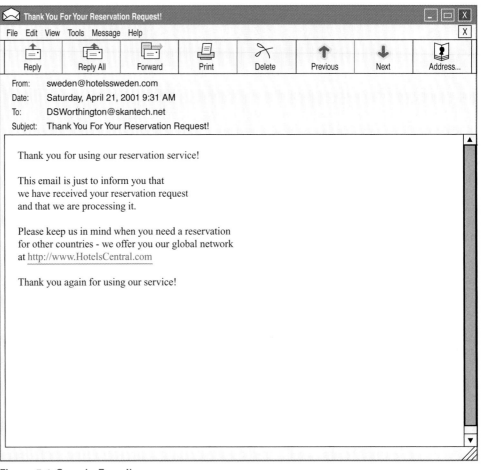

Thank You For Your Reservation Request!

File Edit View Tools Message Help

Reply | Reply All | Forward | Print | Delete | Previous | Next | Address...

From: sweden@hotelssweden.com
Date: Saturday, April 21, 2001 9:31 AM
To: DSWorthington@skantech.net
Subject: Thank You For Your Reservation Request!

Thank you for using our reservation service!

This email is just to inform you that
we have received your reservation request
and that we are processing it.

Please keep us in mind when you need a reservation
for other countries - we offer you our global network
at http://www.HotelsCentral.com

Thank you again for using our service!

Figure 5.1 Sample E-mail

Ayden-Grifton High School

Route 3, Box 172
AYDEN, NORTH CAROLINA 28513
Telephone:
252-555-0183

MEMORANDUM

To: Mrs. Lopez, Ms. Parham, and Members of FHA/HERO

From: Mr. James D. Gray, Principal

Date: February 6, 20—

Subject: CONGRATULATIONS ON HOMELESS SHELTER PROJECT SUCCESS

Congratulations, students, on the outstanding contributions made to the Pitt County Homeless Shelter by the members of FHA/HERO and compliments, Mrs. Lopez and Ms. Parham, for the leadership you provided.

This project involving the entire school and community helped make us all more aware of the difficult conditions faced by many members of our community. I was especially pleased that so many of our students and parents participated in donating food, money, and consumable items for this worthwhile program.

I thank you for organizing and seeing this project to completion. This effort is a great example of teaching and learning.

Member of Southern Association of Colleges and Schools

AYDEN-GRIFTON
HIGH SCHOOL
Pitt County, North Carolina
DEDICATED TO EXCELLENCE

It is the Purpose of Pitt County Schools to Provide
Equal Opportunity Regardless of Race, Color,
National Origin, Sex, or Handicap

Figure 5.2 Sample Memorandum

Ayden-Grifton High School

Route 3, Box 172
AYDEN, NORTH CAROLINA 28513
Telephone: 252-555-0183

6 February 20—

Ms. Janine Wooten, Director
Pitt County Homeless Shelter
2003 Jordan Way
Greenville, NC 27835

Ladies and Gentlemen:

Students, faculty, staff, and friends of Ayden-Grifton High School thank you for the certificate of appreciation in the attractive gold frame you sent us. We have placed it in our library in an area with other honors and awards where everyone can see and enjoy it.

However, we also should thank you for this opportunity. Collecting items and assembling emergency kits for your agency taught all of us valuable lessons. The students not only used skills they are building in the classroom, such as writing letters to the business community requesting donations of products, but also learned that effective teamwork makes even a big task possible. Yet the most important lesson that the students as well as the adults who assisted learned is that one person, no matter what age, can make a difference in the lives of others.

Ayden-Grifton High School looks forward to working with the Pitt County Homeless Shelter on a similar project next year.

Sincerely,

Mr. James Gray

Mr. James Gray
Principal
Ayden-Grifton High School

pts

Figure 5.3 Sample Letter

INTRODUCTION TO E-MAILS, MEMORANDUMS, AND LETTERS

Communication is essential for being able to act and make decisions in the business world. People must be able to share information. Some communication can take place face-to-face, but a great deal is conducted through e-mails, **memorandums,** and letters. All three may be used for brief correspondence; however, each one has its own distinguishing characteristics. For instance, e-mail is the fastest, most efficient means of written communication. A writer can compose a message, send it electronically around the world, and receive an answer immediately.

© GETTY IMAGES/PHOTODISC

Unlike electronic correspondence, memorandums and letters take more time. Of the two, memorandums are more efficient than letters, primarily because memorandums have fewer formal parts and because they are usually directed to an audience within the same organization as the sender. In contrast, letters may have many parts and may be sent by the postal service or a commercial carrier to readers outside the organization.

All brief correspondence seeks the **goodwill** of readers and practices principles of good communication.

GOODWILL

Goodwill is the act of making a friend and then keeping the friend. Goodwill is like good vibes, a feeling of good intentions. Effective business correspondence fosters goodwill through its word choice and message. You can create goodwill in writing the same way you create the bonds of a friendship.

Goodwill, like friendship, is created by being honest and polite. Business friendships grow in an atmosphere of mutual respect and trust. You also foster goodwill by attending to correspondence as quickly as you can. In short, you generate goodwill by treating your reader as you would like to be treated.

PRINCIPLES OF EFFECTIVE COMMUNICATION

In addition to generating goodwill, brief correspondence should be helpful to readers. The list below suggests some of the characteristics of effective brief correspondence as well as traits to avoid in e-mails, memorandums, and letters.

Develops Goodwill	Hinders Goodwill	By
Concise language	Fuzzy, unnecessary words	Taking up readers' time with details they do not need
Accuracy, completeness	Inaccurate, incomplete information	Creating misunderstandings and problems to be solved later
Professional appearance	Sloppy appearance	Making you and your organization appear incompetent
Conventional format	Unfamiliar format	Confusing the reader, making your intent unclear
Logical organization	Illogical organization	Frustrating the reader
Standard English usage	Grammatical errors, misspelled words	Making you and your organization appear careless

Following conventional format and using standard English help make a positive impression on your reader. To ensure that the information in your correspondence is well organized, complete, and free of errors, reread the document before you send it. If you are unsure whether your message is clear, have a colleague read your correspondence and provide feedback.

E-mails, memos, and letters not only help to get the job done, but also serve as a way of evaluating the writer's performance. Managers and administrators can tell from an employee's correspondence whether that employee is solving or creating problems, communicating with or confusing readers, building or ruining relationships, getting the job done or making no progress.

CREATING A SUITABLE TONE

Brief correspondence usually has a conversational, informal tone. In fact, it is appropriate in this type of correspondence to use *I,* the first-person pronoun. "You're busy, so I'll be brief" is the opening sentence of an effective sales letter for a magazine. Note the focus on the reader, the use of first person, and the casual tone. Readers are more likely to cooperate when the message sounds as if a person, rather than a machine, wrote it. This informal writing style is similar to a conversation you might have with a friend, if that conversation were polished slightly.

USING HUMOR EFFECTIVELY

Use humor to create goodwill in difficult situations or with uncooperative audiences. For example, in Figure 5.4, Marissa McIntyre uses humor to convince students to volunteer to donate blood, even if they have not donated before or are a little afraid.

MEMORANDUM

TO: All Students   23 October 20—

FROM: Marissa McIntyre, Volunteer Club Chair

SUBJECT: Giving Up Your Blood!

The Volunteer Club again this fall invites you to give blood when we host the American Red Cross Bloodmobile on campus 28 October 20—. See Mrs. Liang in the main office to schedule an appointment for any free period on Bloodmobile Day. Please show your pride and sign up today!

Mr. DeLeone, the Volunteer Club sponsor, says not to worry if you are afraid of the sight of blood—especially your own. This year he offers blindfolds for the faint-hearted and a shoulder to lean on for those who just plain faint!

Figure 5.4 Using Humor Effectively

Writers, however, should be cautious about using humor. As useful as it can be, humor used carelessly may be harmful. For example, a manager is not likely to laugh when her quality assurance officer writes that the government safety inspectors "were going to kill us" if that manager's daughter had been involved in a fatal car accident. Consider audience, situation, and character of the relationship before deciding whether to use humor.

Stop and Think

What is goodwill and why is it important? Is a formal tone ever appropriate for brief correspondence?

AUDIENCE

Readers of e-mails, memorandums, and letters have some similar characteristics. All expect this type of communication to be brief, to target a specific reader or readers, to have a specific purpose, and to follow conventional format.

Some correspondence is sent to a multiple audience, and some is written with a very select audience in mind. If the reader is only one person, meet the needs of that person. Use language and information he or she will understand and answer questions that reader would ask if he or she were present. If an audience is made up of a group of readers, consider the needs of all of them.

Regardless of how well you know your readers, use Figure 2.3 in Chapter 2 on page 32 to help you focus on your audience. If you know little about your audience, learn as much as you can. Ask others what they know about your audience or read correspondence your audience has written. If you can't learn much about your audience, assume a serious or neutral tone.

Keep your language moderately simple and natural. Work especially hard to build goodwill.

AUDIENCE FOR E-MAILS

E-mail, for personal and professional correspondence, has become a common way to communicate. Readers may be within or outside the writer's organization. So writers will know some readers well and others not at all. Because readers frequently receive a lot of e-mail in a day, they expect writers to focus on a point and keep the message brief, without omitting essential information. Readers expect messages to be relevant and clear; they will not waste their time with messages that are incomplete, confusing, or unclear.

AUDIENCE FOR MEMORANDUMS

Memorandums are used only to correspond inside an organization. Therefore, the reader will be a member of the writer's organization, an **internal audience.**

Within an organization, everyone is likely to receive and read memos. For example, an employee might get a memo from a coworker explaining a procedure change. A memo outlining the facts—implementation time, date, actions, and checklist—provides a written record so the person receiving the notice does not become confused about the details of what is expected.

Communication Dilemma

You are sitting at your desk at Phoenix Fabrication when you receive an e-mail from your college dorm mate. He wants to know how you have been, what types of projects you are working on at work, and whether you plan to attend the class reunion. You want to send him an e-mail and boast a bit about the new product you are developing for your company. Since you haven't seen him in a couple of years, you also want to make plans to meet at the reunion.

Just when you are about to hit "reply," you remember that your boss cautioned you about using company time to conduct personal business. He also told you that if you reveal proprietary information about the company's products, you may be subject to legal action. That sounds pretty scary, you think, but maybe just one little personal e-mail will not hurt. After all, how will anyone know you sent it?

Should you reply to your college dorm mate?

Even though memos are addressed to people inside a company, the writer must consider the audience carefully. The audience may consist of people with a variety of outlooks, backgrounds, opinions, interests, and levels in the organization.

Remember that the internal audience of an international company may have members in Los Angeles and Moscow. Once identified, each audience must be thoroughly studied to ensure that its needs are met.

AUDIENCE FOR LETTERS

While memos are for readers inside an organization (internal communication), letters are for readers outside an organization (external communication). Although you may know a great deal about members inside your organization, you may know very little about readers outside your company, an **external audience.**

A letter is an extension of your organization. The letter will be in the presence of your reader when you are not. If the letter is well written, you will make a good impression and inspire confidence in yourself and your organization.

Stop and Think What are the primary differences in audiences for e-mails, memorandums, and letters?

PREWRITING

Effective e-mails, memorandums, and letters depend on planning. After analyzing your audience, you need to make decisions based on what you have learned. Ask yourself these questions before you write:

© GETTY IMAGES/PHOTODISC

- What do I want to accomplish with this message?
- What should happen after the receiver reads this correspondence?
- What is the main point?
- Does my reader need background information? How much?
- Do I need to make the message simpler for this audience? What definitions or explanations will the audience need?
- Is this reader familiar with the subject matter? Does the reader have previous experiences with this idea?
- What questions should my correspondence answer?

In addition to answering the questions above, you should take notes on the details you need for your correspondence. Gather the facts, such as the situation background, events that occurred, problems created, order/part numbers, accurate descriptions, or questions to ask. Find out the name, title, correct spelling, and correct address of the person you are writing to. Double-check to make sure the information you have gathered is accurate and complete.

Using the answers to these questions, put your ideas on paper. Some writers prefer a list, such as the kind you make for grocery shopping. Other writers like to use freewriting. As you learned in Chapter 4, freewriting is writing everything that comes to mind. Remember that this is the creative part of writing, so do not be critical of your ideas. Get all of the ideas, brilliant or otherwise, on paper.

Whichever technique you use will generate a collection of ideas you want to cover in the message or body. With all of the ideas before you, you can start to be critical. Cut the ones that are unnecessary and change those that do not communicate exactly what you want to say. Prewriting is also the time to rank ideas. Consider what you will place first, second, third, and so on.

PREWRITING E-MAILS

Prewriting for e-mail involves planning to communicate with readers who have diverse needs and expectations. First, remember that busy professionals may receive a great volume of e-mail. Thus, your SUBJECT line must be specific and descriptive; it should immediately show readers how the topic relates to them. If your SUBJECT line is poorly written, chances are the receiver will delete your message without reading it.

Second, consider the reader's expectations for formality and length. If you are sending an e-mail to people within your company or organization, you are likely to know the formality they expect by referring to other e-mails. For instance, the corporate climate may be formal, so readers might expect complete sentences, correct punctuation, and few or no abbreviations.

However, others with whom you communicate electronically may be more comfortable with informal e-mails—incomplete sentences; little punctuation; and the many abbreviations writers have developed to make online exchanges fast, such as *BTW* for *by the way* or *HAND* for *Have a nice day*.

In addition to level of formality, plan the length of your messages to meet readers' needs and expectations. Since people generally read e-mail from a computer screen rather than print hard copies, keep messages as brief as possible so that people can read the text without scrolling through several pages. Short messages also allow for easier response. If you have a long, involved message, send it as several different e-mails or create a document with a word processor and send the long document as an attachment.

Third, plan for differences in e-mail software. Avoid complex formatting, such as bulleted lists, tables, italics, or underlining, unless you know that the recipient's software can read them.

Fourth, clearly explain the context of your message so that all readers will understand. For example, when you respond to a question, make sure readers realize which question you are answering.

Finally, plan for handling emotions effectively. Do not flame. (When writers harshly criticize each other, they are flaming.) Avoid e-mailing when you are angry. Wait until you can handle the issue logically, rather than emotionally. Using all capital letters generally equates to shouting, so use this style only when you intend to shout. For emphasis, you can surround a word or phrase with asterisks or white space.

Another way to convey feelings is through the use of emoticons, symbols created on the keyboard to convey emotions, such as :-), the smiley face. Yet writers must carefully consider how readers will react to the feelings expressed in an e-mail because feelings can be misinterpreted or misunderstood.

SEE THE SITES

To learn about writing processes for all types of correspondence, including business letters, e-mails, and memos, check out Colorado State's writing web site.

To view e-mail makeovers, articles about business writing, checklists to guide your writing, and more, log on to the E-write Online site. You can even take a quiz to test your e-mail know-how!

You can find the url for both sites in the web links on techwriting. swlearning.com.

PREWRITING MEMORANDUMS

As with planning e-mails, prewriting memorandums requires writers to consider the audience's expectations. Readers usually expect memos to be brief and to cover one topic. However, the need to be brief should not override substance. Make sure the memo fully explains the topic, whether it offers a solution to a problem, outlines a change in procedures or policies, or deals with other business concerns.

Furthermore, writers sometimes choose to write memos as documentation (proof) of discussions, decisions, or actions. Perhaps you or your company would like something more substantial or concrete than e-mail to back up an offer made during a meeting or a request for information or an action taken following a safety review.

You should plan to include all of the specific details—names, dates, times, locations, and other details—that your audience might need.

PREWRITING LETTERS

Memos as internal correspondence may, in some circumstances, be informal; and in others, formal. Letters, on the other hand, are almost always formal. Letters usually address external audiences, so letter writers should keep the reader informed.

For instance, the reader may not be as aware of history and background as others inside the organization are. The reader is not likely to know insider language or jargon. In addition, when a person is communicating with an unfamiliar audience, the writer should put his or her best foot forward, carefully choosing words, gauging tone, and focusing on the purpose of the correspondence.

When letters are used internally for special circumstances, such as promotions, dismissals, recommendations, or disciplinary matters, writers should plan for a higher level of formality because of the importance of the subject and the legal implications.

Stop and Think

Why are e-mail privacy and security issues important to consider in prewriting?

FORMATTING

Much as fancy type identifies a formal invitation, the formatting features of e-mails, memorandums, and letters help readers recognize the type of correspondence they are viewing. Specific elements are unique to each type. E-mails, for example, may look like memos, but they typically include e-mail addresses for the sender and receiver. Memos are recognizable by their headings (To, From, Date, and Subject) and the title *MEMO* at the top of the document. Likewise, the mark of a letter is the inside and return addresses, salutation, and complimentary close, features familiar to audiences.

© GETTY IMAGES/PHOTODISC

WARM UP

Think about the information all readers want to know when they receive messages. What are their questions? Compare the answer to this question to the elements of formatting for e-mails, memos, and letters.

FORMATTING E-MAILS

Writers usually do not need to be concerned about formatting decisions when they create e-mails because the e-mail software provider has already made most of the decisions. Most programs, such as Microsoft® Outlook Express®, shown in Figure 5.5, simply ask the writer to click on a light-colored line or in a blank box and type the intended receiver or subject line. Most programs insert the sender's name or address automatically.

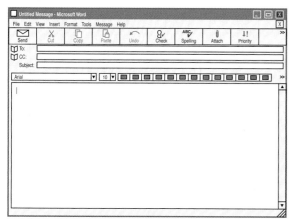

Figure 5.5 Formatting E-mails

FORMATTING MEMORANDUMS

The rough draft of a memo begins with a standard **format** of headings and is followed by the body or message. Like the addresses and salutation (Dear Mr. Roberio:) in a letter, headings make a document recognizable as a memo. Five elements usually appear at the top of a memo:

MEMO

TO:

FROM:

DATE:

SUBJECT:

However, the headings do not always appear in this order. When you begin work, your new employer will probably give you a style manual that shows you the format the company prefers.

Memo templates are included in most word processing software. Microsoft® Word, for instance, provides three memo templates and a wizard to help writers create memorandums. The advantages of working with memo templates are that they are simple to use (even for writers with no experience), are easily modified, and provide attractive document design.

At the same time, these familiar templates have a number of shortcomings, such as overused design (readers will recognize the template) and decisions made without the writer's input or consideration. Because writers do not need to think about design or headings, sometimes these "plug-and-play" templates encourage writers not to think about other decisions relating to their message. Ineffective communication may be the result.

Caption The word *MEMO* or *Memorandum* should be placed at the top of the page. Some preprinted memo forms and most computer software packages provide the caption for writers.

TO Line In the TO section, you name your audience. You can name one person, such as Joanna Jett, or you can name a group, such as the Employee Benefits Committee or the Sterile Manufacturing Division. On occasion, you may need to name several readers who are not connected by a unit or committee. In this case, you may simply list their names.

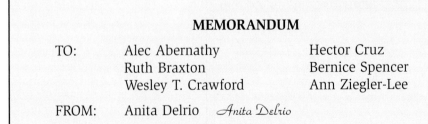

Figure 5.6 Receivers' Names Listed in Columns

The list of receivers' names may be presented in several ways. For example, you can place all names on one or two lines and connect them with commas, as in the model memo at the beginning of this chapter. Another option is to place the names in one column or several columns, as in Figure 5.6. The number of columns you choose depends on how many names you list.

If you list several people's names, enter them in either alphabetical or hierarchical order. In hierarchical order, the people of greatest recognition and responsibility in the organization, such as the president and vice president, are listed first. Others are listed in decreasing order of rank within the organization. Remember, however, if the hierarchal list contains two employees of the same rank, such as two directors, you should place their names in alphabetical order so as not to offend either person.

FROM Line After the FROM heading, you list the name or names of the sender of the message. If you are the only person responsible for the message, your name appears. If the memo comes from a group, the group or unit name is listed, such as FROM: Jefferson Jazz Band.

Some memos are from several people not tied to a group. In this case, list the names of the individual senders in a line joined by commas or in columns, again in alphabetical or hierarchical order. Also, remember to write your initials or sign your full name after the typed name in the FROM section, as in Figure 5.6.

Initialing or signing is especially important on memos that deal with important legal or organizational matters. Memos become legal documents that can be used in a court of law when they are signed and dated. In

Focus on Ethics

Sending a personal e-mail that reveals proprietary information (ideas the company owns) might cost you your good standing with your colleagues or even your job. It might subject you to legal action as well. Do not say anything in an e-mail that you would not say directly to a person and do not write anything that might embarrass you or your organization, regardless of who reads it. E-mail can be deleted, but it never really disappears and may be forwarded anywhere to anyone. Most networks (the sender's and the receiver's) archive and back up all e-mail.

In addition, some people might think that a simple e-mail reply to a friend outside the company is not so bad. If so, then you might ask, "Where do we draw the line?" and "Who draws the line?" If using the office computer to answer personal messages is fine, then is it okay to use the company car to pick up your dry cleaning or the corporate credit card to pay for the dry cleaning? Can you use the office copy machine to run off brochures for your weekend real estate business? Can you use time you have at work to order a gift online for your brother's birthday or pay your personal water bill? What about making a couple of long-distance phone calls to your grandparents on the company phone?

Using company time and equipment to conduct personal business is unwise; it could get your company in trouble legally, and you could be fired.

addition, your initials or signature tells your reader that you have reviewed the memo and accept responsibility for the message, especially if someone else typed the document.

DATE Line The DATE line usually appears after TO and FROM and before the SUBJECT line. It also can appear in the upper right corner across from the TO line. You can choose between two styles for writing the date: international (also called *military* in the United States) or traditional.

International date style is becoming increasingly popular in technical documents because of economy. International style requires no commas. In this style, the writer gives the day first, the month next, and the year last, as in 12 December 1996.

Traditional-style dates, as in June 4, 1955, or April 1, 2006, give the month, the date, a comma, and the year.

SUBJECT Line In most memos, the SUBJECT line logically appears as the last of the headings. It announces the point of the memo immediately before you develop that point. You may see terms such as *Reference, Regarding,* or *Re* (which comes from the Latin *res* meaning "thing" or "matter") used in the same way as the word SUBJECT. In addition to helping the reader predict the topic, the *SUBJECT* line distinguishes one message from another and focuses the writer on one main idea.

> **Predict.** The SUBJECT line should allow readers to predict what the memo will say; in other words, it reflects the main idea discussed in the body. Be as specific as you can when composing the SUBJECT line. A SUBJECT line that reads "Insurance" does little to help the reader predict what the memo will cover; the line is too general to provide insight. "Dental Insurance Open Enrollment Period Set for 20–27 June 2004" is precise enough to tell readers what to expect and encourage them to read the message. The SUBJECT line should not be a complete sentence, but a phrase or clause, more like a newspaper headline.

> **Distinguish.** In addition to helping the reader predict the subject of the memo, the SUBJECT line should make clear the difference between one memo and many others. For instance, servers at a restaurant may read many memos during the year that deal with menu items. Therefore, if the SUBJECT line says only "Menu Changes," the server reading it will not immediately know this message is different from last week's memo. Instead, specific SUBJECT lines, such as "Italian Items Added to Menu for June" or "Lobster Price Increase" or "Salmon Unavailable Until 20 April" tell the server exactly what to expect the message to cover.

> **Focus.** The SUBJECT line also aids the writer. Writing a SUBJECT line forces the writer to focus on the most important idea. It further allows the writer to check the message of the memo against the SUBJECT line. The message should cover the same idea that the SUBJECT line announces.

A memo should cover only one main point. Writers who have two messages for the same audience should write two memos. First, if a memo has more than one message, the reader cannot determine what is truly important. Second, the very busy reader may find the first idea, assume it is the only important information, and quit reading. Third, the memo might be so long that it intimidates readers. Readers generally expect memos to be one to four paragraphs. Finally, some messages are inappropriate to combine, as in Figure 5.7.

TO:	Dr. Joyner	Mr. Umezaki
	Dr. Everest	Ms. Shankowski
FROM:	Hannah Smith, Personnel Officer	
DATE:	June 10, 20—	
SUBJECT:	1. Vacation and Sick Leave Slips	
	2. Death of Mr. Martin's Mother-in-law	

1. Please ensure that all vacation and sick leave slips for this fiscal year (July 1, 20— through June 30, 20—) are turned in to Tammie by June 27, 20—.

2. Dan Martin's mother-in-law and Selma Hale's grandmother, Mrs. Sadie Harper, passed away on Sunday, June 9, 20—. Funeral arrangements are being handled by Belevedere's Funeral Home. Services will be held at Belevedere's Funeral Home at 2 p.m. on Tuesday, June 11. Expressions of sympathy may be sent to

| Dan at: | 811 E. Cooper Street | Selma at: | Route 1, Box 32 |
| | Tylersville, SD 47934 | | Tylersville, SD 47934 |

Figure 5.7 Ineffective Memo with Two Main Ideas

FORMATTING LETTERS

All letters share a similar format. They are constructed in basic parts and may be written in one of several styles. Two possible styles are **block style** and **modified block style.**

Letter Parts The letter model at the beginning of this chapter on page 110 and Figure 5.8 on the next page illustrate the basic parts of a letter: heading, dateline, inside address, salutation, body, closing, signature, and reference initials. Note the description of each part.

Jefferson Gas and Appliance	**HEADING:** complete address (no abbreviations) of the sender as a *return address* (personal business letter) or letterhead (company/organization letter).

Jefferson Gas and Appliance
HWY 17 South
P.O. Box 11
Washington, NC 27889
13 July 20—

Ms. Rhea Tankard
Manager
Malloy's Manufacturing
1023 West Main Street
Washington, NC 27889

Dear Ms. Tankard

Subject: Contract for . . .

Xxxxxxxxxxxxxxxxxx
Xxxxxx xxxxxx xxxx
Xxxxxxxxxxxxxxxxxx
Xxxxxxxxxx xxxxx x
Xxxxxxxxxxxxxxxx

Xxxxxxxxxxxxxxxxxx
Xxxxxx xxxxxx xxxx
Xxxxxxxxxxxxxxxxxx
Xxxxxxxxxx xxxxx x
Xxxxxxxxxxxxxxxx

Xxxxxxxxxxxxxxxxxx
Xxxxxx xxxxxx xxxx
Xxxxxxxxxxxxxxxxxx
Xxxxxxxxxx xxxxx x
Xxxxxxxxxxxxxxxx

Sincerely yours

W. B. (Jeff) Jefferson
President

WBJ/pjm

Enclosures (3)

c: Pat Morgan
   Jon Reardon

HEADING: complete address (no abbreviations) of the sender as a *return address* (personal business letter) or letterhead (company/organization letter).

DATELINE: date the letter was written.

INSIDE ADDRESS: professional (Dr., Rev., Capt., or others) or courtesy title (Mr., Ms., or Mrs.), correct name (first name/first initial and last name), title, and address of the person to whom you are writing (no abbreviations). Name here should match the name used in the salutation.

SALUTATION: exact name of the person you want to read your letter. May be written with or without end punctuation.
SUBJECT LINE (optional)**:** focuses on the topic of the letter.

BODY: usually two to five paragraphs long but can be several pages and may use headings similar to reports. The letter should look balanced on the page.

The BODY of most letters is single-spaced with a double space (one blank line) between paragraphs. The organization depends on the type of letter you are writing.

In standard block style letters, all lines begin at the left margin. In modified block style, all lines begin at the left margin except the date and the closing lines, which are centered. First lines of paragraphs may begin at the left margin or be indented.

CLOSING: friendly but businesslike ending. Common closings include *Sincerely, Yours truly,* and *Cordially* (never *Thank you*). Punctuate in *pairs:* Punctuate *both* the salutation and the closing OR punctuate *neither* the salutation *nor* the closing.
SIGNATURE LINE: typed name and title with space for handwritten signature above.

REFERENCE INITIALS: initials (in uppercase) of the person who dictated the letter followed by the initials (in lowercase) of the person who typed the letter. The two sets of initials may be separated by a slash or a colon.
ENCLOSURE NOTATION: indicates additional documents in the envelope. Often the word *Enclosure* is followed by a colon and the titles of the enclosed documents are listed.

COPY NOTATION: indicates a copy has been sent to other people.

Figure 5.8 Letter Parts

Letter Styles Letter styles vary. Usually, business letters are written on letterhead stationery in either block or modified block style. Personal letters include return addresses instead of letterheads and may be written in block or modified block style.

Block-style letters are easy to type but may look off-balance. Paragraphs are not indented, and every part (except the letterhead, which may be centered) is flush with the left margin. Modified block style is difficult to type but looks more symmetrical on the page. In this style, the dateline, return address (if letterhead stationery is not used), closing, and signature line are typed beginning at the horizontal center of the page. Paragraphs may be indented or typed flush with the left margin. Figure 5.9 illustrates basic differences in block and modified block design.

Two punctuation styles are commonly used in business letters: open and mixed. Open punctuation means no punctuation marks are used after the salutation and the complimentary close. Open punctuation is considered a time-saving style and is often used with a block format letter. When the mixed punctuation style is used, the salutation and complimentary close are followed by punctuation marks. The proper punctuation with this style is a comma after the complimentary close and a colon (for business letters) or a comma (for personal or informal letters) after the salutation.

Block With No Indents

Letterhead
Dateline
Inside Address
Dear Mr. Torres
Xxxx xxxxx xxxxxx xxxxx xxxxxx xxx x xxxxx xx xxx xx xx xxx xxxxxxxx xxxxx
Yours truly

Modified Block With Indents

Letterhead
Dateline
Inside Address
Dear Mr. Torres
Xxxx xxxxx xxxxxx xxxxx xxxxxx xxx x xxxxx xx xxx xx xx xxx xxxxxxxx xxxxx
Yours truly

Modified Block With No Indents

Personal Address
Dateline
Inside Address
Dear Mr. Torres
Xxxx xxxxx xxxxxx xxxxx xxxxxx xxx x xxxxx xx xxx xx xx xxx xxxxxxxx xxxxx
Yours truly

Figure 5.9 Letter Styles

Stop and Think In what order should the names of recipients be listed in e-mails or memos? Should a writer use *Thank you* as a complimentary close in a letter?

Consider this opening line:

Dear Arnie, You're fired.

Does this message work? Will it build goodwill? Could the idea be presented more effectively?

COMPOSING THE MESSAGE

Since all e-mails, memos, and letters begin with a specific purpose, writers must keep that purpose in mind when composing the message.

While formatting the document is important, the headings are only a means for conveying the ideas you want to share. The message or the body is the heart of the document.

© GETTY IMAGES/PHOTODISC

The message section of correspondence should be organized for the reader, not for the writer. Employees are busy and cannot waste time, so correspondence should be organized accordingly. Imagine a busy decision maker opening an e-mail she expects to be one page, only to discover that the message is more than four pages. The receiver may decide not to invest the time to read four pages, especially when she expects e-mail to be brief. Writers who frustrate readers or fail to meet their expectations are not likely to be successful in achieving goals.

The message itself, along with readers' expectations, must be considered. Organize ideas according to the message. Some messages are best presented in a direct, straightforward way. Others, when presented bluntly and directly, are likely to offend readers. And others, such as persuasive messages, require more motivation than a direct approach provides. The strategies for informative and good news messages, negative or bad news messages, and persuasive messages are useful in writing e-mails, memorandums, and letters.

INFORMATIVE AND GOOD NEWS MESSAGES

Brief correspondence usually gives the audience information that is pleasant or at least acceptable. Pronouncements of good news, routine letters of inquiry, responses to letters of inquiry, and letters of appreciation all use a similar positive organizational structure.

You can expect the readers of a good news message to be in a receptive mood as they read your correspondence. Picture a smile, a HOORAY, or at least an affirmative nod from these readers. Because your news is responsible for the pleasant mood, these readers are easy to approach.

Therefore, the strategy is direct: present the main idea first. Explanations, background information, and supplementary ideas follow the main idea.

The model memo at the beginning of the chapter on page 109 and the memo message from the production manager at Imperial Waters, Inc., below are examples of the direct approach to organizing informative and good news messages.

MEMO

TO: All Lab Employees

FROM: Jamir Cayton, Production Manager *Jamir Cayton*

DATE: November 15, 20—

SUBJECT: Deadline to Turn In Leased Chemical Lab Garments

Main idea—what the writer wants the reader to do

Please turn in by December 7, 20—, all leased chemical lab garments checked out to you.

Explanation and supplementary ideas—why the writer is requesting this action and what effect it will have on the reader

We signed a contract and will receive service from a new cleaning company, D & W Garment Care Center, effective December 8, 20—. Benefits of the change you should notice are:

■ Perfume- and starch-free garments.

■ An additional coat each week.

■ Immediate replacement of worn or damaged garments.

Figure 5.10 Memo Using the Direct Approach

Figures 5.11 and 5.12 are examples of positive news letters. Figure 5.11 conveys good news to Regina Williams, the recipient of an $800 scholarship to a local community college. Here the tone is enthusiastic.

PITT Community College Office Of The Dean Of Students

Telephone	**(919) 555-0139**
Fax Number	**(919) 555-0140**

October 26, 20—

Ms. Regina Williams
P.O. Box 2453
Winterville, NCa 28590

Dear Ms. Williams:

I am pleased to award you an $800 PCC Student Government Association Scholarship to attend Pitt Community College for the 2004-2005 academic year. The selection committee recognizes your achievements and your need for assistance in attaining your chosen goal.

The funds will be disbursed during the upcoming academic year. These monies will be available for you to use during preregistration and registration for tuition and fees, as designated in the scholarship. Any remaining funds may be used to purchase books, supplies, or other school-related items in the PCC bookstore. Remaining funds will be given to you approximately four to eight weeks after registration.

I warmly congratulate you and wish you every possible success. We look forward to having you as a student at PCC. If you have any questions, feel free to contact Mr. Rudy Lloyd in Room 12 of our scholarship office in the Vernon White Building or call (919) 555-0164.

Sincerely,

Garrie Moore

Garrie Moore
Dean of Students

ta

P.O. Drawer 7007 • Greenville • North Carolina • 27835-7007
An Equal Opportunity/Affirmative Action Institution

Figure 5.11 Positive Message: Good News Letter

Figure 5.12 shows the body of a letter of inquiry. Correspondence of inquiry, while employing a more neutral tone, still represents positive messages because it shows an interest in a product or service.

Jamie Sitterson
1254 Littlefield Court, Johnson City, NM 40567-9903

3 February 20—

Mr. Robert M. Steiner, Director
William Faulkner Birthplace
P.O. Box 20
Oxford, MS 32145

Dear Mr. Steiner:

I would appreciate any information you can send me on William Faulkner's
life as a young man in Oxford, Mississippi.

Specifically, I am interested in knowing:

1. Why Faulkner joined the Royal Air Force.

2. How old he was when he started to write.

3. Where he got the idea for Benji in The Sound and the Fury.

In addition, I would appreciate any brochures you have that show pictures
of his birthplace, family, and life as a young man. I am working on a
research paper for English and need this information by 12 December if
I am to complete my research in time.

I would appreciate any information you can send.

Sincerely,

Jamie Sitterson
Jamie Sitterson

Figure 5.12 Positive Message: Letter of Inquiry

BAD NEWS MESSAGES

Occasionally the purpose of an e-mail, a memo, or a letter is to share negative
news—information readers will not be pleased to get, such as employee layoffs
or unpopular policy changes. Negative messages can range from serious to
mildly disappointing. A letter with a negative message may refuse a request,
delay an order, or register a complaint. In this case, the direct approach is not
the best choice. If readers see the bad news immediately, the disappointment
might be so great that they miss the explanation entirely. A bad news message
must relay the bad news and still try to maintain the goodwill of the reader.

Therefore, the strategy of bad news messages is indirect. The bad news is
softened by surrounding it with pleasant ideas in this way:

1. Open with a positive statement, or **buffer,** generally some idea about which the writer and reader agree.

2. In the next section of the message, clearly announce the bad news, but place it in the middle or at the end of the section, not at the beginning. Writers may choose to explain the reason for the bad news. Sometimes the explanation is unnecessary or even counterproductive.

3. Close the message on a pleasant note by offering an alternative solution or a different perspective, making a constructive suggestion, or looking positively to the future.

The following memo body written by the owner of Precision Cuts Hair Studio shows how the bad news in the middle is buffered by pleasant ideas in the opening and closing.

Precision Cuts Hair Studio

Memo

To: All Stylists

From: Monza Hairston   *MH*

        Owner and Manager

Date: 6 June 20—

Re: Fashioning a Positive and Professional Image

Positive statement—creativity, something about which reader and writer agree

Being creative folks, we enjoy expressing our individuality in the way we dress. It is stylish and fun to dress flamboyantly.

Bad news statement—new policy that is likely to be unpopular

Some of us, using those creative energies, have been talking about ways to improve our professional image. Toward this end, the shop will adopt a uniform dress policy beginning on the first working day of next month. You may choose from solid navy and solid white outfits or outfits combining the two colors.

Positive close—benefits employees may enjoy

Besides enhancing the shop's professional image, the new policy will save you money because your personal clothes will not be subjected to the chemicals you use every day. Any creative energy you have left can be spent on clients to make our shop the most popular one in town!

Figure 5.13 Bad News Memo with Buffer

The opening buffer protects the reader from the bad news, a friendly close ends on a positive note, and the bad news is strategically sandwiched in between.

Figure 5.14 shows a negative news letter. Abraham Bizmark of Bizmark Gold Studio writes La'Neice Jackson, president of D'Oro Jewelry Stores.

Bizmark Gold Studio
123 Front Street   Rivervale, ND 99743
Telephone 709.555.0110   Fax 709.555.0111

30 September 20—

La'Neice Jackson, President
D'Oro Jewelry Stores
P.O. Box 4091
Tabor City, ND 99712

Dear Ms. Jackson:

Thank you for your recent order from Bizmark Gold Studio. We know you are preparing for the busy holiday season.   **Buffer**

However, the recent trucking strike has made it difficult for us to deliver customers' orders in the southwest region of the state. Therefore, your order for 250 rings (100, #3567890; 100, #7865301; and 50, #9956541) and 300 serpentine necklaces (150, #7643781; 100, #3215431; and 50, #9799773), which would normally reach you in ten working days, will be delayed until the trucking crisis has been resolved.   **Explanation**

We appreciate your understanding and apologize for any inconvenience. The trucking strike has caused similar delays with other businesses in the region.   **Bad news**

We know that gold jewelry says so much more than other gifts for many of your customers; it represents life connections. Since our designs in 14-karat gold are such an important element in your preholiday inventory, we will make sure that your order is on the first truck out of our Missoula studio when the new trucking contracts are signed.   **Friendly close—what the writer CAN do**

Sincerely,

Abraham Bizmark
Abraham Bizmark
Vice President, Marketing and Distribution
c:Ricardo Batista, Shipping and Receiving

www.bizmarkjewelry.com

Figure 5.14 Negative Message: Bad News

Letters of complaint are also examples of correspondence containing negative news. When an individual has a legitimate complaint, the challenge is to present the complaint without alienating the reader. Most complaint letters also include a request to make things right, sometimes a refund, an exchange, extra service, or at least an assurance that the problem will not recur. Figure 5.15 shows the body of a complaint letter to Luigi's Restaurant.

76 Old Tar Road
Homestead, FL 83713
March 19, 20—

Manager, Luigi's Italian Restaurant
Ocean Boulevard
Key Largo, FL 83725

Manager:

Buffer

I have enjoyed dining at Luigi's for a number of years. My parents have visited your restaurant to celebrate special occasions—birthdays, anniversaries, graduations—ever since I can remember.

Last Saturday night I took my date to Luigi's for an elegant meal before our senior prom. However, instead of receiving the special treatment my date and I were expecting, we were treated unfairly.

Explanation and complaint

My 7:40 reservation, made well in advance three weeks ago, was not honored. Instead, I saw the host give the corner table I had requested to another couple. As a result, my date and I had to wait 45 minutes (a very long and hungry 45 minutes) before another table was ready. I was embarrassed, and our late dinner caused us to miss the opening toast at our senior prom.

Request for action

I would like to know that I can look forward to other special dinners at Luigi's. Would you please talk to your host and convey my disappointment? Please let me know that the next time I bring a friend to eat at Luigi's, the service will be improved.

Respectfully,

Zane M. Brecht

Zane M. Brecht

Figure 5.15 Negative Message: Letter of Complaint

PERSUASIVE MESSAGES

A persuasive message is any correspondence in which the sender attempts to convince the receiver to agree with the writer. Persuasive messages are most typically used to sell products or services. Persuasive messages also include requests for assistance, support, or participation, such as a request for an employment recommendation or an invitation to participate in a telethon to raise money for a charity. The memo below written by a sales director shows a persuasive strategy at work.

interoffice memorandum

to: All Sales Representatives

from: Jordan Smithwick, Sales Director   *JS*

date: 12 November 20—

subject: Using the Board to Help Yourself OR
             Putting Your Schedule to Work for You and Others

Would you like the IRS to be able to find you in order to deliver your tax refund check? Would you like customers to be able to find you when they want to place an order?

Hook—uses humor and direct questions to grab attention

If these possibilities are important to you, please help me to help you. Just today I have had five calls for sales representatives I could not locate. That could be five orders that will not be placed, as well as commissions that will not go into your paycheck. To avoid this problem, check in and out on the board. It is still on my office door, and a brand-new marker is attached for your use.

Sell—gives details to convince the reader

Please remember to sign in when you arrive at work and to sign out when you leave for the day, but especially mark times when you leave the building for lunch or sales calls. If you do, I can tell your callers when to call again or when to expect your return call. And I'll even hold your refund check until you return!

Motivate—calls the reader to action

Figure 5.16 Persuasive Memo

Sales Letters Sales letters, because they must convince readers that the product or service is worthy of their time and money, are one type of persuasive message. Many employees write sales letters as a part of their responsibilities. Some sales letters target only one reader, while others target a large audience. Think, for instance, of the junk mail, or direct sales mail, you receive. Many products—magazines, books, vinyl siding, music, videos, seeds and plants, tools, and others—are sold by these mass mailings of sales letters.

Who Reads Sales Letters? Today's sophisticated marketing techniques make it possible to target select audiences for certain products. Knowing your audience's needs and interests is vital to writing sales letters.

Consumers make buying decisions based on a number of psychological and sociological factors. Abraham Maslow, in his work on human motivation, said people try to satisfy the following basic needs and higher-order needs. His system is known as **Maslow's Hierarchy of Needs:**

> **Physiological.** Physical needs for food, water, and air; the need to be free from pain; and the need to have a family
>
> **Safety.** Protection from the environment by adequate shelter
>
> **Love and Belonging.** The need to receive and to give affection, to feel accepted by others
>
> **Esteem.** The need to be respected by others and by themselves; the need for recognition, status, and prestige
>
> **Self-Actualization.** The highest of needs, attained by only a few people; after satisfying the first four needs, self-actualized people fulfill their potential

Basic needs must be met before higher-order needs can be met. For example, individuals must have food and shelter and feel physically secure before they can seek love and belonging. They must feel love and belonging before they can seek esteem.

When writing a sales letter, ask which needs on Maslow's Hierarchy you are addressing. Meet the lower needs first and remember that people's buying decisions can be more complicated than they appear. Wanting particular brand-name shoes may have more to do with a need for acceptance than with a physical need for footwear.

Consider **sociological influences** and buyer involvement. Present circumstances, social class, culture, and family influence buying decisions. Also, some consumers may be more involved in buying decisions than others. Highly involved consumers search for information and evaluate alternatives. Less-involved consumers may be indifferent, buying what is on sale or what is convenient.

Know what your competition has to offer so you can counter with convincing proof of your product. Try to find out how much your reader is willing to spend.

Use these questions to analyze your sales audience:

- What psychological needs does my reader have? (Use Maslow's Hierarchy as a starting point.)

- What sociological factors may influence my reader's buying decision?

- How involved is my reader likely to be?

- What is my competition offering, and how is my offer better?

- What objections will my reader have to my product?

- How much is my reader willing to spend?

Organizing and Composing Sales Letters Persuasion means you make your product or service look appealing. Presenting false information is unethical, but it's considered good business sense to present a product's strengths in a sales letter. To make a product or service look appealing, write sales letters according to the following organizational plan:

- HOOK your reader's attention.

- SELL your product or service.

- MOTIVATE your reader to action!

HOOK Your Reader's Attention. Hooks are attention-getters designed to make you open the letter and start to read. They often start on the envelope itself and continue after the reader opens the letter.

Sometimes an announcement written in boldface precedes the letter itself. The first line of the body sounds exciting. Throughout the letter, the writer "pulls out all the stops": some information is boldfaced, underlined, bulleted, shadowed with color, or set apart from the text. Some letters use headings and different fonts. Some have borders, pictures, or graphics—anything to capture the readers' attention. Figure 5.17 illustrates some familiar attention-getters.

Figure 5.17 Hooks in Sales Letters

The appeals of the attention-getters vary. Some appeal to the desire to get something for nothing. Some appeal to your sense of compassion, need for security, or desire for prestige. Some appeal to your curiosity.

SELL Your Product or Service. Advertisers describe their product (sometimes including pictures) to help you understand, but also to give you a favorable impression of the product. It is unethical (and illegal) for an advertiser to lie, but the words are usually written to sell—to create a favorable impression and a desire for the product or service.

A sales letter should offer convincing evidence of the merits of the product or service. Facts, figures, and statistics can provide objective proof. **Testimonials,** endorsements from real people (often famous people), provide personal stories that the product or service worked for them. Sometimes the advertisers try to compel the reader to try their product free for a limited time. This way they hope the product itself will convince the reader to keep it and pay for it. Often enclosures are included, such as brochures with pictures, order forms, or more testimonials. Sometimes a sales letter is not just a letter; it is a whole packet of materials!

MOTIVATE Your Reader to Action. Finally, the writer must try to motivate you to do something—go to the phone and dial a number, get into your car and drive to the store, write a check, or fill in a credit card number. To move you to action, advertisers make this part as convenient as they can. You have probably heard motivators similar to the ones listed in Figure 5.18.

An operator is waiting to take your call.

COME ON DOWN to Barton's Building Supplies.

Buy **now** and save **15%** off the cover price.

Send your tax-deductible contribution and help a homeless person find shelter from the cold.

Figure 5.18 Motivating Statements in Sales Letters

Figure 5.19 is a sales letter from West Winchester University trying to convince Jennifer Nelson to apply for admission. Using testimonials, a strong focus on Jennifer's needs and interests, and facts, the letter is persuasive. In addition, the use of an enclosed reply card makes it easy for Jennifer to say yes.

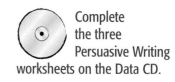

WEST WINCHESTER UNIVERSITY

1203 South Leming Road, Alexandria, Virginia 22314
Phone 202-555-0171 • FAX 202-555-0190

April 17, 20—

Jennifer L. Nelson
764 Lord Fulford Drive
Boling, NC 27878-7873

Dear Jennifer:

We've heard great things about you from the Student Search Office. Based on what we've heard, we thought you would be interested in West Winchester University, one of Virginia's most progressive universities specializing in technology, teaching, and public service.

Here is what others are saying about us:

"WWU trains its students to tackle the tough problems of a technological age."

    -EDUCATION WEEKLY

"WWU's academic program is impressive … Its professors rank teaching as their number one priority."

    -HOW TO GET A GOOD EDUCATION AT A STATE UNIVERSITY
    by Shireen Straker

WWU offers programs under the College of Arts and Sciences and five professional colleges-Architecture, Business Administration, Engineering, Education and Allied Professions, and Nursing. Classes averaging 33 students encourage individual attention. Laboratories are equipped with the most up-to-date facilities. Our 940-acre campus is located in the largest urban area in Virginia.

Want to learn more? Send us the enclosed card, and we will tell you more. Find out why WWU is the right decision for your education.

Sincerely,

Marilyn L. Zavala

Marilyn L. Zavala
Director of Admissions

Figure 5.19 Example of a Sales Letter

Stop and Think

In the Warm Up, you read the following statement: "Dear Arnie: You're fired." Why is the direct approach not effective for bad news messages? What is a call to action in persuasive messages?

POINT YOUR
BROWSER

techwriting.swlearning.com

SUMMARY

1. Three types of brief correspondence—e-mails, memorandums, and letters—are essential tools in the business world.

2. Maintaining goodwill, following principles of effective communication, creating a suitable tone, and using humor effectively are important factors in brief correspondence.

3. Writers must analyze and appropriately address the audience in all three types of brief correspondence.

4. Considering audience needs and expectations, determining goals, thinking about technology and the situation, and freewriting are prewriting steps to successful brief correspondence writing.

5. Each type of correspondence uses specific formatting that distinguishes it from other correspondence.

6. The body must be organized with the type of message and the reader's needs in mind. Writers share good news messages using a direct approach. However, bad news messages require an indirect approach to buffer the unpleasant news. Persuasive messages are best presented with a "Hook, Sell, Motivate" strategy.

Checklist

■ Have I identified and analyzed my audience? If I am addressing a multilevel audience, have I planned to meet the needs of each group or type of reader?

■ Did I establish my purpose or goal in this correspondence?

■ Did I use freewriting to generate the information I want to share with the audience?

■ Did I develop an organizational plan? Does it take into account a good news, bad news, or persuasive message?

■ Does my correspondence follow the correct format and use consistent style? Does it contain correct parts?

■ Is the tone and level of formality appropriate to the audience?

■ Have I asked a respected peer to read my correspondence and give specific feedback on the impact and effectiveness of my message? (Ask this editor if he or she has questions after reading the correspondence. Also, ask if any part is unclear or inappropriate.)

■ Did I proofread the headings for completeness and accuracy?

■ Did I proofread the message for errors in spelling, typing, grammar, and punctuation?

■ When the correspondence was acceptable, did I sign my name or, if appropriate, write my initials to the right of my typed name?

Build On What You Know

1. Here are eight parts to a good news letter announcing that Terrence Heilig has won a cruise to the Caribbean. The parts, however, are mixed up. Rewrite the letter, putting the sentences in proper order. Several combinations may be possible.

   a. To claim your prize, you must call 1-800-CRUISES before April 18 and provide the operators with proof of your identity.

   b. You have just won an all-expenses paid cruise to the Caribbean!

   c. Congratulations, Terrence. We look forward to helping you arrange the vacation of your life!

   d. Enjoy a variety of on-board recreational activities, delectable meals, and superb entertainment at our expense.

   e. Your name, Terrence Heilig, was drawn out of 456,897 entries to be our top-prize winner in the Colombo Publishers Sweepstakes.

   f. Colombo has reserved four nights and five days for you and a guest.

   g. You must schedule your trip between 1 June and 21 September 20—.

   h. Pack your bags, Terrence, and include lots of sunscreen!

2. Read the following writing situations. Select the details you need; then write the headings for each memorandum.

   a. You are manager for your school's soccer team. Normally you coordinate the packing of equipment and supplies for traveling to away games. However, for the next conference game to be played at Midland, you will be out of state attending your cousin's wedding. Therefore, you are writing a memo to Coach Marsh Rivers and your two assistant managers, Brent Abene and Deborah Johansen, to remind them of what needs to be done in your absence.

   b. You are Janice Fitzsimmons, manager of A Helping Hand, a residential cleaning service in San Alto, New Mexico. Six full-time and fifteen part-time employees are under your supervision. To thank the entire staff for their service, you plan to hold a picnic in your backyard. The event will take place on October 1, 20—, from 5 to 8 p.m. You are writing a memo today to invite all employees and their families to the picnic.

3. Mac Erwin of the ABC Detective Agency has just located Nina Reddenberger's car, stolen three months ago from a shopping mall. List information you would include in a letter to Nina from Mac announcing the good news. Make up the addresses. Before making your list, use your imagination to answer these questions: How can Nina get her car back? When can she get her car back? How did the detective find the car? How does Nina feel?

4. If you are currently working on a research project in another class, compose a letter of inquiry to ask for some of the information you need. Begin thinking about this assignment by listing things you want to know.

Apply What You Learned

5. Write a memo from Cheryl Brinkdopke, chief of installation services for Fox Cablevision, to Eric Monroe, an employee under her supervision. Eric has just completed 25 years of service with Fox Cablevision, and Cheryl wants to show her support for his work. Eric has had perfect attendance for the last three years, and his customer evaluations are consistently positive.

6. As assistant to your Quality Assurance Team at World Wide Insurance Association, you are in charge of scheduling meetings. The chair, Janine Leone, has asked you to call a meeting for Monday afternoon, April 24, 20—. She wants the group to discuss a recent employee concern regarding unsafe exercise equipment in the Employee Wellness Center. Janine would like the Quality Assurance Team to gather in Room 124-C at 4:15. She expects the meeting to end at 5 p.m. Write a memo announcing the meeting.

7. You are chief food scientist for Leigh Bakery in Anderson, Wisconsin. Matthew Carlson, president of the Logan Dairy Cooperative, a farmer-owned and -operated sales organization under contract to sell its entire production to your company, has invited you to speak to his members regarding the effect of certain veterinary medicines on the taste of dairy products. On the date the Cooperative requested, Thursday, January 18, 20—, you are already scheduled to attend a meeting of the American Association of Bakers. Write a memo declining the invitation to speak to the Cooperative.

8. Plan and draft an e-mail that announces a new flextime program at Bauman Industries. The program will allow all workers to share the responsibilities of one position among two or three people. Print the e-mail to give your instructor or share it with your classmates or team.

   a. One e-mail should target and address the managerial staff within the company. Consider the needs, concerns, questions, and biases of this audience before composing the e-mail.

   b. The second e-mail should target and address all employees of the company. Remember that you will need to meet the needs and answer the questions of all readers without offending anyone.

9. Conduct an Internet search for the web site of a business or an industry related to a topic you are interested in. Search until you find a web site that provides an e-mail address for contacting the organization.

   a. Write an e-mail requesting information or materials from the company. Before you send it, print the e-mail to give to your instructor or to share with other students. Consider which strategy (good news, bad news, or persuasive message) to use for organizing the body of your e-mail.

   b. Analyze the e-mail you receive in response to your request and share your analysis and the e-mail with your class.

Use the Work Is A Zoo! worksheet and checklist on the Data CD to help guide you through this activity.

Work Is A Zoo!

Next Friday you and Tyrone will meet with the entire Marketing Department (which includes the public relations division).

You hope to present information from other zoos with similar programs. You also are trying to talk to a local science instructor for her thoughts. If you speak with her, you will present your findings from that conversation as well.

Additionally, you are developing a survey that will go out to science instructors in the area.

It is important that the rest of the staff buy in to the ZiPS program because they will be involved in various aspects of it. Their ideas and input are valuable at the start of the program.

Send a memo to the staff telling everyone about the meeting and what it is going to be about. Remember that all memos:

- Include a heading. List the recipients according to rank, starting with the highest. For example, Nevil Kaplan is the head of the entire department, so his name should come first.

- Are accurate and brief. Don't get off track going into all of the details of the presentation; the goal of this memo is to tell people about the meeting.

- Cover one subject only. Now is not the time to invite people to a potluck for the July 4 weekend.

- Explain any actions to be taken. If you need to know how many people are coming, include that in your memo.

From *Words@Work* 1st edition by VANDALAY GROUP © 2000. Reprinted with permission of South-Western, a division of Thomson Learning: www.thomsonrights.com. Fax 800 730-2215.

DOCUMENT DESIGN AND GRAPHICS

GOALS

DESIGN an effective document for your audience and purpose

DETERMINE the audience and purpose of graphics

FORMAT graphics to make them easy to understand

CONSTRUCT graphics for your audience and purpose

See the Data CD for Write-to-Learn and In The Know activity worksheets.

WRITE-TO-LEARN

Using words only, write directions from school to your residence. Then draw a map with arrows to show the same route. Which is easier to understand, the written directions or the map? In a short journal entry, explain why.

In The Know

bar graph a graph using a horizontal axis and a vertical axis to compare numerical data, drawn with heights or lengths of rectangular bars

call outs the names of specific parts of a diagram, connected to the diagram or drawing with lines

chart a drawing with boxes, words, and lines to show a process or an organizational structure

design elements considerations in writing a document that affect page layout; the way a document looks

diagram a line drawing

double bar graph a graph using a horizontal axis and a vertical axis to compare pairs of numbers, drawn with heights or lengths of rectangular bars

double line graph a graph using a horizontal axis and a vertical axis to compare trends and show relationships between two sets of data, drawn with lines

flowchart a drawing with lines and arrows to show a process or series of steps

formal table numerical information set up in rows and columns and drawn with rules; used to present figures

graphics information presented in a visual form, such as tables, graphs, and diagrams

informal table a simple table with two or three items, drawn without rules and stubs

line graph a graph using a horizontal axis and a vertical axis to show a trend or relationship between numbers, drawn with lines

multiple bar graph a graph using horizontal and vertical axes to compare data, drawn with two or more bars for each measurement

multiple line graph a graph using more than one line to compare data

organizational chart a drawing with boxes, words, and lines to show how an organization is structured

pie graph a circular graph showing how parts relate to the whole; the whole equals 100 percent

verbal table information given in rows and columns; uses words instead of numbers

Writing@Work

Dorinda Gunther is a freelance graphic designer and creative director. She has expertise in interactive multimedia design, including Web and CD-ROM, set design, video, corporate identity, printed materials, exhibits, and business meetings. She takes a versatile and integrated approach to design and communications, sales training, and consumer education.

As a freelance designer, Dorinda must communicate with clients to update them on their projects and to earn new business. She mainly uses e-mail to communicate with clients about current projects. To earn new business, she has created several tools that she uses to promote her work. One of these tools is a web site. She uses the web site to promote herself and her work, but she also uses it to upload work in progress for her clients to review.

In addition to the web site, Dorinda has created a letter of introduction and a PowerPoint® presentation to promote her work. Using these tools, she effectively communicates her abilities to prospective clients. Without effective communication, Dorinda would have difficulty obtaining new business.

In the graphic design industry, it is possible to encounter a client who wants a designer to use graphics to intentionally mislead an audience. Dorinda feels strongly about this issue and says, "I don't believe I have ever stretched the truth through design. I would not feel comfortable misleading the audience in any way."

Another ethical issue in the design industry is using pictures from someone else's web site or using pictures whose source you have forgotten. Dorinda is careful about this issue. She uses stock photography when original photography is not available, and she always instructs clients on the rights and usage guidelines of purchased photography.

Dorinda has a bachelor of science degree in design. She has worked for companies as an art director and as an associate creative director. She has been freelancing since 2001.

© 2005 Used with permission

MEMO

TO: Teachers and Students

FROM: Principal Oden

DATE: October 6, 20—

SUBJECT: **Parking Reassignments for Friday, October 14, 20—**

On Friday, October 14, 20—, 16 marching bands from area high schools will be arriving to compete in the Holbrook High School Annual Band Classic. To help our school sponsor this important event, we ask teachers and students with Area A, B, and C parking permits to park in the garment factory parking lot across the street to make room for the 30-35 buses that will be arriving on that day. Please note the following parking reassignments for Friday, October 14, only:

Area A   move to parking lot to the north of the factory

Area B   move to parking lot to the south of the factory

Area C   move to parking lot northeast of the factory

Administration move to Austin Avenue in front of the factory

The map reproduced here and posted on bulletin boards throughout the school will help you locate the proper parking areas:

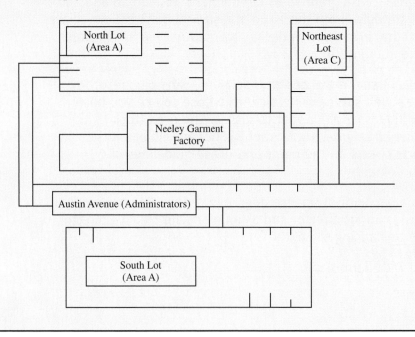

Figure 6.1 Document with Graphics

DESIGNING THE DOCUMENT

When you write, you make many decisions. For example, you decide what to write, how to organize, which words to use, and whether the words reflect standard usage. Indeed, words are important to any writer, but in technical writing, how the words *look* on the page is just as important as what the words say.

WARM UP

Recall a time you went to the library to choose a book for a book report. After looking through several books, how did you make your final choice? Did some books look more inviting than others? Why or why not?

© GETTY IMAGES/PHOTODISC

A cluttered room with poorly designed lighting can make you feel overwhelmed. A cluttered document with poorly designed elements can make your readers feel the same way. Readers may be discouraged if they cannot find the information they need quickly and easily. Good technical writers must learn to design pages that are visually friendly if they want readers to stay focused.

For example, the 3″ × ½″ plastic tab inserted into Lorenzo's potted rosebush included six steps for planting and 57 tiny words squeezed onto the tab. Lorenzo could not read the directions, so he threw out the tab and dug a hole deep enough to plant the root ball of the bush several inches below the ground. Stephanie, the next-door neighbor, showed Lorenzo the 2″ × 3″ set of instructions that came tied around a branch of her newest rosebush. With the instructions having room for an illustration and print
big enough for Lorenzo to see, Lorenzo read the caution against burying the root ball too deeply and adjusted the hole he had dug. In a few months, both neighbors had beautiful roses, thanks to Stephanie's better-designed instructions. Figure 6.2 shows two sets of instructions, one poorly designed and the other designed with the reader's needs in mind.

Tea Rose

Find an area that will receive full sun. Use rich, well-drained soil that contains organic matter. Dig a hole slightly wider than the root-ball. Plant the bush so that the top of the root-ball is exposed. Do not cover the root-ball. Water the area thoroughly and fertilize twice a year: in spring and late summer.

Tea Rose

1. Find an area that will receive full sun
2. Use rich, well-drained soil that contains organic matter.
3. Dig a hole slightly wider than the root-ball.
4. Plant the bush so that the top of the root-ball is exposed. Do NOT cover the root-ball.
5. Water the area thoroughly.
6. Fertilize twice a year: in spring and late summer.

Figure 6.2 Examples of Poorly Designed and Improved Instructions

DESIGN ELEMENTS

In addition to words, writers can use **design elements** to aid comprehension and keep the reader's interest. Elements to consider when designing are white space, text, headings, graphics, and physical features.

White Space White space is space that is white or blank. White space rests the eyes, separates chunks of information, and makes a document look inviting. Writers can create white space in margins, between paragraphs, before itemized lists, and around graphics.

Text Text refers to the words printed on the page. Readers read text more quickly if it is left-justified with ragged-right edges. Left justification means that the text is flush with the left margin of the page. Ragged right means that words lie unevenly along the right margin. This page is set up with left justification and ragged-right edges.

Two differences between fonts, or letter design, are serif and sans serif. (*Sans* is French for "without.") Serif refers to letters with distinguishing lines or "tails" (like this sentence) that make it easy to see the differences between one letter and another. Sans serif refers to letters with fewer distinguishing lines and no "tails" (like this sentence) and is appropriate for something short, such as a title or a heading. The major headings in this textbook use a sans serif font.

Size is measured in points, with a large point number (14 or 16) used for a larger letter. Text in 10 or 12 points can be seen easily. For paragraphs, choose a 10- to12-point serif font that mixes capital and lowercase letters. Do not write an entire document in all capitals; all capitals are hard to read and should be used only for emphasis, for a title, or for a major heading.

Highlighters are print styles that focus the reader's attention on something important. **Boldface**, underline, *italics*, and CAPITALS are effective highlighters, with **boldface** being the most effective and CAPITALS the least effective. Use highlighters sparingly: overuse clutters the page and distracts the reader, drawing attention *away from* the text instead of *to* the text.

Another effective tool for highlighting is an itemized list. To itemize a list, set up a list separate from the text and indented from the left margin. Bullets (•) often precede each item in the list to highlight the information.

For example, Mr. Gorham wrote his students a letter, giving them last-minute instructions for their trip to France. He used a bulleted list to draw attention to the five important items for his students to pack.

> The items below are essential for a smooth, trouble-free trip. Be sure to check and double-check that you possess the following items:
>
> - Your passport—you will not be allowed on the plane without it
> - Your money—credit card, traveler's checks, and some currency
> - Your insurance card
> - Any medication you routinely take
> - Your driver's license

Headings Headings are short titles that introduce the main idea of a selected portion of text. Like a formal outline, headings help your reader see the organization of a document in one glance. Most reports use a system of two headings (first-degree headings and second-degree headings) but can use more. For example, this textbook uses a system of four headings.

Complete the Practicing Systems of Headings Activity worksheet on the Data CD.

Graphics **Graphics** are visual representations of data or information. They include many familiar visual aids such as tables, line graphs, pie graphs, and diagrams, but they also include more sophisticated and less familiar aids such as schematics, pictographs, decision charts, and Internet graphics.

Graphics are used in technical writing any time information can be expressed better in a visual form than in words alone. Sometimes a graphic is used by itself, as in the traffic signs posted on your way to school. For technical writers, the graphic is often used along with text to fully convey meaning.

Whether you use graphics alone or with text, considerations of purpose and audience guide your decision and influence which graphic is appropriate for your document. The last section of this chapter will introduce you to some of the most familiar and easy-to-design graphics.

Physical Features In addition to considering white space, headings, and graphics, writers choose the best physical features, or medium, to use for their document. Possible choices include paper media (heavy stock, 8½ by 11 inches, or a trifold brochure) or electronic media (e-mail, CD-ROM, or web pages). Again, purpose and audience determine which medium you choose. In turn, the medium also will influence the design.

For example, Washington Research Associates (WRA) sent a one-page marketing survey to photography enthusiasts to determine potential customers for a photography supply store. WRA wanted to encourage readers to complete the survey quickly and return it promptly. Because the survey was only one page and the target population was small, the graphic artists decided to use heavy-stock paper with the survey on one side and the return address with prepaid postage on the back. This way, readers could simply refold the document after completing the survey, use the enclosed sticker to seal the "envelope," and put the survey in the mail. The purpose (receiving completed surveys quickly) influenced the medium (the envelope design). Likewise, the envelope design (the medium) influenced placement of the address, the prepaid postage, and the sticker to seal the envelope (the format).

Stop and Think

Why do white space, ragged-right edges, serif font, and headings make text easier to read? What is the purpose of highlighters?

What is being described here?

A circle, 3 inches in diameter, contains three items. At the bottom of the figure, approximately ¾ of an inch from the bottom, is a single line, approximately 2 inches long curved in the shape of the bottom half of a small circle. At the top of the 3-inch circle, approximately ½ inch from the top and 1 inch apart, are two small circles, ¼ of an inch in diameter. A perfect square encloses the 3-inch circle, the four sides of the square barely touching four points of the circle.

WHO READS GRAPHICS?

A picture is indeed worth a thousand words. Graphics can clarify information quickly. At one glance, your readers can perceive more information than they would with words alone. Most complex technical material can be simplified with a graphic: a table, a drawing, a diagram, or a graph. Where academic readers rely heavily on words to understand meaning, technical readers often rely on words *and* graphics to convey meaning.

© GETTY IMAGES/PHOTODISC

AUDIENCE

Technical subjects, such as engineering, marketing, and medicine, rely heavily on data that is presented visually, so readers of technical documents expect to see graphic aids in their reading. However, readers vary in their ability to understand graphics. As with decisions about text, decisions about graphics depend on what your readers are able to understand and what they already know.

Generally, the more data that is included in a graphic, the more difficult it will be to read. When deciding which graphic your audience will best understand, you should always be sure to ask these questions about your reader(s):

- How much does my reader know about the subject?

- How interested is my reader in the subject?

- Do my readers include a technical audience? In other words, do my readers need or expect technical information or figures?

- Will my audience be confused by technical information or figures?

- Does my audience's reading level tend to be higher (tenth grade or higher) or lower (ninth grade or lower)?

PURPOSE AND OBJECTIVES

Audience is only one consideration in deciding what kind of graphic to use. You also must consider the purpose of your graphic, how much information you have, and what type of information there is.

To choose graphics that relay your meaning most effectively, you can ask yourself 1) what the objectives of your writing are and 2) how graphics can help you achieve those objectives. Then choose the graphic that best meets those objectives.

To help you decide which graphic to use, look at the purpose column in Figure 6.3. Turn each purpose statement into a question that begins with an understood "Do I want . . .?" For example, "Do I want to show my readers how to operate a digital camera?" If so, drawing the mechanism of the camera with clearly labeled parts would help achieve that purpose.

Purpose (Do I Want . . .?)	Type of Graphic
to show a mechanism or part of a mechanism?	line drawing or diagram
to show how the whole is divided into parts or how the parts relate to the whole?	pie graph
to present a small amount of data in an easy-to-read format?	informal table
to compare sets of data; to present differences; to depict a trend?	bar graph
to compare several sets of data; to depict a trend?	double bar graph
to show a trend; to show how data is related?	line graph
to show several trends; to compare trends; to show how data is related?	multiple line graph
to present information, especially many numbers, in an easy-to-read format?	formal table
to present a process?	flowchart
to present the structure of an organization?	organizational chart
to show the details of what something actually looks like?	photograph

Figure 6.3 Graphics Purpose

Stop and Think

What are some questions to ask about your audience to help you select an appropriate graphic? Using Figure 6.3, name three graphics you see frequently in textbooks. Give the purpose of each.

WARM UP

Take a close look at the graphics in the following sections of this chapter. What do you notice about each graphic? What do the graphics have in common? Notice some of the differences. In what graphics do the differences occur?

FORMATTING GRAPHICS TO MAKE THEM EASY TO UNDERSTAND

Graphics add critical information to your text and become part of the overall appearance of your document. Good writers create a flow between words and graphics that unifies a document so that readers move along without interruption. To help your reader interpret graphics quickly and easily, you should keep graphics simple and neat, integrate graphics with text, give credit for borrowed graphics, and use color effectively.

© GETTY IMAGES/PHOTODISC

KEEP GRAPHICS NEAT AND SIMPLE

The quality of a graphic is a factor in how carefully it is read. A neat, clean graphic is easy to read and interpret. Leave enough white space to make the graphic look uncluttered and make the graphic large enough to see all parts clearly. Align decimals when they are presented in columns, as shown in the figures below:

8.3

0.525

98.6

In general, a graphic should have one main point. Using two uncluttered, simple graphics to illustrate two concepts is better than using one cluttered graphic to illustrate too many concepts.

Figure 6.4 is an example of a cluttered graphic. Its many lines make it look more like a robotic weapon from a *Star Wars* movie than a line graph predicting trends in community college majors.

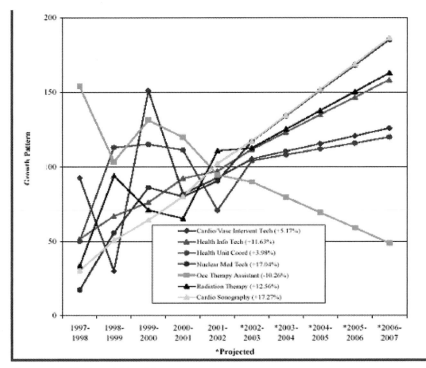

Figure 6.4 Cluttered Graphic

INTEGRATE GRAPHICS WITH TEXT

Refer to each graphic clearly in the text BEFORE you place it on the page. Refer to the graphic when you think your reader will look at it for the first time. Use the word *Figure* to refer to any graphic that is not a formal table. Use the word *Table* to refer to a formal table (a table with rules and titles). Call your reader's attention to figures or tables by 1) incorporating references into your text, 2) using parentheses, or 3) creating stand-alone sentences:

---

1) Table 1/Figure 1 shows the amount of rainfall in Idaho over the past three years.

2) The rainfall in Idaho over six years varied substantially (see Table 1/Figure 1).

2) The rainfall in Idaho over six years varied substantially (Table 1/Figure 1).

3) The rainfall in Idaho over six years varied substantially. See Table 1/Figure 1.

Choose one method and refer to all of your figures and tables the same way. Informal tables need not be referred to as a table or a figure. **Verbal tables** are not always referred to as a table or figure but are often integrated into the text with an appropriate introduction.

Place each graphic in a convenient place for the reader to see. If the graphic is small enough (⅕ to ½ page), try to place it on the same page as its reference. If the graphic is large (¾ to 1 page), you may need to place it on the page immediately following your reference. For graphics used in reports, explain the graphic's significance in the report as you introduce the graphic. Explain in words the relationships you want your reader to see. For example, point out parts of a diagram, trends in a line graph, or important numbers in a table. You need not discuss every part of the graphic, but do point out what is important for the reader to know. Generally, explanations are presented in the introduction preceding the graphic. More complex graphics may require discussion before and after placement of the graphic.

Provide a title for every graphic. Table titles may be centered above the table and figure titles centered below the figure; however, placement may vary. Choose a placement and be consistent throughout your document. Use titles that are specific so the readers can understand what they will learn from the graphic. For example, use

Salary Distribution for 1955-1956	NOT JUST Salaries
Regal Powerboat Model OTY-453	NOT JUST Powerboat

Informal tables do not need titles. Number figures consecutively throughout. Number tables consecutively, but separately from figures, throughout.

GIVE CREDIT FOR BORROWED GRAPHICS

Give credit for a graphic if you do not compile it yourself or if you compile it using borrowed data. Place the word *Source* below your figure and give the bibliographic reference for the source as you would a footnote or an endnote.

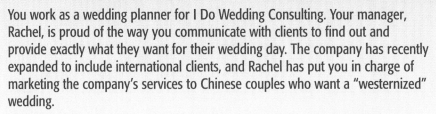

You work as a wedding planner for I Do Wedding Consulting. Your manager, Rachel, is proud of the way you communicate with clients to find out and provide exactly what they want for their wedding day. The company has recently expanded to include international clients, and Rachel has put you in charge of marketing the company's services to Chinese couples who want a "westernized" wedding.

You decide to create a brochure that shows pictures of weddings you have planned in the past. You personally believe the most beautiful weddings have been "all-white" weddings, so you include pictures that show arrangements of white roses and other white flowers on the cover of your brochure. Several weeks after the brochures are distributed, Rachel is upset with you because not a single Chinese couple has called to make an appointment.

Why do you think the brochure was not effective for the target audience? You may need to research color associations in other countries to learn why the brochure was not an effective marketing tool.

USE COLOR EFFECTIVELY

Color draws a reader's attention often before the reader pays attention to the words. Color is a powerful design tool that can be used to:

- Indicate a document's organization. By using the same color for major headings, you give your readers visual cues to the overall organization of a document and help them scan quickly for information.

- Emphasize or clarify an important point. By using a color for a key word, a phrase, an idea, or a part of a graphic, you draw your reader's attention to important information. You also can use color to signify a change or to guide readers through a process.

You can get thousands of free images from a variety of sources to add to your documents. Many web sites have images, graphics, and photographs that are free and do not require permission to use. You also can purchase CD-ROMs that store thousands of images on a disk. These disks are organized by categories, such as business, wildlife, or travel images. Once you purchase the CD-ROM, you may use the images without copyright permission.

© GETTY IMAGES/PHOTODISC

- Support your text's meaning. By using certain colors consistently to convey specific information, your reader begins to associate the color (red with danger, for example) with the meaning and therefore understands text more quickly.

- Make your document attractive. By using colors to break up black and white text, your page will be more appealing.

Color, like any technical writing tool, can be misused. To use color effectively:

- Avoid overusing color. More than three or four colors (including black and white as two colors) can overwhelm a reader, and using one color too often can be distracting.

- Apply color consistently to elements throughout your document. For example, if you set major headings in red and key words in black boldface, do not suddenly switch a major heading to blue or a key word to red boldface.

- Remain sensitive to cultural identifications with colors. International audiences associate colors differently from American audiences. For instance, green is associated with go (traffic lights) to an American audience, and red is associated with danger (a firetruck or stop sign). On the other hand, green is a holy color to a Muslim, and red is a sign of mourning to a South African.

- Avoid unusual combinations of colors. Some colors, such as purple on a blue background or orange on a red background, are simply too difficult to read.

Stop and Think

Why should graphics be neat and simple?

CONSTRUCTING GRAPHICS FOR AUDIENCE AND PURPOSE

As a composer of graphics, you have many choices available to use in your documents. You must make choices about which graphics are most appropriate to use for different audiences and purposes. This section will show you how one writer selected graphics for two articles she wrote on the topic of fitness for two different magazines.

© GETTY IMAGES/PHOTODISC

Theresa has been asked to share the secrets of her successful fitness program with two very different audiences. One article will appear in *Fitness,* a magazine for junior high school students just beginning an exercise program. These readers have little knowledge of fitness and only a moderate interest in improving their health. As younger readers, their reading level is lower, and their experience reading graphics is limited.

The other article will appear in *Mind and Body,* a magazine for college students majoring in physical education. These readers are different from the readers of *Fitness*: they have a solid background in physical education, a keen interest in the subject, a higher reading level, and more experience interpreting graphics. This section will take you through Theresa's decision-making processes as she decides how to present her fitness expertise to the different audiences of *Fitness* and *Mind and Body.*

CONSTRUCTING TABLES

Tables are used to present words or numbers that can be organized into categories of columns and rows. Tables are one of the most popular graphic aids and can be informal or formal. A verbal table, often called a chart, is a variation of the formal table, categorizing words instead of numbers into columns and rows.

Informal Table An **informal table** is a graphic that uses rows and columns drawn *without* rules (lines) or stubs (column headings). In an informal table, the information flows with the text. The explanation of the graphic is a brief summary of the information presented in the graphic.

Theresa wants to motivate the younger readers of *Fitness* to begin their fitness program. Theresa thinks that beginners could benefit from seeing how quickly she saw results. To present her own progress after two months on a workout regimen, Theresa uses an informal table. The informal table is a good choice because the information is simple (only three items to consider) and appropriate for her younger audience. See Figure 6.5 for the informal table and its written introduction.

Over the next two months, Theresa lost a total of 4.2 pounds. For every pound of fat she lost, she gained approximately ¾ pound of muscle.

Fat lost	14.0 lbs.
Muscle gained	9.8 lbs.
Total pounds lost	4.2 lbs.

Figure 6.5 Model of Informal Table

Formal Table A **formal table** is a graphic that presents numerical information in rows and columns with rules (lines drawn). It is typically used to organize numbers in a consistent format.

Theresa wants the readers of *Mind and Body* to know at what rate they should exercise to burn fat. She uses part of a table from a published book. The older and more knowledgeable audience of *Mind and Body* will understand the detailed numerical data. They also will be motivated to locate their own heart rates and will appreciate the information given in the footnotes. Figure 6.6 is part of the formal table Theresa reproduced from *Exercise and You* along with her brief introduction.

Table 1 shows the recommended heart rates by age during exercise. The athlete's training rate is for only the most fit athletes. The average training rate is recommended for a healthy person beginning a fitness program.

Formal table is labeled *Table*

Table 1. Recommended Heart Rates During Aerobic Exercise

Superscript letters direct attention to footnotes

TRAINING RATES[a]			
Age	Maximum Heart Rate	Athlete, 85%[b]	Average, 80%
20	200	170	160
22	198	168	158
24	196	167	157
26	194	165	155
28	192	163	154

Stubs

Rules

[a]Based on average heart rates of 72 beats per minute for males and 80 beats per minute for females

[b]Percentages represent percents of maximum heart rates in Column 2

Footnotes explain parts of the table

Source: Alan Grayson and Susanne Brazinski, *Exercise and You,* Clearview, ND: Mountain Press, 1994.

Source provides bibliographic data

Figure 6.6 Model of Formal Table and Introduction

Complete the Formal Table Activity worksheet on the Data CD.

A formal table is appropriate here because the many different numbers make the information more difficult to read. By presenting numbers in columns, the formal table helps to simplify the information.

Theresa decides to use only a few rules because more would clutter the graphic. The columns are named with stubs. Notice the "a" and "b" superscripts next to the column titles. They direct the reader's attention to the footnotes that give additional information about the table. Underneath the graphic, the word *Source* appears with a footnoted bibliographic entry. Notice that the introduction tells what kind of information is included in the table, but it does not explain every item. The table, with a short introduction, is self-explanatory.

Verbal Table A **verbal table,** also known as a **chart,** is similar to a formal table with its rows and columns. Like a formal table, it uses stubs and may include footnotes and bibliographic information if taken from another source. It is different, though, in the kinds of data included. Formal tables use numerals; verbal tables use words.

Theresa wants to emphasize to both audiences the dangers of poor eating habits and little or no exercise. She needs a graphic appropriate for both audiences. She could write this information in a paragraph but decides that a chart presents the information more efficiently. So Theresa uses the simple verbal table in Figure 6.7 and writes a short introduction.

The following chart shows that some diseases have possible causes in poor eating habits.

Eating Habits	Diseases from Poor Eating Habits
Too much fat	Some cancers, heart disease, strokes
Too much salt	Heart disease, high blood pressure
Too much cholesterol	Heart disease, high blood pressure
Too much sugar	Diabetes, hypoglycemia
Lack of fiber	Some cancers, gallstones
Lack of calcium	Osteoporosis

Source: Marion Newberry, *Nutrition*, New York: Medical Press, 1992, 12.

Figure 6.7 Model of a Verbal Table with Introduction

Theresa believes strongly that both audiences need this information. To avoid overwhelming her younger readers, she does not add data that might interest only the older audience. She knows that the older audience is already aware of the health risks of an inactive lifestyle and needs to be reminded only of possible health consequences. She designs the chart to be simple enough for a younger audience who, she believes, will make the effort to relate to the information.

CONSTRUCTING GRAPHS

A graph is a visual that shows the *relationships* between numerical data. Three types are bar graphs, line graphs, and pie graphs.

Bar Graph The **bar graph** is a graphic using a horizontal axis and a vertical axis to compare numerical data presented in rectangular bars.

Theresa wants to show the readers of *Fitness* how much fat she lost per week for the first two months. She has already given these readers the total amount of fat she lost and wants to follow that information with more specific data. The bar graph is relatively easy to read and is therefore appropriate for the *Fitness* readers. Figure 6.8 shows the bar graph she designed, along with the introduction that tells Theresa's readers which numbers to pay attention to.

Figure 1 shows the progression of fat loss per week for eight weeks. Notice that the greatest amount of fat loss occurred during weeks 1 (3.6 pounds lost) and 2 (2.7 pounds lost). Weeks 3 (1.5 pounds lost) and 4 (1.1 pounds lost) show the least amount of fat loss. Typically, the body will lose more weight at first because of sustained metabolism and significant water loss. Several weeks into the weight-loss program, the metabolism slows down the amount of loss to protect the body from harm. Notice also that after seven weeks on the program, Theresa's weight loss stabilized at a loss of a little more than a pound a week.

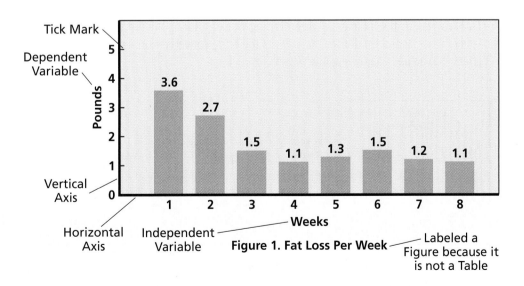

Figure 6.8 Model of Bar Graph with Introduction

In her bar graph, Theresa used the horizontal axis for the independent variable and the vertical axis for the dependent variable. In this case, the independent variable is the number of weeks and the dependent variable is the amount of pounds lost. The independent variable (the variable that changes automatically) effects changes in the dependent variable. Typically, the vertical axis represents the dependent variable, and the horizontal axis represents the independent variable. Often the horizontal axis depicts time or distance.

Here, the number of weeks, which pass automatically, has something to do with the amount of weight lost. Put another way, the dependent variable, weight lost, is affected by the independent variable, the passage of time.

Notice that the specific number of pounds has been added atop each bar for easy reference. To do so is not necessary, but helpful. In fact, Theresa could have left out the numbers next to the tick marks, since the actual numbers were placed atop the bars. The decision to add specific numbers depends on your readers and how specific they need you to be. Additional tick marks between pounds to mark individual ounces or half pounds were not added because the graph was understandable without them. Additional lines would have cluttered the graphic. Note that the bars are the same width and that the space between the bars is one-half the bar width.

Multiple Bar Graph To compare how much fat she lost to how much muscle she gained, Theresa uses the **multiple bar graph,** a bar graph with more than one bar, in Figure 6.9. With just two bars, this **double bar graph** is easy for both audiences to read and offers the *Mind and Body* audience more information than a single bar graph. However, Theresa decides to use the multiple bar graph for only the *Fitness* readers because she wants a graph that emphasizes the *difference* in fat loss and muscle gain in the first weeks.

Figure 2 compares the amount of fat lost to the number of pounds gained. Notice that the amount of muscle gained is small compared to the amount of fat lost during the first weeks. However, as the fat loss stabilized during weeks 7 and 8, the amount of muscle gain is slightly higher. Muscle is denser than fat. As the body converts more fat to muscle, the net effect is to actually gain weight while still losing fat.

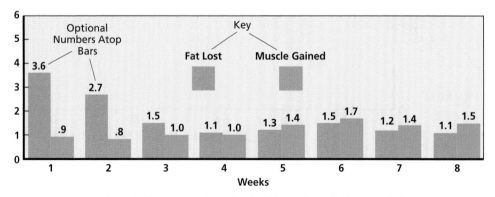

Figure 2. Fat Compared to Muscle Gain, in Pounds (for 8 weeks)

Figure 6.9 Model of a Double Bar Graph with Introduction

Writers have a responsibility to present data accurately without creating distortions that may be misleading. When constructing graphs drawn on horizontal and vertical axes, be careful to begin the quantitative scale at zero and to keep horizontal and vertical axes proportional. In the following graphs, note how misleading the approval ratings for a political candidate can be: Figure 1 minimizes the trend by spreading the horizontal axis out. Figure 2 exaggerates the trend by shortening the horizontal axis. Figure 3 minimizes the trend by taking away the zero point. Figure 4 is the most realistic of all.

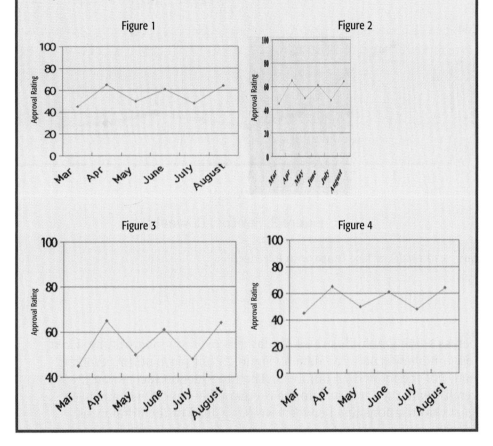

The double bar graph uses two sets of bars on a horizontal and vertical axis to compare several sets of numerical data. With some bars taller than others, the bar graph dramatically depicts differences. Again, the introduction points out what is most important to the reader.

The bars for fat lost are shaded differently from the bars for muscle gained. A **key** is provided to explain the shading. Also, Theresa considers adding the specific pounds atop each bar as she did in the single bar graph. This way, her readers can see the specific amount easily.

Line Graph The **line graph** is similar to a bar graph in that it uses a horizontal axis and a vertical axis to compare numerical data. Instead of bars, however, this graph uses a line that depicts a trend.

Theresa can use a line graph to show the same data she used in the bar graph and must decide which graph is more appropriate for her readers. To experiment with a different graph, she plotted the same eight-week fat-loss data on a line graph. Figure 6.10 shows the same data in a line graph that Figure 6.9 shows in a bar graph.

Figure 3 shows how the fat loss peaked in the earlier weeks, dropped remarkably during the middle weeks, and plateaued during the last four weeks.

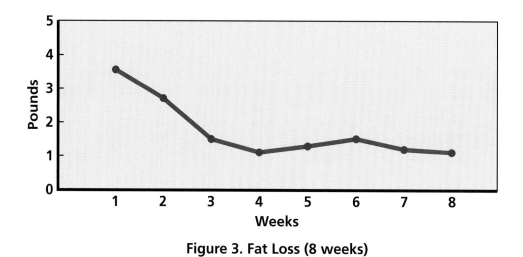

Figure 3. Fat Loss (8 weeks)

Figure 6.10 Model of Line Graph with Introduction

Theresa's line graph illustrates the fat loss over a period of time. Even though it shows the same data as Figure 6.9, it plays up the general trend, not the individual numbers. The introduction focuses on the overall trend: the fat loss "dropped remarkably" and "plateaued." It plays up relationships between weeks instead of the differences between them.

This graph would be appropriate for either audience because the trend is easily interpreted, but Theresa decides not to use this line graph for either article. She believes that the bar graph is more appropriate for the inexperienced readers of *Fitness* because she wants to highlight differences in the fat lost. Instead, Theresa considers using the multiple line graph below for her *Fitness* audience.

Multiple Line Graph Theresa's Figure 6.11 puts the same information as the double bar graph in Figure 6.9 into a **multiple line graph,** a graph using more than one line to compare data. Because Theresa's graph compares two sets of data, think of it as a **double line graph.**

The relationship between fat loss and muscle gain is more closely matched after the first weeks of the fitness program (see Figure 4). During the first two weeks, the amount of muscle gain is minimal and fat loss is at its maximum. As the fat loss plateaus, the muscle gain stabilizes, surpassing fat loss by a few ounces.

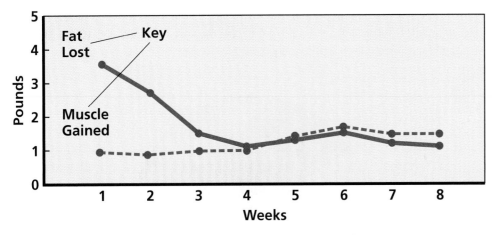

Figure 3. Fat Loss (8 weeks)

Figure 6.11 Model of Multiple Line Graph with Introduction

Theresa decides that the physical education majors would be interested in seeing how the two sets of data interact with each other and would have the educational background to understand how muscle gain affects fat loss. While she will present her *Fitness* readers the same information in *two* bar graphs, she will present her *Mind and Body* readers the same information in *one* multiple line graph.

Notice how the double line graph illustrates the *relationship* between fat loss and muscle gain rather than the *differences* between fat loss and muscle gain. Again, the introduction emphasizes this relationship.

Pie Graph To represent what percentage of her total daily food intake consisted of fat, protein, and carbohydrates, Theresa draws a **pie graph** in Figure 6.12. A pie graph is a circular graphic that shows how the parts relate to the whole.

Complete the Pie Graph Activity worksheet on the Data CD.

The whole totals 100 percent, with each piece of the pie representing a percentage of the whole. Notice that the pie pieces move clockwise from the twelve o'clock position from the largest to the smallest. A pie graph should contain no more than seven sections.

Figure 5 shows the amount of protein, carbohydrates, and fat a person on a fitness plan needs in one day. Surprisingly, the human body needs more carbohydrates (65%) than protein and much less fat than previously thought.

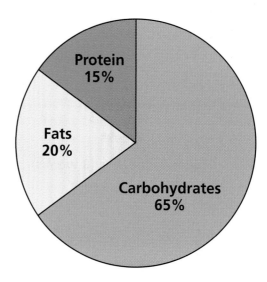

Figure 6.12 Model of Pie Graph with Introduction

The introduction repeats the actual percentages in the pie and points out the significance of those numbers. The readers of *Mind and Body* already know these percentages and do not need to be reminded of them, so Theresa decides not to use the pie graph for this more sophisticated audience. The readers of *Fitness,* who include people just beginning fitness programs, may need this information.

CONSTRUCTING CHARTS AND DIAGRAMS

A **chart** is a drawing with boxes, words, and lines to show a process or an organizational structure. Two popular charts include the **flowchart** and the organizational chart. A **diagram** or drawing shows what something looks like or how it operates.

Flowchart Theresa wants a quick way to show the complex process of converting glucose to fat. She knows the readers of *Mind and Body* already understand what happens to food the body does not use, but the readers of *Fitness* are unaware of this process. She chooses a flowchart, Figure 6.13, to illustrate this process to her less knowledgeable readers. In the flowchart, the arrows lead the reader through the process, and the introduction summarizes the process.

 Complete the Organizational Chart Activity worksheet on the Data CD.

Figure 6 shows what happens when sugars and starches are digested to glucose. The glucose not used by the brain or the muscles is converted to fat.

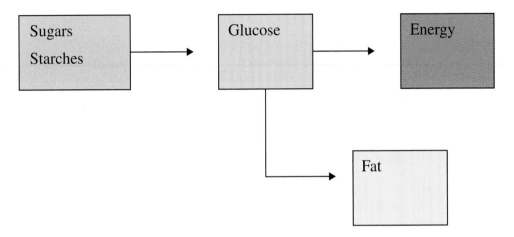

Figure 6.13 Model of Flowchart with Introduction

Organizational Chart Theresa was asked to present her research to the student body during assembly. To make students aware of the school's fitness center, she creates an **organizational chart.** The chart shows the hierarchy of the fitness center employees. Theresa creates her organizational chart using boxes, words, and lines in Figure 6.14.

The following chart shows the organization of the school fitness center.

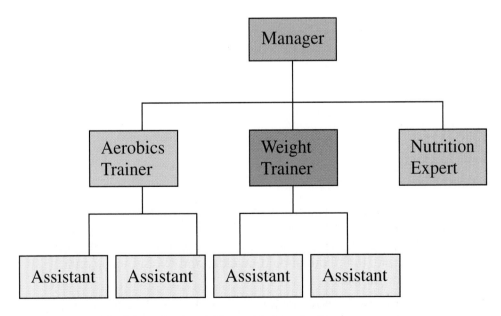

Figure 6.14 Model of Organizational Chart with Introduction

The blocks contain the job titles. At the top of the chart is the highest position. The lines show who is responsible to whom. The introduction describes information in the chart.

Diagram or Drawing For her *Mind and Body* article, Theresa uses a diagram, or drawing, in Figure 6.15 from *Good Health* to show what triglycerides (fat) look like in the bloodstream. She believes her *Mind and Body* readers have the background for this information and hopes the diagram will reinforce the dangers of a diet too high in fat.

Notice the use of **call outs,** names of parts with lines drawn to the appropriate place. The drawing represents a simplified version of the blood arteriole and capillaries. Adding other particles in the bloodstream would complicate the graphic. Here, the author drew only what was needed to make the point.

Figure 8 shows how the blood cells clump together abnormally after a dinner high in triglycerides (fat). Notice that when the triglycerides create sludging, blood flow to the capillaries is impeded.

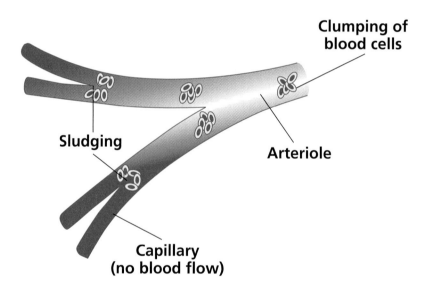

Figure 6.15 Model of a Diagram with Introduction

Photograph A photograph can be inserted into a document when it is important to show what something actually looks like. Photographs include a lot of detail, however, and are not always an appropriate graphic aid to use. To be effective, the photo should be clear and should focus on a particular idea or message.

Theresa decides to set up a web page to promote a healthy lifestyle. Because she thinks exercising with others encourages people to keep up their fitness regime, she decides to post a photograph of friends engaging in a power walk at lunch. Her photo also helps create the mood she is after, that is, to depict fitness in a fun and positive way. Figure 6.16 shows the photo she chose.

The workers at Sampsun Marine Industries, shown in Figure 6.16 below, get together every day for a walk around the grounds.

Figure 6.16 Photograph of Empoyee Power Walk

Stop and Think

Which chart shows a process? Which chart shows an organizational hierarchy? Which graphic shows what something looks like? What is the advantage of using a photograph? What is the disadvantage of using a photograph?

POINT YOUR
BROWSER

techwriting.swlearning.com

SUMMARY

1. To create effective document design, 1) use adequate white space, 2) use left justification with ragged-right edges, 3) use a 10- to 12-point serif font that mixes capitals and lowercase letters, 4) determine a workable system of headings, 5) use highlighters to draw attention to important information, and 6) consider appropriate physical features.

2. Graphics should adhere to basic principles. They should be neat, use figure labels and numbers to refer to anything that is not a table, use table labels and numbers to refer to formal tables, and be located in a convenient place for the reader (usually right after the referral phrase). They also should use specific titles, give credit when necessary, use words to explain, show decimals aligned, and use color effectively.

3. Each type of graphic has a purpose that can be matched to writing objectives and audience needs.

4. Effective graphics include informal, formal, and verbal tables; bar graphs and line graphs; flowcharts, organizational charts, and diagrams; and photographs.

Checklist

- Have I determined my writing objectives and found a graphic to match?

- Have I designed my page effectively with adequate white space, left justification and ragged-right edges, a 10- to 12-point serif font, capital and lowercase letters, a workable system of headings, and appropriate highlighters?

- Have I selected appropriate graphics?

- Have I selected appropriate physical features and an appropriate medium for my writing objectives?

- Have I constructed the graphic neatly?

- Have I referred to the graphic properly as a table or figure?

- Have I placed the graphic in a convenient place for the reader?

- Have I provided a specific title for every graph, every chart, and every formal table?

- Have I numbered the graphics consecutively? Table 1, 2, etc. or Figure 1, 2, etc.?

- Have I given credit for the graphic found in an outside source?

- Have I explained the significance of the graphic?

- Have I kept the graphic as simple as possible?

- Have I used color effectively?

- Have I constructed each graphic according to the criteria required by that graphic?

Build On What You Know

1. Examine several of your textbooks for design features. Describe each design. Which book has the best design and why?

2. Read local newspapers and magazines. Cut out an example of each type of graphic presented in this chapter. Identify the parts of the graphic. Using your checklist, determine whether the graphic designers presented data effectively.

3. Look for graphics that are different from the ones presented in this chapter. Note what is different about them. What has been added or changed? Even though the graphics are different, they will likely fall into one of the categories described in this chapter. Which category do they fall into?

4. Suggest the best graphic to use for presenting the situations below. As a bonus, try to construct the graphic.

   a. Lamar wrote to his father and listed his last test grades in calculus: Chapter 1 Test, 83; Chapter 2 Test, 79; Chapter 3 Test, 92.

   b. Carrie wanted to know how many miles she walked as she went about her everyday activities during a regular five-day school week opposed to how many miles she walked during the first five days of summer vacation. She used a pedometer and estimated her mileage each day on a chart. Here are her figures: School in session: May 25, 1.3; May 26, 1.9; May 27, 2.7; May 28, 1.6; May 29, 2.5. Vacation: June 1, .6; June 2, 1.2; June 3, .9; June 4, 1.4; June 5, 2.0.

   c. Ichiro wanted to show his parents that he had wisely spent the money they gave him for the first month of college. They gave him $800 to buy books and set up his dorm room. In his letter, he rounds his figures to the nearest dollar and uses a graphic with the following information: $562, books and educational supplies; $36, eating out; $115, dorm accessories (rug, poster, sheets, etc.); $25, entertainment; $40, parking fine (which he assures them will not happen again!); and $22, unspent funds.

   d. Crystal is head cashier for a grocery store. She must show her coworkers the procedure for gaining approval for a customer check over $200. The procedure is as follows: politely tell the customer it is store policy to have checks over $200 approved; verify the identity of the customer with a picture ID; make sure information on the check is correct; get two phone numbers from the customer; put your initials on the check; call the manager to the checkout to meet the customer and approve the check.

   e. Alessandra must show her physics instructor the structure of a hydrogen atom and the location of protons, neutrons, and electrons.

   f. Patrick is designing a travel brochure for future Peace Corps volunteers. He wants to show how eager students were to learn English in a Phillipine village where current volunteers recently spent time.

Apply What You Learned

5. Select a photo of you or a friend that you are especially proud of. Write a brief article explaining the significance of the photo and insert the photo. Be sure to title the photo, number it, and refer to it in your article.

6. Convert this survey information into a pie graph. You surveyed 450 clients of Iron Works Gym to determine their preferences for new equipment, facilities, or services. Results were as follows: 175 clients want more weight-lifting equipment, 50 clients want child-care services, 75 clients want a sauna, 50 clients want more trainers, and 80 clients want a juice bar.

7. Use the information from the table below to generate graphics.

Commodity	1980	1985	1990	1995	1996	1997	1998	1999	2000
Milk (plain and flavored)	27.6	26.7	25.7	24.0	24.0	23.6	23.2	23.1	22.6
Whole	17.0	14.3	10.5	8.6	8.5	8.3	8.2	8.2	8.1
Reduced-fat, light, and skim	10.5	12.3	15.2	15.4	15.4	15.3	15.1	14.9	14.5
Bottled water	2.4	4.5	8.0	11.5	12.3	12.9	15.7	17.7	(NA)
Fruit juices	7.4	7.8	7.9	8.7	8.7	8.7	8.5	9.3	8.4
Fruit drinks	(NA)	(NA)	6.3	7.7	7.9	8.2	7.7	7.7	(NA)
Vegetable juices	(NA)	(NA)	0.3	0.3	0.3	0.3	0.3	0.3	(NA)

All measurements are in gallons.

Source: U.S. Dept. of Agriculture, Economic Research Service, Food Consumption, Prices, and Expenditures, annual; *Agricultural Outlook,* monthly; and online at <http://www.ers.usda.gov/data/sonsumption>.

- A bar graph to illustrate the *total* amount of milk consumed from 1996-2000

- A double bar graph to show the amount of whole and reduced-fat milk consumed from 1996-2000

- A line graph to illustrate the amount of bottled water consumed from 1990-2000

- A double line graph to illustrate the amount of whole and reduced fat milk consumed from 1980-2000

- A table of milk, bottled water, fruit juices, and vegetable juices consumed from 1996-1999

- An informal table of *total* milk and *total* vegetable juices consumed in 2000

See the Data CD for an additional Work Is A Zoo! worksheet for this activity.

Work Is A Zoo!

You have gathered your information, and the presentation is taking shape. But you will be presenting a lot of ideas at once, including numbers and comparisons to other zoo programs. Tyrone is worried that people will be overwhelmed.

You mention this problem to Anya, and she says, "Guys, why not make some attractive graphics to help the listeners? I like being able to see numbers presented in graphs. You could even give us some ideas about the kinds of logos that other zoos are using on their promotional materials." Great idea, Anya.

Now your task is to produce graphics to enhance your presentation. You may want graphics to show:

- Logos and promotional material from other zoos.
- Number of zoos with similar programs.
- Overall cost of the program.
- Success rates of the program.
- Information from interviews.

Think about these things as you plan your graphics:

- Complicated and unclear graphics add no value to a presentation.
- Your audience and purpose should determine the kind of graphic you use.
- Graphics should provide *needed* information.
- The size of the graphic should not be too big or too small.

Be sure to use the graphic that best presents the information. You might choose from the following graphics:

- Tables
- Bar graphs
- Line graphs
- Flowcharts
- Organizational charts
- Diagrams
- Photographs

INSTRUCTIONS

GOALS

ANALYZE your audience's expectations and the steps required for instructions

DETERMINE an appropriate format for instructions

PREPARE a clear, concise set of instructions

DETERMINE how to write online instructions

See the Data CD for Write-to-Learn and In The Know activity worksheets.

WRITE-TO-LEARN

Think of the last time you followed instructions. Maybe the instructions were from an instructor, a parent, an employer, or a manual. In a short journal entry, answer these questions: What were the circumstances under which you followed the instructions? Were the instructions easy to follow? If so, why? Were the instructions hard to follow? If so, why? How did you handle any problems created by poorly written instructions? Did the instructions use graphics? If so, what kind? Were the graphics helpful? What kind of medium was used: verbal, paper, or online?

In The Know

active voice refers to a verb whose subject performs the action of the verb

cautions statements designed to keep a person from harming the mechanism he or she is working with

concurrent testing determining the usefulness of a product or an activity by observing someone's performance while he or she is using the product or engaging in the activity

explanations information coming after a step and providing additional data to clarify the step

field test checking your instructions with a small sample of people to see whether the instructions are clear

imperative mood the form of a verb that signals a command or instruction; the subject is "you" or understood "you"

online instructions instructions using computer technology as the medium; some types include help menus, CD-ROMs, or web-based instructions

retrospective testing checking the usefulness of a product or an activity after someone has used the product or performed the activity

second person use of "you" or an understood "you"

set of instructions a step-by-step list of actions necessary to complete a task

step one action in a set of instructions

warnings statements designed to keep a person from being harmed

Writing@Work

Sara Coers is a technical communicator for RDS, a financial software company in Indianapolis. In her position, she is responsible for planning, writing, and editing instructional materials, including tutorials and online help, for her company's software products.

As a technical communicator, it is essential that Sara's written communication be absolutely clear. The clarity of her communication is so important because, before Sara's employment with RDS, the company had a history of documentation that did not meet users' needs. Sara's challenge is to create documentation that is user-friendly. Sara also strives for minimalist writing—she wants to use as few words as possible and still have people understand. And to ensure consistency among her written documents, she tries to reuse as much material as possible.

Sara writes for a wide range of audiences. Not only does she write for external clients, such as credit union employees, but she also must write for internal audiences, such as RDS trainers and developers. Although she will generally write different information for these different groups, she must always consider each group's level of understanding.

Because of the number of users Sara writes for, she must be able to effectively relay information to people of varied educational backgrounds. Her rule is to present information in such a way that the people with the least amount of education or lowest level of comprehension of the product will still be able to understand clearly.

RDS has some clients who base their businesses on different ethnic populations. Sara must consider this when she is writing her instructional materials. She makes sure that her communication is not confusing to any group of users. She also uses what she calls "equal-opportunity examples." When using examples in her writing, she makes sure they will make sense to people of all different cultures.

Sara has a bachelor of arts degree from Indiana University and a master's in technical and scientific communication from Miami University in Ohio. She served two internships with Peregrine Systems, primarily writing user guides and online help, before obtaining her current position with RDS.

At Home Operation

Recording Your Outgoing Announcement

Before using your new answering system telephone, you should record an announcement. This is what callers will hear when the system answers a call. Your announcement may be up to 2 minutes long.

1. Prepare your announcement.

   Example: "Hello. I can't come to the phone right now. Please leave your name, telephone number, and a short message after the beep. I will return your call as soon as I can. Thank you."

2. Hold down ANNC, located under the cassette cover (Figure 1). Continue to hold don ANNC while recording. The system will beep once to indicate that it is ready to record.

3. When the system beeps, speak toward the front of the unit in a normal tone of voice.

4. Release ANNC when you are finished. The tape will reset automatically.

> **NOTE:** Your system cannot record an announcement when messages are on the tape. If you have messages and the MESSAGES light is blinking, first listen to your messages and then let your system clear them. (See page 14, "Listen to Your Messages.") When the MESSAGES light is lit steadily, you can record your announcement.

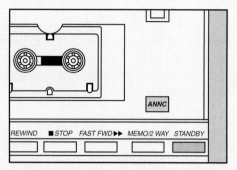

Figure 1

Playing Back Your Announcement

1. If the tape is rewinding, wait for it to stop moving.

2. Set the message VOLUME control (on the right side of the system) to the middle.

3. Tap (quickly press and release) ANNC

> **NOTE:** Be sure that you release the button quickly. If you hold it down for more than a second, your announcement will be erased.

To change your announcement

Follow Steps 1–4 under "Recording Your Outgoing Announcement." Your new announcement will be recorded over the old one.

Figure 7.1 Instructions Model

GETTING STARTED ON INSTRUCTIONS

Imagine that you just purchased a new entertainment center for your television and stereo. You want to assemble the entertainment center quickly because you invited some friends over to watch a movie. Your friends will be arriving in two hours, and you must put together your entertainment center before they arrive. Since you are on a tight schedule, you start to assemble the entertainment center without looking at the instructions. "It cannot be that hard," you think. You are certain that reading the instructions will slow you down. An hour and a half later, you are still trying to connect the parts. You are frantic because your guests will be arriving in 30 minutes, and the entertainment center is still in pieces on the floor. Finally, you look at the instructions.

WARM UP

Do you always read instructions before you attempt a procedure? Why or why not?

 You can view various sample instructions in the sample documents on the Data CD.

WHO READS INSTRUCTIONS?

People who read a **set of instructions** need to perform a task or understand how someone else performs that task. The server who is asked to close a restaurant at night needs to know the procedure for doing so. The surveyor measuring a road for underground pipes needs to know traffic patterns. You, assembling your newly purchased entertainment center, need to know how to set it up as quickly as possible.

You can empathize with a reader trying to follow a set of instructions. Instructions, with their graphics and technical language, can be intimidating. Consequently, some readers will read instructions carefully, paying attention to every word.

On the other hand, a lot of readers, like you in the situation above, are impatient, trying to go through the steps without reading them first. Some readers, thinking they are familiar with the procedure already, will read only a few steps and think they know what to do. Other readers rely more on the graphics for information and less on the words.

To see how your audience affects the way you write instructions, see the Instructions for a Pre-Schooler and Teenager in the Sample Documents on the Data CD.

Whatever their attitude, readers trust the writer of a set of instructions to give them accurate, precise information in the proper sequence. Some instructions—electrical installation and medical procedures, for example—can be matters of life or death. In these cases, readers trust writers with their lives and with the lives of others.

Because your reader trusts you, make sure your procedures are accurate and include enough detail. The amount of detail depends on your audience's knowledge about the process. A beginner, for example, needs more detail than someone with experience. Good instructions keep readers motivated to read carefully.

PREWRITING

Before writing your own instructions, you must understand the sequence of events in the procedure you are writing about. That way, your explanations will be clear to someone reading them. If you do not understand the procedure, your readers probably will not understand it either. Use these suggestions to analyze the process and to better understand the steps involved:

1. Create a flowchart with steps to the process. Write what someone should do first, second, third, etc. Try not to skip any steps. Add steps or remove steps as needed.

2. In your mind, work the process backward. What is the purpose of the procedure? What is done last, next to last, third to last, etc.?

3. Watch a person who is a member of your target audience performing the task for the first time. Take notes. What is the very first step? What is the most difficult step? What steps does the person misunderstand? Would additional steps help this person? Do any of the steps need to be explained?

4. Interview this person about the procedure after he or she has finished. What additional suggestions can he or she give you for improving your instructions?

Stop and Think

What would you tell a four-year-old about making a peanut butter and jelly sandwich that you would not tell a person your age?

ORGANIZING AND FORMATTING INSTRUCTIONS

Now that you have analyzed the steps for your instructions, organize your information into sections for your reader. Then place that information in an easy-to-read format.

WARM UP

Look at the instructions model that opens this chapter on page 172. What do you notice about how the instructions are laid out on the page? What special features do the instructions use? What have the writers done to make the instructions easy to follow?

ORGANIZING INSTRUCTIONS

All instructions include steps of procedures and appropriate **explanations;** however, instructions often contain other parts as well. Whether to include these parts depends on the audience and the purpose of the instructions.

Instructions usually include an introduction, but some do not. Manuals contain an introduction at the beginning but may not contain introductions for one of the parts. Telling someone how to use an appliance would require only familiarity with the appliance, not a list of materials. But telling someone how to make pancakes would require a list of materials and ingredients. Explaining how to answer questions on a job interview would require a different structure from suggesting ways to deal with depression.

Some instructions might require **cautions** against actions that would harm the mechanism. Others might require stronger **warnings** to prevent serious injury to someone using the instructions. When you delete a file from your computer, a message appears to ask whether you really want to send this file to the recycle bin. The instructions telling you how to administer flea and tick protection for your cat warns about the dangers of swallowing, coming in contact with skin and eyes, and using near an open flame. Even your bag of popcorn warns you: "HANDLE CAREFULLY—CONTAINS HOT AIR AND STEAM." You are responsible for including proper cautions and warnings with any instructions you write.

Use Figure 7.2 to determine what sections to add to basic steps.

PROVIDE...	IF...
Introduction	Your reader needs any or all of the following information: background, context, purpose (what readers will be able to do when they finish), whom the instructions are for, scope (what the instructions do and do not cover), organization, something special about how to read the instructions, assumptions about readers' knowledge or ability, motivation to read the instructions carefully.
Definitions	Your reader must learn new terms to perform the procedure. Place six or more terms in a separate list or glossary; define fewer than six terms as you write.
List of Materials, Tools, or Ingredients	Your reader should gather materials, tools, or ingredients before following your instructions.
Graphics	A picture, diagram, or flowchart would make the instructions easier to follow. Also include graphics if the instructions are complicated or dangerous.
Warnings	Your reader could get hurt if he or she overlooks a step or does it incorrectly. Place warnings before the reader is likely to do anything dangerous. Often a symbol or graphic that signifies danger accompanies the warning.
Cautions	Your reader could damage equipment if he or she does a step incorrectly. Place cautions close to where readers need them before they are likely to do anything dangerous. Often a symbol or graphic accompanies the caution.
Notes	Additional information would aid your reader's understanding. This information is not an essential step. Include it immediately after the step to which it is most closely related.
More Explanation of Each Step	Your reader is performing the process for the first time, the procedure is complicated, or the reader needs to know more to perform the procedure correctly.
Less Explanation of Each Step	Your reader has performed the process before or the procedure is simple. You also should provide less explanation for steps in an emergency procedure where reading explanations would prevent the reader from acting quickly.

Figure 7.2 What to Include in a Set of Instructions

FORMATTING INSTRUCTIONS

Because readers are unpredictable and often impatient, format instructions so they are easy to read. Use plenty of white space to make instructions look accessible. Number your steps with Arabic numerals and align the steps in a list.

Another effective way to make instructions easy to use is by incorporating graphics, such as flowcharts and diagrams. Graphics simplify a process and are especially useful for an intermediate reader, one who has performed the process before and needs to be reminded only of the steps. Sometimes different parts of a mechanism are shown at different times during the steps. (See Chapter 6, *Document Design and Graphics,* for help making decisions about your graphics.) Refer to your graphics with an explanatory statement, such as "Refer to Figure 1 to see the location of buttons on the DVD player." Instructions that include these referral statements remind the reader to look at the graphic at the proper time.

Formats can vary. For example, simple instructions may include only a one-sentence introduction and a list of steps. Some may contain pictures only. More complex instructions require several sections and graphics. Figures 7.3 and 7.4 illustrate two simple instruction formats.

Figure 7.3 Instructions Using Pictures Only

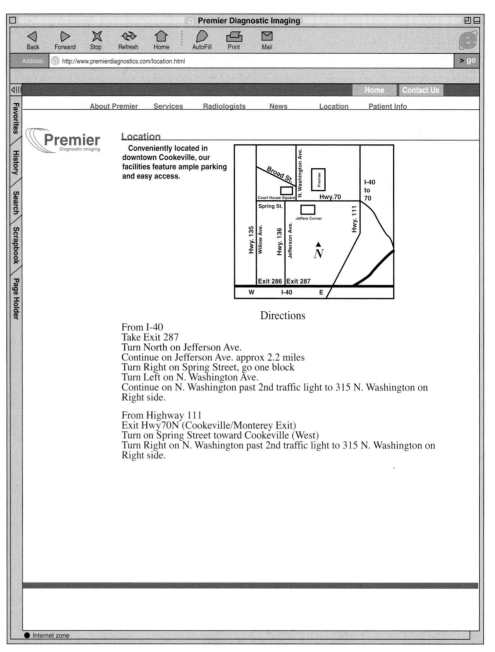

Figure 7.4 Simple Instructions with List of Steps

The browser window contains the following content:

Premier Diagnostic Imaging

http://www.premierdiagnostics.com/location.html

Home   Contact Us

About Premier   Services   Radiologists   News   Location   Patient Info

Location

Conveniently located in downtown Cookeville, our facilities feature ample parking and easy access.

Directions

From I-40
Take Exit 287
Turn North on Jefferson Ave.
Continue on Jefferson Ave. approx 2.2 miles
Turn Right on Spring Street, go one block
Turn Left on N. Washington Ave.
Continue on N. Washington past 2nd traffic light to 315 N. Washington on Right side.

From Highway 111
Exit Hwy70N (Cookeville/Monterey Exit)
Turn on Spring Street toward Cookeville (West)
Turn Right on N. Washington past 2nd traffic light to 315 N. Washington on Right side.

Stop and Think

Why does the organization of a set of instructions change from one set to another? How can page layout help someone read and follow instructions more effectively? Name some graphics that help readers understand instructions.

COMPOSING INSTRUCTIONS

Organization, format, and graphics may vary, but all instructions require chronological steps. Except for instructions written for experienced readers, most instructions require explanations to accompany the steps.

WARM UP

Look at Figure 7.1 at the beginning of this chapter on page 172. Determine the sentences that actually tell the reader to do something. What do you notice about the wording of these sentences? What do the other sentences tell the reader?

© GETTY IMAGES/PHOTODISC

STEPS

A **step** is the action a reader performs, what he or she actually does. Steps have a consistent and unique structure. Use the following guidelines for writing steps:

1. Make sure steps proceed forward in time, with no backtracking to pick up a step that was forgotten.

   ■ Incorrect (Backtracking):

   a. Insert the key into the ignition switch.

   b. Turn the key forward until you hear the engine hum.

   c. Buckle your seat belt before you turn the key.

   ■ Correct (Forward in time):

   a. Buckle your seat belt.

   b. Insert the key.

   c. Turn the key forward.

2. Begin each step with an **active voice** verb in **imperative mood** (a command: verb + what) using **second person**.

- **Incorrect (No verb to start):** The system needs to be cleaned with a tape cleaner.

- **Correct (Action verb to start):** Clean the system with a tape cleaner.

NOTE: Sometimes it's necessary to begin with a modifying word or phrase, as in "Thoroughly clean the system . . . ." OR "If the sound is garbled, clean the system . . . ."

3. Use short sentences.

- **Incorrect (Too long):** Slide the brake lever(s) as close as possible toward the grip without limiting the operation of the brake levers or causing the end of the brake lever to extend beyond the end of the handlebar.

- **Correct (Shorter sentences):** Slide the brake lever(s) as close as possible toward the grip. Do not limit the operation of the brake levers. Do not cause the end of the brake lever to extend beyond the end of the handlebar.

4. Write only one instruction for each step.

- **Incorrect (More than one step):** Buckle your seat belt and depress the brake.

- **Correct (One instruction per step):**
  a. Buckle your seat belt.
  b. Depress the brake.

EXCEPTION: If two steps are closely tied to each other in time, reading them in the same step might be easier for your reader: Release the clutch. At the same time, press the accelerator.

5. Make sure each step is truly a step, something to do.

- **Incorrect (Not a step):** The rope will come back to you.

- **Correct (Step):** Grasp the rope when it comes back to you.

6. Keep the natural articles *a, an,* and *the.*

- **Incorrect (Without articles):** Send electrician notice to connect power to house.

- **Correct (With articles):** Send the electrician a notice to connect power to the house.

7. Place explanations after the step (if you need an explanation).

- **Incorrect (Explanation before the step):** Make sure there is an equal distance between each chain stay tube and the wheel. Securely tighten the axle nuts.

NOTE: Even though *Make* is a verb, it is not a step. It explains how to securely tighten the axle nuts.

- **Correct (Step beginning with the action):** Securely tighten the axle nuts. Make sure there is an equal distance between each chain stay tube and the wheel.

EXPLANATIONS

An **explanation** is an extension of the step it explains. Explanations use the same number as the step they follow and are written immediately after the step.

1. Write the step. *Then* write the explanation.

2. Write the step. *Then* write the explanation.

3. Write the step. *Then* write the explanation.

The number and type of explanations depend on your reader's previous experience. Typical explanations include:

What not to do and why Do not place stray pencil marks on the answer sheet. The computerized scanner may read the stray mark as an error.

Significant details to help the reader understand why something is important Rinse the boiled egg with cold water as soon as you remove it from boiling water. The cold water will cause the egg to contract from the shell, making it easier to peel the shell off the egg.

How to make a decision Wrap a small section of hair around the curling iron. If you want curls to flip up, wrap the hair backward (away from the shoulders). If you want curls to curve under, wrap the hair down (toward the shoulders).

NOTE: This step and explanation also could be written using the following format:

1. Wrap a small section of hair around the curling iron.

    a. If you want curls to flip up, wrap the hair backward.

    b. If you want curls to curve under, wrap the hair downward.

What will happen when the reader does something 1) Press PROGRAM on the remote control. The MENU will appear on the TV screen. 2) To autoscan for a channel, press CHANNEL SCAN on the remote control once. The tuner scans the channels stored in the tuner's memory, stopping on each channel for about two seconds.

More details on how Tighten the axle nuts. Make sure they are tight. There must not be any space between the inner nut, the wheel slip, and the axle nuts. If there is space, tighten the axle nuts more securely.

Quick definitions Beat the eggs until frothy, or until they look like sea foam. OR The antenna is the "signal receiver" that picks up TV broadcasts.

NOTE: If you have six or more definitions, you need a separate section labeled *Definitions* or *Glossary*. If you have fewer than six, define them as you write or place them in the introduction.

Because some readers need more details than others, you must think carefully about how much explanation to add. Consider the answers to these questions:

- What should readers not do? Why? (What did you do wrong the first time you performed the process?)

Communication Update

Many companies use interactive video to train employees. This choice saves companies money by avoiding costly travel expenses incurred when employees must go somewhere else for specialized training. Interactive video places instructional material on a CD. Employees load the CD, study it at their own pace, and interact by typing answers or comments. Training is available on a host of topics, including sales techniques, museum operations, and information technologies.

To apply the concepts in this section, complete the Formatting Instructions Activity worksheet on the Data CD.

- Would readers be more likely to perform the steps correctly if they knew the significance of the action, the reason for performing the step, or more about the process?

- Would pointing out what should happen when readers execute a step help them? (The first time you performed the process, how did you know you had performed a step correctly?)

- Does the reader need help making a decision? Should some steps be subdivided? Refer to the curling iron example in this chapter:

  1. Wrap a small section of hair around the curling iron.

     a. If you want curls to flip up, wrap the hair backward.

     b. If you want curls to curve under, wrap the hair downward.

- Would the reader benefit from a quick definition?

- What questions will readers have? (What questions did you have the first time you performed the process?)

- What are the most crucial steps, the steps that absolutely must be done correctly?

PRECISE DETAILS

Make sure you have included enough precise, specific details to show your reader what to do. Details might include distances, sizes, places, or time.

Focus on Ethics

When you pick up a prescription from the pharmacy, you receive an insert that gives you information about the drug—instructions for use, proper doses, and risks. By giving patients and doctors more information on which to base judgments about good health, drug companies accept an ethical responsibility to protect their consumers. Warnings appear on the inserts in order of the risk severity:

- Contraindications

- Warnings

- Precautions

- Adverse reactions

In addition to these four risk categories, the Food and Drug Administration (FDA) requires another category for selected drugs to indicate special problems that could lead to serious injury or death. These problems are displayed prominently in a box as a warning to consumers and physicians. Based on clinical data, the black box warning alerts physicians to carefully monitor the health of patients taking these drugs.

- Incorrect (Insufficient): The bike chain should have correct tension. Make sure there is some movement, or "give," in the chain.

- Correct (Sufficient): The bike chain should have correct tension. Make sure there is ³⁄₈″ of movement, or "give," between the front and rear sprockets.

- Incorrect (Insufficient): Connect the short wire from the TV/Game Switch Box to the antenna terminals on your television set.

- Correct (Sufficient): Connect the short twin-lead wire from the TV/Game Switch Box to the VHF terminals on your television set.

- Incorrect (Insufficient): Switch the computer on.

- Correct (Sufficient): Turn on the power switch. The power switch is a ½″ wide black oval button under the CD-ROM drive on the front of the central processing unit.

FIELD TESTS

Always **field test** your instructions by asking several people to try them before you send your final copy. Your field testers can provide you with valuable feedback by noting wording that is not clear, steps that are out of sequence, or steps that have been left out altogether. To administer a field test, also called a usability test, you must select a test method, design the test, select test subjects, and make revisions based on the data.

Concurrent testing and **retrospective testing** are two field tests used to evaluate how well users perform your instructions.

Concurrent testing Concurrent testing evaluates a product or an activity while it is being used or performed. In a concurrent test, you observe your subjects reading and performing your instructions. You measure such things as their accuracy, speed, recall, and attitude.

Rhonda adapted an informal method of concurrent testing to evaluate instructions she wrote. Her instructions told AmeriCorps volunteers how to find the campsite for their training retreat. To make sure that all 50 volunteers would find the site, she asked three of her classmates to follow her directions using a map she had drawn. Two classmates did not arrive at the campsite because they turned onto Riverview Lane instead of Riverview Road. As a result, Rhonda knew she needed to revise her instructions to emphasize the name of the correct road and to caution drivers against making the wrong turn. Because of the information Rhonda learned from the field test, none of the AmeriCorps volunteers got lost.

Concurrent testing for longer instructions involves a more formal procedure. For example, Arturo, service manager for Satellite Dish Subsidiaries, wants to know that his instructions for installing a satellite dish for TV and Internet service are clear. He selects five test subjects in a rural community, ranging in age from 21 to 41, since these are the people who will most likely install the dish themselves. He then watches each one install the dish, taking careful notes on the errors they make, the comments they make, the questions they ask, and frustrations they show. After watching the five subjects perform the satellite dish installation, he knows that two subjects had difficulty mounting the dish in the right

SEE THE SITES

Check out the College of Wooster library web site to find an online field test. The purpose of this field test is for the creators of an online literacy tutorial to learn how to improve the tutorial.

The University of Wisconsin-Eau-Claire has an online help collection that gives tutorials about various computing and technical resources. Browse this site and find examples of effective online instructions on a variety of subjects.

You can find the URL for both sites in the web links on techwriting. swlearning.com. You also will find a worksheet for activities.

Practice conducting a field test using the Field Test Activity worksheet on the Data CD.

location at the proper angle. He realizes his steps about placement are confusing because they contain too much information per step. So he makes these steps shorter and adds a roof diagram to show suggested areas for placement.

© GETTY IMAGES/PHOTODISC

To design a useful conconcurrent study, decide whether your subjects should complete the whole procedure or selected tasks. Rhonda and Arturo asked their subjects to perform the entire task. On the other hand, one usability study of a web site advertising cars asked users to perform only selected tasks. These tasks included finding the sale of the day, descriptions of used models, and information on warranties.

As you observe your test subjects, ask yourself these questions:

- Were the subjects able to do what the instructions told them to do?
- How long did the subjects take to complete the task?
- How many mistakes did the subjects make?
- What steps were the most difficult? the least difficult?
- Were the subjects frustrated at any time? If so, explain.
- What did the subjects remember about the task 15 minutes after completing it?
- What did the subjects remember about the task 24 hours after completing it?

You also can ask subjects to think aloud, reading the instructions aloud and saying whatever comes to mind. Through this window to subjects' thoughts, you see how they are reacting to every step. If possible, videotape or audiotape their performance to review more closely later.

Retrospective testing A second way to test instructions is by retrospective testing—asking subjects to complete a questionnaire or to answer questions about a task after they perform it. Many field tests use a concurrent test along with a retrospective test. This way testers gain additional insights into test subjects' behavior.

Surveys are often used with retrospective testing. As you learned in Chapter 3, *Technical Research*, a survey can include different types of questions. Figure 7.5 shows questions Kelsey plans to ask his loan officers after they have field-tested his procedure for completing a car loan application.

Question Types	Questions
Multiple Choice	Was the introduction informative? Yes___ No___
	After filling in the applicant's name, address, Social Security number, and telephone number (steps 1-4), the next step was to
	a. enter the amount of money requested.
	b. include the value of the car.
	c. enter the current interest rate.
Likert Scale	Rank on a scale of 1-10 (with 10 being the most satisfied and 1 being the least satisfied) your satisfaction with the completeness** of this document.
	1 2 3 4 5 6 7 8 9 10
Short Answer	Describe the first step you performed.
	After reading step 6 *(maybe a critical step such as entering gross income)*, what did you think you were supposed to do?
Open	What suggestions do you have for improvement?
	What was the most difficult section and why?

** Kelsey could ask about clarity of the wording or usefulness of the graphics.

Figure 7.5 Survey Questions for a Retrospective Field Test

Regardless of the test method you use, select a reasonable sample of subjects. To ask senior accountants to test instructions for using a machine lathe is not practical because they would not use the instructions. You would ask senior accountants to test instructions for new accounting software and machine shop technicians to test instructions for the machine lathe. Some experts say to use at least five testers, but others think five is not enough—especially for a longer document such as a manual or for more interactive media such as a web site. After completing your field test, compile your data, list problems from most frequent to least frequent, and devise solutions.

Stop and Think

How are steps written? What kind of information do explanations contain? What kind of information makes instructions precise? Why is field testing important? How can a writer field-test instructions?

WRITING ONLINE INSTRUCTIONS

No doubt you have used **online instructions**—perhaps to order concert tickets, track a UPS special delivery, or complete a job application. Online instructions allow users to find out something, get something, or learn something quickly. Online instructions sometimes offer immediate feedback, too. For example, you might learn before you click the Submit button that you forgot to include your Social Security number on a job application.

© GETTY IMAGES/PHOTODISC

TYPES OF ONLINE INSTRUCTIONS

Online instructions, also called computer-based instructions, include help menus, CD-ROMs, and web-based instructions. Help menus are one of the most popular types of online instructions. Most computer programs feature a help menu, typically in the upper right side of your screen. Examples include the Macintosh balloon help (the call out that appears when you point to a menu item) or the animated paper clip in Microsoft® Word (the smiley-faced paper clip that provides a gateway to the help topics). When you use your Hotmail™ or Yahoo® e-mail accounts, or when you log onto AOL® Instant Messenger™, you probably used the help feature to set up addresses, send attachments, or add names to your buddies list.

Think back over your educational career, and you may recall using tutorials (over a network or on CD-ROMs) to teach yourself everything from grammar to math to keyboarding. Your school or community library may have online instructions to the online catalog. Now wireless classrooms at colleges and universities provide students with Internet access to an instructor's syllabus and handouts. As a result, students take laptops instead of books to class. Some classes are taught entirely on the Internet, and students access a teacher's instructions for the class from home through programs such as Blackboard™ or WebCT™.

Communication Dilemma

You have just landed a job as a trainer for an international company that makes engines for fighter planes. Your job is to train new engineers, line managers, and other employees to assemble specific engine parts. Your first training session will be carried out online, and your job is to prepare the online training materials for the session.

On Friday afternoon before the training begins the following Monday, your manager tells you that many employees taking the training are not from the United States. Participants live in Russia, Taiwan, Germany, and Japan. In addition, your boss explains that many of the trainees do not speak English.

How do you revise your training materials so international employees can understand them?

GUIDELINES FOR WRITING ONLINE INSTRUCTIONS

To write online instructions, keep in mind the strategies presented in this chapter for writing and explaining steps, using white space and graphics, and providing cautions and warnings. In addition to the guidelines for writing paper-based instructions, online instructions should:

■ Limit each unit of instruction to one screen size so the user does not need to scroll down the page.

■ Use consistent design—font, font sizes, colors, graphics, and headers—so the reader learns to anticipate the organization and feels comfortable nagivating.

■ Provide a tree or map of the site and topics so readers can see the site at a glance.

■ Insert navigational aids such as a link to the home page and to other important pages.

■ Evaluate the usefulness of the instructions with a field test and revise them if necessary.

Also, if you are teaching users to perform tasks on a screen, configure instructions so they do not take up the entire screen. By configuring your instructions this way, you allow users to work on the screen while they read the instructions.

Stop and Think

What strategies should you keep in mind when writing online instructions?

■ *Chapter 7 Review*

POINT YOUR BROWSER

techwriting.swlearning.com

SUMMARY

1. Readers of instructions can be in a hurry, so writers must learn to compensate with carefully planned writing. Readers trust writers to be accurate and safety-conscious and to provide adequate explanation in their instructions.

2. All instructions contain itemized steps. Most instructions contain an introduction and graphics. Whether or not to include a list of materials, warnings, cautions, notes, or definitions will depend on the process and the audience.

3. Instructions are written in short chronological sentences using active voice and imperative mood. Each step must show an action. Explanations follow steps and tell what not to do, why a step is performed, what the results of a step are, and how to complete a step. Explanations should provide enough details to enable the reader to perform the step correctly and safely.

4. When writing online instructions, remember to limit each unit of instruction to one screen, use a consistent design (font, colors, and graphics), provide a tree or map of the site and topics, insert navigational aids in your home page, and configure instructions so users performing tasks on the screen can see them while working.

Checklist

- Do I thoroughly understand the procedure I am writing about?

- Did I consider using graphics?

- Did I consider using an introduction, a list of materials, cautions, warnings, and notes?

- Have I written steps that move forward in time? Do my steps begin with a verb that commands? Have I used short sentences that include only one action per step? Are my steps truly steps, things to do? Have I kept the articles *a, an,* and *the*?

- Have I considered including explanations that tell what not to do and why? that include significant details to help the reader understand why a step is important? that tell the reader how to make a decision? that include descriptions of what will happen when the reader does something? that give enough details on how something should be done?

- Have I included enough precise details, such as distances, sizes, places, or time?

- Have I considered whether online instructions would be appropriate for my audience? Have I followed the additional guidelines for online instructions?

- Did I field-test my instructions with my target audience?

Build On What You Know

1. Examine each step below. What kind of information would make each instruction more specific?

   a. Rotate the tool several times around the wire, leaving the spring closed.

   b. Draw part of an oval for the head.

   c. If the fitting has a tub spout, make a hole in the wall.

   d. Clean your room before you leave.

   e. Beat the meringue until stiff peaks form.

   f. Place the selvages of the material together.

2. Break up each sentence below into shorter sentences that reflect one step per sentence.

   a. Remove the cover from the mike; press the transit button on your mike; and by using a small screwdriver with a plastic or wooden handle, adjust the transmitting frequency.

   b. Take the two upper sections of the handle; and using the shortest bolt with the nut provided, fasten together as shown in the illustration in Figure 1.

   c. Read the passage and locate all nouns, underlining them with a single line.

3. Rewrite these steps to begin each with a verb in active voice and imperative mood. The "you" can be understood.

   a. The cook should touch the AUTO DEFROST pad to begin the defrosting process.

   b. When you wish to play, you should press the START button.

   c. The aquarium floor requires a layer of gravel that, sloping from the back to the front, is about 6 to 8 centimeters deep at the front wall.

   d. We want you to come to the front of the room and use the available podium.

4. Label each of the following as steps, explanations, cautions, or warnings.

   a. When paddling, keep the canoe in line with the current.

   b. Make sure that the supply voltage matches the voltage specified on the rating plate.

   c. Separate dark clothes from light clothes to prevent colors from running.

   d. Do not overload your dryer. For efficient drying, clothes need to tumble freely.

   e. Designate a high number of rings (10 or more) for your modem calls.

   f. Install the stem correctly, or an accident can occur.

   g. To determine how tight the fasteners need to be, see the Torque Range chart in the back of this book.

Apply What You Learned

5. Which of these guidelines for writing instructions apply to all instructions (print and online), and which apply only to online instructions?

   a. Make sure each step represents only one action, unless the actions are so closely related that they need to be expressed in the same step.

   b. Limit each unit of instruction to one screen size.

   c. Evaluate the usefulness of your instructions with a field test.

   d. Use a consistent design for each screen.

   e. Provide a tree or map of your site and topics.

   f. Do not omit *a, an,* and *the.*

   g. Eliminate your reader's need to scroll down the page.

   h. Insert navigational aids such as links to important pages.

   i. Include appropriate cautions, warnings, and notes.

   j. Use active-voice verbs in imperative mood for steps.

6. For a beginner using a word processing program such as WordPerfect® or Microsoft® Word, list help topics this person would most likely use.

7. In small groups, write instructions on any of the following processes (or other process you are familiar with). Be sure to analyze your audience, follow the guidelines for composing instructions, and provide ample explanations.

making a bed	using a calculator	changing oil/tires
setting up a tent	lifting weights	playing a video game (or any other game)
setting up an aquarium	building a model	playing a sport
brushing/flossing teeth	mowing the lawn	constructing a craft
administering first aid	taking pictures	changing a diaper
cleaning a room	creating artwork	

8. Suppose you are writing a help menu program for a word processing program that you know well. Write a list of step-by-step instructions for one of these:

   - Changing the font type for an entire document

   - Underlining a word

   - Changing the margins

   - Copying and pasting a paragraph

   - Cutting and pasting a paragraph

The Work Is A Zoo! worksheet for this activity is on the Data CD.

Work Is A Zoo!

This morning during a breakfast meeting, Anya told you that the zoo is about to hire extra help before the start of the school year. She explained that when instructors bring their students to the zoo, more employees are needed to accommodate them.

Anya asked you to write instructions for using the zoo time clock. The instructions will be used to train new employees to record the time they work on a daily basis. She explained that some of these employees do not speak English as their first language, so you must accommodate these nonnative speakers of English in your instructions.

Write the instructions for a time clock you are familiar with. (If you have not used a time clock, write the instructions for completing a weekly time sheet.)

First, decide whether your instructions should be paper-based or online.

Include the appropriate sections in your instructions:

- Introduction
- Definitions
- Preparations
- Warnings and cautions (if necessary)
- Steps and explanations
- Closing

If appropriate, include any graphics that will help the audience.

INFORMATIVE REPORTS

GOALS

WRITE two types
of summaries, an
abstract, a mechanism
description, a trip
report, and an
incident report

COMPOSE progress
and periodic reports

See the Data CD
for Write-to-Learn
and In The Know
activity worksheets.

WRITE-TO-LEARN

Think about where you are on the path of your educational goals. You may want to earn a two-year associate degree. Perhaps your career will require a four-year bachelor's degree—or beyond that, a master's or a doctorate degree. Write several paragraphs answering the following questions: What have you achieved toward reaching your long-term educational goals? What do you still need to do to reach those goals? When will you reach your goals? What problems will you have? Your audience can be your parents or guardians, a scholarship committee, or other people who have supported your educational career.

In The Know

abstract a short, concise version of a longer piece of communication; includes only the most important general information

fiscal year the operating or business year, a calendar that runs from July to June, rather than January to December

incident reports reports that objectively relate the details of unusual events, such as accidents or equipment malfunctions

mechanism description a description of a device; includes the purpose of the device and overall description, a description of parts, and the function of each part

periodic report a report, issued at timed intervals, informing the audience of the progress made on all of the projects of an organization during the reporting period

progress report a report that tells the audience what work has been completed and what work remains on one particular project during the reporting period

reporting period the time span covered by a report

summary a condensed version of a piece of communication; includes general information and may include a few important details

spatial order organized through space as in right to left, left to right, top to bottom, bottom to top, or east to west

trip reports reports that tell what was accomplished during a trip and what was learned from a trip

Writing@Work

Bob Colombo is a police officer in northeast Ohio. Bob's responsibilities include basic patrol, initial crime scene investigation, traffic enforcement, and public relations duties.

In his position, Bob must write incident reports. These reports include information about the victim of the crime, any witnesses to the crime, and the suspect. Bob must complete a paragraph explaining what is contained in the report and then use the remainder of the report to describe what happened; what will happen (police follow-up); and, if appropriate, advice for the victim of the crime. Bob's reports must be accurate and clearly written. If a trial takes place, the incident report is the first bit of evidence scrutinized. Officers will generally use incident reports to refresh their memories before a trial. If the report is not accurate or clear, the defense attorney may be able to rattle an officer on the stand. "Sometimes," Bob says, "the initial report can make or break a trial."

Bob's police department has a system of checks and balances to ensure that officers' reports are clear and accurate. A supervisor proofreads all initial reports, which are then sent to the reporting officer for corrections. The report in turn is sent to the executive officer, who proofreads the report again and makes his or her changes and additions. Bob explains, "Reports that are unclear or confusing can lead to charges being dropped against a suspect or a case being dismissed in court. Incidents like this can make a police department look incompetent and cause a community to lose trust and respect for that police department."

Everyone has heard stories of police officers who do not play by the rules. As Bob says, "In every profession there is that 10 percent who make the other 90 percent look bad." When an officer intentionally leaves information out of a report, a guilty person may go free because evidence has been omitted and the testimony is tainted. In addition, omitting information could cost an officer his or her job and create bad publicity for all police officers. "My job is that much harder when other officers do something wrong intentionally, then try to cover it up and get caught. A small portion of people tend to distrust the police to begin with, and when the media gets a story about a police officer on the other side of the law, it further drives a wedge between the people and the police."

Pitt County Communities in Schools

MEMORANDUM

TO: Board of Directors

FROM: Andrew S. Benitez, Executive Director *ASB*

DATE: May 15, 20—

RE: Progress Report: Planning for a Community Outreach Program at Conley
          Community College

Since our meeting in January when you asked my staff and me to begin planning for a community outreach program at Conley Community College next year, I have been amazed by the interest and cooperation this project has generated. This report will acquaint you with the work completed, the work scheduled, and the problems encountered.

WORK COMPLETED (January 15–May 15, 20—)
Many people cooperated and worked hard to make these accomplishments possible.

Public Relations
We developed a brochure defining the community outreach program and its goals. In March, we distributed 1,000 copies. The brochure helped with one of our first and most critical activities, which was to educate faculty, staff, students, and parents about the program.

Faculty Recruitment
We selected Duffy Lincoln as site coordinator. In addition, the three faculty members needed for the program have been named: Mack Jones, Lillian Outterbridge, and Luisa Rojas. All personnel volunteered for the coming academic year with full knowledge of the demands that developing a new program will place on them.

Program Planning
The faculty has adopted a plan for integrating academic and real-life skills in the curriculum to make learning more meaningful. The program will begin with a group of 60 students. Instructors have begun developing lesson plans, integrating English, biology, and history with emphasis on the practical applications to life.

Andrew S. Benitez, Executive Director
209 East Third Street, Greenville, NC 27858
Office (919) 555-0191 • FAX (919) 555-0194

Figure 8.1 Progress Report Model

Board of Directors
Page 2
May 15, 20—

WORK SCHEDULED

As you can see, a number of tasks are on the upcoming schedule, but the workload does not seem impossible. The faculty and I are determined to see this program effectively serving students and the community.

Program Evaluation

The faculty will spend the next three months determining ways to assess the program and the students' progress.

Program Planning

A number of tasks need to be completed in the next reporting period:

1. Before August, we will schedule six field trips for students to regional business sites.

2. Faculty will coordinate the Adopt-a-Grandparent Program over the summer.

3. We will develop a list of guest speakers and mentors for students.

Student Selection

By June 30, the faculty will select 60 students to participate, and by July 15, all students who are selected will be notified by mail.

PROBLEMS/PROJECTIONS

The only problems we have encountered thus far are the good kind. We have experienced overwhelming interest in the program and have had twice as many faculty members apply as we expected. Student interest also has been greater than we expected.

If work continues as it has up until now, we will be ready to begin the program on schedule. We look forward to a productive summer. I will continue to report progress to you.

Figure 8.1 Progress Report Model, cont.

SUMMARY AND ABSTRACT

Professionals in business and industry use specialized reports to convey information about their work. This chapter presents the most frequently used informative reports: summaries and abstracts, mechanism descriptions, trip reports, incident reports, and progress and periodic reports. These specialized reports use standard forms, so once you learn how to use them, you can develop reports using information from jobs or personal experience.

© GETTY IMAGES/PHOTODISC

A **summary** or an **abstract** is a condensed version of a document, usually found at the beginning of a document. When you write an essay, you generate details to develop or support a thesis and topic sentences. Summaries require writers to do the opposite: keep only the general information and most important details. By condensing the report highlights before the audience reads the details, summaries save coworkers time.

Abstracts are more condensed than summaries, reducing documents to a brief thesis. The length depends on the audience's needs and expectations. To write a summary or an abstract:

1. Include the thesis, or main point, of the document in the first sentence.

2. Make clear early on what you are summarizing. With an article, introduce the information by including the author's name and the title in the first sentence. With a speech or a meeting, give the speaker credit in the opening sentence.

3. After determining the main point, in your own words, write topic sentences that support the main point.

4. Decide whether your audience needs a few details or only main ideas.

   ■ For long summaries, include only details that are especially important.

   ■ For short summaries, leave out all details.

   ■ For abstracts, include only the most important general ideas. Be concise. Reduce the original document to the main idea in a few sentences.

5. Keep your summary information proportional to the original. If the author spent four paragraphs on one topic and two paragraphs on another, your summary should give equal time and emphasis. For example, do not include more information from the two-paragraph topic than from the four-paragraph topic in your summary or abstract.

6. Write in present tense.

7. Be sure to paraphrase, not copy word for word.

8. Quote sparingly, if at all, and use quotation marks correctly.

9. Provide transitions to keep the summary from sounding choppy.

Do not give your opinion unless asked. A summary or an abstract should be an objective presentation of what you read or what happened. To prepare for writing a summary or an abstract, try one of these suggestions:

1. With an oral presentation, take notes during the presentation or soon afterward. This way you are less likely to forget what the speaker said.

2. With a written document, read the document twice. As you read for the second time, cross out everything (all details) except the main ideas. Paraphrase what is left. For longer summaries, choose a few important details to include. For abstracts, condense the paraphrased material.

Figure 8.3 contains two summaries and an abstract of the article in Figure 8.2.

A Faster Way to Clean Roots

Agronomists, plant pathologists, and botanists—to name a few—are interested in the effects of soil and crop management practices on crop root systems. But before they can begin their studies, scientists usually have to spend time and energy cleaning soil off the roots. A new invention by the *Agricultural Research Service (ARS)* may help.

Soil scientist Joseph G. Benjamin, of ARS's Central Great Plains Research Station in Akron, Colorado, has created a root washer with a rotary design to automate and speed up the process. Other devices require more attention from the operator. The new device can clean up to 24 samples at a time, more than previous washers.

The washing cycle starts when a technician places a sample of soil and roots in the machine's chambers. As the sample rotates within the machine, it is dipped into and sprayed with water to remove the soil. Mud exits from the back of the machine. The cycle takes about 90 minutes, and the roots, which are not damaged by the machine, are then ready for study. "The root washer works well to easily and quickly separate plant roots and other organic materials from the soil," Benjamin says. He also points out that his device can wash larger samples than other washers can.

Once the roots are clean, a flatbed scanner is then used to digitize images of them for scientists to analyze with computer software. Through mathematical equations, Benjamin is able to determine the surface area of the roots contained in the sample. As Benjamin points out, "The human eye is still the best discriminator at determining what materials are roots and what are not." Benjamin's root washer is an enlarged version of a weed-seed washer invented by weed scientist Lori J. Wiles and others in ARS's Water Management Unit, at Fort Collins, Colorado. Before her invention, there was nothing available commercially to quickly wash soil from seeds.

Source: Elstein, David. U.S. Department of Agriculture. "A Faster Way to Clean Roots." *Agricultural Research*: 2004 (vol. 52, no.1) http://www.ars.usda.gov/is/AR/archive/jan04/roots0104.htm.

Figure 8.2 Article to be Summarized

	LONG SUMMARY OF "A FASTER WAY TO CLEAN ROOTS"
The first paragraph introduces the source (the author's name and the title of the article) and restates the thesis of the article.	David Elstein in "A Faster Way to Clean Roots" announces a technological breakthrough for people who study plants and crop management. While scientists normally have to use considerable time cleaning dirt from plant roots by hand before the plants can be studied, a machine created by soil scientist Joseph G. Benjamin offers help with the process.
The second paragraph includes the next two main ideas and significant details.	Benjamin developed a device to rotate and clean 24 plants at once, decreasing the need for scientists to handle the plants and speeding up the process. During washing, the machine dunks and shoots water at the roots, but it does not harm or change the root system at all. The water takes the mud with it when it drains from the machine.
The third paragraph includes the next two main ideas and significant details.	When the clean roots are taken from the new machine, Benjamin uses a flatbed scanner, computer software, and mathematical equations to calculate the roots' surface area. However, the inventor notes that the machine is not as effective as the human eye at distinguishing roots from other materials.
The conclusion ends with the same idea as the original.	Benjamin based the design of his invention on a weed-seed washer scientist Lori J. Wiles and colleagues at the ARS Water Management Research Unit in Fort Collins, Colorado, invented.

	SHORT SUMMARY OF "A FASTER WAY TO CLEAN ROOTS"
The first sentence identifies the source. The second sentence paraphrases the thesis. The body includes only the main ideas from the original.	David Elstein in "A Faster Way to Clean Roots" announces a technological breakthrough for people who study plants and crop management. Since scientists must painstakingly remove dirt from the root system of plants they wish to study, soil scientist Joseph G. Benjamin's creation of a machine to clean soil and organic matter from plant roots without damaging the roots mechanizes and speeds up the preparation. Benjamin's rotary design wash cycle prepares 24 samples for study faster and with less handling than other machines. When the plants are clean, Benjamin uses a flatbed scanner, computer software, and mathematical equations to calculate the roots' surface area.

	ABSTRACT OF "A FASTER WAY TO CLEAN ROOTS"
The abstract includes only the source and the most important information from the article: the announcement of Benjamin's invention.	David Elstein in "A Faster Way to Clean Roots" announces a technological breakthrough for people who study plants and crop management, soil scientist Joseph G. Benjamin's creation of a machine to clean soil and organic matter from plant roots without damaging the roots.

Figure 8.3 Sample Summaries

 Stop and Think If a summary includes three of an article's five main points, is it effective?

MECHANISM DESCRIPTION

A **mechanism description** describes the main parts of a device or mechanism. It tells what the purpose of the mechanism and overall design is, what the parts are, what they look like, and what their function is.

Mechanism descriptions are used in catalogs, instruction manuals, and employee training. Examples of mechanisms in the workplace include car parts; furniture; kitchen tools; doorstops; pencil sharpeners; and more sophisticated machines, such as an engine or a DVD player.

Consumers can find a mechanism description in a manual that comes with new equipment, such as a computer or can opener. This description tells what the parts are, how they fit together, and what their functions are. Technicians and operators use the description to become familiar with the characteristics of the machine and to troubleshoot problems. New employees use a mechanism description to learn their job responsibilities and safety procedures. Decision makers use mechanism descriptions to reach informed decisions, perhaps comparing current equipment with a piece of equipment being proposed for purchase.

To write a mechanism description:

1. Use **spatial order:** explain the parts from left to right, right to left, top to bottom, bottom to top, or whatever pattern is logical.

2. Open with an overall physical description of the mechanism, a statement that identifies its general purpose (for example, what it is designed to do), and a preview of its parts.

3. Divide the mechanism into its parts and discuss each part under a separate heading. Use the proper names of the parts. Place headings in the same order you used in the preview list.

4. Provide a precise physical description of the parts. Include size, color, location (where the parts can be found), and material (what the mechanism is made of).

5. Include the purpose or function of each part.

6. Provide a graphic of the mechanism. Include exploded (enlarged) views of parts when they are too small to be seen easily. Add call outs to each part.

7. Use active voice where possible.

Do not explain how to operate the mechanism. Instead, describe what it does, what it looks like, what its parts are, what the parts look like, and what each part does. To get started, pretend that you must describe to someone on the telephone a device that person has not seen before. Take notes, describing in detail what every part looks like.

Figure 8.4 is a mechanism description of a handheld can opener.

HANDHELD CAN OPENER

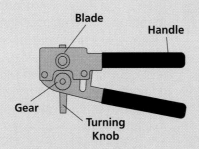

A handheld can opener is used to open standard aluminum and tin cans in which food is stored. It will open cans with a $1/8$-inch lip around the rim and will not open cans (such as soda cans) with a smooth rim. The handheld can opener (see Figure 1) consists of the following parts: handle, blade and gear, and turning knob.

Handle
The handle consists of two 3-inch stainless steel movable prongs that extend beyond the cutting mechanism. Each prong is encased in a $2\,1/2$-inch white plastic sheath to protect it from rust and to make it easy to grip. The user presses the prongs of the handle together to place the blade over the lip on the top of the can and to pierce the top of the can.

Blade
The blade, opposite the gear, is a $1/2$-inch diameter circle, approximately the size of a penny and made of gray metal. The outer edge of the circle is sharp, allowing the blade to cut the lid off the can.

Gear
The gear, located directly under the turning knob, is on the back of the can opener. Approximately $1/2$-inch in diameter, or the size of a penny, it is made of stainless steel. Attached to the turning knob, the gear is placed under the lip of the can to grip the can.

Turning Knob
The turning knob is a $2\,1/2$-inch-long rectangular lever used to move the blade along the outer edges of the can. Located on the side opposite the blade and gear, it is made of stainless steel. The user turns the knob, which, in turn, rotates the blade.

Figure 8.4 Sample Mechanism Description

Stop and Think

In a mechanism description, should a writer describe a metal disk as a) about the size of a penny or b) $1/2$-inch in diameter? What organizational pattern is used in mechanism descriptions?

TRIP REPORT

Trip reports tell supervisors and coworkers what was gained from a business trip. Often businesses send workers to conferences to learn the latest developments in their field. Sometimes associates visit other businesses to negotiate deals or learn about operations. A trip is an investigation, a research mission from which the findings must be shared with other coworkers.

© GETTY IMAGES/PHOTODISC

Trip reports are like a condensed narrative. Often the report does not include everything about the trip, only parts that are most useful to the organization. In this way, the trip report is similar to a summary because you include only the most important details about the trip.

To write a trip report:

1. Report what your audience will find most useful. You do not need to include all trip details; only include what your audience requires.

2. Cover the Reporter's Questions as you write the report: Who? What? When? Where? Why?

3. Preview the report in your introduction.

4. Use bulleted lists for important events or knowledge gained.

5. Decide whether your report needs Conclusions and/or Recommendations. Some trip reports require neither, and some require both.

   a. Use Conclusions to summarize the trip benefits.

   b. Use Recommendations to recommend further action.

The last sentence in the introduction previews the rest of the report.

The Conclusion sums up Thompson's assessment of the trip.

The Recommendation makes a suggestion about what should be done with the information gained from the trip.

6. Choose between chronological order or order of importance.

7. Use *I* or *we* to make the report sound natural and use active voice.

Before you leave, find out what the purpose of the trip is and what you are expected to learn. Investigate these concerns during your trip and address them in the report. Figure 8.5 is a trip report from Linda Thompson to her supervisor relating the important findings of an insurance conference.

MEMO

TO: Cristina Santana
FROM: Linda Thompson *LT*
DATE: 5 November 20–
SUBJECT: Medical Providers HHII Conference

The Medical Providers HHII conference was held in Greensboro, North Carolina, on 28 October 20–. The conference featured speakers from various insurance groups. The seminars focused on new policy changes and the correct way to file a claim. Few changes have been made in filing claims, but Medicaid, Blue Cross Blue Shield of North Carolina, and Workers' Compensation have already implemented new policies.

Medicaid of North Carolina
Effective 1 January 20–, Carolina Access requires that a primary care physician refer a patient. The primary care physician's name will appear on the front of the Medicaid card. The referring physician's authorization number must appear on the claim form for payment of benefits.

Blue Cross Blue Shield
Effective 1 November 20–, copayment to a specialty practice has been changed from $10 to $20 per visit. Patients must pay their copayment on the day services are rendered.

Workers' Compensation
Effective 1 January 20–, treatment provided by a physician's assistant (P.A.) for on-the-job injuries will not be covered. Such claims will be denied.

Conclusion
The seminars were not as informative as they have been in the past, but they gave me an opportunity to meet with other insurance agents. Speaking with them gave me a chance to understand how other physicians' offices are run.

Recommendation
I recommend that we circulate the new policy changes among office personnel and mail letters to clients announcing the changes.

Figure 8.5 Sample Trip Report

Stop and Think   How does a writer decide what to cover in a trip report?

INCIDENT REPORT

Incident reports, also called accident reports, describe an unusual incident or occurrence. The incident could be an accident, a surprise inspection, the outburst of an angry employee or customer, or a near-accident. When police write the details of your fender bender, they are writing an incident report. When your instructor "writes you up" for missing class, he or she is writing an incident report.

WARM UP

Imagine a familiar scene: children are playing together and something is broken. When an adult arrives, he or she asks, "What happened?" What responses do the children provide? Will all of the children give the same account? Will some responses be better than others? If so, how and why? Describe similar situations from your work or academic life.

The report must be carefully written to reflect what really happened, for it can become legal evidence used in court. It also must be written to accommodate a variety of readers.

To write an incident report:

1. Begin with a quick summary of what happened.

2. Add Background as a heading if information about events leading up to the incident would be helpful for your readers. Some incident reports combine the summary and background and do not use a separate heading for this part if it is short.

3. Under Description, tell exactly what happened in chronological order. Be sure to cover the Reporter's Questions: Who? What? When? Where? Why? and the question How?

4. Be honest and objective.

5. Use the Outcome to tell the observable incident results.

6. Use the Conclusion to tell what was learned from the incident and how to prevent it from happening again.

Do not include information that you cannot verify. To get started, carefully note evidence. Interview people separately who know about the incident.

Figure 8.6 recounts an injury at a day-care center. Possible readers include parents, supervisors, insurance agents, and lawyers or a judge if parents find the day-care provider negligent.

Paragraph one summarizes the incident and tells when it took place.

The Description provides more details. It answers the major questions Who? What? Where? When? and Why? It reads like a narrative and covers the incident from the beginning to the end.

The Outcome tells what happened as a result of the incident. It may repeat part of what was stated in the Description.

The Conclusion tells what has been learned as a result of this experience and what will help prevent a similar incident.

INCIDENT OF INJURY AT TINY TOT DAY CARE

Summary

On July 13, 20–, Dennis Lechworth was bitten by another child at Tiny Tot Day Care. Ms. Holland cleaned the wound, and there was no permanent damage. Mrs. Olsen informed both children's parents of the incident. The report was filed in the permanent records of both children.

Description

On July 13, 20–, Ms. Holland and Mrs. Olsen were supervising a group of ten children on the playground. At 10:15 a.m., Dennis cried out loudly and ran to Ms. Holland. Dennis cried hard enough to give himself hiccups. With tears in his eyes, he showed his arm to Ms. Holland. Ms. Holland comforted Dennis by picking him up in her arms and holding him. Ms. Holland took Dennis inside to wash the wound caused by the bite.

While inside, Dennis told Ms. Holland who had bitten him. Apparently, the other child wanted the wagon Dennis was using. The other child grabbed Dennis and bit him on the upper right arm. There was no blood, but the skin was slightly broken. The area was cleaned with soap and water and then dried. Dennis returned to the playground but stayed away from the child who had bitten him. Mrs. Olsen and Ms. Holland talked to the other child about how much it hurts to be bitten and that boys and girls should not bite.

Outcome

No permanent damage was done to Dennis's arm. Incident reports were filed in the permanent records of both children. Parents of both children were informed of the incident.

Conclusion

In the future, both children will be watched more closely. Since biting is a common problem with this age group, it is important to know 1) the children who are under stress and therefore more likely to bite and 2) indirect guidance techniques to help eliminate such aggressive behavior.

Figure 8.6 Sample Incident Report

Stop and Think

The Reporter's Questions should be answered in the Description section of an incident report. What are the questions?

PROGRESS AND PERIODIC REPORTS

Progress reports are documents that report on progress for a period of time; they tell what has been done. Likewise, periodic reports, reports given periodically, also tell about progress. Yet an important difference separates the two report types.

© GETTY IMAGES/PHOTODISC

A **progress report** describes what has been done during a specified time on *one particular project,* such as work completed on the construction of a building. A progress report covers in detail *all* of the achievements toward one project. Anyone in an organization, from the president to a security guard, might need to report the progress he or she has made on a project.

WARM UP

Read the model progress report at the beginning of this chapter. Determine the relationship between the writer and the audience. What is the writer's purpose in presenting this report?

On the other hand, a **periodic report** explains accomplishments for all of the projects of a work group or of the whole organization over a specified time period. For instance, when you listened to your governor make a State of the State address or the President make a State of the Union address, you heard a periodic report. These speeches explore the many ongoing projects of the state or the nation for the year. Periodic reports may cover different periods: a week (weekly), a month (monthly), three months (quarterly), or six months (semiannually).

To write progress and periodic reports:

1. Consider the project schedule or plan (for progress reports) or the activities and accomplishments of the organization (for periodic reports). Begin by noting the time period. Are you sharing information about the last two weeks, the past month, or the fiscal year? (A **fiscal year** is the operating year, such as the academic year, which often runs from July to June.)

2. Meet your audience's needs. What are the audience's concerns, history with the writer and the project or organization, and roles?

3. Organize tasks so you can clearly report them. In a chart, list in one column what was scheduled to be done in a certain period and in another column what was actually done. Include an additional list that covers what should be done next. Once the lists are complete, the categories become subheadings under a major heading.

4. Format for the audience. When the report is written for an internal reader, it is probably formatted as a memo. When the report is written for an external reader, it is probably formatted as a letter.

COMPOSING PROGRESS REPORTS

Since progress reports are meant to inform managers of work being done on a particular project, the reports are organized to answer the readers' most important questions first. The outline below is a typical plan used for progress reports:

Heading in Report	What That Section Covers
Introduction	Report topic, purpose, and reporting period
Work Completed	What has been done
Work Scheduled	What needs to be done
Problems/Projections	What has gone wrong and when the work will be finished

Under each heading, the writer may add subheadings if several ideas will be covered in that section. Figure 8.7 below shows a progress report.

Indicates that this is the third progress report on this project; notes the report topic.

The Introduction describes the project being reported on, gives the reporting period, and states the purpose of the report.

Covers what has been done on the project.

The Work Completed may include subheads if the work accomplished falls under two or more categories.

Covers work yet to be done.

Memorandum

To: Yearbook Staff Members
From: Yearbook Staff Trip Committee
Date: February 1, 20–

Subject: Progress Report 3: Planning for Trip to Disney World

Since our yearbook staff trip to Disney World is less than two months away, we are working hard to make an enjoyable adventure possible. This report outlines the accomplishments, the work remaining, and one problem encountered during January.

WORK COMPLETED (January 1–February 1, 20–)
We are marking a few things off the to-do list. If we can maintain the current level of enthusiasm, we will get there.

Finances
The staff sponsored two doughnut sales to add $350 to the travel fund.

Reservations
Three buses from the White Goose Line have been reserved at a cost of $800 each. In addition, reservations have been made for three nights at the Disney Dunes Hotel and a deposit of $500 has been paid to the hotel.

Chaperones
University policy requires 11 instructors or parents to accompany groups the size of our staff on overnight trips. To satisfy that requirement, four instructors, their spouses, and three parents have agreed to serve as chaperones.

WORK SCHEDULED
The primary responsibilities remaining are earning the rest of the money required for the trip and making additional reservations.

Figure 8.7 Model of an Internal Progress Report

Finances
The fund balance now contains $9,675 of the $11,000 we need to earn for the trip. Five other fund-raising projects have been scheduled before the trip. However, if the future projects are as successful as the last two, we may raise the remaining $1,325 after only three projects have been completed.

Reservations
We will order two-day passes for Disney World and one-day tickets for Sea World next week. Also, Ms. Zhao will make reservations for the Yearbook Banquet at Seaside Restaurant. The Banquet Committee will request a buffet for Saturday evening.

PROBLEMS/PROJECTIONS
The University Board has agreed to consider our request to be excused from classes early on the day we leave. Otherwise, we cannot reach Orlando before three o'clock in the morning. If we arrive in the middle of the night, we will probably waste the day planned for Disney World, catching up on sleep. We might think of changing the schedule if the Board denies our request. Other plans are proceeding as expected, and we should have all work for the trip completed by March 16, two weeks before departure.

Figure 8.7 Model of an Internal Progress Report, Cont.

Omits the subhead *Chaperones* under Work Scheduled because nothing else concerning chaperones needs to be done.

Explains any difficulties that may affect the project; gives a revised completion date if problems have caused delay.

SEE THE SITES

The National Park Service publishes a web site that contains incident reports from many national parks. These reports record information ranging from the loss of a camera to the outbreak of a fire.

Virginia Tech's Writing Guidelines for Engineering and Science Students web site gives user-friendly guidelines for writing all types of informative reports, from progress reports to science lab reports. This web site even has sample reports you can download.

You can find the URL for both sites in the web links at techwriting. swlearning.com.

Drafting an Introduction In the opening or introductory section of the progress report:

1. Name the project.

2. Note the time period you cover.

3. State the purpose of the report (to tell readers the project status).

Using *I* or *we* is acceptable and encouraged. By using first person, you take responsibility for your actions and opinions.

Communication Dilemma

Ellen Hardee-Laking and coworker Andre Carver, soil scientists with CIC Inc., have been working on a 36-acre tract of land to determine whether the land is appropriate for building homes. Until a year ago, this tract was the site of a junkyard stacked high with all kinds of vehicles leaking oil, gas, antifreeze, and other chemicals into the soil.

Hardee-Laking and Carver were assigned to the project by their supervisor when the new landowner contracted with CIC to determine whether she could safely go forward with her plans to develop a luxury townhome community. The landowner and the CIC supervisor are pushing for a rapid decision from the scientists. Feeling the pressure, Hardee-Laking prepares a progress report that indicates test results for twice as many tests as she had actually run. She tells Carver that she used the actual results of tests completed to anticipate the results for tests not yet run. She claims the report shows what they would find if they had time to run all of the tests.

Should Carver sign the report and go along with Hardee-Laking? Or should he report her actions to the supervisor? Should he tell the client? What should Carver do?

Drafting the Work Completed Section In the Work Completed section:

1. Note again the time period you cover (optional; usually beside the heading or in the opening sentence of the section).

2. Use past tense verbs.

3. Use subheadings (to separate jobs) or bulleted lists.

4. Provide enough details and explanations about each job completed to meet the readers' needs.

Since your reader is probably most concerned about what you have done on the project, be certain that this section is clear and accurate. Place your most important ideas first. After all, this is the good-news section; it is your opportunity to tell others what you have achieved.

Drafting the Work Scheduled Section In the Work Scheduled section, tell your audience what work needs to be done in the next reporting period or what remains to be done to complete the project. Use future tense verbs. As with the Work Completed section, you may need to separate and emphasize each major task or job with subheadings.

Drafting the Problems/Projections Section In the Problems/Projections section:

1. Describe any obstacles to complete the job. You may list and number these problems or describe them in paragraphs. Be honest and direct in this section. Unless you need to assign responsibility, report just the facts.

2. Give a completion date for the project. If problems have stalled the project so that the original completion date cannot be met, give your audience a new date.

COMPOSING PERIODIC REPORTS

Remember that a periodic report reviews what an entire organization or work group has done in a specified time period. The report keeps decision makers informed and should be organized so that the reader can find important information easily.

The structure of a periodic report usually consists of:

1. An overview that briefly presents the report highlights.

2. A section for each activity category or work undertaken during the reporting period, with section headings and sometimes subheadings, organized from most important to least important.

3. A conclusion that refers to the next report.

Drafting the Introduction The introduction should be brief and to the point. Keep in mind that the reader is busy and will expect a summary of important points first. The summary should mention each idea included in a major heading. Also, state the **reporting period,** the time for which the document describes progress.

Drafting the Work Progress Sections After the introduction, the rest of the report is determined by the types of work done. The report will have a heading and discussion for each type of work. For instance, the monthly activity report of a U.S. Navy recruiter might include the following work areas (and headings): Job Fairs, School-Based Meetings, Office Conferences, and Public Speaking Events. Under each heading, the recruiter describes, from most important to least important, what he or she

Focus on Ethics

Informative reports, whether they are incident reports, trip reports, or progress and periodic reports, usually are read by many people. For this reason, the writer must be completely accurate and truthful. For example, Yvonne M. Jelenic, an instructor of preschool students with developmental disabilities, stresses the importance of accuracy and precision in progress reports. "Miss Von," as her students know her, says instructors are aware that parents and guardians want their children to succeed academically, physically, and socially. Sometimes instructors are tempted to overstate a child's progress to please the family. But greater disappointment is certain to follow if family members see that the child's true abilities are less than what the family had been led to expect.

has accomplished during the reporting period. The writer also may note in the rest of the report any problems encountered. The writer should report problems factually, omitting personal opinions and allowing readers to draw their own conclusions. Figure 8.8 is an example of a periodic report.

Memorandum

To: Miss Helen Wooten, Adviser
From: Ove Jensen, Student Intern *OJ*
Date: March 5, 20—
Subject: Job Shadowing a Radiologic Technologist at Grove Park Hospital

February has been a productive period in my second month of job-shadowing Ms. Antoinette Clavelle, radiologic technologist at Grove Park Hospital. The month was filled with action and variety. I observed work in the Neonatal Intensive Care Unit, the MRI (Magnetic Resonance Imaging) section, and the Radiology Lab. In addition, I completed one of the three research papers required for earning academic credit.

Neonatal Intensive Care Unit
During my first session with Ms. Clavelle last month, which took place in the Neonatal Intensive Care Unit, I watched radiologists work with medically fragile premature and newborn babies. Ms. Clavelle used an ultrasound machine to obtain images of the brains of two patients.

I further observed Ms. Clavelle use a portable X-ray device to take film of the chest and abdomen of another young patient. Some of the infants in this unit weigh as little as 1 pound and are connected to many pieces of support equipment, such as respirators and heart monitors. These patients present unique challenges to radiologic technologies.

MRI Section
Since Ms. Clavelle is a rotation supervisor, I was able to observe the operation of the MRI machine while she worked in that area. This room-sized piece of imaging equipment serves a variety of purposes in diagnosing patients' problems. During the four hours I shadowed Ms. Clavelle in the MRI section, she worked with the following patients:

1) An 82-year-old stroke patient,
2) A 14-year-old auto crash victim with head trauma,
3) A quarterback for the university football team with a knee injury, and
4) A 36-year-old woman suffering back pain.

Gives highlights of entire report.

Is organized from most important information to least important information.

Provides as many specifics as possible.

Figure 8.8 Periodic Report

One key to effective writing is to be specific and accurate. Another key is to use lists, numbered or set in columns, when possible. In addition, divide long discussions into shorter paragraphs to reflect groups of ideas.

Drafting the Conclusion The concluding section looks to the next periodic report the writer will compose.

Everything about this machine is computer-driven, so I became a little restless in the control room while the patients were undergoing treatment. The problem was that I did not understand the computer jargon used by the technologists, nor did I understand what I was seeing when I looked at the images on the computer screen. Many of the technologists were in a hurry and did not have time to explain the images to me.

Notes and explains problem area.

Radiology Lab
Observing Ms. Clavelle in the Radiology Lab gave me an opportunity to witness a wide range of uses of radiologic technology as well as to see the necessity for accurate reporting. A patient's well-being may depend on the technologist's communication skills.

Researched Reports
As my goal is to earn academic credit toward graduation, I am submitting one researched report, Using Ultrasound in Diagnosing Brain Hemorrhage, along with this monthly report. I am researching now for the second report and plan to finish it by the end of March. I should have the final paper completed by the end of April or the first week in May.

Conclusion
My experiences with Ms. Clavelle in February were worthwhile and exciting. In fact, after observing technologists use several types of equipment, I have found that my interest is greatest in ultrasound, and I am considering work in that area as a career goal. When we meet next, I would like to discuss the educational requirements for such a career and the possibility of shadowing someone during the spring semester who works only with ultrasound.

Looks forward to the next report and meeting.

Figure 8.8 Periodic Report, cont.

Stop and Think

What is the difference between progress and periodic reports?

Chapter 8 Review

POINT YOUR BROWSER
techwriting.swlearning.com

SUMMARY

1. Summaries and abstracts are condensed versions of longer documents. In a summary, the writer clearly and logically presents only main ideas. The length of the original and the writer's purpose determine the length of the summary. Abstracts are shorter than summaries and cover the main idea of the original.

2. A mechanism description describes the main parts of a device or mechanism and tells the purpose of the mechanism and overall design, what the various parts are, what they look like, and what their functions are.

3. Trip reports tell supervisors and coworkers what was gained from a business trip. The report includes only the most helpful details of the trip.

4. Incident reports, also called accident reports, describe an unusual incident or occurrence.

5. Progress reports describe the status of work on one particular project for a specified period.

6. Periodic reports describe the progress of all ongoing projects in an organization or an organization division during a specified time period.

7. Progress and periodic reports require writers to consider the interests of the audience and the schedule of the project or the organization.

Checklist

- Have I designed, organized, and written the document with the audience in mind?

- Have I analyzed my audiences and determined what readers need to know?

- Is my format appropriate for the audience and the situation?

- Have I included relevant background information?

- Are the data under each heading organized appropriately?

- Is the information complete and accurate?

- Have I used lists where appropriate for ease of reading?

- Have I made my document easy to read by using descriptive headings, and do the headings follow parallel structure?

- Is my discussion organized deductively, with an overview or a main idea presented first?

- Do I present accurate, specific details?

- Have I remained objective throughout?

- Have I presented problems as facts, not accusations?

Build On What You Know

1. The statements listed in *a* through *j* will go into a progress report. Identify each statement as Work Completed, Work Scheduled, or Problems/Projections.

   a. We have purchased a site license from NetBright for our network.

   b. The CD-ROM, which was delivered last Friday, was damaged in shipping so that it is inoperable.

   c. We installed screensavers on all computers.

   d. If all work scheduled is completed as we expect, the network will be ready for the team orientation on September 23.

   e. This week the system director will order the serial cable we need.

   f. The hardware security system we requested was $300 over our budget.

   g. Each computer will be named so that users can easily identify it.

   h. A system administrator will have to be trained before we can operate fully.

   i. We connected the laser printer to the network and tested it.

   j. We forgot to order a surge protector for the computer attached to the LCD projection panel, so we cannot use this equipment until the order comes next week.

2. Some sentences below are vague, and some include the writer's personal opinions. Revise each sentence to make it specific and factual. Invent details as needed.

   a. The calibrator is several minutes off schedule.

   b. The phenomenal response to our new computer safety education program shows that this new program will benefit employees.

   c. To get to the warehouse, go down the hall a bit and turn left.

   d. The line was down for a while Friday because of that lecture on safety.

   e. We can assemble the original air purifier in 45 minutes, but the fancy case of the new model causes a much longer assembly time than we planned.

3. Evaluate your progress on a hobby or collection. For instance, if you build sound systems in your room, explain the pieces of equipment, such as speakers and receivers, you have acquired and describe the equipment you will add. If you collect baseball cards or comic books, note the cards or books you possess now and the items you want to trade or buy. Make notes about your progress. Then share your notes with your classmates.

Apply What You Learned

4. Write a long summary, a short summary, and an abstract on one of the following: a magazine article, a textbook chapter, a sporting event, a meeting, a TV show, a movie, a classroom lecture, or a speech.

5. List five to ten mechanisms you know well. These could be mechanisms you use at work, at home, or at school. Consider using VCRs, telephones, curling irons, stereo equipment, car equipment, telescopes, farm equipment, computers, exercise machines, cash registers, or tools. Write a mechanism description for one of the items. Include a diagram of the mechanism in your report.

6. Take a trip to gather information about something that interests you. Before you go, list questions to answer during the trip. You could visit a college, a business, a school's lab facilities or sporting event, a museum, or a historical site. Write a trip report to your instructor, your parent, or a real or fictional supervisor who answers the questions. Use memo format.

7. Think of a time something went wrong. You may have had a problem at school or work. Perhaps you observed someone else's problem. After identifying and analyzing a specific audience, write an incident report describing the incident and what you learned from it.

8. Consider any project you are working on at home, school, or work as a progress report topic. Your audience will be a person or group of people who have an interest in or make decisions about the project. Use the appropriate format and organization for the topic and audience.

9. If you are seeking a summer or part-time job or applying for admission to a school, write a progress report to your adviser or family about how you are accomplishing your goals.

10. Think of groups to which you belong: a family, a club, a neighborhood, a school. With one group and a particular time period in mind, plan and write a periodic report for a specific audience. Describe the ongoing activities for your group or your unit of the larger organization.

11. Write a periodic report using the following case study.

As the Drafting Club chair, you receive organization funds from the Student Government Association (SGA). You report to the SGA twice a semester to tell them what the club is doing. Your next report is due January 6, 20—. In this report, you will discuss Professional Pursuits, Service, and Membership. The club is more active than ever. Over the holidays, five members attended the American Institute of Building Design meeting in Las Vegas and brought back information to share with other members. The club began the school year with 21 members, and two students joined in the second semester. This year's service project is to plan the city's first Habitat for Humanity house. Club members have completed the exterior drawings and submitted them for approval. They will finish the interior drawings before school ends. All 23 members of the club have participated in this service project.

Additional worksheets to assist you with this activity are available on the Data CD.

Work Is A Zoo!

You had a great talk with Dana Schnell yesterday afternoon. She talked about the impact of her class's involvement with the zoo. Over the course of the year, she saw her students' interest in the natural sciences rise. Parents told her that their children were asking to go to bookstores and libraries to find more information.

Dana also had some good ideas about how to get other instructors excited about ZiPS. In fact, she volunteered to write a letter encouraging instructors to attend an information session next month.

Now you need to incorporate your conversation with Dana into your presentation of findings. Tyrone suggests that you take a few minutes to summarize your interview with Dana and then go over your summary with him.

Summarize your conversation with Dana Schnell. A good summary does not restate the entire interview; it should be brief, well written, and accurate.

Think about your audience—Tyrone and the rest of the staff—as you write the summary. Do they need to know every detail?

Arrange the summary cohesively, perhaps around such topic areas as:

- Dana's experience.
- What worked.
- What did not.
- Suggestions for attracting local instructors.

NEWS RELEASES AND SCIENCE LAB REPORTS

GOALS

COMPOSE news or press releases

COMPOSE science lab reports

See the Data CD for Write-to-Learn and In The Know activity worksheets.

WRITE-TO-LEARN

Think of a time when you had information you needed to share with others. Perhaps you learned something that other people needed to know; for example, your school or workplace will close at 1 p.m. because of a broken water main. Write a description of the situation you recall. Then write one or two paragraphs in which you discuss how you would present the information to others.

In The Know

active voice when the subject of the sentence performs the action of the verb

conclusions the logical, inductive leaps made after considering all of the details of an experiment; what is learned from an experiment

date line the feature of a press release that identifies the location of a story

deductive reasoning reasoning from the general to the particular

embargo to prohibit or to request that a story not be published

experiments the controlled observations of natural phenomena

hook in a news story, an opening element whose purpose is to engage the reader, grab attention, and lead into the subject

hypothesis a pattern to help organize knowledge and predict other events

inductive reasoning reasoning from the particular to the general

media a system or means of mass communication

objectivity an attitude signifying that no personal bias or opinion has distorted or slanted a researcher's thinking

passive voice the verb *to be* plus the participle of the main verb; used in scientific writing to focus on the process instead of the performer

PSA public service announcement; news published for the benefit of the public

public relations plans or actions taken by an individual or an organization to create a favorable relationship with the public

results observable effects of an experiment

scientific method using inductive and deductive reasoning and a system of controls to objectively explore natural phenomena

Writing@Work

Janet Gray Coonce is a chemistry instructor at Oxford College of Emory University in Atlanta, Georgia. She lectures in general chemistry, works as a chemistry lab instructor, performs organic chemistry research, and publishes her findings.

Throughout Janet's school and teaching career, she has had to write many lab reports. "As an undergraduate student, I wrote a lab report for each experiment performed in my chemistry, physics, and biology courses. These reports taught me how to present information in a clear and concise manner in order to share my findings quickly and efficiently with others." Now as an instructor, Janet must write lab reports to describe and explain the results of original research to be published as manuscripts in peer-reviewed scientific journals. Janet stresses the importance of clear writing in these reports. "Presenting information as accurately as possible is extremely important in order for others to believe, understand, and reproduce my results."

According to Janet, lab reports are very important. Students must learn to write scientifically so that scientists are able to glance at a report and quickly understand the objective. "As Sir Isaac Newton said, 'If I have seen farther, it is by standing on the shoulders of giants.' You must read and understand the reports of previous researchers to 'stand on their shoulders.' Once you have 'seen farther,' you must share your results with others so they can understand and make improvements." Janet believes that many of the recent advances in science and technology can be attributed to the accessibility of lab reports. Because this is the case, communication in these lab reports must be clear and easily understandable.

Janet discusses some ethical issues that can potentially arise when writing lab reports. Some students may be tempted to present fabricated data to make their findings agree with others; however, in most schools, creating or falsifying data is a violation of the honor code and could result in serious punishment. "As a researcher, recording only correct information is even more important. Although it may be tempting to present wrong or misleading information to support a hypothesis, reports are peer-reviewed and other researchers will expose the lies if they find conflicting information."

Janet has a master's degree in Chemistry from Emory University.

March 5, 20-

Michael Braukus
Headquarters, Washington DC
(Phone: 202 555-1979)

Bruce Buckingham
Kennedy Space Center, FL
(Phone: 321 555-2468)

Release No. 01-33

KENNEDY SPACE CLEANS UP WITH FERTILE INVENTION; WINS NASA AWARD

Faced with the daunting task of reducing hazardous rocket-fuel waste, a team of inventive scientists and engineers from NASA's Kennedy Space Center (KSC), FL, found a way to really clean up, while at the same time produce a commercially successful and safe byproduct.

The team developed a process to convert the hazardous waste to a helpful fertilizer and was honored with NASA's Commercial Invention of the Year Award.

The invention was developed by NASA's Dr. Clyde Parrish, Dr. Dale Lueck, Mr. Andrew Kelly and Dynacs Engineering's Mr. Paul Gamble. Together, they developed the new process in response to a space agency request to reduce the hazardous waste stream captured in a scrubber when a toxic oxidizer is transferred back and forth from storage tanks into the space shuttle's Orbital Maneuvering Subsystem (OMS) and Reaction Control System (RCS) pods. The shuttle's OMS is used for the major orbital and deorbit maneuvers and the RCS is used for orbiter attitude control.

The process was tested and is being implemented at Kennedy, where it is being used on orange groves located on the center's grounds.

"We have a number of talented scientists and engineers on our team and we're proud of them. I believe this is just the first of many such awards for the Kennedy Space Center," said Kennedy Director Roy Bridges. It is the first time Kennedy has won the award, given annually by NASA Headquarters to recognize a significant technology spinoff developed at one of the Agency's centers.

The inventors will be honored at a ceremony at NASA Headquarters in April where the team will receive a check and a certificate from the NASA administrator. The technology will be submitted as NASA's nominee for the Intellectual Property Owners Inc. Invention of the Year award, which is held in cooperation with the United States Patent and Trademark Office.

-more-

Figure 9.1 Press Release Model

"This was very much a team effort," said Gamble, the current lead for the project at Dynacs Engineering. Dynacs is the engineering development contractor at Kennedy. "We're all very proud to have been a part of it. When we're able to commercialize a technology we've developed at KSC, it benefits everyone. It's another example of how the space program makes all our lives better," Gamble said.

Parrish suggested the original idea for the technology and led development of the process, which started while he worked at Dynacs. Parrish had worked on a Navy project team 25 years previously that found an oxidizer used in battlefield illumination flares could be used as a fertilizer. Parrish has many patents and awards to his credit.

The invention has been licensed to Phoenix Systems International Inc. of McDonald, Ohio, an engineering firm that develops technologies applied to utility and industrial fossil fuel. The U.S. Air Force also has expressed interest in the technology for launch facilities at Cape Canaveral Air Force Station, Florida, and Vandenberg Air Force Base, California.

The award represents another success for Kennedy's Technology Programs and Commercialization Office. The office works with KSC scientists and engineers to report new technologies and commercialize them when possible.

"Our office has been striving to create an awareness of all facets of new technology reporting, including the awards program. As a part of this effort, we're seeking to provide more recognition for our inventors and their inventions," said Pam Bookman, a commercialization manager for the office. "Our people have always produced new technologies to cope with the operational challenges we face, but they're realizing more often now that those technologies can often be commercialized."

SOURCE: "NOx Emissions Transformed into Fertilizer." NASA Kennedy Space Center. 5 March 2001 < http://technology.ksc.nasa.gov/WWWaccess/Stories/Scrubber/Index.html > .

Figure 9.1 Press Release Model, cont.

ECOLOGY LAB: HOW LOCATION AFFECTS MICROCLIMATES

To show how just a small change in location can make a difference in microclimate range, a simple experiment was set up at River Park in Walston, South Carolina.

Materials and Method

Min-max thermometers were set up in groups of three locations in the park for a 21-hour period. The thermometers were placed at a pond with minimal shading, at heights of 1 m and 10 cm above the surface and at 10 cm below the surface. Two more thermometers were set up on a floodplain under a canopy of dense foliage, at 1 m and 10 cm above the ground. Two thermometers were placed at the river's edge under moderately dense foliage, at 1 m and 10 cm above the river's edge. The relative humidity was also taken at each location using a sling psychrometer.

Results and Discussion

Table 1 shows the variation in temperature and humidity of the three sites.

Table 1. Temperatures and Humidity of Microclimates at River Park in Walston, SC, 26 August 20—

TEMPERATURE AND HUMIDITY	POND			FLOOD PLAIN		RIVER	
	1 m above	10 m above	10 cm below	1 m above	10 cm above	1 m above	10 cm above
Maximum	32[a]	27	26	26	27	28	31
Minimum	23	24	24	2	21	22	22
Current	25	27	25	2	23	29	24
Range	9	3	2	5	6	6	9
Humidity	96%			91%		100%	

[a]Temperatures in degrees Celsius

The data lead to these observations:

1. The range of temperatures within each location is greater with increased distance from the surface. The wide range is probably due to the insulating effects of the ground and water or perhaps reduced airflow. In fact, the submerged thermometer had the least variation, testifying to the water's insulating qualities.

2. The pond location generally had higher temperatures and a greater range of temperatures due to the lack of cover and the insulating effects of the water. The water's resistance to temperature fluctuations may have kept the higher thermometers warm.

Conclusions

A microclimate can extend to a range as small as a few centimeters. In all, a microclimate must be considered species-specific. An organism will thrive only when the climate surrounding it is within that species' tolerances.

Figure 9.2 Science Lab Report

NEWS RELEASES

News releases, also called press releases, are reports of events or facts prepared to send to the **media.** The goal of the release is to inform the public. Some news releases are news stories, such as an employee promotion or a company expansion.

Some press releases are also known as public service announcements, or PSAs. As the name suggests, **PSA**s differ from other news releases in that they present beneficial facts to the public. PSAs, for example, announce Red Cross blood drives, city council meetings, fund-raisers, and other public events.

News is uncovered by reporters, as Carl Bernstein and Bob Woodward of the *Washington Post* did in uncovering the break-in at Democratic Party national headquarters on June 17, 1972, now known as the Watergate scandal. People and organizations send news releases to the media to share information with the public.

In large organizations, **public relations** departments, responsible for communication between the company and the outside world, write news releases to help the company maintain a positive image. For instance, if an executive is involved in a scandal, the public relations staff may prepare a news release to present the company's view of the situation and to restore public confidence.

In smaller organizations without public relations departments, any employee might write a news release. The maintenance director might write a release describing the company's recycling efforts, a retail sales manager might cover the store's planned expansion, and a volunteer group's administrative assistant might outline the organization's upcoming fund-raising project.

Since the writer sends the release to select news agencies, the first readers are editors and news directors who read critically. They decide whether the news release will be run. If the information is newsworthy and the release is well written so that little editing is required, the chance that it will be run increases. Other influential factors include space and time constraints.

If the release is run, the second audience is the public. In this case, the public is anyone who reads a newspaper or magazine, watches television, or listens to the radio. Specialized media agencies receive news releases that target a particular audience, so the second audience might also be a select group.

For instance, you are probably familiar with television stations that target specific people: MTV targets teen music lovers; TNN attracts country music fans; CNN focuses on people interested in world, economic, and financial news; and the Disney Channel targets children. In any case, various audiences are looking for the same thing—timely and interesting information.

COMPOSING NEWS RELEASES

When an employer asks you to write a news release, where do you start? Technical writers should begin by analyzing their audience. For a news release, consider the editor or news director as well as the public. Also, consider answering the Reporter's Questions, planning for accuracy, planning for credibility, beginning the news story effectively, organizing information in the most reader-friendly way, and taking a news writer's approach to the story.

Reporter's Questions The next step is to ask the classic five "Reporter's Questions": Who? What? When? Where? Why? Answering these questions will provide the most important information to include.

Beyond the Reporter's Questions, ask yourself:

- What will interest my audience?
- What will grab their attention?
- What would they ask if they could?

Accuracy News release writers should be accurate. Writers should check their prewriting notes for accuracy in the following:

- Facts
- Numbers and statistics
- Names
- Locations
- Quotations
- Completeness ("the whole truth")

If your text is correct, your releases will have a greater chance of being published.

Communication Dilemma

In March 2004, the public relations group for a financial planning business owned by three brothers was faced with a great challenge. The youngest brother, Nicholas Castleberry, was arrested for embezzling from the company. He had been transferring funds from company accounts to his private account for three years and had used the embezzled funds to feed his gambling habit.

Should the company have issued a press release? What and how much information should have been told? If you worked for this company, what would you have done?

Credibility Similar to inaccuracies, exaggerations can ruin a news release and destroy a writer's credibility. Exaggerations are overstatements or additions beyond the truth. One way to avoid exaggeration is to use information that can be verified. Another way is to avoid superlatives, such as *the best, the fastest, the first,* and *the worst,* unless you can document or prove the statement.

For instance, if your release opens with "R. J. Birch, the fastest 10K runner in the state," are you being honest or are you exaggerating? If you can prove that R. J. Birch is the fastest runner, that is, if you have recorded race times, then the release is truthful. If, on the other hand, your statement that R. J. Birch is the fastest is based only on your opinion, then you may be exaggerating.

As you compose, be aware that your news release will compete with others for space or airtime. Since the headline will be read first, compose it carefully. Include an active verb. The verb will be present tense for current events, past tense for events already concluded, and future tense for scheduled activities. For example, the headline HALIFAX ACADEMY TO HOST STAR TREK CONVENTION uses an active verb that indicates future time, *to host,* since the event has not yet occurred.

Like the headline, the body must earn a positive response from an editor or a news director as well as from the public. To achieve this goal, the release must open with a **hook,** answer the five Reporter's Questions immediately, and be organized with the important ideas first.

Beginning the Story Begin your news release with 1) a hook to catch the audience's interest and 2) answers to the five Reporter's Questions so the audience gets essential information immediately.

Provide a Hook. Open with a hook—catchy wording or an idea that attracts attention. Dynamic wording or an intriguing idea seizes the audience's attention and encourages further reading, viewing, or listening. Listed below are several examples of hooks used to open news releases:

- The nets are still hanging in Memorial Coliseum after last night's City League upset, but only because the Westinghouse-sponsored Knights expect to return for them during the playoffs.

- When 600 first-year students show up for orientation at Schantz College on Saturday, they will get something besides their dorm assignments.

- The Michaux Farm owns some birds that will never fly the coop.

- The Easter Bunny Brought What?!

All of these opening sentences attract the reader's or listener's attention. If they are effective, the audience will want to know more.

Answer the Five Reporter's Questions. Answer Who? What? Where? When? and Why? immediately. In fact, an effective news release will include the answers to all five questions in the first paragraph. Some will include this information in the first sentence. Figure 9.3 shows an illustration of this idea-packed opening. Notice where the Five Reporter's Questions are addressed in this opening.

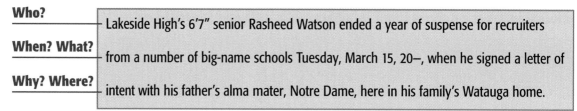

Who?

When? What?

Why? Where?

Lakeside High's 6'7" senior Rasheed Watson ended a year of suspense for recruiters from a number of big-name schools Tuesday, March 15, 20–, when he signed a letter of intent with his father's alma mater, Notre Dame, here in his family's Watauga home.

Figure 9.3 Reporter's Questions in News Release Opening

Organizing Information Order ideas from most important to least important. Organizing from most to least important achieves several purposes:

- You make editors' work easier and the story's publication more likely.

- You help readers find the most important information quickly and easily. Readers will find the most important information even if they do not read the entire article.

- If a release must be cut, you make the work easier and you have more control over how it will be cut.

If a news director has only 20 seconds of airtime (time to deliver a news story) and your news release requires 30 seconds, the news director must cut 10 seconds from your release or choose not to use it.

Likewise, print editors sometimes must cut inches from press releases to fit them into the space available in the publication, as illustrated in Figure 9.4. The triangle shows the part of the release one editor decided to publish. The last two paragraphs, containing the least important information, were cut.

 Complete the Reorganizing an Ineffective News Release worksheet on the Data CD.

CAMELOT
Public Information Office

City of Camelot
Office of the Mayor
1156 West Main Street
Camelot, IL 61808-1908
Phone: (555) 555-0001
Fax: (555) 555-0012

News
August 23, 20—
For Immediate Release

CAMELOT, IL– Roller Art has donated $100,000 to Camelot for the development of a park especially designed for in-line and roller-skating enthusiasts. The park will feature two oval tracks for straightforward skating and another area with five ramps for trick skating.

The 2.45-acre park site is located three blocks west of the city office quad. Roller Art deeded this undeveloped land to the city two years ago.

Construction on the property is expected to begin within the month, and Mayor Margie Huerta says the park, to be named Roller Royale, will be open by early summer.

Maureen Nowicki, spokesperson for Roller Art, said her company is happy to be able to give back to the community that has helped Roller Art become successful. Roller Art employs 48 people who design and manufacture roller skates.

Roller Art has a history of giving to Camelot. In its nine years of doing business in the community, the company has donated a total of $425,000 to the city and an equal amount to local nonprofit groups.

The local company has the top-selling in-line skates on the market, Rold World. Rold World, developed after years of research, combines speed with the maximum in directional control.

-30-

Figure 9.4 News Release Cut by Editor

Taking a News Writer's Approach News will get editors to publish a release. If you are tempted to promote a product or a service in your release, remind yourself that news is who did what where, when, and why, while advertisements are how new, improved, or cost-effective something might be. Editors are unlikely to publish news releases that read like sales literature.

Although your releases should not make a direct sales appeal as an advertisement would, most releases are good news messages intended to create goodwill. The message will be shared with a large audience and may cover positive news, such as introducing a new product, expanding facilities, or hiring employees. For instance, when KFC announced its

Colonel's Rotisserie Gold roasted chicken, the company could not send a letter to all customers. Instead, press releases announced the new product.

FORMATTING NEWS RELEASES

News releases are formatted so information the reader needs stands out, editors can write and make changes easily, and typesetters and news anchors (who might read the text on the air) can easily follow the document. For illustrative purposes, the release is divided into three units: top of the page or introductory information, body or story, and pagination cues. As you read about how to format a news release properly, refer to Figure 9.5.

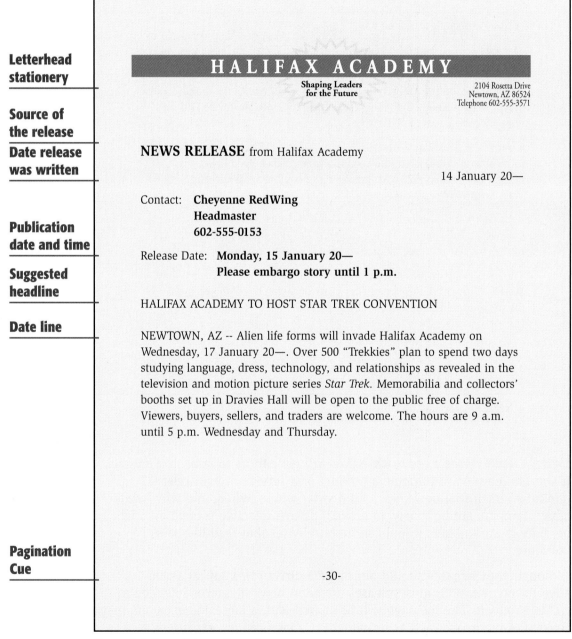

Letterhead stationery

Source of the release

Date release was written

Publication date and time

Suggested headline

Date line

Pagination Cue

HALIFAX ACADEMY

Shaping Leaders
for the Future

2104 Rosetta Drive
Newtown, AZ 86524
Telephone 602-555-3571

NEWS RELEASE from Halifax Academy

14 January 20—

Contact: **Cheyenne RedWing**
          Headmaster
          602-555-0153

Release Date: **Monday, 15 January 20—**
               Please embargo story until 1 p.m.

HALIFAX ACADEMY TO HOST STAR TREK CONVENTION

NEWTOWN, AZ -- Alien life forms will invade Halifax Academy on Wednesday, 17 January 20—. Over 500 "Trekkies" plan to spend two days studying language, dress, technology, and relationships as revealed in the television and motion picture series *Star Trek*. Memorabilia and collectors' booths set up in Dravies Hall will be open to the public free of charge. Viewers, buyers, sellers, and traders are welcome. The hours are 9 a.m. until 5 p.m. Wednesday and Thursday.

-30-

Figure 9.5 News Release Format

Introductory Information Many large companies create special stationery, or letterhead, for news releases. This stationery is printed with the company name, address, telephone number, logo, and the words *NEWS RELEASE*. Writers for organizations that do not have special letterhead use plain 8 ½″ × 11″ paper. Writers then decide how to organize and present the features at the top of the page. Follow these guidelines for introductory format:

1. Begin with the words *NEWS RELEASE*, usually in all capital letters. Key the source of the document in initial caps.

2. Give the contact person's name. Type *Contact* and a colon. After the colon, enter the name of the person who is responsible for the news release. Under the name, enter the person's job title and phone number.

3. Record the date the document was written in the upper right corner across from the contact person's name.

4. Place the words *Release Date* and a colon at the left margin beneath the contact information. Two spaces after the colon, type the date— and the specific time—the information should be made public.

5. Writers occasionally request a release to be held for a period of time before publication. If you want a story to be held, type beneath or beside the release date *Please hold until [desired release time]* or *Please embargo story until [desired release time]*. **Embargo** means to withhold or delay publication.

6. Give the news agency a suggested headline in all capital letters.

Body These guidelines will help you format the body of releases:

1. Preface the body of your release with a **date line** that identifies the location of the story. Type the date line in all capital letters. In Figure 9.5, NEWTOWN, AZ is where the story takes place. After the location, 1) leave a space, 2) type a hyphen, 3) leave another space, 4) type a second hyphen, and 5) leave a final space.

2. Double-space the body. Use double-spaced lines for print media and triple-spaced lines for radio and television.

Pagination Cues News release writers use a special code to help readers follow the text and read from one page to another. To use these cues:

1. Type the word *-more-* centered at the bottom of the page when the release will be continued on the next page.

2. End news releases with *-30-* or *###* centered after the last line.

SEE THE SITES

The U.S. Food and Drug Administration publishes a web site that contains links to press releases of the past decade. Here you will find everything from food and drug research to biologics and radiation protection.

For quick tips on how to write science lab reports, check out the University of Wisconsin-Madison writing center web site. Here you will find a menu that shows how to write each part of a science lab report, from the title to the discussion.

You can find the URL for both sites in the web links at techwriting. swlearning.com.

Stop and Think

Before a news release is published, what group of readers must approve it?

SCIENCE LAB REPORTS

Henry David Thoreau used his creative mind to write *Walden*, a literary and philosophical masterpiece. However, he also used his creative mind to explore Walden Pond using scientific calculations: "I surveyed it carefully, before the ice broke up, early in [1846] with compass, chain, and sounding line . . . . I fathomed it easily with a cod-line and a stone weighing about a pound and a half, and could tell accurately when the stone left bottom, by having to pull so much harder before the water got underneath to help me. The greatest depth was exactly one hundred and two feet . . ." (191).

© GETTY IMAGES/PHOTODISC

Creative genius—the inspiration for writing *Walden*—is also the inspiration for designing the incandescent lightbulb, the theory of relativity, and the binary language of computer programming. In fact, creativity, coupled with curiosity and a sense of adventure, is the driving force behind scientific exploration.

However, scientific exploration adds little to the knowledge community unless the scientist records what was done and what happened. The science lab report is necessary for sharing knowledge.

Two audiences read lab reports: 1) workplace scientists and 2) educators. Both audiences expect data to be presented professionally and ethically. Both read lab reports with great interest and a critical eye. They are experts in their fields, apt to note any inconsistencies in the research.

Work audiences and school audiences, however, read for different purposes. In the workplace, research scientists with a professional or financial interest in the subject read lab reports. The research represents new knowledge, and audiences are eager to get the **results.** Often these lab reports become the basis of more involved science reports submitted to major magazines such as *Analytical Chemistry* and *Journal of Medicine.*

In school, instructors read lab reports. The procedures and **experiments** do not represent new research (except in upper-level classes) but are replicated to teach students scientific concepts. In the classroom, the lab report is a test to see whether students performed an experiment correctly and understood what happened. Here instructors are interested in more detailed explanations than workplace audiences, who are more interested in results.

Whoever the audience, all lab report readers respect, understand, and follow the **scientific method,** the reasoning on which scientific experimentation is based. The scientific method calls for precision, accuracy, **objectivity,** and carefully drawn **conclusions** based on sufficient data. Data must be presented clearly, with much of it in graphics such as tables and graphs.

Thoreau, Henry David. *Walden.* New York: New American Library of World Literature, Inc., 1964.

FORMATTING AND ORGANIZING LAB REPORTS

The structure of a lab report varies little. Sometimes the names of the headings change or something is added, but lab reports always answer these questions: What was the purpose of the lab? What materials were used? What procedure was followed? What were the results? What were the conclusions? A typical lab report typically includes four sections.

1. The Introduction section:

   - Always tells objectives of the lab, what the lab is expected to prove.

   - Sometimes gives the background of the problem under research.

   - Sometimes tells under whose authority the lab was conducted.

   - Sometimes is given a separate heading if the lab report is long.

2. The Materials and Method (also called Experimental Section, Methodology, Procedures) section:

   - Always describes and lists materials and/or instruments used.

   - Always describes the procedure used, including relevant calculations.

   - Always uses chronological order (through time).

3. The Results and Discussion (also called Results or Discussion) section:

   - Always presents test results with relevant calculations; usually includes accompanying graphics—tables, graphs, etc.

   - Always discusses the results and explains why things happened.

   - Usually uses chronological order for results seen and cause-to-effect order for discussion of the results.

4. The Conclusions section:

   - Always includes a brief summary that tells how the test results, findings, and analysis meet the objectives.

   - Sometimes uses chronological order; sometimes uses priority order.

Depending on the lab type and the report length, other sections are added: a Theory section explaining the scientific theory behind the lab, an

Communication Update

New technologies have made modern scientific research possible. The developments of advanced instrumentation and experimental techniques have provided researchers the means to collect many forms of qualitative and quantitative data. Computer programs such as Molecular modeling programs, Ab Initio quantum chemistry programs, Mathcad, Maple, and others help process and analyze huge amounts of data that would otherwise take years to understand.

Complete the
Exercise in
Objectivity
worksheet on the Data CD.

Instrumentation section if the lab tests equipment, a Calculations section if the lab uses lengthy mathematical computations, a Recommendation section if necessary for the assignment. Longer reports also may use an Appendix, a separate section at the end of the report that contains tables and graphs whose complexity and length would otherwise disrupt the flow of the report.

COMPOSING LAB REPORTS

The scientific method determines the science lab report structure. Scientists draw tentative conclusions using inductive reasoning. Reasoning from the particular (I sneeze every time I am around a rose) to the general (the conclusion: roses make me sneeze) is called **inductive reasoning.**

Scientists use deductive reasoning to test conclusions for validity. **Deductive reasoning** takes you from the general (conclusion: I think roses make me sneeze) to the particular (If I send my mother roses, they will make me sneeze; so I will give her candy instead of roses). The tentative conclusion becomes the **hypothesis,** a tentative explanation that helps organize knowledge and predict other events, which is tested in the next science lab experiment.

Results versus Conclusions Experiments require writers to observe results and then draw conclusions. Observable **results,** however, are different from the **conclusions** drawn. When Paul Broca measured women's brains in the mid-1800s, he observed that they weighed an average of 181 grams less than men's brains. His observation, the result of his measurements, was correct. The brains did weigh less. However, he wrongly concluded that smaller brains meant women were less intelligent than men (409). Less weight does not lead to the conclusion that women are not as smart.

A result is not the same as a conclusion. A result is simply what happened; a conclusion goes beyond what happened. A conclusion requires a scientist to draw an inference, to make a point about the results.

Objectivity **Objectivity** is important in scientific thinking. Objectivity means that the conclusion reached is based on facts and not a person's whim or bias. When Broca weighed women's brains in the mid-1800s, his bias that women were intellectually inferior kept him from analyzing his data objectively. Objectivity also means that another experimenter can follow the same procedure and get the same results.

Objective knowledge is different from subjective knowledge. Subjective knowledge, based on personal opinion, is difficult to measure and can vary from one person to another. To say that your hair makes you look sophisticated is a subjective statement, a personal interpretation of sophistication. Not everyone, however, would agree that your hair makes you look sophisticated. To say that your hair is black and cut in a block style with strands approximately 11 inches long is an objective description. Everyone can agree on this description because it is measurable.

Gould, Stephen Jay. "Women's Brains." *The Blair Reader.* Ed. Laurie G. Kirszner and Stephen R. Mandell. Englewood Cliffs, NJ: Prentice Hall, 1992. 407-413.

Complete the Active Passive Editing Exercises worksheet on the Data CD.

Focus on Ethics

Clinical trials are research studies carried out to test the effectiveness of new drugs, vaccines, therapies, and diagnostic procedures. Many of these trials are funded by private organizations. Usually, these sponsoring organizations hope to sell the medicines related to the study. Sometimes these companies have undue influence over the results, design of the study, selection of population, and dissemination of the conclusions of the research.

Changing or "fudging" data can be tempting for funding organizations or any other organization when results of a lab experiment are unexpected or difficult to understand. Unfortunately, false reports can lead other researchers down time-consuming and frustrating pathways that hinder new scientific developments. Inaccurate representation of results in medicinal quality and in clinical trials can lead to patient deaths and other extreme consequences.

Active Voice versus Passive Voice Because objectivity is important, lab reports often use **passive voice.** Passive voice uses a form of the verb *to be* with the past participle of the verb. Passive voice keeps the reader focused on the process instead of on the scientist performing that process. Science strives to be objective, and some people think that naming the person makes the lab report sound too subjective and personal.

Active voice focuses on the person: Dr. Cuomo used the Winkler method to test the oxygen saturation in all three locations. OR We used the Winkler method to test the oxygen saturation in all three locations.

Passive voice focuses on the process: Oxygen saturation was tested in all three locations using the Winkler method.

Most advice in this text encourages writers to avoid passive and write in **active voice.** While active voice sounds more natural in most contexts, the lab report is unique: lab reports typically rely on passive voice. Note the following examples:

- Tiny shifts in blood flow to parts of the brain *were detected* with functional magnetic resonance imaging.

- A 50 ml solution *was prepared* using distilled water in volumetric flasks.

Precision Your grandmother cooked with a pinch of this and a pinch of that—which was a workable measurement system as long as she was doing the pinching. The real problem came when someone else tried to duplicate the recipe. How could someone else duplicate the precise size of Grandmother's pinch?

Precision is extremely important in a lab report. Numbers must be used so other people understand the report the same way. If Grandmother's pinch of salt is equal to ¼ teaspoon of salt, then others can duplicate the pinch with a measuring spoon.

Lab reports use numbers in several ways. Some examples of numbers used in lab reports are:

Chemical Formulas
$A1_2O_3$ (aluminum oxide), NaCl (sodium chloride)

Mathematical Formulas
$y = ax^2 + bx + c$

Metric Measurements
centimeter, millimeter, microsecond

Percentages and Decimals
19.56 cm, 2312.12 cm, 3345.41%

Scientific Notation
A' 10n 3.00' 108

Significant Figures
3.15 cm, 0.315 cm, 0.00315 cm, 3.00 cm

Tables

Table 1. Data on Voltage Measurements			
Resistance	Voltage (measured)	Voltage (theoretical)	Voltage (AC)
3.80	3.25	4.08	6.00
2.20	1.03	1.32	5.2
1.00	0.45	0.60	4.00

Word Choice The science lab report uses straightforward language. The purpose of using language that is straightforward is to include data in the most clear and concise manner possible. This way, the chances of mistakes made from confusing language are few.

Here are examples of typical sentences from different sections of science lab reports:

To Verb + *What* Phrases

- To *determine* what differences there may be between several aquatic ecosystems, samples were taken in early November from three sites in eastern South Carolina.

- This lab is designed to *identify* fatty acids in internal standard, known and unknown mixtures.

Lists

- The system consists of a z-80A microprocessor, 16-bit DAC, 12-bit ADC, 24 K RAM, 60 K ROM, a potentiostatic circuit (current follower/filter), a plotter, a dot-matrix printer, a monitor, a keyboard, a mouse, and an auto cell stand.

- The survey was sent to 25 students, 25 instructors, 10 administrators, and 25 parents.

Description of Processes

- For this experiment, 25 *men and women were selected at random* from the graduating class.

- The *blood was drawn* from the patient's finger and placed on the slide. Then the *sample was examined* under a microscope.

Cause-to-Effect Reasoning

- The data from the table *suggests that* the resolution is highest with the pH 7/45% MeOH buffer solution (alpha = 3.35).

- The warmer temperatures *indicate that* the air is capable of holding more moisture.

© GETTY IMAGES/PHOTODISC

Graphics Think about data that could be presented visually. If that data will help your reader understand your lab report, use a graphic. For lab reports, consider using the following:

- Tables if your results use a lot of numbers

- A schematic if your method or results require an understanding of the circuitry (inside workings) of a mechanism

- A diagram if your method or results involve an understanding of special instruments or mechanisms

- Maps if you are working with an outdoor lab where places are important

- Graphs if you wish to compare numerical data

- Photographs if the actual picture will help your reader understand your data

See Chapter 6, *Document Design and Graphics,* for more information about graphics.

Stop and Think

What is the difference between results and conclusions? Why do writers of science lab reports use passive voice?

Chapter 9 Review

POINT YOUR BROWSER

techwriting.swlearning.com

SUMMARY

1. News or press releases are documents that communicate news of an organization to publishing agencies such as newspapers, magazines, and radio and television stations.

2. Two audiences benefit from news releases: 1) the news directors and editors of news agencies and 2) their readers, viewers, and listeners.

3. Writers of press releases should be accurate and credible. They should answer the five Reporter's Questions (Who? What? When? Where? Why?) and other questions the audience is likely to have about the topic.

4. The news release has a standard format that the audience expects.

5. Lab reports answer these questions: What was the purpose of the lab? What materials were used? What was the procedure? What were the results? What are the conclusions?

6. Workplace audiences are interested in the lab test results. Educators are interested in an explanation and the proper procedure. Both audiences expect the writer to follow the scientific method, presenting data precisely and accurately and using graphics where appropriate.

7. The scientific method determines the structure of the lab report. The scientific method uses inductive and deductive reasoning, maintains objectivity, and records precise data.

Checklist

- Is my press release appropriate for the audience?

- Does my release answer the five Reporter's Questions (and others the audience might have) at the opening of the story?

- Did I properly format features at the top of the first page?

- Did I begin the body of the release with a hook to catch the audience's attention? Did I present the essential ideas early?

- Is my release more news (who, what, when, where, why) than advertisement (what product or service is "new and improved")? Did I avoid inaccuracies and exaggerations?

- Have I answered the basic questions of the lab report: What was the purpose of the lab? What materials were used? What was the procedure? What were the results? What are the conclusions?

- Is my data precise and accurate? Did I maintain objectivity?

- Have I included appropriate headings and graphics?

- Have I written the methods and results using chronological order? Have I discussed and explained the results and not simply stated them?

- Does my conclusion section provide a true conclusion?

Build On What You Know

1. Read the paragraph below, which is the opening paragraph of a news release. Identify which Reporter's Questions are not answered.

NASA: No talk of cutting mission

CAPE CANAVERAL, Florida.– NASA said Sunday it did not intend to cut short Calypso's 14-day mission despite trouble with a fuel line connected to a crucial auxiliary unit. (From Associated Press Reports, *The Daily Reflector,* Greenville, South Carolina, Monday, March 7, 20–PAGE 1)

---

2. Are these statements subjective or objective? Why do you think so?

   a. This is the best English class I have ever had.

   b. This class covers the basic style and formatting of technical writing.

   c. The patient seemed angry, probably because of something that happened on the way to the office.

   d. The temperature is in the mid-80s with little chance of rain.

3. What type of graphics do you think these statements call for? Consider calculations, figures, and tables.

   a. The experiments were designed to demonstrate the properties of inverse functions. We experimented with several types of functions, including transcendental functions and polynomial expressions.

   b. The area of the platinum disk was found using simple algebra.

   c. An energy flow diagram (see Figure 1) was developed illustrating the energy flow and the student's position on the food web.

   d. The circuit in Figure 1 uses an op-amp as a multiplier.

4. Which part of the following statements could be more precise?

   a. The bear drank from the water hole several times in the afternoon.

   b. The decibels were tested at levels too low for human ears.

   c. The robin sat on a few eggs in the nest for a couple of weeks.

   d. The CPU costs around $500, the monitor costs about $350, and the printer costs $398.99 plus shipping and handling.

5. Read these sentences. Where do they belong in a lab report—under Introduction, Materials and Method, Results, Discussion, or Conclusions?

   a. For this activity, four potatoes, four pieces of wood, four cans, and a flame were used to determine evidence of carbon.

   b. The larger the food supply, the larger the guppy population.

   c. The data for absorbencies in Table 1 show excellent correlation and show a strong linear relationship (R = 1.00) for Plot 1.

Apply What You Learned

6. Clip an article from your newspaper (or photocopy an article from a newspaper in the library). Read the article carefully. Then find answers to the five Reporter's Questions in the article and write them down.

7. For each of the situations described below, write and properly format a news release appropriate to the circumstances. Add details as needed and omit any information not needed.

   a. You are the captain of your school's chess team. Your team, having won the regional competition last Saturday, will be participating in the state contest on the first Saturday of next month. The faculty member on campus who sponsors your team has asked you to write a news release announcing your team's success and the upcoming event. The faculty sponsor wants the release sent to the local newspaper and television station.

   b. Write a news release announcing your school's First Annual Metalworks Sale and inviting the public to attend. The sale will feature wrought iron furniture, candlesticks, cookware holders, and fireplace tools. The public may make purchases during the sale with cash, check, or credit card. The sale will be held in Gray Gallery from 6 to 9:30 p.m. on Friday, 28 April and from 9 a.m. to 6 p.m. on Saturday, 29 April 20—. All items are student work and will be sold to buy new equipment for the metalworks laboratory.

8. If your school or your community has a newspaper or radio or television station, visit the news office. Interview the person in charge of news. Ask the news director to show you a collection of news releases. In addition, ask the news director about the editing he or she usually does with press releases before publication.

9. Look for something newsworthy at your school (events, projects, awards, programs, or sports) or in your community (organizational or club news, neighborhood programs and events, or special projects). For instance, you may learn that some of your neighbors are forming a community watch group. Analyze the audience—editors and public. Prewrite, compose, edit, and revise a news release that might be sent to a local news agency, such as the area newspaper or television or radio station.

10. Look through a series of science experiments for children. Scout handbooks, Mr. Wizard's science program, and the Discovery Channel are good sources of simple experiments for children. Try an experiment, keep notes in a notebook, and write a lab report for English class.

11. Think of something about which you would like to know more. Maybe you would like to know under what conditions your car gets better gas mileage; whether some additive makes your car run better; or whether one brand of polish, lipstick, or sunscreen works better than another. Ask your science instructor to help you design an experiment to give you the knowledge you seek. Perform the experiment and write the results.

This activity will help you practice writing effective news releases. Refer to the Work Is A Zoo! worksheets for this chapter.

Work Is A Zoo!

Next week is the zoo's annual Earth Week celebration. Anya has placed you in charge of writing a news release to announce the celebration. The news release will be published in the local newspaper; it also will be read on your local television news station.

What a great way to market the exciting events that are happening at the zoo!

Before you begin writing the news release, you and Anya talk about the details of the celebration. Last year, she says, a total of 45,000 visitors attended the event. This year she expects an even larger crowd because of the birth of a new giraffe calf, Klaya. The birth of Klaya is significant because giraffes are considered to be endangered. Students will get to see Klaya in an exhibit with her mother, Mia, during the celebration.

The celebration also will feature a crafts booth where students can make earth-friendly crafts, an interactive video of endangered species featuring Klaya and Mia, and a demonstration given by the zoo's animal trainer about the safest way to train animals. A special exhibit also will show how the animals' environments are created in the zoo so that they are as similar as possible to their natural environment.

A raffle drawing will occur each day of the week at noon. Students will be able to choose from a variety of zoo-related prizes including free zoo passes for a year.

The zoo's admission for the entire week is $7 for adults and $4 for children under 13.

Write a news release in which you announce the zoo's Earth Week celebration to the public.

EMPLOYMENT COMMUNICATION

GOALS

IDENTIFY the audience for employment communication

PLAN to write employment communication

FORMAT and ORGANIZE resumes

COMPOSE resumes

COMPOSE employment letters

See the Data CD for Write-to-Learn and In The Know activity worksheets.

WRITE-TO-LEARN

Place yourself in the future, ten years from now. Write a one-page description of your life. Where do you live? Are you married? Do you have children? What talents and interests have you pursued? What kind of job do you have? Do you work for a small company, for a large company, or for yourself? Do you telecommute? Do you work by yourself or with others? Are you happy with your job? How much money do you make?

In The Know

chronological resume a traditional resume that provides a history of employment and education in reverse chronological order

electronic resume a resume that is posted on a web site or sent as part of an e-mail or as an attachment to an e-mail

letter of application a letter accompanying a resume; highlights major qualifications for a job

follow-up letter a letter thanking a prospective employer for an interview

functional resume a nontraditional resume organized according to the most important function or skill for the job

keywords important words, especially nouns, in a scannable resume that match the employer's list of key qualifications

online resume a type of electronic resume posted on a web site

parallel structure repeating the same grammatical structure of a phrase or sentence

priority order organized from most important to least important

resignation letter a letter written to an employer or a supervisor stating the writer's intention to resign or leave the company

resume a one- or two-page summary of job qualifications; uses elements of page design to highlight the most impressive qualifications

reverse chronological order organized backward through time

solicited letter a letter of application written for an advertised position

scannable resumes resumes written to be scanned for keywords by an optical scanner

unsolicited letter a letter of application written for an unadvertised position

text file an ASCII plain text file that can be opened by most word processing programs

Writing@Work

Melanie Beccaccio is a human resources manager for a financial services company. In her position, she supports employee selection and staffing, training and development, and employee relations. Melanie sees many types of employment communication in her job. Among them are letters of application, resumes, follow-up letters, and letters of resignation. She looks for all employment communications to contain concise information and correct grammar and spelling, which are essential in portraying a professional first impression.

For letters of application, Melanie recommends stating the employment objective in the first sentence. She suggests you summarize your qualifications that state your sincere interest and the personal characteristics that distinguish you. And she suggests you always indicate how and when you can be reached.

She looks for resumes to contain educational background, employment history, extracurricular activities, and special awards or honors. She says that including references is not necessary unless specifically requested. Making sure your resume is easy to read is also important. Try to keep resumes to one page if possible, be consistent in font and point size, and use bullet phrases rather than complete sentences.

Melanie believes that a separate hard-copy thank-you letter to each person who interviewed you is a nice gesture. "It shows effort, interest, and initiative!" She recommends commenting in your letter about something specific that made your interview experience memorable and suggests that you briefly restate why you are interested in and qualified for the job.

Letters of resignation should always be hard copy rather than e-mail. They should include the current date; your last day of employment (provide at least two weeks notice); your reasons for leaving; and a brief statement of thanks, indicating how you benefited from working there.

Melanie stresses the importance of clearly communicating on your resume and in an interview your skills and experience. "You must be completely honest and thorough when you complete an application, submit a resume, and participate in an interview." She explains that recruiting professionals can use sophisticated background and reference checks to verify information that you present. "Most companies will not offer employment to an individual who has been dishonest or misleading during the selection process."

Melanie has a bachelor's degree in business psychology from Miami University.

© 2005 Used with permission

Matthew R. Abboud
mabboud@mail.com

Temporary
803 Princeton Road
Albuquerque, New Mexico 87103
(505) 555-0173

Permanent
67B Lakeside Apartments
Albuquerque, New Mexico 87103
(505) 555-0172

OBJECTIVE   Computer programmer for a major manufacturer

QUALIFICATIONS
- 3 years' experience in networking and computer support
- A.A.S. degree in Computer Programming
- Experience in C++, SQL server, VB.NET, and Windows NT
- Proficient in all Microsoft Office (2000/XP) products

EDUCATION   **Maddox Community College, San Soma, New Mexico**
AAS, May 2004
Major: **Computer Programming**, GPA 3.9/4.0

Major Courses

Advanced C++	AdvancedVisual BASIC	Systems Analysis/Design
JAVA Programming	Database Concepts	Object Oriented Programming
Windows NT	Database Management	Technical Writing
UNIX/Lennox OS	Internet Programming	Interpersonal Communication

CO-OP EXPERIENCE   **Wadell Computer Industries**   **August 2002–Present**
Columbia, New Mexico
- Design and develop test specifications for software systems
- Evaluate existing computerized systems to improve efficiency
- Served on Quality Assurance Team within IT department

Xenox Computer Designs   **July 2001–May 2003**
Vales, New Mexico
- Set up and maintained clients using Windows™ NT
- Maintained SQL server database
- Answered Help Desk calls

OTHER   **Earned half of college expenses working part-time**   **1998–2001**
EXPERIENCE   Auto Express, Vales, New Mexico, Sales Clerk
AG Shirt Factory, Gabriel, New Mexico, Production Line Worker
Better Burgers, Vales, New Mexico, Cook and Sales Clerk

INTERESTS   Programming, sailing, photography

REFERENCES   Available Upon Request

Figure 10.1 Chronological Resume Model

JUANITA MANUEL
Route 5, Box 332
Charles, Ohio 26785

(414) 555-0195   jmanuel@mail.com

Objective

Part-time work as an administrative assistant in a business environment

Office Skills

- Experience with Microsoft Office
- Knowledge of office procedures
- Strong interpersonal skills
- Knowledge of accounting ledgers

Administrative Activities

MANUEL'S FLOWERS, July 2003–Present
Assisted with clerical duties in family-owned business

BETA CLUB TREASURER, October 2002–June 2003
Maintained account ledger, created annual budget, balanced budget, wrote checks

COCHAIRPERSON, JUNIOR MAGAZINE SALES, January 2002–March 2003
Directed sales staff, planned advertising campaign, sold magazines

Education

Wanoca High School, Charles, Ohio. Expected date of graduation, June 2005
Course of Study: Office Technology
Specialized Courses: Accounting, Office Management, and Word Processing

Interests

Writing, skiing, singing, playing the piano

References

Steve Pollock	Hilda Bracken	Greg Wilms
Business Teacher	Manager, Shoe Bargain	City Treasurer
342 Baily Road	8890 Yellowstone Street	89 Braxton Place
Charles, Ohio 26785	Farmville, Ohio 26798	Charles, Ohio 26785
(614) 555-0189	(614) 555-0187	(614) 555-0135

Figure 10.2 Functional Skills Resume Model

WHO READS EMPLOYMENT COMMUNICATION?

The job you seek may be the long-awaited dream job, a part-time job to help you through school, or a transitional job. Whatever the job, you will need employment communication that is both attractive and effective to highlight your strengths for the job market. You will use your technical writing skills to begin your job search. That is, you will first analyze your audience's needs and then persuade your audience that you can fulfill those needs.

Employment communication includes a **resume** (a one- or two-page summary of your qualifications), a **letter of application** (a letter to accompany the resume), a **follow-up letter** (a letter to thank the employer for an interview), and possibly a **resignation letter** (a letter to announce your intention to resign). Resumes and accompanying letters are important because:

- They make you look professional and ready to work.

- They allow you to control the presentation of your skills.

- They encourage an employer to call you promptly to arrange a time for an interview.

- They give employers something to look at before you fill out any applications they may require.

- They maintain goodwill between you and your employer after you leave a job.

To write the best employment communication possible, you must always understand your audience by considering the employer's perspective and expectations.

EMPLOYER'S PERSPECTIVE

Employers are looking for a good match. Generally, employers seek someone whose credentials meet their company's needs, whose personality fits with their current staff, and whose career plan complements their own. Prospective employers are interested in your work habits, skills, education, and experience.

Prospective employers also want to know whether you can get along with others, solve problems, and communicate. Most importantly, they want to know whether you have personal and professional integrity.

Your resume and letter of application show employers that you have the skills they need. At this stage, the resume and letter are the only means employers have of knowing who you are and what you can do for them.

If you have done a good job writing, you may be asked to meet face-to-face in a job interview. In the interview, you have an opportunity to persuade an employer that you are the candidate the company seeks. The goal, then, of a resume and letter of application is to create enough interest in you to be granted an interview. The goal of the interview is to persuade an employer to hire you.

Audience awareness is especially important in writing a resume and letter of application. Focusing on the reader of the resume may be difficult because the resume is primarily about the writer. Nonetheless, the reader is the one who hires, so the reader's needs are most important.

EMPLOYER'S EXPECTATIONS

Your prospective employer expects your communication to conform to standard employment protocol. Employment communication must:

1. Contain no errors. Resumes with misspellings, typos, nonstandard dialect, and punctuation errors are routinely cast aside during initial screenings.

2. Look neat and professional. For example, a resume corrected with correction fluid and strikeovers or one whose print is too light makes the writer look careless. To look professional, resumes should be printed in letter-quality print on bonded (heavy, stiff) paper.

3. Follow an accepted format. A resume that is too long, for example, or one printed on purple paper or written using an eccentric design looks as if the writer did not know how to properly format a resume.

4. Emphasize your best qualities (even if you think that you may be bragging).

Stop and Think

Why do employers discard some resumes intially? Why do employers read selected employment communication carefully?

Use the questions on the Find Out About Yourself worksheet and the Find Out About Your Employer worksheet on the Data CD to help you research the information you will use to write a resume and letter of application.

GETTING STARTED ON EMPLOYMENT COMMUNICATION

To get started on an employment package, find out about yourself, find out about your employer, and choose your references.

© GETTY IMAGES/PHOTODISC

FIND OUT ABOUT YOURSELF

Good employment communication begins with self-assessment. To get started on your employment package, think about your skills, aptitudes, goals, education, interests, and experience.

Write the answers to the following questions to assess your strengths as an employee. When you finish, highlight or circle the three most important things about your employable self.

- What are your special talents and skills?
- What kind of work do you think you have an aptitude for?
- Have you received any honors or awards? If so, what were they?
- Which of your accomplishments in the past two years might impress a prospective employer?
- What school and community activities do you participate in? In your activities, have you worked on committees or been responsible for certain projects? If so, what were they?
- What are your hobbies or interests?
- What is your GPA (Grade Point Average)?
- What special classes have prepared you for a particular job?
- What past jobs have you held? Write the dates for each job. Describe what you did in each job.

FIND OUT ABOUT YOUR EMPLOYER

In any persuasive communication, the better you know your audience, the better you can tailor your communication to its needs. To approach a prospective employer, you should learn all you can about this person, the organization, and the job. Call the human resources office and find out about the company's hiring practices. You also can get information on major American companies in *Hoover's 500: Profiles of America's Largest Business Enterprises.*

To continue researching information for your employment package, take notes by answering the following questions. Then highlight or circle what you think are the three most important pieces of information.

- Who will be responsible for making the decision to hire you, an individual or a committee?

- If an individual, what position does the individual hold? What does he or she expect from an employee?

- If the responsible party is a committee, who is on it? What are their positions? What do they expect from an employee?

- What is a typical interview like? Who conducts the interview? Will you be expected to take a test or perform a task as part of the interview?

- What can you find out about the company—its mission statement or philosophy, its current projects, its organization, its openings, or its past record?

- What can you find out about the specific position you would be applying for? What would you be expected to do, and with whom would you be working?

CHOOSE YOUR REFERENCES

A reference is a person who knows you well enough to vouch for your skills and your character. This person should feel comfortable making positive statements about your performance at work, giving examples of your accomplishments, and answering specific questions from a prospective employer.

Choose at least three people to include as references. Work references—people for whom you have actually worked—make the best references. After all, your employer is interested in knowing how well you perform on the job. Educational references, such as instructors, advisers, and guidance counselors, also can attest to your knowledge and reliability.

Before you list someone as a reference, ask the person if he or she will agree to be a reference for you. If this person hesitates or says no, ask someone else. Do not risk listing someone who may not be a strong advocate.

Stop and Think
List three people who might agree to be a reference for you. What do you think each person would say about you?

FORMATTING AND ORGANIZING RESUMES

Look at the Abboud and Manuel resumes at the beginning of this chapter for ten seconds and then look away. What do you remember from this ten-second glance? Look back at the resumes. To what three parts of each resume are your eyes drawn?

Complete the Chart for Analyzing Resumes worksheet on the Data CD.

Because employers may spend no more than 15 to 45 seconds looking at your resume during the initial screening, you must make the resume memorable. Here you have the opportunity to show off your skills with page design using special features, appropriate headings, and organizational schemes to make your resume look outstanding!

© GETTY IMAGES/PHOTODISC

MAKING YOUR RESUME STAND OUT

Designing a resume is like designing a newspaper ad. Have you ever noticed how some words in a newspaper ad jump out at you? They may be in bold type, for example, or bulleted to draw your attention. A newspaper ad is designed to create an immediate impression in a small space.

Like a newspaper ad, the resume must impress a reader in a short amount of space. After all, you are designing an ad and you are selling yourself, your skills, and your expertise to a prospective employer. You want your most impressive qualifications to jump out at the employer during his or her first ten-second glance at your resume. For a high school student or newly graduated college student, the resume should be only one page long. For people with several years of impressive work experience, a two-page resume is acceptable. Electronic resumes may be longer, for they are generally scanned by a computer program for the initial screening and not by a human being.

Part of the design strategy is to consider how the resume looks. It should look symmetrical and balanced. White space allowing ample margins results in a resume that is uncluttered and easy to read. Special features such as **boldfacing,** underlining, *italicizing,* CAPITALIZING, • bullets, or * asterisks make important information stand out. Headings should be easy to spot. Use an easy-to-read font (Times New Roman or Arial, for example) in 10- or

12-point type. Be careful, though: too many special features will make your resume look cluttered and busy. See Chapter 6, *Document Design and Graphics*, to review design elements.

ORGANIZING RESUMES

To organize text for your resume, follow this sequence:

1. Include all of the basic headings.

2. Decide which optional headings to include.

3. Highlight your strengths in either a chronological resume or a functional resume.

4. Use priority order (from most important to least important) and reverse chronological order (backward through time) to write sections.

DECIDING WHICH HEADINGS TO INCLUDE

Making decisions about which headings to include is like making decisions about your daily wardrobe. You must put on certain clothes—jeans, shirts, shoes, socks—whatever your basic wardrobe consists of. However, you can choose accessories, items such as jewelry, caps, scarves, and belts. The accessories help you express your individuality; they set you apart from others. Similarly, a resume must include the basic headings. Optional headings, like accessories, highlight your strengths and minimize your weaknesses.

Basic Headings Basic headings include your identification, education, employment experience, and references. Figure 10.3 illustrates what *must* and *may* be included under each basic heading.

	Must Include	May include
Identification*	Name, complete address, phone, and e-mail address	Permanent or temporary address
Education	Name, city, and state of school; dates of attendance and graduation or expected graduation; and major or course of study	List of courses, if helpful to employer; academic honors, if any; GPA, if good; and extracurricular activities
Experience	Name, city, and state of company; position or title; and description of duties, if related to job sought	Promotions and special accomplishments and description of duties, even if not related to job sought
References	One of these: References Available Upon Request; name, title, address, and phone number of three references	
*Identification is not a heading. It merely describes the information given at the top of the resume.		

Figure 10.3 Basic Headings

Optional Headings Optional headings let you show off your strengths and minimize your weaknesses. Many different optional headings appear on resumes, but some of the most popular headings are *Career Objective, Qualifications, Skills, Interests and Activities, Achievements and Honors,* and *Military Experience.*

Figure 10.4 suggests when to use these headings and when not to use these headings.

	Use if . . .	Do not use if . . .
Objective	You are applying for a specific job. The company prefers you to include an objective.	You are not applying for a specific job. The company prefers to decide in which position to place you.
Qualifications	You wish to summarize your strengths. You have the qualifications listed in the ad for employment. You have impressive technical skills.	You are not sure what skills the employer needs. You do not have special skills.
Interests and Activities	Your employer wants to know more personal information and qualifications. Your interests complement your qualifications. You want your employer to see you as well-rounded and human. You have space to fill on the page.	Your employer wants to know only about your work. You do not have space.
Achievements and Honors	You have honors and awards. You achieved other significant goals.	You do not have any honors or awards.
Military Experience	You gained military skills you want to highlight. You have impressive experience.	You have included military experience under another heading. You do not have military or ROTC training.

Figure 10.4 Optional Resume Headings

You may choose other names for some headings. Relate the name to the information you are giving. Here are a few variations:

Objective:	Job Objective, Career Objective, Professional Objective
Experience:	Work Experience, Related Experience, Co-op Experience
	You can divide Experience into two areas: Related Work Experience and Other Work Experience; Co-op Experience and Other Experience; Related Experience and Military Experience
Education:	Military School, Licenses, Certificates
Qualifications:	Major Qualifications, Summary, Skills
Interests:	Interests and Activities, Activities
Honors:	Honors and Achievements, Achievements, Awards

CHRONOLOGICAL RESUME

The **chronological resume** takes an employer backward in time through your educational and employment record. A chronological resume offers an approach that most employers recognize and accept. This resume:

- Provides a history of employment and education, regardless of the job.

- Accounts for every year out of school with no gaps in time.

- Tends to emphasize dates in resume design.

- Uses predictable, traditional headings.

- Places education and work experience early in the resume.

The chronological resume offers several advantages. First, it is familiar and readily accepted. Second, it can be read quickly. Third, it draws attention to a steady and impressive work history.

Even though the chronological resume is widely used, it is not ideal for everyone. First, a lengthy work history may make the resume too long. Second, the format is so structured that it may limit someone whose qualifications do not fit into its framework. For example, it may not be flexible enough for someone with little or no work experience. Third, it may be so similar to other resumes that it will not stand out. In other words, it may get lost in the "sameness" of other chronological resumes.

The Abboud resume at the beginning of this chapter is an example of a chronological resume. Abboud is applying for a job directly related to his degree. With only two years of related work experience, he believes his degree is his strongest asset and his related work experience (co-op) is his next strongest asset. He lists his other work experience last because it is not so impressive as his related work experience. The dates, separated from the main text of the resume, stand out. Notice that he does not describe this work experience because it is not as impressive as his co-op experience. Most of his employers will understand what these part-time jobs entailed and will note these only because he worked part-time to support himself in school.

SEE THE SITES

A good place to start your job search is to browse the *Occupational Outlook Handbook*. This handbook is published annually by the U.S. Department of Labor and can be found online. It gives information about the job outlook, salaries, and job conditions.

Monster.com is an interactive site that gives you resume advice and career tips. It also allows you to post an electronic resume and search thousands of job listings in a variety of fields. You can find the URL for both sites in the web links at techwriting. swlearning.com.

FUNCTIONAL RESUME

Resumes organized according to function or purpose are more flexible than chronological resumes. Tailored to suit the requirements of a particular job, a **functional resume:**

- Summarizes the most important qualifications for the job.

- May not account for every year out of school.

- Emphasizes skills, accomplishments, and job titles regardless of time frame.

- Uses less predictable, nontraditional headings designed for the job.

- May present education and work experience later in the resume.

The functional resume offers several advantages. First, it helps the employer judge what skills and accomplishments are useful for the job. Second, the functional resume can be used in a variety of circumstances. For example, functional resumes are useful when you have plenty of work experience and skills that would take up too much space on a chronological resume. On the other hand, functional resumes are also useful when you are applying for a job for which you have no formal education but for which you have marketable skills. For example, perhaps you have carpentry skills taught to you at home. Even though you do not have a degree, you still have the skills.

While the functional resume offers flexibility and a more original format, employers may want to discuss items such as "holes" in resumes (time lapses that are not explained). In a job interview, be prepared to account for such lapses.

Manuel's resume at the beginning of the chapter is a functional resume. Manuel's circumstances are different from Abboud's, and a functional resume meets her needs. Manuel is not applying for her first full-time job upon graduating from college; she is applying for her first part-time job while she is in high school. Because she does not yet have a degree, her job skills are more important than her education. She has no work experience, so she capitalizes on her club and community volunteer work to show she can handle office responsibilities.

ELECTRONIC RESUME

Technology is changing the way people look for and apply for jobs. Today the Internet and e-mail capabilities offer electronic ways to send and post resumes. An **electronic resume** may take one of the following forms:

E-mail resumes	Sent as an attachment to an e-mail or as part of an e-mail message
Scannable resumes	Sent as an attachment to an e-mail or part of an e-mail message and then scanned by the company
	Mailed and then scanned by the company
Online resumes	Posted on a company's or job search web site
	Posted on your own web site

E-mail Resume When sending an e-mail resume, you should, whenever possible, send it as an attachment that saves your formatting (boldfacing, bullets, italics, columns). Let your employer know what software program and version you used to create the document and ask whether another one is preferred. If the company to which you are applying has the same word processing program you used to create the resume, sending an attachment is the best option. There is little difference, then, in the actual appearance of an electronic resume and the traditional print resume. The only difference is how the resume is sent.

On the other hand, if the company does not have the same program you used to create the resume or if you are not sure about the program your employer uses, you will need to explore other options.

One option is to send the document as part of the e-mail message itself. In this case, the employer will receive the resume, but it may look jumbled when the e-mail is opened.

Another option is to attach the resume to the e-mail as a plain **text file** (ASCII) using the electronic format specified in Figure 10.5 on the next page. Most word processing programs allow the option of saving a document as a text (.txt) file. The advantage of a text file is that users can open it regardless of the word processing program they use.

For example, a resume written using an older version of WordPerfect® but saved as a text file should open on a personal computer that uses a current version of Microsoft® Word. By using the text file, you ensure that anyone can open your file. You can format to a limited degree, but you lose the attractiveness of your carefully designed print resume.

To key a resume that you intend to save as a text file, use the electronic formatting suggestions in the left column of Figure 10.5. You can read the rationale for each formatting suggestion in the right column.

Scannable Resume **Scannable resumes** are mailed as a print document, sent as an e-mail, or posted online to be scanned electronically for **keywords.** A keyword search compares qualifications on the resume to qualifications the employer needs and determines whether the resume has enough matches to warrant a closer reading. The second column in Figure 10.5 shows the similarities and differences between a scannable resume and a text file resume.

Online Resume An **online resume** is posted on a web site. Typically, it is one you create, one your company or school hosts, or one sponsored by a web-based job-hunting service such as Monster Board or CareerPath. Job-hunting services give instructions for posting resumes online at each of their sites.

Another option is to design your own web site from which you post your resume and set up links to your portfolio, references, or professional organizations. Be aware, however, that employers are not likely to seek your personal web site for initial screening. Send your resume—print, e-mail, or scannable—and note that you have a web site if the employer would like additional information.

Communication Update

Many people seeking a job post web sites that contain not only their resume, but also links to work samples. These web sites are sometimes known as electronic portfolios. With such a site, employers can quickly view your resume and work samples on their computers and do not need to wait for you to send them. Most word processing software allows you to create such portfolios easily by converting your text to HTML, a language used to create web pages.

ASCII Text File	Scannable Text	Rationale
Use plain fonts: a large, open, no "tails" font, such as Arial.	Use plain fonts: a large, open no "tails" font, such as Arial.	Text files will convert standard fonts. If either file is printed, it will be legible. Scanners cannot read small or fancy fonts.
Use 10- to 12-point font size.	Use 10- to 12-point font size.	If either file is printed, it will be legible. Scanners cannot read small fonts.
Use one column, flush with left margin; do not use side headings or tables.	Use one column, flush with left margin; do not use side headings or tables.	Text files do not always convert columns into a readable form. Scanners will not interpret columns in the correct order.
Use capital letters to signal heading titles and other important information.	Use capital letters to signal heading titles and other important information.	Both text files and scanners will interpret capital letters. Capital letters give you a way to set apart important information.
Use commas to indicate small breaks, semicolons to indicate breaks in a longer list, colons to set up a list, and periods to end sections.	Use commas to indicate small breaks, semicolons to indicate breaks in a longer list, colons to set up a list, and periods to end sections.	Both text files and scanners will interpret standard punctuation. Use as you would for more traditional resumes.
Use space bar instead of tab keys.	Use space bar instead of tab keys.	Both text files and scanners may have trouble interpreting a tab.
Avoid boldfacing, italics, or underlining.	May use boldfacing. Still avoid italics or underlining.	While the text file may have difficulty interpreting boldfacing, the scanner will not.
Save as plain text file (.txt).	Save as a word processing document unless in doubt about the employer's ability to open a file you are sending electronically.	Text files must be saved as a plain text file. Print documents for scanning will likely be mailed or posted on a company's web site.
Send with e-mail. Employer prints.	If you print, use dark black ink on white paper.	The scanner will read darker, larger print better than smaller, lighter print.
Send with e-mail. Employer can reset margins when printed.	Use wide margins, setting up lines with only 60 to 65 characters.	Scanners set to read only 60 to 65 characters will read your entire line and not "chop off" any words.
Send with e-mail. Employer prints.	If you print, do not staple or or fold pages.	Loose pages are easy to scan. Folded pages may cover up words, and the folds may be interpreted as a line.
Send with e-mail.	If you print, mail in a large envelope.	A large envelope will allow the resume to lie flat.

Figure 10.5 Electronic Formats

ORGANIZATIONAL STRATEGIES

Two organizational strategies govern the writing of all resumes: **priority order** and **reverse chronological order.**

Priority Order Major sections (except for *References*; they are placed last) are presented from most important to least important. Most important should be what is most important to your prospective employer. If you have impressive work experience, that work experience may be more important to your employer than education. If so, place work experience before education. If you are a recent graduate without much work experience, you may want to list education first as the most important qualification. A skills summary that provides an overview of your qualifications should be placed early in the resume. Employers quickly skimming your resume can focus on your major qualifications even if they do not read further. Within each section, lists of skills, duties, awards, and interests also are organized from most important to least important.

Reserve Chronological Order Some parts of the resume are presented in reverse chronological order (backward through time). The priority here is time: what is most recent is considered to be most important. In particular, past jobs and schools attended should be listed in reverse chronological order. For example, when presenting your work experience, list your most recent job first, your second most recent job second, your third most recent job third, etc.

Communication Dilemma

Tim, age 28, spent two years in the state penitentiary for shoplifting when he was 19 years old. Since that time, he attended classes, obtaining an associate degree in accounting, and spent three years in the U.S. Army. He now has a family and is an involved and respected member of his community.

Tim is applying for a job with D & J Accounting. The application asks if he has ever been convicted of a crime. Since his shoplifting offense, Tim has been a law-abiding citizen.

Should Tim tell about the shoplifting?

Stop and Think Which optional headings would you include in your resume? Compare the advantages and disadvantages of the chronological resume and the functional resume. Which type of resume will best meet your needs? Why will this type of resume best meet your needs?

Look closely at the wording of Abboud's resume and Manuel's resume. How would you describe the wording? Do the writers use fragments or clauses? How are the resumes punctuated?

Complete the Finding Famous Parallel Statements worksheet on the Data CD.

COMPOSING RESUMES

After you have analyzed your audience and assessed your strengths as an employee, you are ready to compose the parts of your resume. From the questions you answered about your employer and the employment self-assessment, review the six items you circled as being most important. Add one more item to the list: your name. Now that you know from this list what information to highlight, you are ready to compose your resume.

© GETTY IMAGES/PHOTODISC

WORD CHOICE

When writing a resume, you want to make sure you have presented information in as few words as possible and have placed information in an easy-to-read format.

The word choice in a resume is probably unlike anything you have written before. A resume has its own grammar rules: sentences and paragraphs are out. They take too long to read. Instead, resumes are written in lists using the following:

- nouns or nouns + descriptive phrases
- verbs + what phrases

When creating lists for resumes, use **parallel structure** (repeating the grammatical structure already in place). Parallel structure makes the resume straightforward and easy to read. For more information about parallel structure, see The Inside Track: Tech Writing Tips on Parallelism on page 382.

Nouns or Nouns + Descriptive Phrases For naming *Interests, Activities, Honors, Achievements, Awards,* etc., simple noun lists and nouns + descriptive phrases are most useful.

Some examples of nouns or nouns + descriptive phrases are:

Nouns	
Interests:	sailing, reading, programming, gardening (gerunds that name)
Activities:	aerobics, Girl Scout leader, Key Club member, choir member
Honors:	Chief Marshall, speech contest winner, Honor Society member or Who's Who, Honor Society, Quill and Scroll
Nouns + Descriptive phrases	
Skills:	Knowledge of both Windows and Macintosh environments Ability to program in a variety of languages including Lotus Notes, C++, and Java Experience installing and configuring networks

The structure of these lists is parallel because the listed items start the same way each time. Can you see that there is an understood "I have" before each item in the Skills section? ("I have" knowledge of _____).

Verbs + What Phrases *Verbs + What* phrases are quick, effective ways to describe skills, qualifications, and work experience. Use action verbs to stress what you can do for an employer. Performance is more impressive than qualifications. Notice that the phrases have an understood "I" or "I can" before each item ("I" troubleshoot; "I" program; "I" assemble). The greater the variety of verbs, the more dynamic and effective the resume is.

Skills: Troubleshoot hardware and software malfunctions

Program using ASP.NET

Assemble PCs including laptops, desktops, towers, and minitowers

Be sure that the lists are consistent in tense: present tense for jobs you currently hold and past tense for jobs you no longer hold. If you had (or have) a title, before your list of duties, include the title followed by a colon.

Present Tense Phrases to Describe Jobs You Currently Hold

encode data	install equipment	wait tables
provide child care	repair VCRs	take orders

Past Tense Verb Phrases for Jobs You No Longer Hold

sold merchandise	analyzed data	assisted customers
stocked groceries	filled reports	evaluated procedures

Be sure to view the many different resume samples on the Data CD.

Title before Verb Phrase

Cashier: operated register, greeted customers, and stocked shelves

Supervisor: supervised 15 workers, enforced safety measures, and handled payroll

Figure 10.6 shows other action verbs you may wish to consider.

accomplished	completed	earned	initiated	reduced
achieved	composed	established	led	revised
administered	contributed	evaluated	maintained	saved
analyzed	coordinated	expanded	operated	sold
applied	created	headed	organized	solved
assisted	designed	identified	performed	streamlined
built	developed	implemented	planned	supervised
communicated	devised	improved	produced	trained
compiled	directed	increased	promoted	wrote

Figure 10.6 Action Verbs

KEYWORDS FOR SCANNABLE RESUMES

When selecting keywords for a scannable resume, the rules of resume writing change. The print resume relies on verbs to demonstrate skills peformed. The scannable resume relies on nouns that list skills, qualifications, and job titles. It even includes a separate heading called KEYWORDS to list these credentials.

To help you name your abilities, complete this sentence: I am capable of ____. Job-related skills might include C + + programming, graphic design, marketing, statistical analysis, training, or database management. Other skills often sought include communication, problem solving, management, organization, or attention to detail. Job titles might include computer specialist, manager, supervisor, director, administrative assistant, chair, or facilitator. Special qualifications might include membership in professional organizations, licenses, certifications, degrees, or awards.

A machine can scan a three-page resume as quickly as a one-page, so when in doubt, include more information rather than less when preparing a scannable resume. Print resumes strive to save time for the reader by restricting length and using concise wording; scannable resumes are thorough.

Using several synonyms for one word increases the odds that your keywords will match your employer's keywords. For example, the words *graphic arts* and *graphic design* are synonyms for computer-aided design. Include all three terms if your resume will be scanned.

Focus on Ethics

Recently the city manager of a small town was fired because he listed a degree in city planning on his resume that he did not actually have. He was two classes short and decided that was as good as the degree—except that it was not. It was a lie.

Many people have skeletons in their closets: a court conviction, a substance abuse problem, or an unfinished degree. It is true that on paper, someone with a conviction does not look as good as the person with a sterling record. Someone without the proper degree does not look as good as the person with the degree. However, the truth is better than any lie conceived to cover up the "skeleton." If a person cannot be trusted to complete employment data honestly, then this person is not a good risk for a company.

The bottom line is this: falsifying employment data carries serious consequences, immediate termination, or prosecution. Some events in the distant past may have little bearing on the job hunt and need not be disclosed. However, if you are asked about something, *do not lie.*

Complete the Editing Faison's Resume worksheet on the Data CD to practice correct formatting.

PUNCTUATION

Since resumes do not contain complete sentences, applying traditional punctuation rules is hard. If one piece of information ends naturally on a single line, you may choose not to put an end mark there at all. For other marks of punctuation:

- Use periods to break up large blocks of thought or to indicate a change in information.
- Use colons to introduce lists.
- Use commas to separate simple lists of three or more items.
- Use semicolons to separate complex lists (lists that already contain commas) of three or more items.

Refer to the models in the chapter to see how these resumes are punctuated. Whatever system you adopt, use consistent punctuation throughout the resume.

Stop and Think

What will be the hardest part of writing a resume? Why? What action verbs can you use to make your own resume dynamic? How does the wording of an essay differ from the wording of a resume? How does a traditional print resume differ from a scannable resume? What are the advantages and disadvantages of the print resume? of the electronic resume?

WARM UP

Look closely at the letter of application in Figure 10.7 on page 260 that Abboud wrote to accompany his resume. How is this letter of application like a sales letter?

COMPOSING EMPLOYMENT LETTERS

Employment letters give you another opportunity to sell your skills. Unlike the resume, they are written in traditional paragraphs and complete sentences, so they also show the employer how well you express yourself. Three primary types of employment letters are letters of application that accompany the resume and highlight the applicant's strengths; follow-up letters that thank the employer for the interview; and in some cases, resignation letters that announce your decision to leave the company.

© GETTY IMAGES/PHOTODISC

LETTER OF APPLICATION

A letter of application is really a sales letter, a persuasive letter that sells you as the product or service. As you recall from Chapter 5, *Brief Correspondence,* sales letters are composed of three parts: the hook, the sell, and the motivation to action. Abboud's letter in Figure 10.7 on page 260 gets his reader's attention by expressing interest in the job opening. Then Abboud spends two paragraphs summarizing his strengths and explaining how these strengths make him a good match for Minelli Industries. In the last paragraph, Abboud motivates his employer to call him to arrange an interview.

Parts of a Letter A letter of application is composed of an opening (attention-getter or hook), a summary of qualifications (proof or sell), and a request for an interview (motivation to action).

> **Opening.** The first paragraph should get the reader's attention. It should:
>
> 1. State your interest in the job.
>
> 2. Explain how you found out about the job.
>
> 3. Quickly summarize your major qualifications for the job.

Some letters are **solicited;** that is, they are "asked for" or advertised. With solicited job openings, refer to the advertisement in the opening sentence: "I am uniquely qualified for the nursing position you advertised recently on the County Hospital's web page of job openings."

Sometimes, however, you may seek employment with a company that has not solicited or advertised a vacancy. Not all companies advertise their jobs, and you will not know whether there is an opening unless you ask. It is possible that your skills are in such demand that a company would create a position for you if employers knew you were available.

Writing an opening to an **unsolicited letter** is more of a challenge. You must generate interest immediately, or your letter may be discarded. Name-dropping may stimulate interest if the person whose name you are mentioning is a respected employee with some influence: *Julia Perea suggested I contact you about an opening in your radiology department.*

Sometimes a more dynamic opening that emphasizes your advantages to your reader is a better attention getter: *With degrees and certifications in medical sonography, radiography, echocardiography, and computed tomography/magnetic resonance imaging, think how valuable my services would be to a small rural hospital with a limited staff. My bedside manner is impressive, and I am available for employment.*

Summary of Qualifications. The second (and maybe third and fourth) paragraph justifies your claim that you can work for the company by proving your credentials. The letter is not meant to be a copy of the resume. It should highlight qualifications but not repeat the resume word for word. In the letter, you have the opportunity to add information about your character, your work habits, your people skills, and any other information you believe is relevant to the job. To provide specific proof that you can perform the job:

1. Describe your education.

2. Describe appropriate work experience.

3. Describe related skills.

4. Explain some of your abilities that you do not mention in the resume itself.

Request for Interview. The last paragraph in the letter of application motivates the reader to action by asking for an interview and making contact with you convenient. Be sure to:

1. Refer to the enclosed resume.

2. Ask for an interview.

3. Tell how and when you can be reached by including your phone number or e-mail address.

Figure 10.7 on the next page is an example of a letter of application that Abboud wrote to Dell Yamsung, personnel director at Minelli Electronic Industries, Inc.

Practice varying your sentence structure by completing the Editing Kyle's Letter worksheet on the Data CD.

803 Princeton Road
Albuquerque, New Mexico 87103
15 June 20—

Dell Yamsung, Personnel Director
Minelli Electronic Industries, Inc.
3902 West Broad Street
Charleston, Arkansas 72203

Dear Mr. Yamsung:

My education and work experience qualify me for the position of computer programmer you advertised in the *Daily Register* last week. Because of my interest in Minelli Industries and my desire to relocate to Arkansas, I would like to be considered for this position.

I earned an associate's degree in Applied Science in Computer Programming from Maddox Community College. At Maddox's UNIX-based computing lab, I learned to program in HTML, Visual BASIC, and C++ languages. In addition, I gained valuable experience in Microsoft Office (2000/XP) as many of our class assignments were completed using an application in the Office suite. My instructors praised the detail with which I wrote programming specifications. Maddox's up-to-date facility has given me the knowledge and confidence I need to adapt to any computer environment.

In addition to my education, I have experience meeting the computing needs of business and industry. At Wadell Computer Industries, I used C++ and Visual BASIC.NET to design and develop test specifications for their software systems. Just before I graduated, I served on a quality assurance team to set up help desk protocols and improve user satisfaction. At Xenox Computer Designs, I installed and configured operating systems including Windows NT, Windows 2000, and Windows XP/Professional. Other responsibilities included maintaining an SQL server database and taking turns at the help desk. My supervisor at Xenox gave me superior evaluations, ranking me high in problem-solving skills and the ability to work with people.

My resume is enclosed for your consideration. I would be happy to schedule an interview to discuss my qualifications. You may reach me at (501) 555-0172 after 3:00 p.m or e-mail me at mabboud@mail.com.

Sincerely,

Matthew Abboud

Matthew Abboud

Enclosure

Figure 10.7 Letter of Application

Sentence Structure When composing your letter of application, vary your sentence structure. Although it is easy to begin every sentence with *I* when writing about yourself, try to begin some sentences with words other than *I*. To achieve variety, consider beginning sentences with prepositional phrases, introductory clauses, and transitional words. See Abboud's letter to observe how he achieved sentence variety.

FOLLOW-UP LETTER

A follow-up letter, sometimes known as a thank-you letter, is sent immediately after you have participated in a job interview. The follow-up letter should:

1. Thank the employer for the interview.

2. Remind the employer of something positive said or done during the interview.

3. Explain why you are the best candidate for the job.

4. Express continuing interest in the job.

Sending a follow-up letter lets employers know you are still interested. They also are encouraged to remember something specific about you. Figure 10.8 shows a follow-up letter that Abboud wrote to Mr. Yamsung after his interview.

803 Princeton Road
Albuquerque, NM 87103
29 June 20–

Dell Yamsung, Personnel Director
Minelli Electronic Industries, Inc.
3902 West Broad Street
Charles, AR 72203

Dear Mr. Yamsung:

Thank you for considering me for the position of computer programmer with your company. I enjoyed touring your facility and discussing ways to improve the SQL server database. As you may remember, I have had two years' experience with installing and configuring operating systems, in particular with Windows NT. I would welcome the opportunity to put my knowledge to work for your company. My desire is to return to my home in Arkansas, and I am very willing to relocate to any of your subsidiaries in the state.

I look forward to hearing from you soon. If you have additional questions about my qualifications, please call me at (501) 555-0172, or e-mail me at mabboud@mail.com.

Sincerely,

Matthew Abboud

Matthew Abboud

Figure 10.8 Follow-up Letter

RESIGNATION LETTER

People change jobs for many reasons: the relocation of a spouse, a higher-paying job, dissatisfaction with a current job, or a career change. Whatever the reason, writing a letter of resignation to inform your current employer of your plans is professional courtesy.

Keep in mind that your former employer will probably be contacted for a job reference. A well-written letter of resignation that gives reasonable notice helps maintain goodwill with your current employer. Later, when asked to provide a reference for you, he or she will likely say positive things about you. To maintain the goodwill of a former employer, your letter of resignation should:

■ Address the letter to the proper person. Find out the expected protocol (company procedure) and chain of command. Normally you would write the letter to your immediate supervisor, who would, in turn, pass the letter up the chain of command. In a small work unit made up of people with whom you work closely, use the supervisor's first name, as you would in memos. In larger work units with a more formal structure, use the supervisor's last name.

■ Announce your intention to leave the company. Be clear that you are writing a letter of resignation.

■ State the last day you will work. Be sure that date provides adequate notice, or more if possible, according to company policy and your knowledge of company operations. The more time you give, the more time an employer has to make decisions about hiring a replacement or redistributing your responsibilities.

■ Use courteous language. Use your manners (*please, thank you*) and qualifying words (*might, probably, most likely, seems*) if necessary.

■ Compliment your employer and the company. Thank your supervisor for any opportunities or special help provided. If you are leaving because you are dissatisfied with the work environment, you can find something positive to say about the organization, even if it is short.

■ Offer to help the company prepare for your absence. Your company is accustomed to depending on you to discharge certain responsibilities. How can you help minimize any stress or confusion created by your leaving? You can offer to train your replacement or complete work projects ahead of time.

■ Volunteer a reason for leaving only if you feel comfortable stating it. Your employer may be interested in your plans, and you may wish to share them. Sometimes, though, the employer-employee relationship is strained. In such cases, you may leave out the reason or provide a simple one, such as the desire to pursue other interests. When there is a real problem at work, such as sexual harassment or discrimination, you need to think carefully about explaining the reason.

■ Close by saying something positive. Thank your employer once more or say something positive about your upcoming plans.

Marlene wrote the letter in Figure 10.9 to Roger Staton, the director of Charter Disability Services, resigning the position that she has held for nine years. Marlene has enjoyed a close working relationship with her supervisor.

1080 Oak Trace Road
Atlanta, GA 78214
30 November 20–

Roger Staton, Director
Charter Disability Services
503 North Chester Street
Atlanta, GA 78214

Dear Roger:

Please accept this letter of resignation, effective two months from now. January 30, 20– will officially be my last day as interpreter for the Hearing Impaired for Charter Disability Services. My husband has accepted an administrative position at Dare Regional Hospital in Clements, Virginia. After much discussion, we believe it is in our best interest to move to his job location.

I have enjoyed nine years working as lead interpreter. Your guidance, in particular, has enabled me to learn new skills and grow professionally. I am proud to have been a part of the Charter team and to have contributed to its fine work as an advocate for disability services.

Before I leave, I will complete the annual evaluations of my clients. Furthermore, I will be happy to spend my last week training my replacement. After I leave, I will be available by phone to answer any questions.

Again, thank you for the opportunity to work for Charter Disability Services. My husband and I will miss you and the staff, but we look forward to new opportunities in Virginia.

Sincerely,

Marlene Meyers

Marlene Meyers

Figure 10.9 Letter of Resignation

Stop and Think

What is the purpose of a letter of application and a follow-up letter? Why should you give as much notice as possible in a letter of resignation?

Chapter 10 Review

POINT YOUR BROWSER

techwriting.swlearning.com

SUMMARY

1. After initial screening, prospective employers read employment communication carefully, so writers should write and design effective employment communication.

2. Before you can write a resume and letter of application, you should find out information about your employer, assess your strengths as an employee, and choose your references.

3. For a resume to stand out, it should look symmetrical, include ample white space, and use an easy-to-read font. Special features, such as boldfacing and bulleted lists, make important information stand out.

4. Basic headings include Identification (applicant's name, address, telephone, and e-mail address), Education, Experience, and References. Other headings are optional, used to enhance your resume.

5. Resumes generally fall into three types: 1) chronological resumes, 2) functional resumes, and 3) electronic resumes.

6. Resumes use one of two organizational strategies: priority order and reverse chronological order.

7. Resumes are written using phrases and lists in parallel structure. Sentences and paragraphs are not used because they take too long to read.

8. Applicants may write three kinds of employment letters: letters of application, follow-up letters, and resignation letters.

Checklist

- Are all documents (resume, letter of application, and follow-up letter) free from grammar, spelling, and punctuation errors? Remember, there should be *no errors* in employment communication.

- Are all documents reader-centered rather than writer-centered?

- Have I addressed the qualifications for the job (either the qualifications listed in an employment ad or the qualifications I think the job requires)?

- Have I chosen the most effective resume for my situation: chronological, functional, or electronic?

- Is my writing organized to reflect my strengths?

- Does my first sentence in my letter of application grab the reader's attention?

- Have I explained in my letter of application how I possess the skills necessary for the job, referring in particular to any skills mentioned in the ad or job description?

- Did I give enough information so that I could be reached easily?

- Is the tone in my letter of application and follow-up letter positive and polite?

- Have I addressed my communication to the proper person in an acceptable way?

- Have I complimented the supervisor and the company in my letter of resignation?

Build On What You Know

1. Important information is left out of each of the following resume excerpts. What is left out?

   A. Address
   Kareem S. Saleeby
   589 Mohican Avenue
   St Thomas, FL

   B. Reference
   Haley VanStaldinuin
   New Dresden, NY
   (518) 555-0124

   C. Experience
   Neuse Sport Shop, Carnival, NM
   * Assisted customers on the floor
   * Operated cash register
   * Stocked shelves

   D. Education
   Danville Technical and
   Vocational College
   Associate in Applied Science
   GPA: 3.5/4.0

2. Here is an ad for an administrative assistant followed by an excerpt from a letter of application for this position. Decide whether the excerpt addresses every qualification in the ad. What, if anything, is left out?

ADMINISTRATIVE ASSISTANT

High-energy, detail-oriented team player for our Greenville office to learn many office responsibilities. Prefer knowledge of Microsoft Office. Send resume to . . .

As a graduate of Montclair Technical Institute, I have gained skills in word processing. In particular, I have worked extensively with all aspects of Microsoft® Office.

I also am familiar with the most up-to-date office management systems. A part-time job with Apex Industries gave me the opportunity to work in an office with an extremely efficient office manager. From the office manager, I learned important tips about filing, turning out timely correspondence, and scheduling appointments.

3. Make parallel the following descriptions for music director: Music Director: I selected music for weekly performances for the choir. Also, I ordered music from companies. When there was a special occasion, I put together a cantata of musical selections. The organ and piano—I played them, too, and sometimes handbells. Oh, and I sang for weddings.

4. The following sentences from letters of application are not specific enough by themselves. They do not provide the details that prove the skill or qualification listed. What kind of information should be added?

   a. I have educational experience with personal computers and basic programming.

   b. I have worked in my family's construction business for the past seven years, so I have extensive knowledge of how a building should be put together. I have worked on every phase of a job.

   c. I am a 20— graduate of Vancouver Community College with an associate degree in medical office technology. Throughout my college career, I gained many skills.

Apply What You Learned

5. Beaumont has listed the following seven people as possible references on his worksheet. Look at the descriptions and help Beaumont decide which references to include and exclude on a resume for a construction job.

- Joe Garriet: Beaumont's high school drafting teacher

- Rosie Montero: Beaumont's neighbor, high school secretary

- Dr. Gretchen Wiggins: head of local Habitat for Humanity for which Beaumont has volunteered (Habitat for Humanity helps build and finance houses for people who could not otherwise afford them.)

- Rochelle Currier: neighbor, architect in local firm, supervised a high school construction project that Beaumont worked on

- Roy Deleon: manager of a building supplies store, has sold supplies to Beaumont

- Meredith McDougan: Beaumont's 12th-grade English teacher

- Chevron Johnson: Beaumont's uncle

6. Write a letter of resignation (to Harold Schumaster, state Democratic chair) for Sophie Benet who is resigning as the Democratic Party chair for her region. She has been chair for one year. Sophie has just found out she can no longer devote time to the political cause. As chair for one year, she organized campaign assistance for local democratic representatives and attended the state Democratic convention. She plans to order materials for the next rally and will set up the booth at the Fall Festival. Her last day as chair will be October 14, a week after Fall Festival. The calendar of events has not yet been determined, but she has ideas for next year and contact numbers that she will be glad to share with the new chair. Sophie has met many interesting people and helped elect two Democratic representatives to the state house and three Democratic city council members. She describes her experiences as "fun" and "fulfilling." She is grateful to Harold, who showed her the ropes and gave her advice during her year as chair.

7. Pretend it is three to five years from now. You just completed the degree you have always wanted, with an impressive GPA. Make up a resume and a letter of application to help you get your dream job.

8. Write a resume for yourself for a job in your area. Use Manuel's resume as a model. Write a letter of application to accompany it.

9. Rewrite the resume you wrote for item 7 or 8 as an electronic resume. Choose between a text file resume or a scannable resume.

10. Write a resume for an adult friend or a relative (any adult who has been in the work force for five years or more). Using the questions in the Getting Started on Employment Communication section, take notes for the resume. Decide whether this adult needs a chronological resume or a functional resume. Ask the adult to supply you with a job objective and a description of a job he or she would like to have. Write a letter of application to accompany the resume.

Work Is A Zoo!

WORK IS A ZOO
In addition to researching the marketing field, research jobs at a zoo to learn what specific knowledge and experience is required. If you can, talk to someone who works at a zoo to learn more. Use the worksheet on the Data CD to help you write your letter of application.

You have decided to apply for an associate marketing position at the zoo. Even though you are already working at the zoo, you must go through the application process again. Because the job is important to you, you want to spend plenty of time getting the process right. You know that several other candidates are being considered, and you need to keep your options open in case the new position falls through.

In addition, you need to be prepared to discuss salary and job expectations if you are offered the position. Your Uncle Mark is a marketer with a publishing company in New York City, and you know he is respected in the field. But you aren't as familiar with career opportunities in the marketing field as you'd like to be. You decide to spend a little time getting familiar with the industry.

Do some research in the marketing field using publications, the Internet, and personal contacts. Do a web search for "marketing." Other key words might be "careers," "public relations," or "marketing salaries." Numerous publications provide business and industry information. For example, the Department of Labor publishes the Occupational Outlook Handbook. Another source might be the Occupational Outlook Quarterly, which includes up-to-date information about employment trends, new occupations, and employment outlook. Check your library and the Internet for these sources.

You updated your resume to include your current position at the zoo. You also added Anya as a reference. Now it is time to write the letter of application.

Remember, letters of application usually include comments about:

- The job you are applying for.

- Your familiarity with the type of job.

- Your attached resume.

- The best way to contact you.

Write a letter of application to the head of the zoo's marketing department, Nedra Kaplan. Remember to state why you are interested in the job and what you think you bring to the job. Is your current experience an asset? What has your current experience taught you?

ORAL PRESENTATIONS

GOALS

LEARN to plan for your audience, your topic, and stage fright

DETERMINE how to organize and compose presentations

PREPARE note cards and graphic aids

REHEARSE for a presentation and PRESENT with confidence

ORGANIZE a group presentation

See the Data CD for Write-to-Learn and In The Know activity worksheets.

WRITE-TO-LEARN

Recall speakers whose performance you have enjoyed. For instance, you may have an instructor who holds your attention from the moment you sit down until the end of class. Perhaps you appreciated a speaker you heard at a club meeting or special event. Consider what makes these speakers effective communicators. List the qualities and actions you think help these speakers effectively reach their audiences. Your list might include:

- Opening with a good joke.
- Using language you can understand.
- Walking through the audience.

In The Know

adrenaline a stimulant, something that excites and creates extra energy

anecdote a short narrative

auditory relating to the sense of hearing or perceived through the sense of hearing

direct approach a presentation strategy in which you state the main idea first and then explain and support that idea with details

external audience listeners outside an organization

feedback the verbal and nonverbal response to a communication process or product

indirect approach a presentation strategy in which the main idea is not presented up front; you build evidence to convince the audience of your point

internal audience listeners within an organization

preview statements an overview of the order of ideas in a presentation

rhetorical question a question designed to provoke thought; a question for which the speaker expects no answer

sans serif type faces without cross strokes on the tops and bottoms of letters, such as Arial

serif type faces with cross strokes on the tops and bottoms of letters, such as Times New Roman

stage fright anxiety or fear experienced when a person speaks to or performs for an audience

Writing@Work

Denny Kramer is a relationship manager at a large financial services company in Covington, Kentucky. In his position, he helps companies set up and administer retirement plans. He also maintains and upgrades these plans.

Denny often meets with current and prospective clients and those who may take their business elsewhere. He presents information about the products and services his company offers and the fees for these services. He answers questions about setting up, maintaining, and upgrading retirement plans.

Denny says: "Winging a presentation does not work. Inevitably you are asked a question that you should have been ready for, but were not." Preparation is the key to a productive, informative presentation. An important part of preparation is learning about your audience. In Denny's case, the president of the company may have different concerns from other members of the audience. Knowing all these concerns is helpful. Denny offers these tips: Do not go in blind; do research ahead of time; and consider any possible issues your audience might have and how they might react.

Many people find that using notes refreshes their memory when making presentations. Denny suggests including only key words or phrases so you are not tempted to read. Another suggestion that Denny offers is to videotape your presentation before you give it. "It helps," he says, "to then watch the presentation with the sound off, listen to the presentation with the video turned off, and then watch and listen to the video. This technique will help you evaluate your body language and hear any unnecessary pauses or extra words."

When you present to an audience, keep in mind several key factors. A good start is to summarize your agenda. Making eye contact with members of your audience is important. Paraphrasing questions from the audience to make sure you have understood them correctly is also a good idea. If appropriate, put humor in your presentation–the more conversational your presentation, the more likely you are to hold the audience's attention. Denny suggests checking periodically to make sure no one has any questions. "I always try to resolve issues that I am aware of up front. That way, I feel more confident that the audience will be paying attention to the rest of the presentation."

Denny has a bachelor's degree in management from Xavier University. He has been in his current position for six years. Prior to this job, Denny worked in several positions at two different banking institutions.

© 2005 Used with permission

Sales by Division, 2004

- **Internet sales**
  - Consistent for year
  - Each quarter high

- **Catalog sales**
  - Holiday season high
  - Other quarters weak

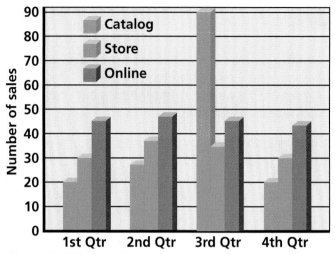

Figure 11.1 Sample Graphic Aid for Oral Presentations

PLANNING

You have many opportunities to speak before groups in business, industry, and school. The success with which you handle oral reporting may determine your success in your profession. You might have the best new product idea your company will ever see. For your idea to become a reality, however, you must effectively communicate it to the management team and convince them to try the product. This chapter tells you how to effectively plan, organize, compose, prepare, rehearse, and present oral reports.

WARM UP

Think about your public speaking experiences. Perhaps you have given a report in class or led a club meeting. If you have not had many speaking opportunities, imagine what the experience would be like. List things you like and dislike about public speaking and share your list with the class.

The higher up the corporate ladder you move, the more you will give oral presentations. The audience, formality, and purpose may vary. For instance, you will give some presentations to **internal audiences,** perhaps above or below you in the organizational hierarchy—or both. You will give some presentations to **external audiences,** such as suppliers, vendors, or customers. Some oral presentations will be as informal as an impromptu gathering where you answer questions. Others will be elaborate, carefully prepared sessions.

The purpose of some oral reports will be to inform; others will be designed to persuade, such as a sales presentation; others will be designed to inform *and* persuade. During the course of your career, you may be asked to propose solutions to problems; outline the results of investigations; announce new policies or procedures; report on the progress of a project; sell an idea, a product, or a service; represent your organization at a conference or community group; or train personnel.

The planning stage is an important part of creating presentations. This is the stage in which you begin to work on audience analysis, a topic, and **stage fright.**

SEE THE SITES

The Internet offers many sites related to effective oral presentations. To start your search, check out the Powerful Presentations web site, which includes tips from dressing for a presentation to making impromptu speeches.

The Executive Speaker web site contains 117 tips for better presentations. These tips include how to control nervousness and advice from professional speakers.

You can find the URL for both sites in the web links at techwriting. swlearning.com.

AUDIENCE

Analyzing your audience is as important in an oral report as it is in a written report. You need to know how your audience feels about your topic. Start by referring to the audience analysis questions in Chapter 2, *Plan for Your Audience and Purpose.* For most presentations, you will probably use the direct approach. With the **direct approach,** you state the main idea first and then explain and support that idea with details. Stating the main idea first lets your listeners know what subject you will address, what points you will make, and how you will proceed.

If, on the other hand, you realize that your audience opposes the point you support or you want to be especially persuasive, you should consider an indirect presentation. With an **indirect approach,** you can build your evidence, convincing the audience of your point.

TOPIC AND MESSAGE

Sometimes speakers are able to choose their own topics. However, when asked to speak at work (and in school), you often will be assigned a topic. Frequently in business, managers ask employees to prepare a written document, such as a report on progress, a solution to a problem, or a report on an incident. After submitting the written report, the employee may be asked to make an oral presentation of the same information. For instance, Edith Frost, a machinist at Tarboro Machine Corporation, wrote a report that suggested three new safety measures for all machine operators. The report was submitted to the plant safety officer, the president and vice president, and all division heads. Frost's supervisor then asked her to present her plan orally at the next managers' meeting.

STAGE FRIGHT

You may think it odd that a textbook tells you to plan for stage fright when most people want to avoid it. Yet stage fright is not something to eliminate; it is energy you should use. Many professional speakers will tell you that you cannot eliminate nervous reactions when speaking, even if you want to. Those reactions, they say, are natural responses to stress. So instead of trying to suppress stage fright, let it work for you. To harness this energy, you should:

- Note how your body responds to anxiety.

- Expect and plan for these reactions.

- Use excess **adrenaline** and energy to give your introduction and important points extra emphasis.

Stop and Think Would an audience of your classmates be more interested in how school policy affects taxpayers or how school policy affects students?

ORGANIZING AND COMPOSING

When you are presenting, listeners cannot refer to a previous page when ideas are unclear or confusing. So you should organize and compose your oral presentations for the listeners' situation and needs.

WARM UP

Think of messages you have prepared for oral delivery, such as planning to ask someone for a date or a favor. Compare oral composing with written composing. Note differences and similarities in a brief journal entry.

PREVIEWING ORGANIZATION

Regardless of the organizational strategy you use, give the audience a preview so they know what plan you are following. The preview is like a map that shows a driver where to turn and how far to go. Your preview explains the order of your ideas. Here are two examples of typical **preview statements:** "This recommendation contains four major parts: review, staffing, operational policy, and production." or "The standard operating procedure for student interns involves completing treatment plans, writing instruction memos, and recording patient progress."

COMPOSING THE INTRODUCTION

Listeners recall the first and last points they hear. Therefore, plan for a strong introduction and conclusion. If you are uncertain how to introduce your presentation, think as your audience might. What would get your attention? You would want to know the topic; the points the speaker will support; and how this issue affects you, the listener. Your introduction should announce your topic and the points you will make. In addition, you should give the listeners something to which they can relate, some connection. For example, an address by a young woman to her small town's board of commissioners began this way: "My friend Miguel died last month. He should not have been in the path of a car going 45 miles per hour, nor should any of your children, grandchildren, or neighbors. Our town must protect its citizens by providing bicycle paths and enforcing the helmet laws."

Depending on your audience and purpose, try one of several introductions. Some openings include using:

- A direct quotation (usually from a well-known source).
- A **rhetorical question.**
- A startling fact or statistic (that would grab a listener's attention).
- A statement you then disprove.
- An **anecdote** or a humorous story.

For example, if you were making a class presentation on the advantages of modern medicine, you might begin this way:

> If you were born in the United States in 1990, at the time of your birth you had a life expectancy of 75.4 years. On the other hand, people born in 1970 were expected to live only 70.8 years. According to these statistics, you will outlive your mother and father by 4.6 years. (United States: National Center for Health Statistics)

The startling fact that the audience's generation is expected to live 4.6 years longer than their parents' should grab the listeners' attention, especially since these statistics relate to the audience's own mortality.

COMPOSING THE BODY

These guidelines will help you compose the body of an oral presentation:

- Address people. Remember that your audience is made up of people much like yourself. Include the words *you* and *your* early and often.
- Use words your audience will know. Define unfamiliar terms.
- Use simpler sentences than when writing. You should not have to say so many words that you cannot catch your breath.
- Give your audience the information they want or need. Explain to listeners how your information impacts them; make it relevant. Remember, it is as easy to ramble in speaking as it is in freewriting, so avoid that pitfall.
- Emphasize main points and make transitions from one point to the next. Since listeners take in only a small percent of what they hear, emphasize the essential ideas. Repeat or restate main points. Announce transitions so the audience will not miss the connection, as if you are saying to the listener, "Now we are leaving the discussion of Point A to move on to Point B. Follow me."
- Consider questions your audience is likely to ask and include those answers in your presentation.
- Plan for a time limit. Determine what your audience expects and frame your report for that time—or less.

Focus on Ethics

You live in an age when a lot of business is conducted globally. That means at some point in your career, you may have an opportunity to attend a meeting in Japan, give a presentation in Australia, or create and present a training course via videoconferencing in Brazil.

Because business is increasingly being conducted globally, knowing the proper method for presentations across cultures is extremely important. Beginning with the presentation planning stage, you must be aware of how cultural practices and expectations of your audience are different from your own. You must research the audience's culture and plan for differences to ensure a well-received presentation.

For example, while presenting to an international audience, you should be aware of gestures that are not universal. In Greece, nodding your head means "no," not "yes." In Australia, a "thumbs up" gesture is considered inappropriate.

You also should research the formality of the culture. Jokes are not appropriate for some audiences. Dressing too formally makes other audiences uncomfortable.

No matter what cultural differences you face, the most effective rule to remember is to respect those differences.

COMPOSING THE CONCLUSION

Conclusions are important because they are the last point or topic the audience will hear; therefore, they require as much planning as introductions. An effective conclusion should hold the audience's attention, summarize the key points, and call for action if requested.

Stop and Think

John wants to persuade his parents, who do not let him drive long distances alone, to let him drive 55 miles to the basketball tournament. Ideas he plans to share with his parents are (a) driving is the least expensive and safest way to get to the tournament, (b) John has behaved responsibly when given other opportunities, and (c) the bus does not go to this location and cab fare would be three times more than the cost of driving. Place these ideas in the most effective order for John to present to his parents.

PREPARING

After you complete the planning process, you need to prepare notes, graphic aids, and your own image. These preparations will help you effectively deliver your presentation. Your risks are huge if you neglect preparation. Without notes, you are left with your memory, which sometimes fails, especially in stressful situations. Without graphic aids to clarify and enhance your words, listeners may wear puzzled frowns, adding to your stress level. And without personal preparation, you may become preoccupied with your clothing or hair, feeling greater frustration and losing even more ground with the audience.

© GETTY IMAGES/PHOTODISC

OUTLINES AND NOTES

A practiced performance using an outline or notes yields an informal, conversational style. Speakers may either generate an outline using presentation graphics software, such as Microsoft® PowerPoint®, or develop an outline independently. By using an outline or notes written on index cards or sheets of paper, you will be able to talk to your audience rather than read to them.

Before you reach this point in the process, you must organize your ideas in the most effective manner. If you were writing a report, your next step would be to compose sentences, build paragraphs, and create a document. For an oral presentation, however, you should avoid extended writing. A complete paper with long sentences and dense paragraphs might encourage you to read the text, rather than interact with your audience, when you are under pressure. On the other hand, fearing you might lose your place in all of that text, you might avoid the text entirely and try to speak without any assistance.

An outline or notes should show each main point in your presentation. Under each main point, list any facts, figures, or quotations that support that point. For example, the outline below shows one section of an oral report on progress toward upgrading computers in a warehouse:

III. Shipping and Receiving

    Area 1

        4 installations

        Problems with location of wiring, Module MJD364

    Area 2

        Work completed; 3 installations

        Approval of supervisor

    Level 3

        Work incomplete; 1 installation

        Relocation of shelving unit, Module SDP21

        Network concern

        Scheduled 9 December 20–

For precision and accuracy, do not trust your memory for such specific information, especially when your adrenaline surges in front of an audience.

For the first point of an outline or note card, write a word or a phrase that will trigger your memory for this opening point. Then go on to each idea, example, and illustration in your speech.

For each idea, prepare a point in an outline or on a note card similar to the one in Figure 11.2. This sample card reminds the speaker that this section of the talk is about tsunamis, the giant, destructive waves that sometimes strike Hawaii and Japan.

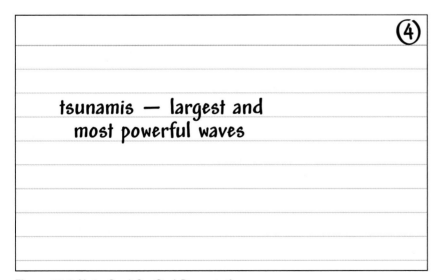

Figure 11.2 Note Card for Oral Presentation

If you are developing computer slides for your presentation, most software packages will allow you to add notes that reinforce the logical flow of the discussion and highlight content details, such as statistics, quotations, and important facts. For instance, PowerPoint® allows you to print handouts with two, three, four, six, or nine slides per page, most of which have space for notes.

Figure 11.3 shows such a PowerPoint® handout you can use to either write notes for yourself or pass out to the audience so they can write notes as you talk.

What do you expect from a career?

- Income?
- Reputation or fame?
- Creativity?
- Geographic location?

- Service to others?
- Title and position?
- Balance in your life?
- Use of your strengths?

SLIDE 4   © SOUTH-WESTERN PUBLISHING

What do your peers expect?

- One in three intends to have a professional career.
- Nearly 10 percent plan to be doctors.
- Few dream about blue-collar or service industry jobs.
- Almost all expect to have a high-status job with high pay.
- Many expect to graduate with a bachelor's degree.
- Many think a bachelor's degree is a vital success tool.
- A large majority expect to earn a PhD.

SLIDE 5   © SOUTH-WESTERN PUBLISHING

What is reality?

Student choices:
- Marine biologist
- Physical therapist
- Doctor
- Lawyer
- Teacher

Fast-growing occupations
- Computer engineer
- Computer support specialist
- Systems analyst
- Database manager
- Desktop publishing specialist
- Paralegal and legal assistant
- Personal care and home health aide
- Medical assistant
- Social and human services assistant
- Physician assistant

SLIDE 6   © SOUTH-WESTERN PUBLISHING

From Pkg:Discovering Your Career, SE/CD 1st edition by Jordan/Whaley. © 2003. Reprinted with permission of South-Western, a division of Thomson Learning: www.thomsonrights.com. Fax 800 730-2215.

Figure 11.3 PowerPoint® Handout with Space for Notes

When preparing outlines or notes, remember these important points:

- Do not write notes as complete sentences, long phrases, or clauses. Even experienced speakers would be tempted to read if the card contained long clauses or sentences.

- Prepare neat notes that are surrounded by adequate white space so you can read them easily.

- Structure notes uniformly: numbered lists, bulleted lists, outline form.

- If you are using cards, write only one idea on each note card; if you are using printed notes or outlines, use a large, easy-to-read **serif** font. Also, print on paper that will allow you to turn pages smoothly without distracting the audience.

- Number notes or cards from beginning to end. On note cards, place the card number in the upper right corner and circle the number, as in Figure 11.2. Should your cards become disorganized, the numbers will help you sort them quickly.

- Use outlines and notes to spark your memory. Glancing at the words, you should be able to look at your audience and deliver a portion of your speech. In this way, you can truly converse (in a polished way) with your audience.

GRAPHIC AIDS

Research suggests that an audience takes in less than 25 percent of what a speaker says. So a speaker should try to increase an audience's comprehension. One way to help your audience is by using graphic aids. Graphic aids clarify ideas and highlight important information, allowing audiences to see and hear the message. The audience has two ways to comprehend your ideas.

Guidelines for choosing what to illustrate When you think of adding graphic aids, how do you know where they would be the most effective for your audience? You can ask these questions:

- What information is most important?

- What data is the most complex or difficult to understand?

- What statistics or figures are particularly important for my audience to comprehend?

Once you answer these questions, you will have selected ideas your audience needs to understand and, as a result, ideas to be illustrated. The next question is how to best illustrate a particular idea to enhance the audience's understanding.

Types of graphic aids Graphic aids can include photographs, line drawings, charts, tables, objects, multimedia, or even people. For instance, a presenter discussing environmental hazards might use a flip chart to diagram the amounts of certain chemicals found in groundwater. A student speaking to her class about erroneous ideas associated with cerebral palsy brought in her brother, a police detective with cerebral palsy, as a graphic aid.

The various types of graphic aids—flip charts, transparencies, slides, multimedia, dry-erase boards, handouts, physical objects, and more—range from simple and inexpensive to complex and costly. The development time and cost must be considered along with effectiveness when choosing graphic aids for your presentations. You would not want to spend a great deal of time or money to create a working prototype of a new product for an internal presentation in which no action or decision was expected. The time and expense could not be justified for a simple informational presentation. However, the investment might be reasonable if production decisions were to be made.

In addition to time and cost, the location (room or space) and audience size are factors in determining the types of graphics to use. Flip charts and posters, for instance, are appropriate for small audiences in close spaces. Objects, demonstrations, marker boards, and transparencies may work well with a medium-sized group, as long as everyone can easily see the graphic. For audiences in a large auditorium, hall, or meeting facility, multimedia presentations and films provide images that are large enough for many people to see at once.

Other factors to consider are artistic talent (your own or your company's) and equipment. If your organization has a graphic arts department that can produce quality graphs, charts, photographs, films, or electronic aids, your only challenges may be selecting the ideas you want to have illustrated and choosing from the image options the artists suggest. On the other hand, you may be required to rely on your own skills and talent. When professional graphic designers are not available, you may need to choose a simpler graphic aid because you can prepare it more effectively than a complex graphic. That is, you might create a simple slide presentation rather than planning, developing, adding sound and captions to, and editing a film.

Guidelines for creating graphic aids When you develop graphics, keep your audience's needs in mind. These guidelines will help you:

- Make the graphic large enough for everyone to see easily—even people sitting in the back of the room.

- Do not crowd numbers or images on a graphic aid.

- Remember that although attractive design counts, the message is more important. Bright colors cannot replace solid ideas. For more information on effective design principles, see Chapter 6, *Document Design and Graphics.*

- Consider handouts your audience can keep if you want listeners to think about your ideas later.

The following tips are for use specifically in presentation graphics software:

- Select landscape layout for your slides (it gives longer lines for your text, particularly if you are using columns).

- Select a font that can be read easily from a distance, such as **Times New Roman Bold** or **Arial Black.** Do not use *italic,* decorative, or condensed fonts.

- Because serif fonts, the fonts with feet or cross strokes on the top and bottom of each letter, improve readability, use a serif font for the text. Likewise, since **sans serif** fonts, those without the cross strokes, present a cleaner, crisper image, use a sans serif font for slide titles.

- Choose a font size that is readable and that suggests the hierarchy of elements within the slide. Use a bolder font for the slide title than for the text. Generally, these sizes are appropriate:

    a. Titles: 24–36 points

    b. Other text: 18–24 points

    c. Source notes: 14–16 points

- Use initial caps, rather than all uppercase, in slide titles. Words in uppercase are difficult to read.

- In bulleted lists, capitalize only the first word (and, of course, proper nouns and proper adjectives). Beginning each word in a list with a capital letter requires your readers to move their eyes up and down through each line, decreasing readability. Capitalizing only the beginning words helps readers scan the list and improves readability.

- Use the Notes section for inserting notes to remind you of your next point; specific facts, figures, or quotations to ensure accuracy; cues when someone else will be advancing the slide; or reminders, such as "Smile," "Make eye contact," or "Hold up the trophy for everyone to see."

- Select colors or templates with the audience in mind. Avoid colors or designs that will distract or offend.

- If you have clip art or an image that supports the text on a slide, place it in the lower right corner. The viewer's eye will be drawn from the title or heading at the top left down through the text to the image. Remember, however, to add graphics only when they enhance and support the text, not simply to brighten a slide.

- Keep slides simple and uncluttered.

- If you use transition effects between slides, make the effect meaningful. For example, choose one effect for each major section of your presentation. Or select one effect for slides that mark the beginning of a new section and another effect for all slides within sections. Since transitions may include sound, be careful not to get carried away with the bells and whistles. A presentation that boxes in one slide, fades out another, checkerboards across a third, and wipes out a fourth, complete with four different sounds, will distract viewers from the topic.

- On your speaker's notes pages, number the slides so you can easily move to a particular slide when someone asks a question.

- If available, use the spelling and style check.

PERSONAL APPEARANCE

In addition to note cards and graphic aids, image has a big impact on the way listeners receive a speaker's message. You probably know how appearance can affect communication in everyday situations, such as the way some salespeople treat you when you are in your worn jeans and an old T-shirt. If you have not experienced this treatment yourself, you likely have seen others treated differently because of their clothing or grooming.

When you select clothing for a presentation, consider the audience's expectations and the situation in which you will be speaking. For instance, someone addressing your city council would probably dress as formally (business suit) as its members typically do. On the other hand, a speaker addressing children at a youth center would dress more casually. Whatever you wear, make sure the outfit feels comfortable. If you feel good about the way you look, you will speak with confidence.

If you have done everything you can to prepare for success, you are ready to move to the rehearsal phase.

Communication Dilemma

Ariane Rouse, a participant in her company's executive training program, learns that 15 percent of the employees will be laid off within the next four months as part of a corporate downsizing plan when she mistakenly receives a confidential memo meant for her supervisor. However, she sees the director of informational services and public relations rehearsing a presentation for an annual company meeting in which he assures employees that all is well with the organization, that a bright future awaits. He does not mention the impending layoffs.

Rouse is disturbed by the deception she believes the director intends. She has choices to make. Should she go to upper management and protest? Should she tell her closest associates and ask their advice? Should she provide an anonymous tip to the news media?

Stop and Think
Could a machine part be a graphic aid? Explain.
Would running shorts ever be appropriate dress for a presentation? Explain.

REHEARSING

WARM UP

In other skills you have developed—sports, music, art—how much practice is enough? What does this tell you about oral presentations? Respond to these questions in a brief journal entry.

Expert presenters will tell you that you must practice in order to give a successful presentation. Practicing helps you develop a conversational style. In fact, good speeches are a conversation between speaker and audience, only slightly more polished than the conversations you have with friends. Practice provides experience, experience that soothes nerves and builds confidence, too. After several rehearsals, with adjustments each time, you will have a presentation you are pleased with. Then you believe the presentation will go well.

© GETTY IMAGES/PHOTODISC

Using your note cards and graphic aids, practice your speech. When you first deliver the talk, you will see parts you like and dislike. Delivering the speech a second time, you may change what you do not like. When you are comfortable with your delivery, you have rehearsed enough. You have reached a conversational style.

Speakers practice speeches in different ways, including using a tape recorder, mirror, video camera, or live audience. With experience, you will decide which methods work for you.

USING A TAPE RECORDER

After recording your presentation, take a break. After you have gained some distance and perspective on the speech, listen to the tape for the following:

- Rate (how fast you talked)

- Volume (how loudly or how softly you talked)

- Pronunciation (the distinctness of your words)

- Inflections (the changes in pitch or tone)
- Time (the amount of time you took to present your ideas)

USING A MIRROR

Watch yourself in a mirror as you practice your presentation. Put yourself in the role of the audience. What do you see that will enhance or detract from the message? Check for:

- Appropriate facial expressions
- Effective use of your body and hands. (Do your hand movements emphasize major points, or do they distract your listener from the topic?)

USING A VIDEO CAMERA

Do not review the tape immediately. Wait until you have greater perspective, perhaps in an hour or in the next day or two. When you do view the tape, pretend to be your audience. Look for strengths as well as weaknesses. With this **auditory** and visual **feedback,** check for the following:

1. How you sound
2. How you look
3. What message you deliver

USING A LIVE AUDIENCE

Ask a friend or family member to listen to you practice your presentation. After delivering the speech, invite comments and suggestions. Try some of these questions:

- What was my speech topic?
- What point did I try to prove?
- Did I make eye contact?
- Did I speak loudly enough?
- Did I tend to use *and uh, um,* or *like?*
- Was my conclusion effective?
- Did I correctly pronounce words?

 Stop and Think While a tape recorder gives useful feedback during rehearsal, what will it not tell you? In small groups, discuss your answers.

PRESENTING

Once you have thoroughly prepared for your presentation, you can present with confidence. Before you are ready, however, you must prepare the environment in which you will make your presentation.

WARM UP

Discuss these questions with your classmates: Can oral presenting be fun? How can you make presenting fun?

© GETTY IMAGES/PHOTODISC

CHECKING THE ROOM

Arrive early for your presentation if possible. During that time, make sure listeners will be comfortable and can see and hear well. Consider seating, lighting, temperature, equipment, and graphic aids.

Seating Check how chairs are placed. Are they arranged to let you communicate effectively? For instance, if you want group discussion, the chairs should be placed so that people can see each other. Also, make sure everyone in the room will be able to see you easily.

Lighting Make certain your audience will have enough light to see. In addition, correct any glaring and overly bright spots. With an appropriately lighted room, your audience can comfortably see and concentrate on your message.

Temperature Check the temperature controls. People who are shivering from cold or sweltering from heat will not be good listeners.

Equipment and Graphic Aids Make sure all equipment is working and prepare for possible problems. Remember Murphy's Law: If something can go wrong, it will! Make sure you have an extra bulb for the projector, markers, computer disks, and anything else you might need.

Consider visibility and access when you place graphic aids. Graphics need to be located where:

- Everyone in the room can easily see them.

- You can point to the graphic as you talk.

- You can reach equipment, such as overhead projectors, to make adjustments.

- The equipment will have a power supply.

Determine before the event how you will post or display your materials.

DELIVERING THE MESSAGE

Having prepared for the presentation, you are ready to enjoy talking with your audience. Use the pointers below to help you be as effective as possible.

- Use appropriate facial expressions. For example, if you are talking about the positive outlook for jobs, an occasional smile is suitable.

- Maintain eye contact. By acknowledging your listener with eye contact, you show interest and concern for that person.

- Explain every graphic. Since each person may see or understand something differently, tell people exactly what you want them to learn from the graphic aid.

- Post or distribute handouts only when you want the audience to use or read them. Otherwise, your listeners may be flipping noisily through pages and reading what captures their attention rather than listening to you. If you do not want to disrupt your presentation but want to distribute your handouts at the appropriate time, ask someone to distribute them for you.

- Consult your notes, but do not read from them. Consult your notes only enough to follow your outline and to cue yourself to key details for your presentation. When you read directly from your note cards, you break eye contact with your audience and lose their interest and attention.

- Continue to talk even when something goes wrong. Recover the best you can, but go on with the show. Do not call attention to a mistake.

- Remember that your audience wants you to succeed. Your audience's desire for an effective presentation, along with the self-confidence you gained from being fully prepared, will ensure a positive experience.

- Give your audience an opportunity to ask questions unless the program does not allow time for questions. If you cannot answer a question, respond in a positive way: "I'm sorry that I don't have the answer to your question, but I will be happy to check my sources and get back to you later this week."

Stop and Think Should you display your poster before you begin to speak? Is eye contact with your audience desirable?

ORGANIZING A GROUP PRESENTATION

Presenting with others requires special consideration. Collaboration provides many opportunities to share diverse perspectives and expertise. However, group presentations require careful planning if they are to be effective. Collaborators must act as a team and plan for dividing a topic, setting time limits, moving between speakers, providing graphic aids and handouts, answering questions, and managing the presentation.

WARM UP

Imagine that three employees walk into a meeting expecting to make a sales presentation. They all expect to make the presentation alone, but when they arrive at the meeting, all three are asked to speak. How do you think the presentation will go?

© DIGITAL VISION

DIVIDING THE TOPIC

When collaborating on a presentation, speakers must plan roles and responsibilities. One important issue to discuss is who will be responsible for presenting what information. For example, three employees making a planning proposal might divide the discussion in this way: Speaker 1—introduction of speakers, their qualifications, and the problem prompting the proposal; Speaker 2—the proposed solution and the budget; and Speaker 3—the conclusion and the requested action. Topic division, therefore, may dictate the order of presenters.

In addition, sometimes a particular speaker's expertise will require that he or she deal with one aspect, such as an accountant explaining the budget. If speakers are equally qualified to present the material, the group will need to define other reasons for assigning roles.

SETTING TIME LIMITS

Just as individual speakers must plan for their presentations to fit within a time limit, group presenters have an obligation to stay within a time frame as well. After the group determines the length of the entire presentation,

the members should decide the total time to allot each member, keeping in mind the material each member will cover and its relative significance. The team members presenting the planning proposal, given a 30-minute slot in the day's agenda, might divide their time this way:

Speaker 1	introduction of speakers and their qualifications; problem prompting the proposal	10 minutes
Speaker 2	proposed solution and budget	15 minutes
Speaker 3	conclusion and requested action	5 minutes

Speaker 2 is allotted the most time because explaining the plan that the group is proposing and justifying its budget are critical. If the audience does not understand this information, the proposal will not be approved. Speaker 2 also receives the greatest portion of time because of the importance of proving that a significant problem exists. Speaker 3 needs less time, not because concluding is unimportant, but because conclusions should be direct and brief, giving the audience time to ask questions.

Members of groups should be even more watchful than individual speakers in preparing to stay within their time limits. If one speaker goes over his or her time limit, the time must be taken from another presenter.

TRANSITIONING BETWEEN SPEAKERS

If you have ever been in an audience when an unidentified person begins to speak, you probably remember how uncomfortable you were. People expect to be introduced to speakers. In a collaborative presentation, members may choose to be introduced or introduce themselves at the beginning of the session. Or each speaker may be introduced as he or she begins to speak.

When various speakers will be answering questions, listeners prefer to be reminded of the respondent's name. Often a moderator will name the presenter as he or she asks that a particular speaker address the question, such as "Dr. Quan, would you like to answer the question of profiling?"

PROVIDING GRAPHIC AIDS AND HANDOUTS

Group presenters should discuss the use of graphic aids and handouts when planning the presentation. Coordinating the appearance of slides, transparencies, and handouts adds to the professionalism and positive impressions of a group presentation. For example, members could agree to use one slide template; a certain color, scheme, or typeface; or the same headers and footers. Members should plan when to distribute handouts. Will all handouts be provided to listeners at one time, or will each presenter be responsible for distributing his or her own? Since some speakers do not want the audience reading handouts while they speak, those speakers may prefer to distribute all handouts at the end of the presentation. Other speakers may want listeners to have copies of their materials for taking notes during the discussion. So speakers should discuss and agree on a plan before the presentation.

Speakers also need to decide which equipment they will require. For instance, when two speakers plan to use overhead transparencies and the third wants to use an LCD projector, they should agree on where to place both pieces of equipment and know whether any equipment must be moved between presenters. Presenters using the same machine for multimedia should know their software needs and make certain the equipment is compatible with the presentation they developed.

Use the Oral Report Evaluation Form worksheet on the Data CD when you practice oral presentations. This worksheet will give you the opportunity to learn from the evaluation and the advice from listeners.

ANSWERING QUESTIONS

Participants of group presentations should anticipate questions and plan how to answer them. In some presentations, the group may decide to allow each speaker to take questions when the speaker ends his or her portion. Other groups will answer questions only after all presenters have completed their speeches. Presenters also should know whether a moderator will assign each question to a particular presenter or whether the presenters will be responsible for assigning the questions. Speakers are smart to plan answers for questions they expect to be asked; therefore, collaborators might divide the topic areas so that each presenter could prepare for questions in a certain area.

MANAGING THE PRESENTATION

Groups may perform more effectively with leadership. For that reason, many groups have a lead presenter, a chairperson, or someone who manages the process. The lead presenter often represents the group in discussions with meeting planners and acts as liaison, then corresponds with group members to keep them informed. The lead presenter sometimes speaks first, previewing the presentation or stating objectives, or last, summarizing key points and moderating the questions. The group may choose to give the lead presenter other responsibilities as well, such as:

- Keeping speakers on schedule, calling time for those who talk too long.

- Keeping questions moving, preventing arguments and monopolization.

- Responding to requests for more information, mailing additional materials.

An effective leader will assure that all group members' talents are used and that all opinions are heard.

Stop and Think

In a collaborative presentation, how do speakers determine who will speak when? Do groups need a lead presenter or chairperson?

■ Chapter 11 Review

POINT YOUR BROWSER

techwriting.swlearning.com

SUMMARY

1. Your ability to effectively present your ideas orally to others will affect your success in the workplace.

2. Plan for your audience, the topic and content of your presentation, and stage fright.

3. Use audience analysis to decide how to organize and preview the organizational plan to help listeners follow you.

4. Preparing involves creating an outline or notes and graphic aids and making adjustments in your image.

5. After planning and preparing, rehearse to polish your presentation using a variety of methods.

6. Check the seating, lighting, temperature, equipment, and graphics to create the best possible listening environment.

7. When presenting as part of a team, think about how the team will divide the topic among presenters; what amount of time to allot each speaker; how to move between speakers; how to handle graphics, handouts, and questions; and who will manage the presentation process.

Checklist

- Have I carefully analyzed my audience?

- Do I have a clearly defined and focused topic?

- Have I planned how I can use my response to stage fright?

- Does the beginning of my report preview the report's organization?

- Have I composed a strong and effective introduction? body? conclusion?

- Will my outline or notes allow me to deliver a conversational performance, rather than reading a speech or speaking without aid?

- What ideas will I present that need clarification or emphasis?

- What type of graphic will be most effective for enhancing the idea and for the speaking situation? Have I prepared for an appropriate and professional appearance?

- Have I rehearsed and gathered feedback for improvement?

- When presenting, have I checked the room for seating, lighting, temperature, equipment, and graphics?

- Have I effectively delivered the message using facial expressions, eye contact, graphics and handouts, notes, confidence, and questions?

- If participating in a collaborative presentation, have my team and I divided the topic among speakers, established time limits, planned transitions, coordinated graphics and handouts, planned for questions, and considered the selection of a team leader or chairperson?

Build On What You Know

1. You have been asked to speak to your nephew's fifth-grade social studies class about Mexico and your work as a volunteer for Habitat for Humanity. The social studies class lasts 50 minutes. If the teacher does not give you a time limit but tells you to talk as long as you like, what factors might you consider?

2. Mrs. Nicci, a counselor, has asked you to explain to a group of 35 first-year students how to complete their registration cards. The entire process involves using decisions the students have made previously and entering data on a preprinted form. Choose a room in your school with which you are familiar and imagine this as the location. What would be the most effective way to arrange chairs for this presentation? Consider the graphics you might use. Consider how much, if at all, you want the students consulting with each other. Another factor could be the size of the room and location of permanent features, such as built-in cabinets.

3. Using one of the topics listed below or a topic your instructor supplies, develop an idea for an effective attention-getting introduction for your peers, other students in your school. Remember to state your topic and to preview the points you will make as well as to connect with your audience.

cost of prescription drugs	teen employment	mass transit in rural or urban United States
globalization	Internet and entertainment	local pollution concerns

4. Fast-forward your life several years and imagine the time when your supervisor first says to you, "Great job on this report! Now you can present the report at the _____ (fill in the blank with managers', stockholders', team, committee, or other appropriate term) meeting." Suppose you have six weeks before the date of the presentation. Develop a timeline with the tasks you will undertake to prepare for an effective oral presentation. The plan should identify what you will do and when you will do it during the six weeks. Remember that you already have a written report, but you need to develop an oral presentation appropriate for a different audience. Also, remember that this is your first on-the-job presentation, so you will want adequate rehearsal time and constructive feedback to build your confidence level.

5. Select or create a graphic aid that you can use in a two-minute presentation to clarify or emphasize an idea. For example, you might bring a tool and demonstrate how to use it. Or you could draw a graph or chart and explain the process or statistics it illustrates. You also could show a photograph, poster, or painting and explain the idea or concept it supports.

Apply What You Learned

6. Review an oral report you presented recently—in school or elsewhere, formal or informal. List some changes you would make to improve your effectiveness if you were able to present again.

7. Attend the presentation of a speaker at school, in the community, or at work. If a live presentation is not possible, watch a video of a speaker, perhaps a politician, an editorial commentator, or a promoter from an infomercial. As you watch and listen to the speaker, make two lists: one for positive elements, things that make the speech work, and a second for negative elements, or things that detract from the presentation's effectiveness.

8. Choose any written report you have previously completed or find a model in a textbook. Write an essay about decisions and changes you would need to make to present the written information in an oral report.

9. Research the career you are currently considering. Look for information on employers, salaries, working conditions, educational requirements, and hiring rates. You could go to the library, talk with a counselor, visit someone working in the field, or talk with an instructor in that curriculum area. When you have as much data as you need, think of making an oral presentation to classmates who might be interested in the same career.

   a. Write a brief analysis of your audience. Refer to Chapter 2, *Plan for Your Audience and Purpose*.

   b. Decide on the focus or main idea for your presentation. Write this focus in one complete sentence.

   c. List at least two ideas for information that could be enhanced with a graphic aid.

   d. Create at least one of the graphic aids listed in item c.

   e. Prepare the outline or notes you would use for this presentation.

10. After reading an article or a speech supplied by your instructor, on a folded sheet of paper, prepare a question relating to the reading. Your instructor will collect the questions in a bag or basket. One by one you and each of your classmates then comes to the front of the room, draws a question, and answers that question. Use this activity to practice question-and-answer sessions.

11. Plan a speech that you could deliver to your own graduating class. Consider audience and purpose when planning. Will you need graphic aids for your speech? If so, what kind of graphic aids would be appropriate? Share your topic and notes with other students to gain feedback. Finally, deliver the speech to your peers and ask for additional feedback.

Use the Work Is A Zoo! worksheet for this chapter on the Data CD to guide you in your planning.

Work Is A Zoo!

The presentation is going to be a first for you. And since you also are hoping for the associate position, you want to do a great job.

You have completed some research, and you have prepared the agenda. Without knowing it, you have already done a lot of work.

Now is the time to think about what you are going to present and how you are going to present it. Think about why you are speaking and whom you are speaking to.

Are you and Tyrone the only speakers? Are you going to have a question-and-answer period? Will there be a relaxed feel to the meeting with opportunities for comments along the way?

Given the information you have found, write an outline for your presentation.

Include Tyrone's ideas for how the new logo can be used for promotional purposes.

Here are a few tips to help you plan:

- Start by grabbing your listeners' attention. Is there an interesting statistic you could use? or a crazy animal fact?

- Guide your listeners as you go. Do not get sidetracked.

- Give supporting evidence. Cite other zoos as backup.

- Develop a strong conclusion. Where do you intend to go? What do you want other staff members to do? How can they be involved?

From *Words@Work* 1st edition by VANDALAY GROUP © 2000. Reprinted with permission of South-Western, a division of Thomson Learning: www.thomsonrights.com. Fax 800 730-2215.

RECOMMENDATION REPORTS

WRITE-TO-LEARN

Think of the last time you had to make a choice between two things. Maybe you had to decide between two classes, two cars, two outfits, or two restaurants. In a one-page journal entry, describe the process you went through to make your decision.

GOALS

DETERMINE how a recommendation report is used and adjust the structure to accommodate the reader

DEVISE criteria for evaluation after determining the problem and possible solutions

ORGANIZE a recommendation report using the appropriate format

COMPOSE a recommendation report by evaluating criteria and drawing conclusions using a point-by-point analysis

See the Data CD for Write-to-Learn and In The Know activity worksheets.

In The Know

appendixes the plural of *appendix;* usually the last elements or special parts of a report; places to include documents, data, or graphics not necessary to the discussion in the report but perhaps helpful or interesting to the audience

criteria the plural form of *criterion;* the factors on which a decision is made; things to consider when making a decision. *The criteria are cost and safety.*

criterion singular; a factor on which a decision is made; something to consider when making a decision. *The criterion is safety.*

field research research done in the field, especially through surveys and interviews

persuasive writing writing to convince others

point-by-point organization a comparison/contrast structure that covers two or three items under one criterion

rank the relative importance of one criterion to another; usually ranked from most important to least important

receptive audience readers who are open to ideas or suggestions in a recommendation report

recommendation report a report that helps decision makers compose choices; after comparing and contrasting two or three choices to a common set of criteria, it recommends (strongly suggests) one choice over the other(s)

solicited report a report written in response to readers' requests for alterations

standard the limits to a criterion; further defines each criterion

subcriteria a smaller category of criteria that falls under a criterion, the larger category; helps to define the criterion

unreceptive audience readers who are not open to ideas or suggestions

unsolicited report a report that has not been asked for; the audience is not expecting the recommendations

Writing@Work

Judy Roberson is the Assistant Director of Community Services for the Upper Cumberland Area Agency on Aging and Disability, located in Cookeville, Tennessee. In her position, she is responsible for monitoring and providing technical assistance to service providers in fourteen counties.

As the Assistant Director of Community Services, Judy writes formal recommendations for policy changes and the initiation of programs. When writing these reports, Judy must keep in mind all stakeholders because these stakeholders, or clients, are the most important part of any system. Often, clients' comments and questions identify unmet needs or flaws that need to be addressed in the system. As a result, recommendations should always address or attempt to resolve clients' concerns.

In Judy's case, her reports are often sent to more than one group of stakeholders. She must also keep in mind service providers, funding agencies, and public officials when writing her recommendation reports.

Judy stresses the importance of clear, concise writing in all of her reports. Because people receiving her reports have varied educations, backgrounds, and experiences, clear, concise recommendations are essential to ensure accurate communication. Judy suggests having a third party review all reports to ensure that the message is being presented clearly—this is a practice she uses when writing her own reports.

When writing her reports, Judy follows a format based on certain criteria. Specifically for her reports, she must include information about on-sight observations made, documentation checked, and technical assistance provided. Then she makes her recommendations. She also makes a point to include an area for comments after her recommendations.

Judy has a bachelor's degree in human ecology. Her work experience has all been service oriented.

MEMO

TO: Roberta Boles

FROM: Lisa Stuckey and Rodrigo Reyes LS RR

DATE: July 15, 20—

SUBJECT: Purchase Recommendation for New Swing Set

INTRODUCTION

The purpose of this report is to recommend which new swing set Tender Care Center should purchase. The old swing set is rusted and poses a safety hazard to the children. We have narrowed our choices to two sets: Play Time Gym Set and Kiddie Swing Set. To determine which set to recommend, we developed the following criteria:

1. Safety

2. Special features

3. Cost

RECOMMENDATION

We recommend that Tender Care Center purchase the Play Time Gym Set. First, the plastic slide and rounded edges make the set safe for the children. Second, this swing set offers more of the special features we want. Third, the cost of the Play Time Gym Set is within the allocated budget.

SCOPE

The Center's directors have suggested that we rank safety as the first criterion. Concern for the children and compliance with federal guidelines require us to be safety conscious.

Special features are our second criterion. The teachers have said that the children play less on the old swing set because there is no special equipment to interest them. We would like the new swing set to have special features that provide variety for the children.

To make sure we stay within budget, we have ranked our third criterion as cost. The director has allocated $700 for a new swing set.

The remainder of this report will compare both swing sets to the three criteria.

Figure 12.1 Recommendation Report

Roberta Boles
Page 2
July 15, 20—

DISCUSSION

Safety

A new swing set must include:

    a. Smooth edges with no rough places that can cause cuts and scrapes.

    b. Few cap covers to wear thin and reveal rough edges that may cut.

    c. A slide under 10 feet long so children can climb safely.

    d. A slide that will not absorb heat and thus burn children's skin.

Play Time Gym Set. We visited Shifferly Sales to see the Play Time Gym Set. The Play Time Gym Set has plastic seats with rounded edges.

Fewer caps are needed because of the rounded edges. The slide is 6 feet long. In addition, the slide is plastic and will not absorb heat from the sun.

Kiddie Swing Set. According to the Fun and Exercise catalog, the Kiddie Swing Set has galvanized steel frames with rounded edges and requires more caps to cover the sharp edges. The slide is under 10 feet long, but heat from the sun will make the metal slide hot.

Conclusion. The Play Time Gym Set meets the subcriteria, while the Kiddie Swing Set has rough edges, more caps, and a metal slide that will absorb heat.

Swing Set Special Features

The swing set must include a variety of activities to maintain the children's interest. The preschool teachers suggest the following features:

    a. Glide ride

    b. Swings

    c. Two-passenger swing

    d. Slide

Figure 12.1 Recommendation Report, cont.

Roberta Boles
Page 3
July 15, 20—

Table 1 depicts a comparison of subcriteria for both swing sets.

Table 1. Comparison of Swing Set Features

FEATURES	PLAY TIME GYM SET	KIDDIE SWING SET
Glide Ride	Yes	Yes
Swings	Yes	Yes
Two-Passenger Swing	Yes	No
Slide	Yes	Yes

Play Time Gym Set. The Play Time Gym Set has the features that the preschool teachers want. Other features, such as the pony ride and the adult swing, are not necessary.

Kiddie Swing Set. Although the Kiddie Swing Set meets most of the subcriteria, it does not have a two-passenger swing. Like the Play Time Gym Set, the Kiddie Swing Set includes a pony ride and an adult swing, which are not needed.

Conclusion. The Play Time Gym Set meets and exceeds our subcriteria for special features. The Kiddie Swing Set lacks a two-passenger swing.

Cost

The cost of the swing set must not exceed $700.

Play Time Gym Set. Carlton Muroulis, sales representative for Shifferly Sales, said the total cost of the Play Time Gym Set is $682.99. The cost breakdown follows:

Play Time Gym Set	$649.99
Tax	15.00
Delivery and Setup	18.00
Total	$682.99

Figure 12.1 Recommendation Report, cont.

Roberta Boles
Page 4
July 15, 20—

Kiddie Swing Set. The total cost of the Kiddie Swing Set is $626.39. Cierra Dickenson, sales manager for Fun and Exercise, gave us the following cost breakdown:

Kiddie Swing Set	$589.99
Tax	11.40
Delivery and Setup	<u>25.00</u>
Total	$626.39

Conclusion. At $682.99, the Play Time Gym Set meets the third criterion. The Kiddie Swing Set, at $626.39, also meets the third criterion—the budget allowance for the swing set.

Figure 12.1 Recommendation Report, cont.

WHAT IS A RECOMMENDATION REPORT?

The **recommendation report** is a problem-and-solution report, a written answer to a need that arises in the workplace. Most problems, however, have more than one solution. The recommendation report recommends the best solution to a problem or need. In other words, it helps readers make a choice. Employees write recommendation reports in the workplace to help decision makers choose the best possible solution. Recommendation reports help people solve large and small problems, from hiring new employees or constructing a new building to selecting a new computer or coffee supplier.

© GETTY IMAGES/PHOTODISC

Sometimes the recommendation is the purchase of equipment. In the model at the beginning of the chapter, Lisa Stuckey and Rodrigo Reyes examined two swing sets and recommended the Play Time Gym Set for Tender Care Center. Throughout this chapter, you will look more closely at some of the decisions Stuckey and Reyes made while writing their report.

Sometimes the report recommends a course of action. For example, Hennepin Logging has decided to expand and has narrowed the location of its new plant to three towns in West Virginia. A recommendation report will compare and contrast the three sites against the **criteria** the company thinks are important. Finally, the report will recommend a location. Later in this chapter, you will see how the writer of this report gathers data and plans the report.

The last time you bought school supplies, you chose from among several alternatives. Knowing that you needed a three-ring binder, you probably examined several different three-ring notebooks. The choice you made depended on factors including cost, special features such as clipboards or zippered pencil pouches, durability, and color. Companies go through this same thinking process when they make choices.

Communication Dilemma

Beth Schroeder is an accountant for Gildstein's Business Managers. She has the tough job of recommending to her supervisor which construction company should build a small office building: Wilmore Construction Company Inc., or Galloway Builders. Wilmore is a larger company and has a better reputation for finishing tasks on schedule.

Bids from both companies fall within Gildstein's budget, but it is imperative that the office building be up in time for holiday sales. Galloway Builders is owned by Schroeder's brother-in-law, Jeff Galloway. The Galloways have a child with a serious medical condition and really need the money they would earn from this contract. Schroeder's husband wants her to recommend his brother's company for the job. He claims families should look out for one another.

What should Schroeder do?

Decision makers who have the power to implement your recommendations read recommendation reports. Sometimes one person reads the report; often a committee or board votes on recommendations. The report is usually written to a supervisor, but sometimes recommendations are made to coworkers.

The report can be **solicited** (asked for) or **unsolicited** (not asked for). In solicited reports, your reader asks you to analyze several alternatives. This reader understands the need and will be more receptive to your suggestions.

In an unsolicited report, your audience is not expecting your recommendations. You may have difficulty gauging this reader's reaction. Your reader may be receptive and may appreciate your initiative in helping to make decisions. On the other hand, your audience may be unwilling to accept your recommendations for a variety of reasons. For example, Kamiela, a production supervisor at a large wholesale nursery, was asked by her manager to help select the walkie-talkies to be issued to all employees so they can communicate with one another while working in the various greenhouses. Since Kamiela's supervisor was already committed to purchasing the walkie-talkies, he was receptive to her recommendation.

However, Latroy received a different reaction from his supervisor. Latroy, a landscape maintenance technician, took the initiative to develop a recommendation report in which he suggested buying three golf carts to be used in maintaining the grounds. Latroy believed the golf carts would be helpful in carrying chemicals for spraying, moving new plants, and getting around the grounds to inspect for pests. However, his employer, who had not requested the recommendation report, did not agree that a golf cart was necessary or would improve the quality of work. As you can see, Latroy's audience was not receptive.

An analysis of your audience's attitude may affect how you organize your report. A **receptive audience** will be ready to read the recommendation up front, early in the report (as is presented in the model at the beginning of this chapter). An **unreceptive audience** will require more careful research and supporting information up front, with the recommendation coming last. You need to lead this reader carefully to your recommendation. Figure 12.2 shows the strategies for accommodating receptive and unreceptive audiences.

RECEPTIVE	UNRECEPTIVE
Introduction	Introduction
Recommendation	Scope
Scope	Discussion—with more details
Discussion—with fewer details	Recommendation

Figure 12.2 Strategy for Receptive and Unreceptive Audiences

Recommendation reports are persuasive. **Persuasive writing** requires you to analyze audiences carefully, for your job is to convince your reader to act on your recommendation. Researched facts, opinions of authorities, and logical thinking are the tools you need to be convincing. Find out what information your reader expects in the final report and how detailed the research should be. For example, in the previous situation, Kamiela knew that her audience approved of purchasing the new equipment but had not chosen the brand or model. As a result, she could focus her report on comparing the types of walkie-talkies.

Latroy, on the other hand, did not have his audience's support from the beginning. He was concerned not only with comparing the different golf carts, but also with convincing the audience that golf carts were needed. Further, if Latroy had analyzed the audience, he would have learned that three years earlier mechanics inside the plant ordered two golf carts to move tools from machine to machine. But the carts were removed when employees were found to be playing with and abusing them. If Latroy had been aware of the previous incident, he could have prepared his report to account for this history and explain how it would not be repeated. Review the information about audience identification in Chapter 2, *Plan for Your Audience and Purpose,* to help you analyze your audience.

Stop and Think

If the reader of the swing set recommendation had been unreceptive, where would you have placed the recommendation section? Why must writers of persuasive reports analyze audiences carefully? Name several possible readers for the swing set recommendation report.

GETTING STARTED ON RECOMMENDATION REPORTS

After you have analyzed your audience and before you can begin writing a recommendation report, you must define your problem, brainstorm solutions, and devise criteria.

WARM UP

Some television commercials help viewers define a problem. Some are problems people know about already. Others are problems listeners may not have considered before. List some of the problems commercials define.

DEFINE YOUR PROBLEM

In a solicited report, the person or group who requested the recommendation report has identified the problem. The problem is usually evident, but put it into words anyway. In the model, Reyes and Stuckey stated the problem in one sentence: "The old swing set is rusted and poses a safety hazard to the children." Problems that initiate recommendation reports range from the selection of a copier or computer to more complex choices, such as the best strategy for improving communication among departments or the best site for building a business.

In an unsolicited report, the problem may need more explanation. Unlike the solicited report, the unsolicited report is not requested; no one except the report writer has noticed the problem or considered solutions. Therefore, you must make certain readers see the problem and its importance clearly. If the problem needs more explanation than one or two sentences, consider placing the explanation in a separate paragraph in the introduction.

State the problem as specifically and precisely as possible, remembering to define terms the audience will not know. For example, "The cedar shake roof of Roosevelt Farms Bed and Breakfast's west wing leaked during the October 2, 2004 hurricane and stained the dining room ceiling" is a better problem statement than "Roosevelt Farms Bed and Breakfast had a leak."

BRAINSTORM SOLUTIONS

Now brainstorm solutions to the problem. You may need others to help you generate possible solutions. Explain the problem to your colleagues and tell them you would like their ideas on possible solutions. Point out that no idea should be considered foolish or impossible, that the focus is creative problem solving, and that the time for criticism will come later.

Take notes as ideas emerge. You could act as moderator, keeping the group on track and stopping any criticism that might creep in. Next, narrow your choices to two or three. Again, you may use the advice of others to help you narrow your choices.

When Reyes and Stuckey brainstormed solutions to the rusted swing set problem, they generated a list of six kinds of equipment they would like to have on the playground. Their list included a jungle gym, an eight-swing gym set, and a swing set and slide combination. They narrowed the list of six to two when they decided that a swing set with special equipment would give them more variety for the price.

DEVISE CRITERIA

After you have narrowed your choices, decide what criteria to use. Interview people in your organization to help you decide what is important to

Focus on Ethics

Writers, especially writers of recommendation reports, should consider the interests of all stakeholders or all parties and people involved in an issue. Since the decisions made based on information and analysis in the recommendation report could affect the stakeholders, a report that represents the views of only one or a few is unfair. This report could even be detrimental to the health of an organization or a company.

For instance, a report recommending an accounting firm with a reputation for racial discrimination to a company with diverse employees and stockholders, if acted upon, could cause significant damage. The writer should consider all stakeholders before recommending such an accounting firm.

Highway construction is an example of a situation in which many opinions and perspectives result in the best recommendation. Building a new road affects many people. The highway location, design, and size can improve or destroy businesses, increase or decrease property values, bypass or relocate homes, and change the character of communities.

Because of this impact, public hearings, city council meetings, and other gatherings are usually held for people to review the choice of plans and to hear other people's ideas. While the meetings provide opportunities for many people to participate, the process takes a great deal of time, possibly five or ten years or more. However, the process is vital to the fairness of all stakeholders.

consider when making the choice. Ask all concerned: administration, workers, people who may have used one of your solutions before. Getting different opinions is important so that the solution you recommend works for everyone.

Richard West was asked to write a report for Hennepin Logging to recommend a West Virginia town for a new plant. After several management meetings, three sites in West Virginia were selected as possible locations. After the sites were chosen, West consulted with others to help him devise criteria. Figure 12.3 shows some of the preliminary information he gained after consulting the administration at Hennepin Logging, the workers who will relocate, and a local furniture manufacturer who purchases wood from Hennepin Logging.

FROM	TOWN SHOULD HAVE
Administration	• 10-acre plot of land • available workforce • adequate power supply
Workers who will relocate	• good schools • affordable housing
Local furniture manufacturer	• good roads • good water supply

Figure 12.3 Preliminary Notes for New Plant Location

From this preliminary list, West was able to classify like items under larger categories. The categories—resources, utilities, and living conditions—became the criteria for his first draft. The smaller units under each category became the **subcriteria:**

Resources	Utilities	Living Conditions
land	power	schools
workforce	water	housing
roads		

Next, he worked to further define each of the subcriteria. Again, he went back to his colleagues and asked these questions: What is a fair price for the land? How many people are needed in the workforce? What kind of labor is needed, skilled or unskilled?

If your list of criteria is longer than four or five, reevaluate their importance to limit your list to no more than five. Working with more than five criteria might overwhelm your readers.

Stop and Think

Should writers of solicited recommendation reports define the problem? Is brainstorming for solutions best done alone or in collaboration?

FORMATTING AND ORGANIZING RECOMMENDATION REPORTS

The recommendation report is a highly structured report using a consistent outline and a comparison/contrast discussion. You may have seen such reports written as multipage paper documents. However, the best format for a recommendation report may not be a multipage paper document. In fact, there are many formatting choices for these types of reports.

If you are submitting a report to a prospective client, you might send it as an e-mail attachment, post it to a web site, create and send a CD-ROM, or provide hyperlinks in a Microsoft® Word document. As with other decisions, you should base format choice on the audience's needs.

© GETTY IMAGES/PHOTODISC

For instance, an audience who frequently uses the Internet would appreciate the ease and speed of access of a web site. In contrast, some readers are more comfortable with a traditional print document, so the writer could submit a paper copy or send the document as an e-mail attachment. Whatever the format, recommendation reports follow the same basic outline.

OUTLINE

The recommendation report consists of introductory material, a recommendation (summary of discussion), scope (what the report covers and why), and discussion (analysis of criteria—the factors used in making the decision).

Introduction

The introduction section:

- Gives the purpose of the report.
- Briefly explains the problem.
- Narrows the choice to two or three items.
- Gives a criteria list.
- Previews the rest of the report.
- May include the investigation method.

The model introduction in Figure 12.4 on the next page orients the readers to the information in the body of the report, that is, the site recommendation for a real estate license review course. This model introduction explains the history and the problem, the recommended solution, the criteria, and the investigation method.

MEMO

To: Marcia Yates, President
Realtors Association
From: Robin Thaxton, Site Coordinator *RST*
Date: November 22, 20–
Subject: Site Recommendation for March 20– License Review Course

At the June 20– Realtors Association meeting, the board agreed to sponsor a review course to be held in March before the spring licensing exam. Board members believed that a six-hour review course held before the state licensing exam would increase the pass rate, helping members to move from salesperson to broker. You asked that I send you my site recommendation by the end of November so that you could include the announcement, prices, and registration information in the December newsletter.

This recommendation report suggests the site I think will meet our needs. After consulting with the Visitors Bureau and other meeting planners as well as examining sales brochures from meeting facilities, I narrowed the options to two locations: the Paradise Hilton and the Narona Garden Club. Each meeting space has been evaluated using the criteria, listed below from most important to least important element, suggested by board members:

- Location
- Cost of meeting rooms
- Equipment
- Food service

Figure 12.4 Sample Introduction

Recommendation

- Makes the recommendation
- Uses criteria to summarize reasons for the recommendation

Since readers want the important information first, the recommendation section appears early in the report, unless the report is unsolicited. As Figure 12.5 below shows, this section may be brief. In longer reports describing more complex situations, the section could be several paragraphs.

Recommendation

I recommend the March 20– review course be held in the meeting rooms of the Paradise Hilton. This venue offers a central location, reasonable cost for use of the facilities (when the hotel serves the luncheon), access to requested electronics with on-site technicians for service, and hot and cold menus.

Figure 12.5 Sample Recommendation

Scope

The scope section:

- Lists criteria, in descending order from most important to least important, that were given in the introduction.
- Explains why the criteria were chosen and why they are ranked as they are.

This discussion assures writers and readers that they agree on important factors in the decision. This section also explains how information is analyzed, as shown below in the description of criteria and explanation of why each criterion was chosen.

SCOPE

Board members noted that location is critical because most of our members registered to take the exam are already employed in the business and will not want to be away from work any longer than necessary. Therefore, the driving time to this review session should be as short as possible. Location is the first criterion.

Since the cost of meeting rooms for the course must be passed on to participants through their registration fees, the prices for facility use must be reasonable. Thus, charges for the use of rooms are the second criterion. Presenters who will teach the review courses have requested an overhead projector with a screen and a computer with a projection system. To be certain the electronics work within the meeting rooms, I prefer that the facility provide them rather than having us rent them or having presenters bring their own equipment. Availability of equipment, therefore, is the third criterion.

To fit six hours of training into a one-day drive-in format, board members suggested that the program and its pricing include a meal and refreshments for two breaks. For that reason, in-house food service is the fourth criterion. The recommendation report will compare the Paradise Hilton and the Narona Garden Club to these criteria:

1. Location

2. Charges for the use of rooms

3. Availability of equipment

4. In-house food service

Figure 12.6 Sample Scope Section

Discussion

The discussion section:

- Analyzes each of the criteria thoroughly.

- Draws conclusions about which item is better for each criteria.

Organize the discussion section of the report by criteria, starting with the most important and moving to the least important. Give each criterion a major heading. Each criterion is introduced with an explanation of essential elements or features. Then each item being considered is compared to the ideal set in the introduction. Finally, a conclusion shows the results of the comparison for the criterion. Figure 12.7 presents one part of a discussion section.

Remember, receptive readers are interested primarily in the recommendation, so it appears early in the report. Unreceptive readers, however, are more likely to be persuaded if the recommendation is placed last, after the discussion.

DISCUSSION

Location

The site for the review course should be within a one hour's drive for all members in our region. The location should be easily accessible from a major highway and well marked on the city bypass.

Paradise Hilton. The Paradise Hilton, in the historic district in the city center, is five minutes from Interstate A1 and within 45–50 minutes of all members. The hotel has many billboards advertising its location on major highways outside and within the city. In addition, the state highway signs direct travelers from the bypasses to this hotel and two other hotels in the historic area. Visitors say the Paradise Hilton is easy to find.

Narona Garden Club. The Narona Garden Club is located in a residential neighborhood just south of the capitol and southwest of the historic area. It is within one hour's drive for our members. While many signs within the city point to its location, no signs on the highway and only one on each bypass make this location difficult for out-of-town visitors to find.

Conclusion. While both locations meet the criteria, the Paradise Hilton is most central and is easier to find because of better signs.

Figure 12.7 Discussion Section

COMPARISON/CONTRAST DISCUSSION

Most recommendation reports follow an organizational plan called **point by point,** as in the model at the beginning of the chapter.

Point by point zigzags from one item to the other, comparing or contrasting some aspect of one item to the same aspect of another item. Under the safety heading in the swing set model, the writers compare the safety features of the Play Time Gym Set to the safety features of the Kiddie Swing Set. Both swing sets are collected under one point or **criterion,** in this case, safety. Figure 12.8 shows the zigzag from one item to another.

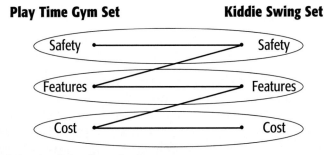

Figure 12.8 Point-by-Point Organization

Figure 12.9 links a general outline for this section to the headings found under the discussion section in the swing set model.

CRITERION 1	SAFETY
Item 1: Explain everything about item 1	Play Time Gym Set
Item 2: Explain everything about item 2	Kiddie Swing Set
Conclusion: Which item is better and why?	Conclusion
CRITERION 2	FEATURES
Item 1: Explain everything about item 1	Play Time Gym Set
Item 2: Explain everything about item 2	Kiddie Swing Set
Conclusion: Which item is better and why?	Conclusion
CRITERION 3	COST
Item 1: Explain everything about item 1	Play Time Gym Set
Item 2: Explain everything about item 2	Kiddie Swing Set
Conclusion: Which item is better and why?	Conclusion

Figure 12.9 Point-by-Point Organization in Swing Set Model

APPENDIXES

Appendixes are another component of some recommendation reports. **Appendixes,** the plural of *appendix,* are supplementary materials that appear at the end of a document. Report writers may decide to attach any information, documents, or supporting materials they believe will aid the audience in understanding the report.

Each document or supplementary item is entered and labeled as a separate appendix. Usually, elements that become appendixes are not directly involved in the report but are closely aligned to information presented.

For instance, a recommendation report suggesting that four part-time sales clerks, rather than one full-time employee, be hired could include a company salary scale as Appendix A and a chart of employee shifts and positions as Appendix B. Some information drawn from these documents would probably be used in the report, but the entire documents might be too distracting to include. So they appear at the end of the document as appendixes, where readers may refer to them.

 Stop and Think What heading of a recommendation report contains the most diverse information? What does it mean to "provide a preview of the rest of the report"? Which part of the report will be the most difficult for you to write? Why?

COMPOSING RECOMMENDATION REPORTS

While decisions regarding formatting and organizing a recommendation report are likely to have an impact on readers' perceptions, those elements are secondary to decisions made in composing: setting criteria, evaluating criteria, and researching criteria.

SETTING CRITERIA

Criteria, the factors on which you base a decision, play an important role in the recommendation report. Figure 12.10 tells where and how criteria are used.

CRITERIA ARE		
Introduced	in the	Introduction
Summarized	in the	Recommendation
Explained and ranked (Why chosen and ranked?)	in the	Scope
Evaluated (one by one)	in the	Discussion

Figure 12.10 Criteria

The criteria you choose depend on what you, your audience, and your colleagues think is important. Safety, special features, and cost are the important factors in choosing a new swing set for Tender Care Center, as noted in the introduction of the report in Figure 12.1. After you select criteria, you must present them in a logical, consistent way.

All criteria must be presented with a name, a rank, and a standard. Choose a simple name, usually a noun, that is parallel to the other criteria. Some reports turn criteria into questions, such as *What is the cost?*

Give each criterion a **rank** to show its relative importance to the other criteria. Which is the most important criterion? second most? third most? List them in descending order, from most important to least important. The rank of criteria may change depending on the circumstances.

For example, younger workers with families moving with the Hennepin Logging operations to West Virginia might rank the criteria for an acceptable town as schools (first), family entertainment (second), and medical facilities (third). Older workers might rank the criteria as medical facilities (first), family entertainment (second), and schools (third).

Finally, determine the **standard** of (or limit to) the criteria. For example, if Tender Care Center will not pay more than $700 for a swing set, then $700 sets the standard for cost.

You may need help refining your criteria. In the swing set model, the playground equipment had to meet several subcriteria under safety and special features. In your report, list subcriteria when you get to the appropriate criterion section. Like criteria, subcriteria should be listed in descending order of importance. Figure 12.11 summarizes how to develop the criteria in your report.

NAME	noun, noun phrase, or question
RANK	criteria listed from most important to least important
STANDARD	a limit that clarifies each criterion (cost, size, quantity, etc.)
SUBCRITERIA	a list of more detailed criteria that fall under one criterion heading

Figure 12.11 How to Develop Criteria

EVALUATING CRITERIA

Evaluating criteria is a step-by-step process. Look at the three subheadings—Play Time Gym Set, Kiddie Swing Set, and Conclusion—under safety in the opening model. Under Play Time Gym Set, the writers discuss the safety subcriteria for one set of swings. Under Kiddie Swing Set, the writers discuss the *same* safety subcriteria for another set of swings. Figure 12.12 shows how the discussion checks off the subcriteria, one by one.

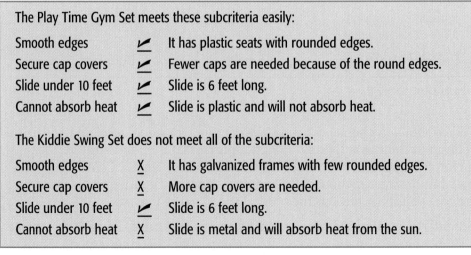

The Play Time Gym Set meets these subcriteria easily:

Smooth edges	✓	It has plastic seats with rounded edges.
Secure cap covers	✓	Fewer caps are needed because of the round edges.
Slide under 10 feet	✓	Slide is 6 feet long.
Cannot absorb heat	✓	Slide is plastic and will not absorb heat.

The Kiddie Swing Set does not meet all of the subcriteria:

Smooth edges	X	It has galvanized frames with few rounded edges.
Secure cap covers	X	More cap covers are needed.
Slide under 10 feet	✓	Slide is 6 feet long.
Cannot absorb heat	X	Slide is metal and will absorb heat from the sun.

Figure 12.12 Checklist to Evaluate Swing Set Safety

The checklist shows at a glance that the Play Time Gym Set meets the preschool's needs for safety more completely. The Play Time Gym Set meets four out of four needs; the Kiddie Swing Set meets one out of four needs. A simple count shows that the Play Time Gym Set wins in the safety category. After the comparison is made, the results are easy to summarize in the conclusion, which follows the discussion of each item.

Suppose that the Kiddie Swing Set had met only the special features and cost criteria and the Play Time Gym Set had met only the safety criteria. Then you would make a judgment call. Safety is ranked as the first concern, more important than special features and cost. You would, therefore, recommend the Play Time Gym Set.

Suppose, however, that both items meet the criteria. Then you should look for some deciding factor. Maybe the cost of one is lower. Maybe the delivery is quicker, the guarantee better. In those rare cases where there is truly no difference between the two items, you are free to recommend either one—or you may want to set other criteria.

RESEARCHING CRITERIA

Research data for a recommendation report can come from a variety of places. Much of the research you conduct for a recommendation report will be **field research,** research using surveys, interviews, and visits. Web sites, manuals, and catalogs can provide product information. Print media in the library can be useful, too. *Consumer Reports,* government publications, business indexes, professional journals, and the many ways to research electronically can all provide data you need. Refer to Chapter 3, *Technical Research,* for more information on researching a topic.

Richard West, in his recommendation report to Hennepin Logging, used several sources. He interviewed his coworkers and workers of another logging operation. He surveyed the employees who would move to the new site. West visited the three towns in West Virginia and interviewed town officials. He reviewed government tax-base documents on the Internet.

Because the writing task was not as involved, the writers of the swing set model in Figure 12.1 did not need to conduct as much research as West. Preschool personnel, sales brochures, a visit to a store, and sales representatives provided all of the information the writers needed.

Be alert to opportunities to present research data in graphics. The swing set model uses tables of costs and features. Other possibilities for graphics are pictures or diagrams of equipment, pie graphs of survey results, and bar graphs to compare items. Refer to Chapter 6, *Document Design and Graphics,* for more information on visual presentation of data.

Stop and Think

Name the sources you might use to research the following recommendation report topics: bass fishing boats, novels, and uniforms for nurses.

■ *Chapter 12 Review*

SUMMARY

1. Decision makers read recommendation reports. Reports can be solicited (asked for) or unsolicited (not asked for). For receptive audiences, place the recommendation section early in the report. For unreceptive audiences, place the recommendation section later in the report.

2. Get started on a recommendation report by defining the problem, generating possible solutions, and devising criteria. Interview colleagues and others to help you with the prewriting process.

3. The recommendation report follows a tight structure using a consistent outline and a comparison/contrast discussion. The major sections include an introduction, the recommendation, the scope, a thorough discussion, and appendixes. The comparison/contrast organization follows a point-by-point pattern that discusses all solutions under one heading or criterion. The recommendation report may be presented in one of many different formats. The format is based on the audience's needs.

4. The introduction contains basic information. The remainder of the report examines criteria. Criteria are presented in the introduction, summarized in the recommendation, explained in the scope, and thoroughly analyzed in the discussion.

Checklist

- Have I devised a reasonable set of criteria by which to judge the items under analysis?

- Have I further defined the criteria by setting standards and including appropriate subcriteria?

- Does my introduction give the purpose of the report, define the problem, narrow the choices, and introduce the criteria in their order of importance?

- Have I considered whether my audience is receptive or unreceptive? If the audience is unreceptive, did I adjust the placement of the recommendation and the number of researched details to accommodate an unreceptive audience?

- Does the scope explain why the criteria were chosen and why they were ranked as they were?

- Is the organization of the discussion clear? Does it follow a point-by-point organizational pattern?

- Have I used graphics appropriately and designed the document to be attractive?

- Have I considered what type of format is appropriate for my audience and what appendixes would help the audience make an informed decision?

Build On What You Know

1. Using the Internet, research one of the products listed below. Then determine an audience, a person or group who might use the product. Using the information you gather on different types or models and different manufacturers' products, devise a reasonable set of criteria by which to judge the items under analysis. Name and describe the audience and list the criteria in order of importance. Also, explain each criterion along with why it was selected.

   a. Golf clubs

   b. PDA (personal digital assistant)

   c. DVD player/recorder

   d. Digital camera

   e. Cosmetics (choose cosmetics for women or men)

2. Suppose you work for a real estate management company. In one of the office buildings your company manages, the heating and air conditioning unit stopped working today. The technician assigned to repair the equipment says that the unit cannot be fixed and should be replaced. The tenant cannot run her business without adequate heating, so she expects action immediately. The technician suggests TempPro heating units as well as Environease machines. He says both are good products with a five-year warranty.

   a. Other than warranty, what criteria might the real estate management company establish?

   b. Suggest a standard for one of the criteria.

   c. Write a problem statement for a recommendation report using this situation. Add specific information as needed.

   d. What graphics might be useful in the recommendation report developed in this case?

3. Travis's doctor has told him to eat a nutritious diet low in fat, cholesterol, and salt and high in complex carbohydrates. Help him evaluate the butter substitutes listed below. What conclusion can you draw from your evaluation?

Substitute	1 tbsp. margarine	1 tbsp. table spread
#1 Low in fat	17% fat	11% fat
#2 Low in cholesterol	0% cholesterol	0% cholesterol
#3 Low in salt	4% salt	5% salt
#4 High in complex carbohydrates	0% complex carbohydrates	0% complex carbohydrates

Apply What You Learned

In small groups, use one of the following scenarios to answer items 4–8. You do not need to use the same scenario for all five questions.

    a. You are on the Entertainment Committee to decide which band to hire for the annual Holiday Ball. According to the survey you sent, employees are evenly divided among a choice for three groups: Newton Jazz Ensemble, Midnight City Rock Band, or Down and Dusty Country Band.

    b. You are on the Hampton Scholarship Committee. Hampton Company gives a $1,000 scholarship to a deserving student every year. The guidance counselor has chosen Wilhelm Nagorski and Annetta Jurevicius as the top two contenders for the scholarship. You and the committee must select one of these students.

    c. You are on Ammsco Chemical's Quality Circle that must decide what goes into the new employee lounge. You have narrowed your choice of microwaves to two: the Trimstyle Model 1400 and the Even Cook Model 550. You, along with the members of your Quality Circle team, must choose the new microwave.

4. Write an introduction to a recommendation report for item a, b, or c. Add details if necessary. Look at the model and at the outline under the Formatting and Organizing Recommendation Reports section in this chapter. You may begin your introduction with "The purpose of this report is to...."

5. For any two of the preceding scenarios, brainstorm a list of criteria. Narrow your list to the top three or four. Rank them in order from most important to least important.

6. Choose one of the lists of criteria from item 5. Apply a standard, or limit, to each of the criteria. Devise subcriteria for one of the criteria.

7. In an oral or written scope section, tell your classmates why you chose your criteria and why you ranked them the way you did.

8. Generate an outline for two of the scenarios. Follow this format. For now, make your best guess for the conclusion under each criterion.

Criterion 1	Criterion 2	Criterion 3
Item 1	Item 1	Item 1
Item 2	Item 2	Item 2
Conclusion	Conclusion	Conclusion

9. List some problems in your community. Focus for a moment on one you care about most. Could two or three courses of action solve this problem? Write a report to your city official recommending a course of action. Research your courses of action using the library or other resources.

Use the Work Is A Zoo! worksheets on the Data CD to guide you through this activity.

Work Is A Zoo!

Anya calls you into her office to tell you that an anonymous donor gave money to the zoo. She says that this person would like the money to be directed toward purchasing new multimedia tools for the students who visit the zoo.

Specifically Anya wants to use the money to purchase new computers for the zoo's learning center. She wants visitors to be able to view web sites that contain information about the zoo's latest programs as well as fun animal facts. She would also like users to be able to download video presentations about the animals' lives at the zoo. She says that with the purchase of the new computers, the zoo may hire a learning center director who might offer classes in the learning center.

Anya explains that the computers will be used by visitors of all ages. The visitors will also have varying computer experience, so the computers should be as easy to use as possible for the less experienced users.

"This will be a great addition to our ZiPS program!" she says. "That's where you come in," she goes on to tell you. Anya explains that she would like you to research new computers for the program and write a recommendation report offering your top three choices. She then gives you her list of criteria.

The computers must:

- Be under $700 each.

- Come equipped with word processing and graphics software.

- Have at least 256 MB of memory.

- Contain both a DVD and diskette drive.

- Come equipped with deluxe encyclopedia software.

PROPOSALS

GOALS

DEFINE proposals and determine their purpose

PLAN to write proposals

COMPOSE informal proposals

COMPOSE formal proposals

See the Data CD for Write-To-Learn and In The Know activity worksheets.

WRITE-TO-LEARN

Think of a time when you have had a successful sales experience. This experience may have been a situation in which you persuaded a person or a group of people to purchase a product or service or to agree to an idea. In a brief journal entry, write a narrative of that experience. Include ways in which you prepared to make the sale as well as a description of your audience.

In The Know

appendix usually the last element or special part of a formal report; a place to include documents, data, or graphics not necessary to the discussion in the report but perhaps helpful or interesting to the audience

executive summary a short synopsis of what a proposal is about; written to meet the needs of a busy decision maker; located at the beginning of a formal proposal

glossary an alphabetical listing of terms accompanied by their definitions, located at the end of a proposal

letter of transmittal a letter formally or officially conveying a formal report from the writers to the external audience

limitations factors or situations that prevent problem solving

memo of transmittal a memorandum formally or officially conveying a formal report from the writers to the internal audience

scope what you examine in your efforts to solve a particular problem

pagination the assignment of sequential page numbers within a document

prefatory material parts or elements of a report that come before the main text (introduction, body, and conclusion)

proposals persuasive documents that offer a solution to an identified problem or need

RFP request for proposal, an advertisement seeking proposals to solve a problem or fill a need and often listing criteria for the solution

solicited proposal a proposal that is written in response to an RFP or upon the request of a supervisor or manager

unsolicited proposal a discovery proposal, one that is written because the writer discovered a problem or need and has a solution to offer

Writing@Work

Marcia Spaeth is the CEO of a nonprofit organization called Tender Mercies, Inc. Tender Mercies owns and manages six buildings that have 150 residents who have been homeless and have a chronic mental illness. Marcia is responsible for the day-to-day operations of the organization and for budget and residential needs. Her job is to ensure that these 150 residents have permanent homes.

As a nonprofit organization, Tender Mercies depends on receiving grants from outsiders. Requesting this money is something else that Marcia is responsible for. Her philosophy in asking for donations is to be direct. "Fund-raisers cannot be afraid to ask—anybody and everybody. If you believe in what you are doing, the 'ask' should be easy." In general, Tender Mercies must raise over $500,000 each year to keep their doors open—and this is just to meet their operating budget. So obviously, Marcia has a big job to do.

When writing grant requests, Marcia says that grant guidelines must be followed to a tee. "In writing government grants, every single *i* must be dotted or you will not get funded, or you may get de-funded." Because of the strict guidelines that must be followed, clear, concise writing is essential. Marcia believes that for an organization's credibility, one proves worthy by following directions. Clear, accurate communication reflects on an organization. "Explain your program/project clearly and simply, or you risk not being funded."

Marcia stresses the importance of using money received as specified in a proposal. This is another reason why clear communication is imperative. "To prove to your donor that you are fiscally responsible, using monies received as stated is extremely important. Otherwise, you risk losing funding in the future." Tender Mercies, specifically, has each year an independent audit performed that holds them accountable for doing exactly as they say.

Marcia majored in education at Edgecliff College, and she has an honorary Doctor of Humane Letters degree from the College of Mount Saint Joseph. She initially became involved at Tender Mercies as a board member and a volunteer. As a result of her passion for the organization and her ability to talk to people about its mission, she became the CEO in 2000.

© 2005 Used with permission

Donovan Phillips, President
3301 Heritage Plaza/ Columbus, Ohio 43209/ 614•555•9854

MEMO TO: Donovan Phillips, Owner
FROM: Carl S. Cordova, Management Intern *CSC*
             Convenient Mart #27, Newsome, Ohio
DATE: 10 March 20—
SUBJECT: Proposal for Improving Traffic Flow

SUMMARY

Customer complaints, accidents, congestion, and delays in service point out the need for improvements in traffic patterns through our parking and gas service areas. The addition of guide rails and painted traffic lanes throughout the lot would add order and increase the speed with which we can serve customers. Dimpoulos Paving Company, with reasonable prices and reputable work, offers the best solution to our problem. The project would take less than two weeks from the date of approval, and customers are certain to appreciate the convenience and safety added to the good value they already receive every time they shop at Convenient Mart #27.

STATEMENT OF PROBLEM

Convenient Mart #27 has wide entrances (30' and 50') from two streets, and the entire back property line is open to the Tunbridge Shopping Center parking lot. Therefore, traffic may enter our lot from all directions except the west, the Burger Barn property line. Customers walking to the store after pumping gas are in danger of being hit by a moving vehicle, and customers attempting to wedge themselves between two other vehicles to get gas have bumped into our pumps. Having drivers enter from any direction they choose and park anywhere they choose creates serious safety and efficiency problems.

SOLUTION

Dimpoulos Paving Company can remedy our problem by installing six guide rails and painting traffic lanes and parking spaces on our lot. Guide rails (metal tubes filled with concrete) at the end of each pumping station will keep vehicles in the proper lanes. Likewise, standard-size painted traffic lanes with yellow directional arrows will improve the traffic flow as well as our ability to offer speedy service. In addition, parking spaces will give in-store customers easy access to the store without impeding gas customers.

BACKGROUND

Our current situation will not improve unless we take action. Congestion and accidents will continue. Three collisions, minor yet causing costly damage—more than $750 for each incident—to the cars involved, have occurred in the last two months. Slow service is another result, according to a survey of customers conducted 20–28 February 20—. Observations over the past three weeks show that gas customers cannot get to the pumps, and other customers cannot get to the store. In addition, these problem situations harm our reputation.

Figure 13.1 Informal Proposal Model

Donovan Phillips
Page 2
10 March 20—

METHODS

Dimpoulos will install six guide rails, one at the end of each pumping station. Workers will fill these round metal tubes with concrete to make them stable and paint them yellow to make them visible. Dimpoulos' engineer said that we have room for five parking spaces around the store. Four will be painted white, and one for handicapped access will be painted blue.

The company also will paint yellow traffic lanes with directional arrows on both sides of each pumping station to create six lanes. As you can see in Figure 1 below, three lanes will enter from the north, one exiting to the east on Myrtle Street and two to the south into Tunbridge Shopping Center. One lane will enter from Myrtle and exit to the north onto Highway 102. The other two lanes will feed from the south, vehicles entering from the Tunbridge lot, and exit onto Highway 102.

Figure 1. Proposed Traffic Lanes, Guide Rails, and Parking Spaces

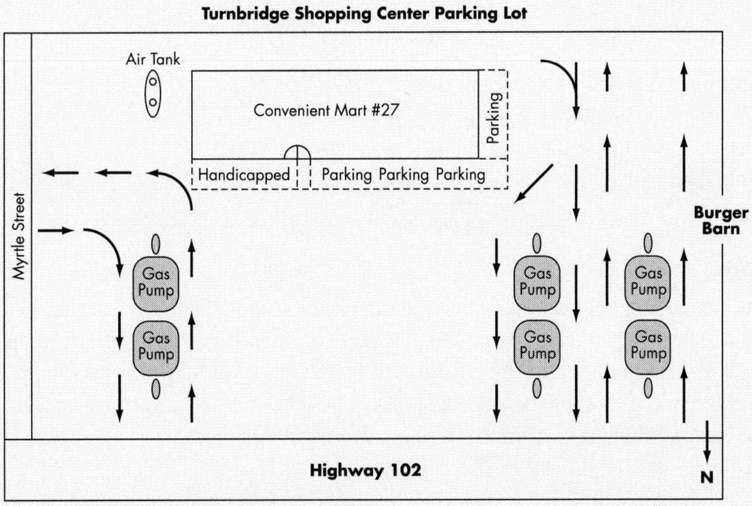

Figure 13.1 Informal Proposal Model, cont.

Donovan Phillips
Page 3
10 March 20—

SCHEDULING
The construction schedule will run as follows:

April 20	April 27	May 2
installing guide rails	painting lanes, arrows, and parking spaces	job completed

Dimpoulos' site supervisor has assured me that all work can be done at night or during our least demanding hours.

BUDGET
The following is a budget for the improvements I suggest:

Six guide rails	$1,049.00
Paint—2 gallons of white	32.86
3 gallons of yellow	48.24
1 gallon of blue	18.98
labor	2,499.00
engineering costs	945.00
	$4,593.08

CONCLUSION
Congestion, accidents, delays in service, and customer response all require that Convenient Mart #27 do something to improve traffic flow. I recommend that you authorize the placement of six guide rails and the painting of traffic lanes and parking spaces to enhance order and efficiency in the way we do business. I believe that the improvements in customer satisfaction and goodwill will more than repay the $4,593.08 cost.

Figure 13.1 Informal Proposal Model

MEMORANDUM

TO: Barkley Wolfe, Manager
           Eastbrook Shopping Center

FROM: Delores O'Malley, Chief of Operations *DO*

DATE: November 23, 20—

SUBJECT: Proposal for Improving Exterior Lighting at Eastbrook

I am submitting for your review my department's proposal to upgrade the exterior lighting system at Eastbrook Shopping Center. This document responds to our October 15, 20-, tenants' meeting and subsequent discussions with you regarding safety on the property.

Of special note are the following sections addressing questions you or our tenants brought up:

Customer attitudes (in Figure 1) 2
Standard illumination levels (Methods) 3
Cost estimate 5

Thank you for reviewing our data and suggestions. We look forward to your response. If you decide to accept our proposal, we are eager to implement the needed changes.

Figure 13.2 Formal Proposal Model

PROPOSAL FOR IMPROVED EXTERIOR LIGHTING
AT EASTBROOK SHOPPING CENTER

Prepared for
Barkley Wolfe, Manager
Eastbrook Shopping Center

Prepared by
Delores O'Malley, Chief of Operations

November 23, 20—

Figure 13.2 Formal Proposal Model, cont.

TABLE OF CONTENTS

EXECUTIVE SUMMARY iv

INTRODUCTION 1

    Problem 1

    Solution 1

    Objectives 1

    Background 1

    Data Sources 2

    Scope and Limitations 2

DISCUSSION 2

    Methods 2

    Scheduling 4

    Materials and Equipment 4

    Cost 5

CONCLUSION 5

GLOSSARY 6

WORKS CITED 7

APPENDIX A. Police Security Ranking for Shopping Centers and Malls 8

List of Illustrations

Table 1. Attitudes Regarding Eastbrook's Exterior Environment at Night 2

Figure 1. Exterior Light Intensity and Proposed Fixture Additions 3

Figure 2. Schedule for Improving Eastbrook's Exterior Lighting 4

Figure 13.2 Formal Proposal Model, cont.

EXECUTIVE SUMMARY

Evidence from our security office, police records, and customer attitude survey proves that Eastbrook Shopping Center has a problem with inadequate lighting outside the building at night.

To improve the lighting so that it meets recommendations of the Illuminating Engineering Society and other experts, we need to exchange our current 150-watt bulbs for 400-watt bulbs and install five new pole lights and six new wall-mount lamps.

The recommended changes will cost less than $1,700 and will improve our security level, liability rating, and public image along with decreasing our energy costs.

Figure 13.2 Formal Proposal Model, cont.

INTRODUCTION

Problem

Inadequate illumination in Eastbrook Shopping Center's parking areas is a serious concern. As good corporate citizens, we have a responsibility to the community to maintain a safe environment. As merchants, we recognize that shoppers and employees expect and have a right to a safe environment. We risk losing customers if Eastbrook doesn't maintain a secure, peaceful image. We also must watch expenses. However, it is evident from our research that, as a result of poor lighting, safety on our grounds is not assured.

Solution

Problems with lighting can be eliminated if we upgrade our exterior lighting system to meet recommendations of local law enforcement and utilities personnel and Illuminating Engineering Society (IES)* guidelines. (Terms designated by an asterisk are defined in the glossary on page 6.) To increase illumination sufficiently in all areas outside the building, we must exchange our 150-watt mercury vapor* bulbs for HPS* bulbs as well as add six wall-mount lights and five new poles in the parking areas.

Objectives

The purpose of this proposal is to improve the quality of exterior lighting at Eastbrook Shopping Center so that customers, employees, and staff feel safe moving to and from the building and their vehicles and so that our parking area does not become the site of illegal activities.

Background

Our records for the last six months prove that we do, indeed, have a problem:

8 incidents of shoplifting (unresolved)	3 purse snatchings
1 assault and battery	1 kidnapping

Further, the police department rates the relative safety of Eastbrook to be low, compared to other shopping centers. (See Appendix A.)

In addition, the survey our marketing agency conducted last month showed that more than 50% of the 400 respondents feel some concern for their safety in entering or exiting our building after dark. Refer to Table 1 for the breakdown of the responses.

Figure 13.2 Formal Proposal Model, cont.

Table 1. Attitudes Regarding Eastbrook's Exterior Environment at Night

(by percentage)

Respondents By Age	Extremely Comfortable	Slightly Comfortable	Comfortable	Slightly Uncomfortable	Uncomfortable
18-20	5	31	15	42	7
21-35	15	19	39	15	12
36-50	5	14	22	23	36
over 50	1	9	13	28	49
TOTAL	26	73	89	108	104
PERCENT	7	18	22	27	26

If this unsafe image continues in the public mind, we will begin to lose valuable customers and eventually lose business occupants of our shopping center. Note particularly the high rate (49%) of persons over 50 who are uncomfortable. With the "graying of America," this group includes a large number of customers we cannot afford to lose. Businesses will move to a location where they and their customers feel safe. Moreover, we risk a lawsuit if incidents occur that we could have prevented.

Data Sources

The data used to create this proposal came from our security records, interviews with Edison Electric public safety directors at other shopping centers, a customer survey we commissioned, data and recommendations from law enforcement and the Illuminating Engineering Society*, and an experiment conducted by our staff.

Scope and Limitations

In seeking solutions, we wanted to increase safety without creating the image of an armed fortress. The solution must appeal to the public and our business occupants. In addition, any changes we make should be visually attractive and not unpleasant for our commercial and residential neighbors. We also have considered cost and energy consumption.

DISCUSSION

Methods

To determine the amount of light currently being produced, we used a footcandle meter* at the base of each pole. An Edison Electric representative recommended an average of one footcandle* per square foot (Smith). Research revealed that IES Lighting Handbook supports this recommendation, suggesting 0.9 or more footcandles (Kaufman 20-26).

Figure 13.2 Formal Proposal Model, cont.

Our results indicated that Eastbrook's lights are generally lower than the suggested illumination. The readings ranged from a high of 1.8 to a low of 0.4, as you can see in Figure 1 below.

Figure 1. Exterior Light Intensity and Proposed Fixture Additions

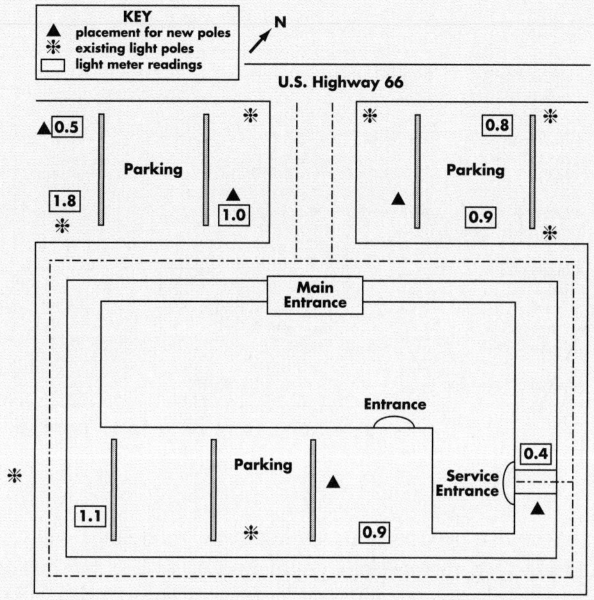

Additionally, a videotaped experiment revealed that in landscaped sections of our parking lots, a person could stand undetected beside a tree or large shrub until the observer was as close as 2 feet. Our research shows almost all parking and pedestrian walkway areas need increased lighting.

Given the videotaped experiment and the footcandle meter readings we collected, an engineer at Edison Electric recommended placement of five new poles outside our building, as indicated on the map in Figure 1 above. Along with the new pole lights, the engineer said that six wall-mount lights installed on the building should bring illumination up to the standard recommendation levels. The six lights will be mounted as follows: one on each side of the main entrance and one on each side of the back entrance, with the remaining two going on the northeast and the southwest walls (Smith).

Figure 13.2 Formal Proposal Model, cont.

Scheduling

We would like to make the suggested improvements as soon as possible. Once equipment has been ordered and received, the project should take less than two weeks, as you can see in Figure 2.

Figure 2. Schedule for Improving Eastbrook's Exterior Lighting

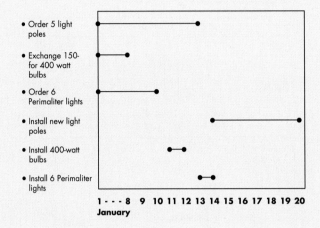

The installation of the five new poles according to IES guidelines will require an outside contractor. Edison Electric has the special equipment needed and can install the poles in one week. The utilities company also will need to replace our 150-watt bulbs with the new 400-watt bulbs since we do not have the cherry picker required to do this job. This task should take approximately one day. Three members of our own maintenance staff can install the six wall-mount lights in less than one day. The entire project should be complete and lighting improved within a month.

Materials and Equipment

We can purchase the 400-watt bulbs from our current supplier, Witherspoon Inc., for only $10 per unit more than we are paying now for the 150-watt bulbs. Moreover, Witherspoon will exchange our current stock of 150-watt bulbs for 400-watt bulbs.

Edison Electric will order the materials and erect the five new poles we need. We should contact with Edison to service the pole lights since we do not own the equipment to do so ourselves.

Figure 13.2 Formal Proposal Model, cont.

Cost

The adjustments necessary to upgrade exterior lighting and implement IES guidelines will cost $1,688.75. The following budget details the expenses for this project:

Five 40-foot metal poles	5 @ $211.95	$1,059.75
Six Perimaliter lights	6 @ $70.00	420.00
Shipping charges for exchanging bulbs		34.00
Edison Electric service fee		175.00
		$1,688.75

In addition to the one-time installation costs, service costs will affect our budget. Operating costs will decrease if this proposal is implemented. Two reasons for the decrease are the longer life and the lower energy consumption of HPS lamps. Mercury vapor lamps have an average rated life of 18,000 to 24,000 hours (Kaufman 8-102) while HPS lamps are likely to be good for 24,000 hours or more (Sorcar 57). In addition, Edison Electric experts suggest we will see an 8-10% reduction in energy use with the HPS lamps, even taking into account the increased wattage (Smith).

CONCLUSION

If Eastbrook's exterior lighting is not improved, future problems are likely to occur. We might face a decrease in the number of customers willing to shop with us in the evening hours and an increase in our insurance rates as a result of liability suits. This proposal is a corrective as well as a preventive measure that increases the safety level for everyone on the property at night. Eastbrook will benefit from a stable environment, night and day.

We recommend that $1,688.75 be allocated in this quarter's operating budget for the installation of 5 new 40-foot metal light poles and 6 new wall-mount fixtures along with the replacement of all 150-watt mercury vapor bulbs with 400-watt HPS lamps. These changes will enhance our security and our image at a reasonable cost.

Figure 13.2 Formal Proposal Model, cont.

GLOSSARY

bulb. A synthetic light source operated with electricity.

footcandle. A unit of illuminance.

footcandle meter. A meter that indicates the amount of light one candle will produce in one foot of space.

HPS. high-pressure sodium. A bulb whose light is derived mainly from sodium vapor.

IES. Illuminating Engineering Society of North America, a professional organization founded in 1906 and dedicated to the theory and practice of illuminating engineering.

lamp. A synthetic light source operated with electricity.

mercury vapor. A bulb whose "light is mainly produced by radiation from mercury vapor" (Sorcar 333).

Figure 13.2 Formal Proposal Model, cont.

WORKS CITED

Abbott, Marvin, Chief of Security, Golden Crossing Mall. Personal Interview. 5 November 19—.

———. IES Lighting Handbook: The Standard Lighting Guide. 5th ed. New York:
    The Illuminating Engineering Society, 1972.

Kaufman, John E., ed. IES Lighting Handbook: A Reference. New York: Waverly Press, 1984.

Smith, Jason, Chief Engineer, Edison Electric. Personal Interview. 1 November 19—.

Sorcar, Prafulla C. Energy Saving Lighting Systems. New York: Van Norstrand Reinhold, 1982.

Figure 13.2 Formal Proposal Model, cont.

APPENDIX A. Police Security Ranking for Shopping Centers and Malls

Metropolitan Police Quarterly Report
June 20— Security Ranking—Shopping Centers and Malls

1 = Most Secure Environment   5 = Least Secure Environment

Rankings are based on a formula including reported incidents, severity of crime, victims, and cost.

Monrovian Heights	1	Wrightly Way Mall	3
Riggan's Place	1	Anandana Plaza	3
Crossroads Mall	2	Caruso's Crossing	4
South Dunbury Center	2	Eastbrook Shopping Center	4
Newtown Shopping Center	2	Benton Shopping Center	5
Village Mall	2	Bargain Hunter's Way	5

Figure 13.2 Formal Proposal Model, cont.

WHAT IS A PROPOSAL?

Persuasive documents that offer a solution to an identified problem or need are **proposals.** Proposals attempt to sell an idea, a product or service, or a new concept or plan. Proposals may be brief or long. The one-page request for a room assignment change you write to your club adviser and the 2,000-page multivolume document selling a new type of amphibious tank to the Department of Defense are both proposals.

WARM UP

As you think about each area of your life—school, home, work, community, and organizations—list problems or needs for which you might seek solutions.

© GETTY IMAGES/PHOTODISC

The term *proposal* hints at the use of this type of document. *Propose* is the base word from which *proposal* comes. Have you "proposed" a party idea to your friends recently? You might think of one person who has proposed marriage to another. If you are thinking of "to suggest" or "to make an offer," you are beginning to understand the proposal's purpose.

A proposal can be a request for support. For instance, the local Boys and Girls Club may direct a proposal to the United Way for money to resurface the club's tennis court. Another proposal might offer a customer goods and services. If a school organization carries out a fund-raising drive by selling candy, the project probably began with a proposal from the candy supplier.

The successful proposal persuades your audience to accept your offered solution and to invest in your idea, product, plan, or service. Employees can use proposals to respond to problems, rather than merely complain about them. The proposal provides a professional means of presenting the employees' ideas for change, which can be empowering.

As Figure 13.3 illustrates, proposals may be divided into several different categories relating to the audience: 1) internal or external; 2) formal or informal; 3) solicited or unsolicited; or 4) sales, research, grant, or planning.

Category	Definition of Category
A. internal	within the organization
external	outside the organization
B. formal	contains parts used in formal reports
informal	omits elements of formal reports; is often briefer
C. solicited	written in response to a request
unsolicited	written independently, without a request
D. sales	attempts to sell a product or service
research	seeks approval for a research study
grant	asks for funding for a project
planning	attempts to persuade the audience to take a certain action

Figure 13.3 Types of Proposals

INTERNAL AND EXTERNAL

Readers of some proposals will be internal; that is, inside the writer's organization. Other readers will be external, or outside the writer's organization. Internal proposals usually attempt to sell an idea or a plan, such as how providing on-site day care can reduce the absentee rate at work, how merit-raise funds should be distributed, and how eliminating classes on the day before finals can ease stress and improve scores. External proposals frequently try to sell goods or services as well as ideas.

INFORMAL AND FORMAL

A proposal is called informal or formal based on the degree to which conventions of formal report writing are followed, how "dressed up" the document looks. Formal proposals contain more parts than informal proposals. Writers decide how formal a document should be based primarily on the audience and its needs.

Because they frequently address an internal audience who understands why the document was written, informal proposals are often brief, generally from one to eight pages. An informed audience eliminates the need for background information or an explanation of the problem. In addition, the report has a flexible organizational plan, uses less formal language, and is frequently presented as a letter or memo. Occasionally, however, a brief informal proposal may be written to an external audience when the subject matter and offered solution are simple and require little explanation.

A proposal going to someone close (in the ranks of the organization) to the writer is usually informal. Likewise, a problem and solution that can be explained in a simple manner are presented in an informal report. The proposal writer would not invest the often lengthy preparation time involved in a formal proposal to suggest something as simple, for example, as changing lunch schedules to allow for a company-wide meeting.

Formal proposals, on the other hand, usually address an external and often unfamiliar audience. They are organized according to standard elements of formal researched reports: cover page, letter of transmittal, title page, table of contents, list of illustrations, **executive summary,** body discussion divided by headings and subheadings, appendixes, **glossary,** and bibliography.

SOLICITED AND UNSOLICITED

A proposal is labeled solicited or unsolicited depending on the audience's role in its initiation. A **solicited proposal** is one the reader asked the writer to create. Sometimes the request comes from a manager at work who sees a problem. The manager then asks for a solution to be presented in a proposal. The request also might appear in an **RFP,** or request for proposal. The RFP states exactly what the customer seeks; proposal writers then prepare their documents to address the needs stated in the RFP. On the other hand, the **unsolicited proposal** is begun when the writer "discovers" a problem, such as an inefficient production line or a lack of water fountains for wheelchair-bound employees. The writer independently identifies a problem, explains it, and offers solutions.

SALES, RESEARCH, GRANT, AND PLANNING PROPOSALS

Based on function, or what the writer wants the audience to agree to do, proposals fall into one of four categories: sales, research, grant, and planning. The sales proposal tries to sell a product or service. The research proposal asks for approval to begin a study or an investigation. A marine biologist at a university, for instance, might request approval (and perhaps funds) for a study of the acid rain effect on a particular fish species. The grant proposal seeks money for a specified project, such as beginning a horseback riding program for children with cerebral palsy. The planning proposal attempts to persuade an audience to take a particular action, as in a plan to improve food service at a pizza restaurant's drive-through window by rearranging preparation tables for efficiency.

A single proposal may combine several categories mentioned here. As you read proposals, you may discover that as many as four categories apply to one document. For instance, the informal proposal presented at the beginning of this chapter is brief and familiar, identifies a problem, speaks to an internal audience, and attempts to persuade readers to take action. So the report is an informal, unsolicited, internal planning proposal.

FORMATTING

The best format for a proposal is determined by the audience's needs and the function or type of proposal. If writers are submitting a formal proposal to a prospective client, they might want to prepare a bound booklike document for decision makers to read and review. The writers of an informal proposal suggesting ways to improve recycling efforts within a printing company could send their proposal to the manager as an e-mail attachment.

A company that installs electronic cable in public buildings could post a proposal to a web site for viewers' access. Some proposal writers could take advantage of images and hyperlinks to persuade the audience by sending a CD containing sound and video as well as links to useful sites.

Decision makers in many different positions in business and industry read proposals. Yet most of these proposal readers read only a portion of the document. They read the section or sections that deal with their area of interest and expertise. Thus, readers evaluate the proposal and accept or reject the suggestions based on the data presented in the section they review.

Stop and Think

Read the models beginning on pages 320 and 323 and review the definition of *proposals* in the *In The Know* section. How do these models fulfill the definition of a proposal?

GETTING STARTED ON PROPOSALS

Now that you know about the different types of proposals, you are ready to plan for writing one. The proposal begins with a problem or a need. The problem may be one you have discovered yourself or one someone pointed out to you, as in an RFP or in a memo or letter from another professional.

© GETTY IMAGES/PHOTODISC

A problem-solving strategy, such as the one listed below, can make your work as a proposal writer easier and can help you focus on the problem:

■ Determine whether you have a problem.

■ If you do, define the problem and your purpose.

■ Conduct preliminary research.

■ Determine the **scope** and **limitations** of your study.

■ Identify the factors or subparts of the problem.

■ Brainstorm possible solutions.

■ Gather data to support the possible solutions.

■ If possible, test and evaluate solutions.

Once you have gone through the problem-solving process and are ready to write your proposal, several strategies can help you appeal to your audience. Create a chart using a sheet of paper with a line drawn down the middle. On the left half of the page, write everything you think the readers need or want in the solution. For instance, if you have an RFP, the criteria, as with a job advertisement, are probably noted there. If you have no RFP, make the list based on your research and insight into the problem and audience.

On the right half of the page, list what your solution offers that the reader wants or needs. In other words, for every want or need in the left column, explain how your plan will fulfill that want or need. Thus, you will have persuasive tools ready for composing your proposal. The following example relates to a sales proposal for football helmets.

Criteria	Response
protects players	■ 1 inch of solid tempered plastic covered with fiberglass for resistance ■ ¾-inch foam padding from ear to ear ■ adjustable liner for greater protection
economical	■ $29.90 per unit, 10% less than the average ■ 10-year warranty/automatic replacement

Complete the Prewriting worksheet on the Data CD.

Another technique some proposal writers use in analyzing audience is to imagine how the reader thinks and feels. Anticipating the readers' questions and concerns may help you understand the readers' point of view and anticipate their needs. Another technique you might try is to gather audience information relating to the proposal issues, as in the following examples:

Problem	■ Is the reader aware of the problem? ■ How much does the reader know about the problem? ■ What factors of the problem most concern the reader?
Solution	■ What do the criteria (perhaps in an RFP) established by the audience tell me about the audience? ■ Prioritize the decision maker's concerns: personnel, money, time, production, public image, and ethics. ■ How open-minded or how critical will your audience be?

You can add other questions to this audience analysis list as you consider the problem, solution, and benefits of the solution.

Focus on Ethics

Sean Walker is an administrative assistant at Pathmark House, a nonprofit agency that serves children from low-income families. The director, Nicole Bainbridge, has recently expanded Sean's responsibilities to include writing grant proposals. Sean enjoys the work and is good at it; already three of his proposals have been approved, bringing in a total of $65,000. Last week the board of directors, whose members Sean is getting to know, called him into a meeting to thank him for the good work.

Nicole wants to hire an assistant to help with the office work, but there is not enough money in this year's budget. Nicole tells Sean that they will pay the assistant's salary with the $15,000 Shilling Foundation grant, a grant that Sean wrote. The Shilling Foundation specified that the grant monies be used specifically to purchase computer equipment and to pay for classes for Pathmark House clients. What should Sean do?

Stop and Think

Why should proposal writers define or state the problem?

COMPOSING INFORMAL PROPOSALS

The organizational strategy of the informal proposal, like that of many technical reports, is designed with the busy decision maker in mind. The proposal usually opens with the most important information the reader needs to know. So writers give information about the problem and solution at the beginning of the report. The organizational plan for the rest of the proposal is flexible to fit the many different situations writers are likely to encounter in their working environments. No matter how you organize your own proposals, you must remember your audience throughout the writing process and ask yourself if you are responding to all readers' questions and doubts.

Informal proposals begin with an Executive Summary or Abstract. Following the summary information, they contain the same parts as any written document: an Introduction, a Body, and a Conclusion. The summary or abstract is a condensed version of the proposal. The introduction presents the problem, solution, and whatever background the reader needs. The body of the proposal is the main section; it covers the facts, the specific evidence to convince the reader that the plan is worthy.

The conclusion, then, wraps up the report and spurs the reader into action.

The specific information contained, and thus the headings used (with the exception of the Executive Summary or Abstract), within each section may vary from situation to situation. Depending on the needs of the problem and solution being proposed, the writer decides which subsections to include and which to omit. Possible headings to be used in each section are listed below.

Section	Possible Headings
Introduction	Problem Addressed and Solution Objectives of Proposed Plan Background Data Sources Scope and Limitations
Body	Methods Scheduling Capabilities, Qualifications of Personnel Materials and Equipment Expected Results Plan for Evaluating Results Feasibility Budget (usually in tabular form) Justification of Budget Items, where necessary
Conclusion	Summary of Key Points Request for Action

DRAFTING THE SUMMARY

The summary or abstract is designed with the busy decision maker in mind. In a short informal proposal, this section may appear on the title page or, typically, as the first paragraph in the report. It provides a brief overview of the essential ideas presented in the proposal. The summary should include a problem statement, the proposed work objectives, the project impact, and the work plan. Cost is not usually discussed in the summary because writers want to present all their evidence to persuade readers first; then the writers hope readers will not be "turned off" by the cost but will be able to justify the expense.

DRAFTING THE INTRODUCTION

The introduction answers the "why" in the reader's mind; it explains why the proposal was written. You must identify the problem up front. Another important element of the introduction is your proposed solution to the problem. This statement should be clear but brief. Later, in the body, you will provide further details and justify your proposal.

The introduction further explains your objectives, or what you hope to accomplish, and clarifies the value of the work and why it is worth the investment you seek. This section also may require a brief historical background of the problem.

For example, a proposal recommending a change in the way student newspapers are distributed might be viewed more seriously if the writer can prove that the current distribution system encourages littering:

> Because the papers are placed in stands near doorways only one hour before students leave campus, students have papers in hand as they walk outside and away from recycling bins and waste receptacles.

Such an explanation of the background will prove to your reader that you have a grasp of the problem. In addition, the introduction may explain the need for a solution. Some readers may ask, "Why not simply leave things as they are?" In this case, note the effects of ignoring the problem.

Another element of the introduction is to discuss how you or other personnel are qualified to solve this problem. In addition, you might describe where you will seek information to help solve the problem. Data sources could be printed materials (such as books, reports, or brochures), interviews, observations, or experiments. The introduction also might define scope or the extent you will search for solutions as well as limitations or boundaries of the project, such as restrictions on time, space, equipment, money, or staff.

DRAFTING THE BODY

After the problem and solution have been described in the introduction, the body of the informal proposal becomes more specific about your plan. The specific details—the facts, figures, statistics, dates, locations, and costs—are the ammunition you use to persuade your audience. For this section, you might address the topics on the next page as needed.

Methods	Explain your methodology, what your approach to the problem will be, what criteria (perhaps from the RFP) you will meet, and what outcome or product you will deliver at the date you specify. Justify your plan of work and any exceptions to the RFP, as needed.
Scheduling	Present a calendar of the work planned and expected completion dates to assure your audience that you anticipate efficiency. Effectively illustrate scheduling, as appropriate. Flowcharts or timelines are excellent for visual presentation of timetables.
	List personnel, numbers, and qualifications of personnel.
	Describe facilities, both available and needed, to be used.
Capabilities	Assure your audience that you can deliver the work you propose by 1) noting the abilities of people involved and 2) describing the successful track record of your organization.
Materials and Equipment	Review materials and equipment to be used. This section is particularly important in scientific projects. Even in a proposal dealing with construction of a building or another product, the type of fabrication material is likely to be critical to the audience.
Expected Results	Explain what you think the result of your work will be.
Plan for Evaluating Results	Outline your plan for evaluating the success of the solution once it is implemented.
Feasibility	Explain how you find the conclusion reasonable to implement.
Budget	Present, typically in a chart, the costs for the work, including salaries, equipment, materials, travel, communication costs, services, and other expenses.
Justification	Clearly (and persuasively) explain the reason for any expenses your audience may question.

DRAFTING THE CONCLUSION

The conclusion should be straightforward and brief. It might include a summary of key points, such as those noted in the summary section, and it should call for the audience to take action. Make the call to action specific and clear, including dates and amounts.

EXPLORING THE COMPOSING STRATEGIES WITH A MODEL

Consider a sample problem to illustrate the composing process: Kimi Chey, a student at Martinique College, has noted that the local newspaper, *The Martinique Times,* contains little information from her school. Occasionally *The Times* carries a report of a football, soccer, or basketball game or some other sporting event, but she would like to see the newspaper cover other school news as well. You will follow Chey through the process of writing a short informal proposal in which she suggests a solution to the editor of her hometown newspaper, Gary Cedillo. Chey decides to write a summary and place it on the title page, but she will wait until later to write it. After the proposal is written, she will pull major ideas from it for her summary.

To help *The Martinique Times* editor understand the problem she has identified, Chey considers the "why" question. She writes a clear statement of the problem: **Except for sporting events, no news from Martinique College appears in *The Martinique Times*.** Beneath that statement, she lists her goals:

- Include club news.

- Note the dates of special events.

- Report on students who deserve attention for academics or other achievements.

- Highlight instructors and their contributions.

- Provide a forum for students.

- Encourage more students to read the local paper.

These goals are the things she would like to have happen as a result of her proposal.

Chey then brainstorms about how these objectives could be met. She thinks of several alternative solutions: 1) develop a student-owned, student-operated paper, 2) request that students be given space for contributions, 3) ask the newspaper to cover the school's news in a more comprehensive manner, or 4) suggest that the school administration submit articles occasionally. She also thinks about the need for the action she proposes: Is there any other way to accomplish these goals? Is anyone else concerned?

The next step Chey takes is to move from brainstorming to analysis, to become more critical in her thinking. For each of the alternate solutions she developed, Chey lists positives and negatives. For example, under solution 1, developing a student-owned newspaper, she lists the following:

Positive	Negative
Students would have complete control.	A great deal of money would be needed.
Students would learn by doing.	Would students have the time to do a good job?
Students would read and support their own paper.	Would work and quality be maintained with student turnover?

Chey realizes her proposal is directed to a business leader interested in the effects of her proposed action on his or her work: profits, personnel, schedule, and public image. She knows that a solid plan with accurate facts and figures is necessary to convince her reader. Having chosen the plan with the most "positives" and the least "negatives," she again brainstorms ideas to be included in the body of her proposal.

Chey decides that the best solution to the problem is to have a student-written column placed weekly in *The Martinique Times*. She then must assure the editor of a sound plan for implementing this idea. She notes who will be involved and their qualifications, who will be responsible, and how the work will be done. Using the outline for the body of the proposal, Chey explores the information she will need to convince her audience. To make the work schedule clear, Chey develops a chart that depicts each step in the development of the student-written column. The chart is labeled to identify the person responsible for each phase. She uses this chart to check for factors she might have overlooked in getting the column into the paper.

Chey prepares to write her conclusion by reviewing her strongest selling points. She knows that her closing should include a clear statement of exactly what she wants the editor to do: Does she want him to announce the beginning of the new column in the paper, call the school's president with an invitation, write to the school journalism instructor, or speak with students or a student group? To see the result of Chey's brainstorming, researching, analyzing, critical thinking, drafting, revising, and editing, read her final draft in Figure 13.4 below and continued on the next page.

Route 1, Box 704
Martinique, MI 12002
23 October 20–

Mr. Gary Cedillo, Editor
THE MARTINIQUE TIMES
113 South Main Street
Martinique, MI 12002

Dear Mr. Cedillo:

As a senior at Martinique College who is interested in pursuing a career in commercial art, I read your newspaper regularly. I have been impressed with the innovative designs and attractive page layout of your publication. However, I also have noticed one element of the TIMES that could be improved.

Problem
The problem is lack of news from Martinique College. Your reporters cover sporting events very well, yet many other events and activities supported by the student body go unmentioned. I believe that students and your other readers are interested in information about Martinique College's special events, academic and other achievements, instructors and their contributions, and club activities as well as sports.

Solution
News from all areas of interest at Martinique College could be covered and at no expense to the TIMES. If you include a weekly column devoted to Martinique College news, students can serve as reporters, gathering and writing the stories. Other students can take photographs to accompany the articles. To assure you of high-quality work, the column can be managed through the Journalism Club; Mr. Jan Justesen, English instructor and club adviser, can supervise this activity.

Objectives
Including student news could have several effects. A change in coverage probably will increase the number of students buying and reading the paper. Thus, the students will benefit by being better informed and by improving their time spent reading. Further, the paper will benefit by developing readers (customers) early in their lives. In addition, the community, by being made more aware of college events, may become more supportive of education and become avid readers of the school column. Moreover, being given a forum certainly will encourage some students to become better writers and readers, better athletes, better at whatever they do.

Figure 13.4 Informal Proposal for an External Audience

Mr. Gary Cedillo
Page 2
23 October 20—

Methods and Scheduling
If you accept this proposal and invite students to submit a weekly column, informing the student body and organizing participants should take no more than one month. During that time, we will choose a name for the column and assign specific duties. Mr. Justesen will develop a chain of command and guidelines for everyone. We currently have experienced writers in the Journalism Club, some who have previously contributed to your paper. These writers will help new staff and photographers polish their work.

Our workflow, as illustrated in Figure 1 below, is designed so that all work will be done well and on time. Once organized, we will have an editorial board; their job will be to review story ideas, select the best, assign writers and photographers, help with editing, and submit work to Mr. Justesen. Mr. Justesen will supervise the entire process and will approve all work before submission to your office.

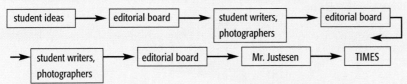

Figure 1: Workflow Process for Substituting Articles

Maintaining the Column
During summer break and school holidays, the column could be suspended. On the other hand, you could retain readers by continuing the column. Perhaps a student intern could report on Martinique College holiday activities.

Conclusion
A student-generated column in the TIMES will be beneficial in many ways. It will sell papers by creating new readers. It will keep readers informed of all areas of Martinique College. It will not cost the paper anything in time or wages. It will encourage students to be their best. It will bring us all closer together. Please help us make these things happen by allowing space for a student column in your paper. Please call Mr. Justesen at 555-0169 with an invitation now.

Sincerely,

Kimi Chey

Kimi Chey

Figure 13.4 Informal Proposal for an External Audience, cont.

Stop and Think

In a large organization, different people are likely to read only the sections of a proposal relating to their area of expertise. Name the sections the following employees might read: CEO (chief executive officer), technical expert, and comptroller (financial officer).

COMPOSING FORMAL PROPOSALS

In the last section of this chapter, you read about informal proposals. Informal and formal proposals are similar. They are both persuasive documents that offer the writers' answers to readers' problems or needs. In both types, writers choose from the same optional subsections in the same order under Introduction, Body, and Conclusion.

© GETTY IMAGES/PHOTODISC

Formal proposals may differ from informal proposals in several ways:

■ Tone, such as the detached, professional voice writers might use with a high-level official

■ Additional report parts, such as the Glossary, Appendix, and the transmittal correspondence

■ Complexity of the outcome, such as the construction of a new building or the $2 billion purchase of jet airliners

Although not used as frequently as informal reports, formal proposals are called for in many circumstances. The following examples are typical:

■ A marine biologist, disturbed by the fish kills in a local estuarine system, wants to study the effect of municipal wastewater dumping on the fish. The biologist seeks funds from the State Department of Fish and Wildlife for a five-year project.

■ Having received an RFP (request for proposal), a major defense contractor proposes its plan for a new amphibious tank. The potential customer is the U.S. government, and the price is over $3 billion.

■ A mechanic in a ball-bearing plant is inspired to improve the precision of a robotic welding machine after studying similar machines at another facility. Having decided on the adjustments needed and the cost in work hours and materials, the mechanic requests approval from the new plant manager.

PREWRITING

Prewriting techniques should help you plan to write a formal proposal. During the prewriting phase, you collect and organize data and determine your objectives. Since a formal proposal is often longer and more involved than other technical reports, prewriting is especially important.

Planning for Persuasion Formal proposal readers need to be convinced, as a salesperson convinces a customer. If you are to be a successful proposal writer, you must address your audience effectively and prevent any skepticism. Here are some guidelines for convincing your audience:

- Collect as many facts as you can to support your proposed plan.

- Be accurate. Plan to check your data. If your reader discovers a discrepancy, an exaggeration, or a mistake, you lose credibility.

- Study your audience and the situation so that you understand the reader's point of view. Planning with an understanding of the reader allows you to write a more convincing proposal.

- Be realistic in your planning. Do not propose to do a job in two weeks to make the sale if you honestly believe the work will take a month. You may suffer the consequences later since your proposal becomes a legal document when it is accepted.

Planning for Integration Another goal of prewriting the formal proposal is planning for integration. The entire document must come together as a logical whole. The description of the problem, for example, will affect how the reader views the effectiveness of the solution. When different writers are composing different sections, a primary writer or editor must consider the entire report, not just one section, as he or she plans and edits.

Communication Dilemma

A team of employees at Blue Vale Packing worked for two months on a sales proposal to a major national mail-order company. The proposal offered to supply all foam-packaging materials for the business. Since this proposal could represent a major portion of Blue Vale's business, the team worked diligently to develop and present the best plan possible. However, a serious problem arose that the team had not anticipated. Most sales proposals must be approved and signed by a person or people at the head of the organization. The team scheduled time for researching, prewriting, composing, and editing before the submission deadline. What they did not anticipate was the president of Blue Vale leaving on a four-week business trip ten days before the due date. Therefore, the president would not be available to approve or sign the proposal in time to meet the submission deadline. What could the team do? Could they salvage the situation and meet the submission deadline? How?

Planning for Graphics, Definitions, and Supplemental Materials As you gather data, consider whether a graphic could help your audience understand the information. Then decide what type of graphic aid will most clearly depict the idea. (Refer to Chapter 6, *Document Design and Graphics,* for more help with planning graphics.)

Plan for terms you will use and whether your readers will need definitions for them. If the proposal needs definitions, decide whether you better serve your audience by placing the definitions within the report or in a glossary at the end. If you need to give only a few definitions, it may be easier for you (and your reader) to include definitions within the text. However, proposals that need numerous definitions should probably include a glossary after the body of the report.

In addition to graphics and definitions, think about materials you might like your readers to have access to but do not want to include in the body of the proposal. Consider placing relevant, but not necessary, materials in an **appendix.** For example, if you have used the results of a survey in your proposal, you may wish to show interested readers exactly how you gathered data by including the survey instrument as an appendix.

PARTS OF FORMAL PROPOSALS

The format of formal proposals is designed to aid the readers. Each formal proposal follows the same basic plan so that readers and writers know what to expect and where to find information they seek. Remember, many expert readers review only one or two sections of a formal proposal.

The parts listed below make up the formal proposal. (Those parts followed by an asterisk are used in informal proposals as well.)

Letter/Memo of Transmittal	Body (or Discussion)*
Title Page	Conclusion (or Summary)*
Table of Contents	Glossary
List of Illustrations	Appendixes
Executive Summary (or Abstract)*	Works Cited
Introduction*	

Letter/Memo of Transmittal The **letter** or **memo of transmittal** is similar to the cover letter mailed with a resume. It is an official greeting and introduction of the document to the reader. Write a letter to accompany a proposal when addressing an external audience and a memo when addressing an internal audience. Use any accepted letter or memo format.

Since the message is usually good news for the audience, this letter or memo uses the direct strategy:

1. Begin with the purpose, the fact that you are submitting a proposal. Name the proposal topic and explain whether you are responding to an RFP, responding to a request, or initiating the proposal on your own.

2. Note any areas of special interest to the reader.

3. Thank the audience for reviewing the proposal. You may offer to provide more information or answer questions.

Complete the Composing and Formatting a Title Page worksheet on the Data CD.

The letter/memo of transmittal is usually written last, after the rest of the proposal is complete.

Title Page The title page of a formal proposal, like a book cover, gives the reader important information about the document. In designing the title page, use white space to make the page attractive. Be clear, accurate, complete, and precise in composing the title page. Provide the following:

- A descriptive title of the proposal

- The company or companies involved

- The names of the writers

- The date the proposal is being submitted

Some internal proposal writers include, as part of the title page, a routing list of readers who will review the document.

Note that a precise title, such as *Proposal to Develop a Policy Governing Substitute Staffing for Absentee Technicians in the Fiber Twist Area* or *Proposal to Purchase and Install the Evermorr Secure 3120 Security System in Glynndale Condominiums* is useful because it gives readers more information than a vague title such as *Proposal to Deal with Absent Workers* or *Proposal to Improve Security in Glynndale Condominiums*.

Table of Contents The table of contents should be designed so that it is attractive, easy to read, and clear. The table of contents may appear alone on a page, or it may be combined with the list of illustrations on a page. The words *Table of Contents,* in all capital letters or initial capitals, should be centered at the top of the page. Beneath these words, the list of contents should, by indentation, visually demonstrate relationships between ideas. For example, section headings may be at the left margin while less important ideas are indented toward the right.

You may choose to double-space a short list for a table of contents, but a longer listing should be single-spaced to make reading easier. Enter headings and subheadings on the left side of the page, **pagination** on the right, and dots (periods) between the heading and its page number.

List of Illustrations Begin with the words *List of Illustrations* (in all capital letters or initial capitals) centered at the top of the page or two to four lines beneath the last table of contents entry. Two to four lines beneath the title, provide the label, number, and descriptive title of the graphic on the left and the page location on the right.

Executive Summary (or Abstract) At the top of the page, centered (in all capital letters or initial capitals), key the words *Executive Summary* or *Abstract.* The executive summary is usually written in paragraph form, two to four paragraphs, on a page by itself. It may be single- or double-spaced.

Write the executive summary after you have finished the rest of the report. Keep the reader in mind as you compose. This section, as the title Executive Summary implies, is designed with the administrator in mind. Busy

executives want the story quickly and only the essential information: the problem, the solution, and the benefits of the solution. Because these readers are concerned with the big picture, the overall health of the organization, they may not read the specific information in the body of the proposal, only the summary. However, proposal writers should plan the summary for all readers, not just executives.

Introduction, Body of Discussion, and Conclusion In long reports (perhaps 20 pages or more), each of these major section headings may begin a new, separate part of the formal proposal. Each section starts on a new page with the heading name, such as *Introduction,* in all capital letters or initial capitals centered at the top of the page. In shorter reports, the entire body may flow from one section to another without page breaks.

The Introduction. The introduction is the framework to prepare readers for the body of the proposal. The introduction answers the questions *what* and *why*. No matter which subparts of the introduction you include in your document, clearly state for your readers the problem and a solution or alternate solutions. If you determine that the readers need background information, summarize the situation and the proposer's qualifications. Include information about your company and personnel, such as the number of years in business, staff and equipment resources, previous clients, and success with similar projects, that will enhance the credibility of your proposal. Since any proposal reviewer might read the introductory material, remember to communicate so that administrators, managers, technical experts, and financial managers can all understand.

The Body of Discussion. If the introduction sets the framework of ideas, the body of a formal proposal is the crux of the argument, the specifics of persuasion. The body is the section in which the technical data prove that your idea (solution) will work. Describe methods for carrying out the project, specific tasks, time schedules, personnel, facilities, and equipment. Include an organizational chart of people working on the project so the reader will know who is responsible for a particular area. In addition to outlining what you will do, these specific details convince the reader that your approach is the best one for the situation. The project's budget should clearly show specific costs and perhaps justify the costs. The graphics you have planned should enhance the text of your proposal, not take the place of the text.

The Conclusion. Be concise and direct when you write the conclusion for your formal proposal. You have already provided all of the information to sway your audience to your point of view. This is not the time to add to your sales pitch. Instead, summarize your most convincing points regarding the importance of the project and the benefits of the solution. Then suggest a course of action.

Glossary If you choose to include a glossary, design it so it is easy to read. In the text of the proposal, designate words appearing in the glossary by using asterisks, italics, or some other highlighting technique. Include a footnote or a parenthetical note beside the first entry, telling the readers that they can find definitions in the glossary.

At the top of the glossary page, center the title Glossary. Use all capital letters or just an initial capital *G*. Make the entry word, the word being defined, stand out by using boldface or columns. When using columns, place the entry words on the left and definitions on the right. Alphabetize all words, acronyms, and symbols, as dictionaries do.

Choose words to define and determine the extent of your definitions based on your audience's needs. Do not define words the audience already understands. At the same time, if your proposal will have several reviewers, define a term even if only one of the readers needs the definition. Write definitions using language the readers understand and consider including graphic aids if they will help the readers' understanding.

Appendixes Appendixes are materials that you want your reader to have access to but that are not a primary part of the proposal. In the body of the proposal, where the topic an appendix supports is mentioned, refer readers to the appendix, as in "See Appendix C." Each appendix must be labeled with the word *Appendix* (can be in all capitals) and given a number (or a letter of the alphabet) and a descriptive title, similar to the system for identifying graphics. Make every document an individual appendix.

Works Cited If your proposal has used ideas or words from a source you need to credit, prepare works cited or documentation pages according to the guidelines of the style manual you are using. Consult the style manual your organization or the RFP requires and follow it precisely.

Page Numbers Assigning page numbers for formal proposals works the same as pagination in books. **Prefatory material,** as in the preface or before the report begins, is numbered with lowercase Roman numerals. Prefatory material includes these:

- Letter/memo of transmittal
- Table of contents
- Title page
- List of illustrations

Since the letter or memo of transmittal is the first page, no page number is needed. In addition, a title page is not numbered. Therefore, the table of contents, the third page, would be numbered iii. Use Arabic numerals for the remainder of the proposal, except for the first page of the report itself, which usually begins with the introduction. This first page carries no page number. Place an Arabic 2 on the next page. Number all other pages of the body of the proposal, glossary, appendixes, and works cited with Arabic numerals in sequence. For pagination, follow the style manual you are using or place page numbers centered at the bottom or in the upper right corner of the page.

Complete the Revising Glossary Entries worksheet on the Data CD.

Stop and Think

Who reads the Executive Summary or Abstract of a formal proposal? Where should terms be defined in this type of report?

■ *Chapter 13 Review*

SUMMARY

1. Proposals are persuasive documents that suggest a solution to a problem or a change.

2. Proposals are defined and categorized according to the audience and their needs: internal or external; informal or formal; solicited or unsolicited; or sales, research, planning, or grant.

3. In prewriting, consider how your solution meets the audience's needs.

4. Proposals may be presented in memo, letter, or manuscript format, the choice being determined by the audience and complexity of the proposal. Headings and subheadings within the proposal delineate sections of the introduction, body, and conclusion.

5. The introduction identifies the problem and offers a solution, along with any background information the audience might find helpful.

6. The body uses facts, figures, statistics, graphics, and other evidence to convince the readers to accept the solution or change.

7. The conclusion restates key points and calls on the audience to take action.

8. Formal proposals include many special parts that have unique formatting guidelines. These parts may include a letter/memo of transmittal, a title page, a table of contents, a list of illustrations, an executive summary (or abstract), an introduction, a body (or discussion), a conclusion (or summary), a glossary, appendixes, and a works cited or bibliography.

Checklist

- Have I identified the problem I wish to see resolved?

- Have I carefully analyzed my audience and then listed the audience's needs?

- Have I brainstormed for alternate solutions? Have I listed positives and negatives for each solution on my list?

- Have I thought about and listed my goals?

- If my readers are unaware of the problem, have I explained the problem clearly in the introduction?

- Does the body of the proposal give my readers enough information to make a decision?

- Have I provided enough evidence, such as facts, figures, and testimony?

- Does my conclusion contain the most important ideas from the proposal? Does my conclusion also call for action from the readers?

- Have I made information easy for my readers to use by including headings and subheadings?

- If my proposal is formal, have I included all of the needed parts?

Build On What You Know

1. Interview an employee concerning a particular problem as well as the solution for which that employee was responsible. Write a description of the problem, the methods the employee used to solve the problem, the effectiveness of the solution, and the satisfaction of the employee with his or her work.

2. Use library research or interviews to learn more about a great problem solver or innovator, such as Thomas Edison, Mother Theresa, Albert Einstein, Eleanor Roosevelt, or Jonas Salk. Find out as much as you can about the methods the person used in seeking solutions. Make an oral presentation of your findings to your class.

3. Interview a proposal writer to find out how his or her company uses formal proposals, who else (within the writer's organization) writes them, and how successful the proposals have been. Ask what this writer thinks is essential in preparing an effective formal proposal.

4. Using the Internet or regional or state newspapers or professional journals in your school, public, or home library, search for requests for proposals.

    a. Copy the RFPs and bring them to class for discussion.

    b. From a careful reading of one RFP, identify the problem that needs to be solved.

    c. Identify the audience the proposal writer needs to address.

    d. Brainstorm to create a list of ideas to include in the proposal introduction.

5. Choose two problems for which you would consider proposing a solution. Write a paragraph or two describing the problem and the decision maker (audience) for each.

6. List possible solutions to a problem or need you have identified.

7. Using a problem whose solution has already been implemented, re-create the thinking proposal writers might have done by:

    a. Developing a list of positive and negative aspects of the solution.

    b. Creating a list showing how the solution meets the needs of the audience or solves the problem.

8. Write a proposal convincing your parents to take you (or to allow you to go with friends) on the perfect vacation. Identify the problem, explain the solution, convince them of the reasonableness of your plan, and justify the cost by preparing a budget.

9. Critique a proposal from business or industry. Analyze how the writers met (or did not meet) the needs of the audience. Review formatting features. Determine organizational patterns. Share the results of your critique orally or in an essay.

Apply What You Learned

10. Imagine that you have asked your parents for a car. They have said, "Yes, but—." Your responsibility will be to pay for insurance, gas, and maintenance if they purchase this car for you. In an informal proposal:

    a. Explain the type of car you want and why.

    b. Describe how you will pay for the car's expenses if you do not have money and your parents do not want you to work more than 10 hours a week, such as would be required at a restaurant, grocery store, or department store. Identify your problem and consider alternate solutions. Be creative! Think of ways to earn money other than holding a regular job. List as many options as you can.

    c. Write the solution you would propose to your parents.

11. Write an informal sales proposal to Karen Grissom, owner of Mason Office Center. You own an indoor plant service, Green Thumb Planting, and you are asking Grissom to become a new client. After visiting the office complex, you determine that the building could use 31 large and 14 medium-sized low-light plants. Your service provides plants and pots, weekly maintenance, and monthly replacement of imperfect plants. If Grissom accepts your proposal, you are ready to install the plantings within one week. For your service, Grissom will pay a $350 installation fee and a $35 maintenance fee each month thereafter. Your proposal should persuade Grissom to sign a service contract. Create and use any additional details or graphics you need to prepare an effective document.

12. With a group of classmates who share your interests, write a formal proposal to solve a specific problem. Identify a problem at school, at work, or in the community that must be dealt with by decision makers distant from you on the organizational ladder; for example, a superintendent, president, or member of the board of trustees. Your proposal should require some research. Here are examples of problems to solve:

School	Work	Community
new or improved equipment	equipment or work space	sidewalks/bike paths
access for the computer lab	wages or department budget	zoning or use of land
snack bar	improved working conditions	street/traffic signs
new club or sport	sponsorship of sports team	access for people with disabilities to neighborhood stores
needed programs	insurance/benefits	street/park lighting

Use the brainstorming worksheet on the Data CD to think of ideas for the learning café. Be sure to follow the problem-solving steps to come up with an argument for the proposal.

Work Is A Zoo!

One weekend as you are relaxing in an Internet café surfing the Internet and drinking a glass of lemonade, you suddenly have a great idea for the zoo. You believe that older students as well as instructors would like a place where they could get a bite to eat and something to drink while they surfed the Internet to learn more about their favorite animals at the zoo. Currently the zoo does not have a café, nor does it have a place where students can learn more about animals on their own time. You become excited as you think about how much the students could learn on their own in the café. They could even form discussion groups in the café, led by zoo employees, to talk about issues at the zoo and environmental concerns. You believe that this learning café would encourage older students to spend more time at the zoo.

Even though you have this great idea in your head, you must communicate it to Anya and Tyrone so they will agree that it is a good idea. You know that the zoo just received funds from an anonymous donor, so you could explain to Anya and Tyrone that part of the money should go toward the much-needed café.

Plan and write an informal proposal to Anya and Tyrone about opening a learning café for older students at the zoo. Remember to:

- Define the problem and your purpose.
- Conduct preliminary research.
- Determine the scope and limitations of your study.
- Identify the factors or subparts of the problem.
- Brainstorm possible solutions.
- Gather data to support the possible solutions.
- Test and evaluate solutions, if possible. You also can discuss a plan for evaluating possible solutions.

TECHNICAL READING

GOALS

RECOGNIZE the differences between literary reading and technical reading

USE strategies for reading technical passages

WRITE-TO-LEARN

How does your science or computer textbook differ from your literature textbook? Do you read scientific or technical material differently from the way you read literature? If so, how? Which type of material do you prefer to read and why? How often do you read scientific or technical material? How do you remember this kind of material?

In The Know

anticipate to guess or predict before actually reading a passage what kind of reasoning it might present

background knowledge knowledge and vocabulary already learned that a reader calls upon to better understand new information

formal outline a listing of main ideas and subtopics arranged in a traditional format of Roman numerals, capital letters, lowercase letters, and numbers (I., A., 1., a.)

graphic organizers portray notes visually with a system of circles, rectangles, and connecting lines that show the relative importance of one piece of information to another

informal outline a listing of main ideas and subtopics arranged in a less traditional format of single headings and indented notes

literary reading reading literature such as short stories, essays, poetry, and novels

margin notes notes made in the margins of text

pace to read efficiently; to read at a rate that is slow enough to allow the mind to absorb information but fast enough to complete the reading assignment

preview to look over a reading assignment before reading it; to determine the subject matter and questions you may have about the material before reading it

professional journals magazines or other periodicals published by and/or written exclusively for a particular discipline, such as a journal written specifically by engineers for engineers or by physicians for physicians

schematics drawings or diagrams

technical reading reading science, business, or technology publications

technical vocabulary specialized words used in specific ways unique to a particular discipline

Writing@Work

John Arthur is Principal Consultant for Siebel University, a division of a software company called Siebel Systems, Inc. In his position, he is responsible for ensuring customer satisfaction through user adoption of Siebel software. He manages projects from the discovery phase through the creation and facilitation of customized instruction.

In John's position, he must read technical information from other writers and from web courses about particular software programs and develop step-by-step instructions for users. John meets with clients and interviews some future users to determine what they currently do and their comfort level with computer programs in general. Based on his findings, John determines what information his clients seem to be missing and proposes solutions to the clients. Once topics of instruction have been agreed upon, John does some additional research by reading and begins to write. John stresses the importance of writing for users of different skill levels. After determining users' comfort levels with computer programs, John adjusts his style of writing through word choice and sentence length.

When John is reading and evaluating the material he will eventually write about, he must be certain that the information is accurate and up to date. "User adoption is highly dependant upon credibility. I thoroughly test the application against the previously written documentation and then against my documentation." If John were to publish documentation that was not evaluated for truth and updated information, his credibility would be harmed and client satisfaction would be diminished. "The client could experience a delay in return on investment through lack of user adoption, and I could experience opportunity loss through a damaged reputation."

John's ability to read technical material and then communicate that material clearly and accurately is absolutely essential in his role as principal consultant. He has always believed in clear communication and says he was strongly influenced by a high school teacher who was fond of saying, "Every word shall be a perfect gem of truth and clarity." John says, "I have lived by these words ever since with my writing."

John has a bachelor's of business administration in marketing. He held two positions at Siebel Systems, Inc., prior to obtaining his current position of Principal Consultant.

Satellite Oceanography

The National Aeronautics and Space Administration (NASA), organized in 1958, has become an important institutional contributor to marine science. For four months in 1978, NASA's **Seasat,** the first oceanographic satellite, beamed oceanographic data to Earth. More recent contributions have been made by satellites beaming radar signals off the sea surface to determine wave height, variations in sea surface contour and temperature, and other information of interest to marine scientists.

① Seasat

② TOPEX/Poseidon

The first of a new generation of oceanographic satellites was launched in 1992 as a joint effort of NASA and the Centre National d'Etudes Spatiales (the French space agency). The centerpiece of **TOPEX/Poseidon,** as the project is known, is a satellite orbiting 1,336 kilometers (835 miles) above Earth in an orbit that allows coverage of 95 percent of the ice-free ocean every ten days. The *TOPEX/Poseidon* satellite is supplied with a positioning device that allows researchers to determine its position to within 10 centimeters (4 inches) of Earth's center! The radars aboard can then determine the height of the sea surface with unprecedented accuracy. Other experiments in this five-year program include sensing water vapor over the ocean, determining the precise location of ocean currents, and determining wind speed and direction.

10cm – precise!

③ SEASTAR

SEASTAR, launched by NASA in 1997, carries a color scanner called SeaWiFS (sea-viewing wide-field-of-view sensor). This device measures the distribution of chlorophyll at the ocean surface, a measure of marine productivity.

measures – how?

NASA's ambitious **Jason-1,** . . . launched in December 2001, is designed to operate in tandem with *TOPEX/Poseidon. Jason-1* uses a scatterometer to measure ocean surface winds, a radiometer to sense water vapor, and an even more accurate radar altimeter to report sea-surface height.

④ Jason-1

A satellite system you can use every day? The U.S. Department of Defense has built the **Global Positioning System (GPS),** a "constellation" of 24 satellites (21 active and 3 spare) in orbit 10,600 miles above Earth. The satellites are spaced so that at least four of them are above the horizon from any point on Earth. Each satellite contains a computer, an atomic clock, and a radio transmitter. On the ground, every GPS receiver contains a computer that calculates its own position with information from at least three of the satellites. The result is provided in the form of a geographic position—longitude and latitude—that is accurate to less than 1 meter (39.27 inches), depending on the type of equipment used. The use of the GPS in marine navigation and positioning has revolutionized data collection at sea.

⑤ Global Positioning System (GPS)

IMPT

Other uses?

Figure 14.1 Technical Reading Model

TECHNICAL READING VS. LITERARY READING

Your company has just replaced the old photocopier in your office with a new one. The *old* one was easy to operate: you placed the paper on the glass plate and hit "Start." Simple enough. The *new* copier collates, copies front and back, reduces, enlarges, changes paper trays, prints transparencies, and displays messages in a small window. Learning to operate this copier will require that you use your technical reading skills to read the manual unless you are lucky enough, of course, to have an assistant who will tackle the new copier for you.

Along with reading copier manuals, you may be asked to read a number of technical documents on the job: business letters, government regulations, computer manuals, compliance audits, legal briefs, financial reports, feasibility studies, and statistical analyses.

In addition, each discipline has its own **professional journals** or newspapers that you may consult regularly: *New England Journal of Medicine, Aerospace and Electronic Systems Magazine, Audubon, PC World,* and *The Wall Street Journal,* to name a few. Even outside of work, you will read technical documents: family medical books, business magazines, car manuals, house plans, and product labels.

© GETTY IMAGES/PHOTODISC

Technical readings are distinguished by technical subject matter, an emphasis on precision, and descriptions of mechanisms and processes. The vocabulary is highly specialized, and graphics are common. Technical reading covers subjects in science, business, and technology. The biology course, marketing course, accounting course, and computer course you take all involve technical reading.

Technical reading differs from **literary reading.** Reading literature requires you to make associations and draw inferences—to interpret and read between the lines. It asks you to use your imagination when you read. Technical reading does not ask you to make emotional associations, draw inferences, or interpret symbolic language. It requires you to understand what is on the page, to understand the logic presented to you. It is packed with detailed and precise information.

Because technical documents are an important part of any workplace, your ability to read and understand them helps you contribute to your organization. An employee who takes initiative to look up information to solve a problem is an asset.

Information changes daily, and those who are able to digest technical information quickly can stay on top of the latest developments in their field. Reading can keep you and your coworkers safe, too—some equipment and chemicals are hazardous when not used properly.

Focus on Ethics

According to a study by Urban & Associates of Sharon, Massachusetts, 23 percent of newspaper readers find factual errors in the daily news stories of their local newspapers at least once a week. So your mother was right: "You can't believe everything you read."

Discriminating readers use their critical-thinking skills to be on the lookout for information that is inaccurate, biased, sensationalized, or lacking in pertinent details.

When you use data from your reading, you have an ethical obligation to double-check that data, looking for other sources that also report the same findings. Publications that must be produced quickly—such as newspapers, magazines, or books on the latest technology—are subject to error. Information published with few, if any, editorial guidelines—such as some articles on the Internet or stories in tabloids—are subject to unscrupulous uses.

The next time you pull up an Internet article that promises the fountain of youth or hands you a get-rich-quick scheme, be skeptical and remember: your mother was right.

Stop and Think

What distinguishes technical reading from literary reading? How can good technical reading skills help you contribute to the workplace?

STRATEGIES FOR READING TECHNICAL PASSAGES

WARM UP

What strategies do you currently use for reading and studying?

Because technical reading is different from other kinds of reading, you must approach technical reading with a plan.

© GETTY IMAGES/PHOTODISC

When reading technical documents, you should:

- Preview the material.
- Take notes.
- Repeat more difficult notes aloud.
- Understand the vocabulary.
- **Anticipate** the line of reasoning.
- Know how to read graphics.
- Pay close attention to numerical data.
- Pace yourself.
- Read more in the subject area.

PREVIEW THE MATERIAL

Previewing warms up the mind for reading just as stretching warms up the body for exercise. After previewing, you read with greater efficiency and retention because you know what to expect.

While previewing, make sure you understand the passage layout. Skim the introduction for an idea of the subject matter. Turn headings into questions; anticipate the information to follow and see where information is placed. In a manual, for example, thumb through the pages to see where the

Use the Technical Reading: Passage 1 worksheet on the Data CD to practice with margin notes.

schematics, description of parts, and glossary are located. Also, use the **preview** to activate your knowledge of the subject. The more **background knowledge** you can activate, the more meaningful the passage will be.

The opening model shows a technical passage on satellite use in oceanography. Figure 14.2 shows how one student previewed this passage. The student first determined the subject and then skimmed the passage, turning the headings and other information into questions.

Subject: The title "Satellite Oceanography" and the first sentence suggest that the passage will talk about how satellites are used to study the ocean.

Questions: How are satellites used to study the oceans?

What kinds of data do satellites give us?

How useful is the data?

Figure 14.2 Sample Preview

TAKE NOTES ON THE READING PASSAGE

Writing about what you read is important for retaining information. As you write, you activate more areas of the brain and, therefore, understand and retain more information. When taking notes, use abbreviations, note what is significant, consider outlining the passage, consider using graphic organizers, and answer questions.

Use Abbreviations To help you write about what you read, devise or borrow a system of abbreviations for marking information. Here are a few examples:

IMPT or !	important information	b/c	because
EX	example	?	questions
∴	math symbol for *therefore*	①, ②, ③	items in a sequence

Note What Is Significant When you write about what you read, take notes on the following:

- Summary of information, especially by sections
- Main ideas
- Definitions
- Lists and series
- Answers to questions you posed during the preview
- Descriptions of processes
- Sections you do not understand and need to review or ask questions about

If you own your book, you can mark important information with **margin notes.** If you prefer to take notes in a notebook, write the same information there. The opening model shows a technical passage with margin notes. Notice how the student has devised symbols and abbreviations. The notes summarize, list information, ask questions, define new terms, note something significant, and mark information the student does not understood.

Consider an Outline Figure 14.3 shows two outlines on the oceanography passage. Such outlines help you see major divisions in a passage. They are also effective summaries. The outline can be formal, as illustrated in the first outline, or the outline can be informal, as illustrated in the second outline.

Communication Update

Mind-mapping software, such as Visual Mind™ and MindManager®, allows you to organize notes you take into a usable outline. The software also allows you to convert those notes into a presentation or lecture. When converted, the presentation can easily be e-mailed to another person or group. Such software is also ideal for groups of people who are working on the same project. As group members take notes, they can consolidate and organize the notes using complex mapping techniques.

Formal Outline

Satellite Oceanography

I. NASA's *Seasat* 1978

II. NASA's *TOPEX/Poseidon* 1992

    A. Determined satellite positioning within 10 cm of Earth's center
    B. Measured height of sea surface
    C. Sensed water vapor
    D. Located ocean currents
    E. Determined wind speed and direction

II. NASA's *SEASTAR* 1977

    A. Measured chlorophyll amounts
    B. Measured marine productivity

III. NASA's *Jason 1* 2001

    A. Measures surface winds
    B. Measures water vapor
    C. Measures sea height

IV. Department of Defense's Global Positioning System (GPS)

    A. Determines geographic position
    B. Has revolutionized marine navigation

Informal Outline

Satellite Oceanography

Satellites:

    Seasat 1978

    TOPEX/Poseidon 1992

        Satellite positioning within 10 cm of Earth's center
        Data on height of sea surface, water vapor, ocean currents, wind speed and direction

    SEASTAR 1977

        Data on chlorophyll and marine productivity

    Jason 1 2001

        Data on surface winds, water vapor, and sea-surface height

    Global Positioning System (GPS)

        Data on geographic position, accurate to less than 1 m
        Revolutionized marine navigation

Figure 14.3 Sample Formal and Informal Outlines

Consider Graphic Organizers Some students prefer to draw **graphic organizers** that map the relationship between ideas with circles, blocks, and lines. A circle or block represents the central idea. Lines drawn to other circles or blocks show how smaller parts of the topic relate to the central idea. Figure 14.4 below and continued on the next page shows the ideas in the oceanography passage illustrated graphically in two ways.

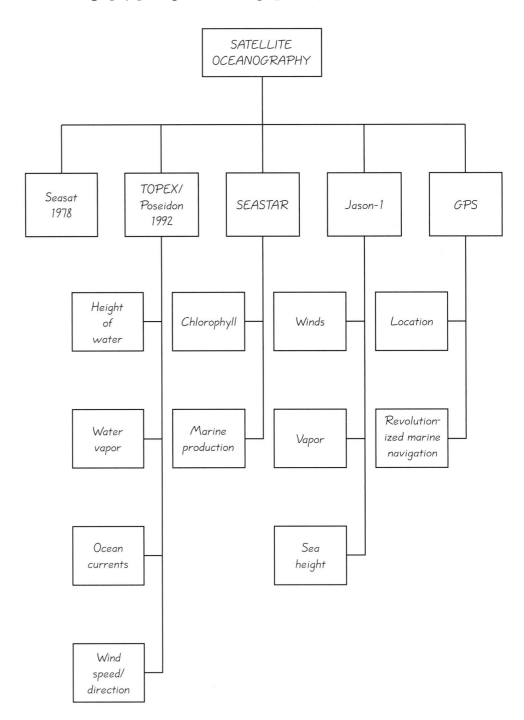

Figure 14.4 Graphic Organizers

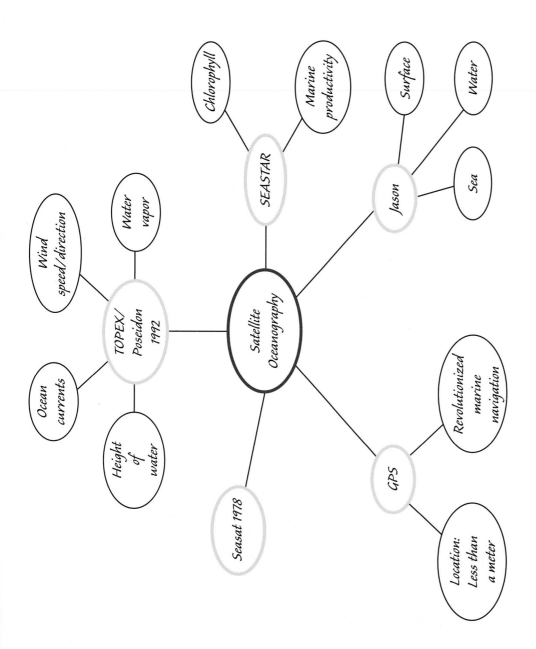

Figure 14.4 Graphic Organizers, cont.

Answer Questions In addition to previewing, taking notes, and outlining, answering questions is also a helpful note-taking tool. The questions can be your own, your instructor's, or the end-of-chapter exercises in a textbook.

In Figure 14.5, one student answers in a notebook the questions posed during the preview in Figure 14.2. Also in Figure 14.5, another student begins to answer the questions at the end of the chapter.

1) Older satellites beam radar signals off the surface of the ocean. Newer satellites use a color scanner (SeaWiFS) to measure the distribution of chlorophyll, a scatterometer to measure ocean winds, a radiometer to measure water vapor, and a radar altimeter to report sea-surface height.

2) Satellites give us information about ocean currents, water vapor, marine productivity, wind direction and speed, and sea height. GPS satellites give us information about location and position.

3) The data is extremely useful because of the variety of information, its precision, and its accuracy. The GPS has revolutionized marine navigation.

Answers to end-of-chapter questions:

How long have satellites been giving scientists data about the ocean? Since 1978

How does the GPS work? Twenty-four satellites (21 active; 3 spare) orbit 10,600 miles above Earth. There are at least four satellites above the horizon at any time from any place on Earth. Each of the satellites has a computer, an atomic clock, and a radio transmitter. On Earth, receivers have a computer that can calculate its position from three of these satellites in lines of longitude and latitude. The position is accurate to within 1 meter.

Figure 14.5 Sample Answers to Questions

REPEAT MORE DIFFICULT NOTES ALOUD

Hearing what you have written and read in silence may help you retain difficult information. Try repeating the following notes aloud several times:

Freud divided the personality into the id, the pleasure principle; the ego, the reality principle; and the superego, the morality principle. Freud divided the personality into the id, the pleasure principle; the ego, the reality principle; and the superego, the morality principle. Freud divided the personality into. . . .

After reading this passage, a student probably could name the three parts of the personality and describe each one.

MAKE SURE YOU UNDERSTAND THE VOCABULARY

When reading in literary subject areas, you often can determine vocabulary in context. In technical reading, however, everyday words can be used in unusual or limited ways. Technical reading also uses specialized words.

When **technical vocabulary** is not defined in the text, look up the unfamiliar word. Textbooks often have glossaries that define technical terms. You may need to ask an expert in the field to define the word for you.

When vocabulary is defined in the text, the definition usually follows the term: after a linking verb, in parentheses, or in an appositive. Figure 14.6 shows several terms defined in the text. Note that some words, such as *cookies,* do not have the same meaning for a computer programmer as they do for you. So even terms that are familiar may be used in different ways for the technical reader. Notice also the use of acronyms (letters to stand for a long or complicated term or series of terms).

"*Parasites* live in or on other living organisms—their hosts—and feed upon specific host tissues for part of their life cycle." (Starr and Taggart 854)

"A *market* is a group of buyers and sellers of a particular good or service. . . . A *competitive market* is a market in which there are many buyers and many sellers so that each has a negligible impact on the market price." (Mankiw 64)

"A *cookie* is a *name = value* pair that a web server sends to a browser. The browser stores the cookie received and will return it in well-defined future requests to the same server." (Wang and Katila 545)

Childhood vaccines include the MMR (measles-mumps-rubella) vaccine and IPV (inactivated polio vaccine).

Figure 14.6 Examples of Technical Vocabulary Defined in the Text

Some definitions need more than a phrase or sentence and extend to a paragraph or more. Figure 14.7 illustrates an extended definition of the term *desert*. The examples and description help the reader gain a more complete understanding of the term. Often an accompanying graphic can convey in a single picture the concept at a glance.

Deserts form on land with less than 10 centimeters or so of annual rainfall and high potential for evaporation. Such conditions prevail at latitudes of about 30 degrees north and south. There we find great deserts of the American Southwest, of northern Chile, Australia, northern and southern Africa, and Arabia. Farther north are the high deserts of eastern Oregon, and Asia's vast Gobi and the Kyzyl-Kum east of the Caspian Sea. Rain shadows are the main reason these northern deserts are so arid.

Deserts do not have lush vegetation. Rain falls in heavy, brief, infrequent pulses that swiftly erode the exposed topsoil. Humidity is so low that the sun's rays easily penetrate the air. They quickly heat the ground's surface, which radiates heat and cools quickly at night.

Although arid or semiarid conditions do not favor large, leafy plants, deserts show plenty of biodiversity. In a patch of Arizona's desert . . . you might find creosote and other deep-rooted, evergreen, woody shrubs; fleshy-stemmed, shallow-rooted cacti; tall saguaros; short prickly pears; and ocotillos, which drop leaves more than once a year and grow new ones after a rain. Annual and perennial species flower briefly but profusely after seasonal rains. Deep-rooted plants, including mesquite and cottonwood, commonly grow near the new streambeds that have a permanent underground water supply.

From Ecology and Behavior 10th edition by STARR/TAGGART. © 2004. Reprinted with permission of Brooks/Cole, a division of Thomson Learning: www.thomsonrights.com. Fax 800 730-2215.

Figure 14.7 Extended Technical Definition

ANTICIPATE THE LINE OF REASONING

Knowing the typical lines of reasoning in technical reading will help you anticipate how to read.

Most technical reading calls on the reader to understand the following:

- A process or procedure (steps; how something works).
- A cause/effect relationship (what makes something happen).
- A mechanism (what something looks like and what it is supposed to do).

Figure 14.8 shows a process description of air flow in coastal regions. In this process description, however, are also several cause/effect relationships. One action causes another action. As a result, this chain reaction is also responsible for the process. Notice, too, the importance of knowing the vocabulary.

Land breezes and sea breezes are small, daily mini-monsoons. Morning sunlight falls on land and adjacent sea, warming both. The temperature of the water doesn't rise as much as the temperature of the land, however. The warmer inland rocks transfer heat to the air, which expands and rises, creating a zone of low atmospheric pressure over the land. Cooler air from over the sea then moves toward land; this is the sea breeze (Figure 7.12a). The situation reverses after sunset with land losing heat to space and falling rapidly in temperature. After a while, the air over the still-warm ocean will be warmer than the air over the cooling land. This air will then rise, and the breeze direction will reverse, becoming a land breeze (Figure 7.12b). Land breezes and sea breezes are common and welcome occurrences in coastal areas.

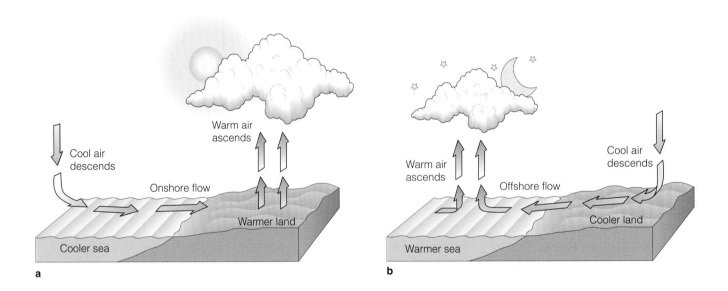

Figure 14.8 Process Description of Flow of Air in Coastal Regions

Figure 14.9 shows another process, a set of instructions, the first steps involved in setting up a web site directory. The reasoning here is linear, a chronologically organized sequence of events.

Site Organization

Now let's consider using hyperlinks to organize pages within a web site for our enterprise web site.

- Organize the pages for a site into a hierarchy of files and directories (folders) stored on the hard disk of the server host. Avoid nonalphanumeric characters in file and directory names. Otherwise, the file name must be URL encoded before becoming part of a URL.

- Place the site entry page (usually, index.html) in the *server root* directory.

- Use subdirectories such as images/, products/, services/, contractors/, members/, and affiliates/ to organize the site. The index.html page within each subdirectory is usually the lead page for that part of the site.

- Keep the organization simple and avoid using more than three levels of subdirectory nesting.

- Design a navigation system that is clear, easy to use, and effective in getting visitors where they want to go in your site.

- Use partial URLs exclusively for linking within the site and make sure the link is in one of these forms:

    1. relative to the host page itself (href=*"file"* or href=*"dir/file"*)
    2. relative to the server root (href=*"path-to-file"*)

If all links are of the first kind, then the pages of the site can be moved as a group to a different location in the file system or to a different hosting computer without change. If you have both types of relative links, then the pages can be moved to the server root on another host without change.

From An Introduction to Web Design and Programming 1st edition by Wang / Katila. © 2004. Reprinted with permission of Course Technology, a division of Thomson Learning: www.thomsonrights.com. Fax 800 730-2215.

Figure 14.9 Step-by-Step Process

Figure 14.10 shows cause-to-effect reasoning as the text explains how changes in the minimum wage affect teenage workers.

Many economists have studied how minimum-wage laws affect the teenage labor market. These researchers compare the changes in the minimum wage over time with the changes in teenage employment. Although there is some debate about how much the minimum wage affects employment, the typical study finds that a 10 percent increase in the minimum wage depresses teenage employment between 1 and 3 percent. In interpreting this estimate, note that 10 percent increase in the minimum wage does not raise the average wage of teenagers by 10 percent. A change in the law does not directly affect those teenagers who are already paid well above the minimum, and enforcement of minimum-wage laws is not perfect. Thus, the estimated drop in employment of 1 to 3 percent is significant.

From PRINCIPLES OF ECONOMICS 3rd edition by MANKIW. © 2004. Reprinted with permission of South-Western, a division of Thomson Learning: www.thomsonrights.com. Fax 800 730-2215.

Figure 14.10 Cause-to-Effect Relationships

Figure 14.11 shows a mechanism description that describes the function of each part of a hard drive.

Hard-drive structure and function have not changed; however, modern hard drives have two or more platters that are stacked together and spin in unison. Read/write heads are controlled by an actuator and move in unison across the disk surfaces as the disks rotate on a spindle (see Figure 6-1). PCs can use many types of hard drives, all using a magnetic medium; the data on all these drives is stored in tracks and sectors, and data files are addressed in clusters made up of one or more sectors.

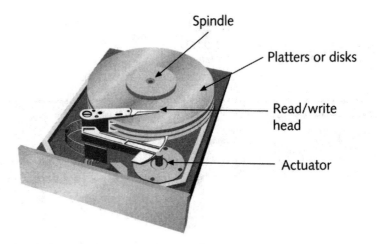

Figure 6-1   Inside a hard drive case

From Enhanced Guide To Managing and Maintaining Your PC, Third Edition Introductory 3rd edition by ANDREWS. © 2001. Reprinted with permission of Course Technology, a division of Thomson Learning: www.thomsonrights.com. Fax 800 730-2215.

Figure 14.11 Mechanism Description of Hard Drive

LEARN HOW TO READ GRAPHICS

Be prepared to think visually when reading a technical passage. Draw a picture of what you are reading—on paper or in your mind.

Most technical reading puts information in visual form to help you see what is happening. To read graphics, make sure you understand the purpose of each type of graphic. Then study the graphic closely as well as the author's explanation of the graphic.

Understand the Purpose of Each Type of Graphic   Figure 14.12 shows the purpose of the most often-used graphics. When you see a diagram, for example, you should know that the purpose of the diagram is to help you see what something looks like. You can then read the graphic specifically with that purpose in mind. See Chapter 6, *Document Design and Graphics,* for more information about graphics.

TYPE OF GRAPHIC	PURPOSE
simple line drawing or diagram	to show a mechanism or part of a mechanism
pie graph	to show how the whole is divided into parts, to show how the parts relate to the whole
informal table	to present a small amount of data (especially numbers) in an easy-to-read format
bar graph	to compare several sets of data; to present differences in a dramatic way; sometimes to depict a trend
double bar graph	to compare several sets of data; sometimes to depict a trend
line graph	to depict a trend; to show how data is related
multiple line graph	to depict several trends; to compare trends; to show how data is related
formal table	to present information, especially a lot of numbers, in an easy-to-read format
flowchart	to present a process
organizational chart	to present the structure of an organization
photograph	to show the details of what something actually looks like

Figure 14.12 Purposes of Common Graphics

SEE THE SITES

The Internet is a seemingly never-ending supply of technical information. Many sites let you download entire technical articles and books. Newspapers.com is a site that provides links to many newspapers, journals, and specialty publications all over the world. The Online Books Page allows you to download entire books on such wide-ranging subjects as anthropology, folklore, ethics, Mediterranean regions, and zoology.

You can find the URL for both sites in the web links at techwriting. swlearning.com.

Read the Graphic Closely After you have noted what kind of graphic you are reading and what its purpose is, read the graphic closely, noticing everything about it:

- Read the title to determine the graphic's subject matter.
- Look for keys to understanding the graphic.
- Read the legend.
- Read the call outs.
- Read the Y-axis and X-axis information.

Next, relate the information in the graphic to the author's discussion of the graphic. Use your fingers to trace the graphic while you read the explanation. Compare the author's discussion to the graphic. The discussion should point out what information in the graphic is important. You can then take notes on the important aspects of the graphic. If you will be asked to remember a diagram, you may wish to draw the diagram yourself.

A number of the technical reading passages presented so far illustrate the importance of graphics. Figure 14.8 uses a picture and arrows to represent the creation of land and sea breezes. Figure 14.11 includes a diagram of a hard drive to make the description easy to follow. Each graphic presents technical information quickly and clarifies the explanation given in words.

PAY CLOSE ATTENTION TO NUMERICAL DATA

Resist the temptation to read too quickly through discussions using numbers. Note that the number $1,231.49, while only six digits long, actually stands for nine words—one thousand two hundred thirty-one dollars and forty-nine cents. Figure 14.13 shows a process description of a capital statement. Even though the digits save space on the page, remember to take time to process the digits as words in your mind.

The computation of the debit to Payroll Taxes was

FICA–OASDI:	6.2% of $14,162.77 = $ 878.09
FICA–HI:	1.45% of $14,162.77 = 205.36
FUTA:	0.8% of $ 3,280.00 = 26.24
SUTA:	3.5% of $ 3,480.00 = 121.80
Total Payroll Taxes $1,231.49	

Payroll Taxes $1,231.49	
FICA Taxes Payable–OASDI 878.09	
FICA Taxes Payable–HI 205.36	
FUTA Taxes Payable 26.24	
SUTA Taxes Payable 121.80	

From Payroll Accounting 13th edition by BIEG. © 2003. Reprinted with permission of South-Western, a division of Thomson Learning: www.thomsonrights.com. Fax 800 730-2215.

Figure 14.13 Technical Reading Using Numbers

PACE YOURSELF

Runners **pace** themselves in order to expend their energy evenly throughout a race. You, too, should pace yourself when you read by following these suggestions:

■ Read slowly. Technical reading is packed with details. Often the details include numbers that you can misread if you are not careful. Because the reading is dense, you should read slowly, making sure you take in all of the details.

■ Read small amounts of information for short periods (maybe 10 to 15 minutes). Then take a brief break and summarize or take notes on what you have read.

- Read the selection twice. The first time you read anything, there will be parts you do not read as carefully. A second reading will enable you to see what you missed the first time. Also, a second reading will allow you to see how the parts of the passage fit together because you will notice transitions and see relationships.

READ MORE IN YOUR TECHNICAL SUBJECT

The more you read in a certain subject area, the better reader you will be in that subject area. For example, if you are used to reading car magazines, you will read a new article about cars better than someone who is used to reading computer magazines.

You will build a knowledge base in the subject and become familiar with vocabulary typically used in the subject. Additional readings build on that knowledge base and vocabulary. So if you want to be a good technical reader, you should read more in your technical reading subject. You also can expand your knowledge base by reading less familiar subject areas. As you can see, the more background knowledge you bring to a subject, the better reader you will be.

Communication Dilemma

You are a chemist at a pharmaceutical company who has been given the task of determining the effects of a controversial medicine on humans. You are not given much time and money to complete your research, however. Because you do not have a lot of time to spare and because your company would like to be able to claim the medicine is safe, you find only two articles from the same journal and use information from them in your report. You would like to check other articles just in case the information you found has been discredited, but the findings might mean that your company cannot sell the medicine. You submit the report, which states that the medicine is safe for humans. Over the next couple of months, your study is discredited because of the negative side effects many consumers experienced when they took the medicine. What could be the effects of this discovery on you? What are the effects of the discovery on your company?

Stop and Think

List the strategies that can help you become a more proficient technical reader.

■ *Chapter 14 Review*

SUMMARY

1. Technical reading differs from literary reading. Technical reading does not require readers to make emotional associations, draw inferences, or interpret symbolic language.

2. Technical reading includes densely packed, precise details. Technical readings are distinguished by technical subject matter, an emphasis on precision, descriptions of mechanisms and processes, frequent use of specialized vocabulary, cause-to-effect reasoning, and use of graphics.

3. Because technical documents are an important part of any workplace, your ability to read and understand them helps you contribute to your organization.

4. Strategies for becoming a proficient technical reader include the following: preview the material, take notes (in the margins of the text or in a notebook), repeat difficult notes aloud, make sure you understand the vocabulary, anticipate the line of reasoning, learn how to read graphics, pay attention to numerical data, pace yourself, and read more in the subject area.

5. Strategies for taking good notes include the following: summarize information (especially by sections), identify main ideas, define words, write lists and series, answer the questions you posed during the preview, describe a process, and note what you do not understand and need to review or ask questions about.

Checklist

- Have I previewed the material I am preparing to read?

- Have I taken notes on the reading passage?

- Have I noted what is significant?

- Have I considered outlining the material?

- Have I considered using graphic aids when taking notes?

- Have I answered important questions about the passage?

- Have I made sure I understand the vocabulary?

- Have I anticipated the line of reasoning? Is the reasoning a process or procedure, a cause/effect relationship, or a mechanism?

- Have I learned how to read graphics?

- Do I understand the purpose of each graphic?

- Have I looked at the graphic closely?

- Have I paid close attention to numerical data?

- Have I paced myself?

- Have I thought about reading more in my technical subject?

Build On What You Know

1. How did you read technical passages before you read this chapter? Will you change anything about how you read technical passages now? If so, what?

2. List vocabulary in a technical field with which you are familiar. Ask your classmates if they understand the vocabulary.

3. In your own words, list the characteristics of technical reading.

4. In your own words, describe the difference between reading technical material and reading literary text.

5. Explain how to read technical material. List suggestions for technical reading that appeal to you.

6. Interview people who work in technical fields. Determine how much reading they do on the job.

7. Conduct a poll of 20 people you know. What kind of reading do they prefer—technical reading or literary reading? What kind of technical reading do they prefer?

8. Analyze your textbooks or technical magazines. Isolate one chapter or one article. How much of the vocabulary is new to you? How much technical vocabulary is in the passage? How many graphic aids are there? Do some of the passages use numbers? How are numbers used?

9. Look back at the chapter or article you used in item 8. How would you chunk (divide up) some of this information? Which parts would be clearer if you repeated them aloud?

10. Read these sentences. Underline the technical word and the part of the sentence that defines that word.

   a. "Impulses originating from these cells (hairlike cells in the inner ear) provide an awareness of body position or balance, called equilibrium, which makes it possible to maintain an upright posture."

   SOURCE: Parham, Christine A. *Psychology: Studying the Behavior of People.* 2nd ed. Cincinnati: South-Western Publishing Co., 1988.

   b. "Sort keys can be unique or non-unique. Sort keys are unique if the value of the sort key field for each record is different. Sort keys are non-unique if more than one record can have the same value in the sort key field."

   SOURCE: Ageloff, Roy, Scott Zimmerman, and Beverly Zimmerman. *Micro Computer Applications for Business.* Cambridge: Course Technology, Inc., 1993.

   c. "Auditing is a field of activity involving an independent review of the accounting records. In conducting an audit, CPAs examine the records supporting the financial reports of an enterprise."

   SOURCE: Warren, Carl S., James Reeve, and Philip E. Fess. *Financial and Managerial Accounting.* 4th ed. Cincinnati: South-Western Publishing Co., 1994.

Apply What You Learned

11. Preview the reading in the following passage. Write your preview and then read it to your classmates.

Ivan Pavlov (1927), a Russian physiologist, . . . inserted tubes into the salivary glands (of dogs) to measure the amount of saliva produced when he fed the dogs. He became perplexed when, after being in the laboratory for a while, the dogs would salivate before they were given food. . . .

Pavlov demonstrated classical conditioning by immediately following the ringing of a bell with the presentation of food to the dogs. Initially, the dogs did not salivate when the bell rang. After following the bell with food several times, Pavlov rang the bell without presenting food. He discovered that the bell alone now produced salivation in the dogs. A form of learning currently referred to as classical (earliest model) conditioning had occurred. The dogs responded differently to an environmental event (bell) as a result of an environmental experience (pairing of bell with food). Originally, the bell was neutral; it did not bring forth a specific response in the dog. After the bell became associated with food, it came to signal presence of food in the mouth—salivation. Classical conditioning had occurred by associating a neutral stimulus with an unconditioned stimulus.

A neutral stimulus is a person, place, event, or object that does not bring forth a specific response from the organism. An unconditioned stimulus is some phenomenon that brings forth a specific response, even the first time it is presented—a reflex response. A reflex response is referred to as an unlearned or unconditioned response.

SOURCE: Parham, Christine A. *Psychology: Studying the Behavior of People.* 2nd ed. Cincinnati: South-Western Publishing Co., 1988. 192.

12. Read the passage you just previewed. Pick out the technical reading elements. First, describe the thought processes. Which parts would you describe as process description? In which parts do you see cause/effect reasoning? Which words represent the specialized vocabulary of the subject area? Are they defined in the text?

13. Practice taking a variety of notes—margin notes (only if your instructor provides a copy you can take notes on) and notebook notes. In your notes, be sure to summarize, define, list, and mark what you have questions about.

14. Would you benefit from repeating parts of your notes aloud? If so, which parts?

15. Read the passage again. Which parts do you understand more clearly because you read them twice?

16. Create a graphic that could be added to help make the reading clearer. Share the graphic with your classmates. Have your classmates answer the following questions about your graphic: Was the graphic immediately clear? What is significant about the graphic?

This Work Is A Zoo! exercise will help you practice finding sources that are relevant to a subject and up to date. The exercise will also help you build your own virtual library from which you can find technical information for future assignments.

Work Is A Zoo!

Anya has just received a phone call from the president of the zoo, who would like to talk to her about improving the quality of life for the animals at the zoo. The president gives Anya two weeks to read and study relevant information. At the end of the two weeks, Anya is expected to summarize in a report the information she finds.

Anya calls you into her office, and you find her buried in a mound of books, magazines, and papers. She explains that she needs you to help her sort through all of the information and find the best sources for her project so she can write the report quickly using the most relevant information.

"I'd like you to give me a list of books, magazines, newspapers, and other specialty publications that concern the quality of life of zoo animals. I need the most recent information, so be sure to check the dates on the articles. Check the Internet first to start your list. You can get information quickly—and that's important!"

Develop a list of relevant articles or books to help Anya with her research. Remember to get a variety of readings so her research will be credible. In addition, help Anya write her report more quickly by reading a few articles and making margin notes for her to review. Remember, when reading technical documents, you should:

- Preview the material.
- Take notes.
- Repeat difficult notes aloud.
- Understand the vocabulary.
- Anticipate the line of reasoning.
- Know how to read graphics.
- Pay close attention to numerical data.
- Pace yourself.
- Read more in the subject area.

The Inside Track
TECH WRITING TIPS

ORGANIZING WITH THE DIRECT APPROACH

The way you organize ideas in conversation and the way you organize for writing can be quite different. To understand the difference, think of a recent exciting event in your life. Imagine telling friends about this event in a casual conversation. Now write a one- or two-paragraph description as if you were speaking to friends. In your description, include a sentence containing the main idea. Compare the organization of the two messages. Where did you place the main idea?

In many technical reports and documents, the main idea should be placed first for the convenience of the reader. Use this strategy to organize good news and informative memos. This strategy calls for putting the most important idea, or the information the reader needs most, first and reserving explanatory and supplementary ideas for later in the memo. Figure 1 illustrates the direct approach to organizing a message.

MAIN IDEA

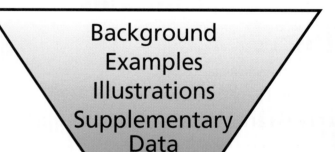

Figure 1 Model for Direct Approach to Organization

As Figure 1 shows, when you organize for your reader, you place the main idea first. Then you add other statements in order of most important to least important. As the writer, you must decide how much information your reader needs and how far to continue with background and explanation.

The Inside Track: Apply What You Learned

1. Identify the most important idea for the employee (reader) from each group of sentences below.

   a. Sonja fell and broke her leg last night.

   b. You need to operate the Ricoh 2086 in her place today.

   a. The electrician checked the thermostat by turning the power off and attaching VOM clips to the two leads from the thermostat to the motor.

   b. The thermostat failed the test and needs to be replaced.

   c. When the electrician turned the power on and moved the thermostat control button to the top of the scale, the reading was not 120 volts as it should have been.

   a. I took a calligraphy course last year and loved it.

   b. In overseeing most of the weddings here at Maui's Special Occasions, I have found calligraphy, the art of beautiful handwriting, to be a valuable skill.

   c. If you wish to study calligraphy, I will pay for your tuition and supplies.

   a. You may sign up to take the seminar series here at work, free of charge.

   b. The seminars will be held from 5-6 p.m. on Tuesdays for five weeks, beginning March 24.

   c. Please sign the registration sheet on the bulletin board by noon on Friday if you want to take advantage of this opportunity.

   d. I recently completed The Winning Presentation seminar series, and I am so impressed with the results.

2. Use main-idea-first or direct organization to arrange the following information. Write the rearranged version in a paragraph for an audience of professional chefs.

   Shalon cookware is made of heavy-duty anodized aluminum.
   It has nickel-plated cast iron and steel handles.
   Its dark surface absorbs and conducts heat evenly.
   Shalon is one of the most highly recommended cookware products on the market.
   It does not interact with foods.
   Shalon cleans easily.

TONE

Tone refers to the emotional overtones that words emit. Not only do words give you information, but they also convey emotions that make you feel good or bad about something. Because human beings are both rational and emotional creatures, tone can affect the way readers react to words.

Unlike the objective tone in technical reports, letters give writers an opportunity to show a range of emotions—from apathy to warmth, from enthusiasm to anger. While some unanswered complaint letters may appropriately display anger, most of your letters should convey a positive, upbeat, reader-centered tone.

Read this passage. Describe the tone. Which words contribute to that tone?

> Dear Parents,
>
> Don't be late picking up your child. The bowling class is held from 11:00 to noon. Pick up your child promptly at noon. If your child is not picked up by 12:10, your child will be taken out of the bowling program.

Here you see that the short, terse style creates a negative tone. The words *If your child is not picked up by 12:10* may spark anger in parents who perceive that they are being treated like children. A better version would have been this one:

> Dear Parents,
>
> We enjoy having your child in our bowling classes.
>
> Please try to pick up your child from bowling class by 12:10. Our instructors must be at the tennis courts at 12:30 and may be late unless you are on time.
>
> Thank you for your cooperation. If you have any questions, please contact . . .

A positive tone makes people more likely to cooperate. You can create a positive tone in the following ways:

Avoid Negative Words. A number of words carry such negative messages that you should avoid them if possible. Words such as *never, not, failed, cannot,* and *regret* can often be replaced by more positive words.

Use Tact. Choose your words with care. Be sensitive to their impact. Instead of saying you *don't like a hat,* try saying *it shows personality.*

Accentuate the Positive. Be optimistic. Most people would prefer to do what is right and best for all concerned. Remember the old example: The cup is half full (accentuating the positive) instead of half empty (accentuating the negative).

Remember Your Manners. Say *please* and *thank you.*

Note the differences in the examples below. What did the writer do to change a negative tone in the first column to a more positive tone in the second column?

Do not sign the evaluations.	Keep the evaluations anonymous.
If you fail to sign the form, your return will be late.	Please sign the form to avoid unnecessary delays.
We insist that you include a deposit.	Please enclose a deposit.
We received your fax in which you claim we sent you damaged goods.	Your faxed letter of 5 July indicates you received damaged goods.
If you decide to visit our museum . . .	When you decide to visit our museum . . .
Your essay is disorganized.	Concentrate on organizing your ideas.

The Inside Track: Apply What You Learned

Make the following statements more user-friendly by rephrasing them to sound more positive.

1. If you will attend the first meeting, I'll buy you lunch on Friday.

2. We told you to be at work by 8 a.m!

3. You claim to have had a flat tire on the way home?

4. We cannot allow you to make failing grades.

5. You have had more than enough time to pay the small amount shown on the enclosed bill.

6. If you cannot be at the practices on time, you cannot be on the team.

7. Our sweatshirts will not shrink.

8. You will not encounter any problems with our software.

9. Do not walk on the grass. Stay on the sidewalks!

10. If you do not contact us before 17 November, we will not have time to process your request.

11. Your bill is now delinquent.

12. Our stores are never closed.

13. If you decide to contribute to the children's fund, your money will never be unwisely spent.

14. You claim that we did not send you a refund.

15. Your outfit is too loud for the commercial. Mr. Carlson will not like it. It will clash with the background.

16. You are working too fast to be accurate. You're making careless errors.

PARALLELISM

In writing, two sets of words are parallel because they repeat the same grammatical structure.

Your ability to recognize parallel structure depends on your ear and your knowledge of grammar. Words, phrases, and clauses joined by coordinating conjunctions and used in lists should be parallel.

PARALLEL WORDS, PHRASES, AND CLAUSES

Can you hear that these sets of words are *not* parallel?

1. I like running, biking, and to paint.
2. He told us to wash our dishes and that we must sweep the floor.
3. I like to paint portraits, play the piano, and to read science.

Here is the grammatical structure of these sentences to help you see where the break in parallel structure occurs:

   S V   Gerund Gerund Infinitive

1. I like running, biking, and to paint.

        Infinitive phrase   Dependent clause

2. He told us to wash our dishes and that we must sweep the floor.

   S V   to + verb/object   verb + object   to + verb/object

3. I like to paint portraits, play the piano, and to read science.

In Sentence 1, the infinitive breaks the parallelism because the list was started with *-ing* words, gerunds. In Sentence 2, the dependent clause breaks the parallelism because the list was started with an infinitive phrase. In Sentence 3, the *to* wasn't repeated in every part of the list, so the parallelism was broken.

Here are improved versions of the above sentences:

1. I like running, biking, and painting. I like to run, bike, and paint.
2. He told us to wash our dishes and to sweep the floor. He told us to wash our dishes and sweep the floor. He told us that we must wash our dishes and sweep the floor.
3. I like to paint portraits, to play the piano, and to read science. I like to paint portraits, play the piano, and read science.

PARALLEL LISTS

The itemized list below is not parallel. Which parts of the list are more alike than other parts?

> At the next Spanish Club meeting, we will discuss these items:
> - Next year's budget
> - Which person to nominate for chair
> - Implementing our attendance policy
> - Whether to donate money to the senior class project
> - Elections

The list on page 382 is not parallel because one item is a noun preceded by an adjective, two are listed as questions, one starts with an *-ing* word, and one is a simple noun. To make the list parallel, start each part of the list the same way. Use all *-ing* beginnings, all questions, all nouns, or all nouns preceded by adjectives.

You can make the list parallel by beginning every part the same way. The following list makes the entire list parallel to the first item by repeating the adjective(s) + noun structure:

- Next year's budget
- Chair nominations
- Attendance policy
- Senior class project donations
- Upcoming elections

PARALLEL ORDER

Using the same order of information also makes parts of a resume parallel.

For example, if you present the work experience of Job 1 in this order, NAME (of business), CITY/STATE (of business), DATES (of work), and JOB TITLE, you must present the work experience of Job 2 in the same order. Don't put DATES first, NAME second, ADDRESS third, etc.

The following example shows three job descriptions that use correct parallel order.

Taylor Computer Manufacturing, Nashville, TN, July 2002 – December 2004, Project Manager

Hix Landscaping Service, Franklin, TN, May 2001 – September 2001, Assistant Landscape Architect

BookWorld Publishing Services and Discount Books, Franklin, TN, October 2000 – June 2001, Sales Clerk

The Inside Track: Apply What You Learned

1. Make the unparallel example list on page 383 (At the next Spanish Club meeting, we will discuss these items) parallel in other ways. Make the whole list parallel to the second item, "Which person to nominate for chair." Then make the list parallel to the third item, "Implementing our attendance policy." Which do you prefer?

2. Make a list of your morning routine. Set up your list with this statement and a colon. Every morning I follow the same routine:

3. Make the items in this list parallel:

Activities

- Chairperson of Booster Club
- Delivered Meals on Wheels to shut-ins
- United Way: accepted pledges
- Recorder for Debating Team

4. Correct these sentences for faulty parallelism.

   a. The letter directed us to preview the contracts, sign them, and to return them promptly.

   b. The rules were fair but that they could not be enforced.

   c. Magdalena and Jenna were told to be home at 2:00 and that they had to refill the car with gasoline.

   d. She had trouble explaining her position and which decision to make.

   e. Johnny can't read, Johnny can't write, and math performance is poor.

   f. The new product line is noted for its durability, its attractiveness, and it is reliable.

5. Make the following sets of job descriptions parallel in structure.

   a. Baylor Industries, Glenville, VA. June 20— to April 20—. Sales Representative: called on customers and kept accounts.

   b. Sales Director. January 20— to August 20—. United Sales Corporation, Oakdale, Virginia. Duties included supervising sales personnel, training new personnel, and calling on customers.

   c. Cookeville, TN, May 20— to September 20—, Murphy's Art Supply, Sales Clerk, ordered art supplies, created company newsletter, arranged displays, and wrote proposal to acquire funds to open a coffee shop in the store.

   d. Branyon Fine Arts Group, taught piano and voice lessons, Cookeville, TN, October 20— to present, served as music teacher.

ECONOMY

Good technical writing is economical. As good food is rich in nutrition and low in fat and sugar, good technical documents are rich in meaning and low in unneeded words and phrases. Technical writers who think of their readers try to write clearly and concisely so that documents take less time and trouble to read. As a writer, you also save production time and costs when economy is the rule. This section provides tips for cutting unnecessary words and phrases.

Avoid *There is/There are* openings. Revise sentences starting with *There is* or *There are* to give the sentence a subject at the beginning, where it will get more attention, followed by an action verb. *There is* and *There are* sentences are not wrong, but they are weak sentences that waste words. Getting directly to the point of the sentence is better. Look at the examples below:

WEAK:	There are 10 units of amoxicillin stored in the warehouse.
IMPROVED:	Ten units of amoxicillin are stored in the warehouse. (passive voice)
	The warehouse stores 10 units of amoxicillin. (active voice)
WEAK:	There is a direct relationship between speed limits and fatalities.
IMPROVED:	Fatalities relate directly to speed limits. (active voice)

The technique for revising these sentences is as follows: 1) Mark out the *There is* or *There are* opening. 2) Move the real subject of the sentence to the opening position. 3) Create an action verb, sometimes from a word that follows the subject.

Eliminate *It* sentence openers. Sentences should not start with *it* unless the *it* refers to a specific person, place, or thing already mentioned. If you see that *it* in a sentence is incorrectly used, omit the *it*. Revise the sentence to give a stronger meaning without the unneeded word. Refer to the examples below:

WEAK:	It gives me great pleasure to introduce our new quality assurance officer, Rebecca Bielby.
IMPROVED:	I am pleased to introduce our new quality assurance officer, Rebecca Bielby.
WEAK:	It is the thermostat that received an electrical surge.
IMPROVED:	The thermostat received an electrical surge.

Delete unnecessary modifiers. In the examples given below, you can see that the modifier placed before each word is unnecessary. These words do not need modification. For instance, can something be very essential? No, something is either essential or not essential. Here are other common examples of unnecessary modifiers:

highly satisfactory	extremely competent
very rare	slightly expensive
barely visible	perfectly clear

Avoid redundancy. Redundancy is needless repetition. Redundancy adds words but does not add meaning. You should omit unnecessary repetition. You can probably think of other redundant expressions to add to the list below.

refer back	advance warning
blue in color	large in size
the month of June	the state of Nevada
basic fundamentals	cancel out
3:00 a.m. in the morning	

Reduce needless phrases. Writers sometimes pad their writing, either intentionally or unintentionally, with unnecessary phrases. Do not use an entire phrase when a single word will do. Each phrase listed below would be better replaced by its single-word equivalent on the right:

due to the fact that = because	prior to = before
be aware of the fact that = know	at a rapid rate = rapidly
in this modern day and age = today	in the event that = if
in many cases = often, frequently	at a later date = later

Replace -*ion* nouns with stronger action verbs. Use of -*ion* nouns often adds words without advancing meaning. These nouns can usually be omitted, making the sentence shorter and stronger.

Refer to the examples on the next page. Notice that the -*ion* nouns have been turned into action verbs.

WEAK:	The Food and Drug Administration, under public pressure, took into consideration the adoption of several new AIDS drugs.
IMPROVED:	The Food and Drug Administration, under public pressure, considered adopting several new AIDS drugs.
WEAK:	Heidi came to the conclusion that the report was a summation of court procedure.
IMPROVED:	Heidi concluded that the report summarized court procedure.

Avoid cliches and overused expressions. Most of the overused expressions listed below will probably sound familiar to you because you have read or heard them often. While these cliches may be easy to write because they jump from your memory, they are not exciting to read. Each cliche below is followed by a possible replacement to its right.

every effort will be made—we will try	attached herewith is—attached
as per your request—as you asked	upon receipt of—having received
as a general rule—generally	under separate cover—separately
I will be most grateful if—Please	afford an opportunity—allow
for the reason that—because	based on the fact that—because of

Avoid strings of prepositional phrases. Some prepositional phrases may be necessary to join ideas, but too many of them can be distracting. Whenever possible, revise sentences to remove excessive prepositional phrases.

WEAK:	The drop in deposits by students in their accounts at the bank is of great concern for management.
IMPROVED:	Decreasing student bank deposits concerns management.
WEAK:	The EPA office in Lawrence plans to send out warnings to residents about possible contamination from lead in the water.
IMPROVED:	The Lawrence EPA office will warn residents about possible lead-contaminated water.

The Inside Track: Apply What You Learned

1. Revise the following sentences to omit the *There is/There are* and *It* openings.
   a. There are ten cases of welding rods on order.
   b. It is certain that the SCSI cable to connect the CD-ROM to the computer is missing.
   c. There is a solution that strips the silver from the film to create the photographic contrast.
   d. It is phosphate that encourages growth of algae in the river.

2. Revise the following sentences to eliminate unnecessary modifiers, redundancies, and needless phrases.
   a. The new packaging, which is oval in shape, has proven "quite satisfactory" in tests in the northeast market.
   b. The CAD software is 5 percent faster than it was prior to the upgrade.
   c. Designers should be aware of the fact that hidden cameras record their production process.
   d. In this modern day and age, we expect almost all jobs to involve computer use.

3. Revise the sentences below to replace the *-ion* nouns with stronger action verbs.

    a. The bulletin provides a description of a closed electrical circuit.

    b. The committee took our amendment into consideration.

    c. The continuation of Patrice's project depends on the financial support of UpStart.

    d. The Research Division presented a recommendation that all toxic wastes be disposed of through Standard Corporation.

    e. The synthetic fibers make an action like natural filament.

4. Revise the following sentences to omit cliches and unnecessary prepositional phrases.

    a. As per your request, I am sending the antenna to fit your AS302 model.

    b. The combinations of fragrance seem to sell well in areas of large metropolitan population in the United States.

    c. The toner cartridge for the LaserWriter needs to be replaced with care.

    d. With precision and swiftness, the photographer loaded the film into the camera.

    e. I will be most grateful if you can afford me an opportunity to interview for the vacant position in your accounting area.

USING NUMBERS

The following rules are generally accepted as guidelines to help you decide when to write numbers as figures and when to write numbers as words in technical documents.

1. Generally, use *figures* for numbers 10 and above. Use *words* for numbers one through nine.

> Oleander Community College presented 22 partial scholarships and 15 full scholarships to first-year students.
>
> Two of my cousins and four of my friends accepted part-time employment.

2. Use *figures* when a series contains numbers above and below 10.

> Her fortune included 5,498 acres of land, 173 paintings, 3 mansions, and 5 horses.

3. Use *figures* when several numbers (including fractions) are presented in a single sentence or in several related sentences.

> Fry 2 cups of sliced apples in ¾ cup of honey, ⅛ cup of apple cider vinegar, and 1 tablespoon of cinnamon.

4. Use *figures* for units of measurement. Note that the unit of measurement may be expressed as a word, an abbreviation, or a symbol.

18 meters	5 ⅓	4.25 liters	55 mph
5.5 centimeters	66 ⅔	75 MHz	35 mm film
0.05 margin of error	14.4 K baud	32°	8″ x 10″

5. Use *figures* for fractions and decimals presented with whole numbers.

5 ⅓	66 ⅔	72.6	10.25

6. Use *figures* to express exact amounts of money.

$181.95	8¢	$0.95

7. Use *figures* for data presented in tables and illustrations.

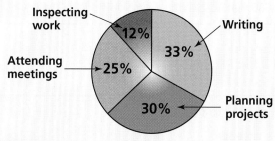

Figure 1 Time Spent on Tasks

8. Use *figures* for addresses and dates.

Route 5 Box 182   103 East Maple Street   January 3, 1865

9. Use *figures* to express age.

3 years old   man in his 20s   an 18-year-old woman

10. Use *figures* for identification numbers.

> The correct number is 378-18-3555.
>
> The engine number is JEMH00347WE99678.

11. Use *figures* for one of two numbers written next to each other.

two 37-cent stamps   16 two-liter drinks

12. Use *figures* to indicate time not expressed with o'clock.

8 a.m.   12:10 p.m.

13. Use *figures* for statistics and scores.

> The odds were 3 to 1 in her favor.
>
> The Grover Bears won the basketball game, 76–74.

14. Use *figures* for page and volume numbers.

> Turn to page 45 in volume 2 of your manual.

15. Use *figures* and *words* for very large numbers (over 6 digits).

$6 trillion   4 million people   5.3 billion years

16. Use *words* at the beginning of a sentence. Rewrite awkward sentences so that the numbers are written as figures within the sentence.

> Nine thousand seven hundred and sixty-six citizens signed the petition.
>
> The petition contained 9,766 signatures.

17. Use *words* for indefinite or approximate numbers.

> More than one hundred people attended.
>
> Approximately fifty tickets were sold.

18. Use *words* for fractions not connected to whole numbers.

> Approximately three-fourths of the children have been vaccinated.

19. Use *words* for ordinals below 10. Use *figures* plus last letters of the ordinal for ordinals over 10.

   third base   ninth inning   10th person   21st birthday

The Inside Track: Apply What You Learned

Using the guidelines above, rewrite the following passages to present numbers as figures and numbers as words.

1. Penguin is the common name for fifteen species of flightless marine birds. They live on four continents in the Southern Hemisphere. One penguin, the Galapagos, lives within six degrees of the equator. Penguins can swim through the water at speeds of up to twenty-five miles per hour. The largest species, the emperor penguin, ranges from three to four feet tall. The smallest, the Adelie, stands about two feet tall.

2. On the twenty-third of February in the year nineteen hundred and eighty seven, one hundred forty-two mallards were tagged off the coast of Florida. For five years, researchers tracked approximately seventy of the mallards over three hundred and ninety-seven miles. The ducks survived in temperatures as low as minus ten degrees Celsius. A report was distributed to twenty-seven agencies in seven states. The research cost six thousand forty five dollars and fifty-six cents. It is estimated that seven and one half million mallards inhabit the southeastern area of the United States. Biologists estimate that ninety percent of the mallards follow predictable patterns of migration.

CLARITY

Good technical writing is clear. To make your writing clear, follow these suggestions:

1. Use traditional *S-V-MODIFERS, S-V-OBJECT,* or *S-V-COMPLEMENT* word order.

   - *Incorrect:* Over the river and two streets down is where we live.

   - *Correct:* We live over the river and two streets down.

   - *Incorrect:* The dishes she washed.

   - *Correct:* She washed the dishes.

   - *Incorrect:* Windy was the day.

   - *Correct:* The day was windy.

2. Write moderately short sentences (12-24 words).

   - *Incorrect:* The registration procedure begins with the student making an appointment with his or her adviser at which time the adviser and student will discuss the student's career goals, placement test scores, and transcripts to determine a schedule of classes that the adviser will enter into the computer and that the student will pay for before the registration period ends—that is, unless the computers are down, in which case the student must come back another time.

   - *Correct:* The registration procedure begins with the student making an appointment with his or her adviser. At this time, the adviser and student will discuss career goals, placement test scores, and transcripts to determine a schedule of classes. Next, the adviser will enter the schedule into the computer. The student will pay for the classes by the end of the registration period. If the computers are down, the student must come back.

3. Place the main idea (the subject or topic) first.

   - *Incorrect:* Kittens like to chase balls of string around the floor. They also enjoy chasing their mothers' tails. Kittens like to pretend they are attacking something that's hiding under a table. Kittens like to play.

   - *Correct:* Kittens like to play. They like to chase balls of string around the floor. They also enjoy chasing their mothers' tails. Kittens like to pretend they are attacking something that's hiding under a table.

4. Use *active voice*—unless you have a good reason to use *passive voice*.

   - *Incorrect:* The new computers were purchased by the school board.

   - *Correct:* The school board purchased the new computers.

(See also The Inside Track: Active Voice and Passive Voice on pages 394–396)

5. Use parallel structure.

- *Incorrect:* Orientation consisted of the following activities:
  - Meeting our adviser
  - Tour the campus
  - Placement tests

- *Correct:* Orientation consisted of the following activities:
  - Meeting our adviser
  - Touring the campus
  - Taking placement tests

(See also The Inside Track: Parallelism on pages 382–384)

6. Use *first person* (*I* or *we*) whenever possible.

- *Incorrect:* The defective parts were returned to the company.

- *Correct:* We returned the defective parts to the company.

7. Choose precise nouns and verbs.

- *Incorrect:* Last night the local school team won the football game against a nearby rival.

- *Correct:* Wednesday, October 16, 20—, the Midland Junior Varsity Bears defeated the Chocowan Junior Varsity Mountain Lions 26–0.

The Inside Track: Apply What You Learned

1. Using the suggestions presented above, rewrite this paragraph to make the sentences and the message clearer.

   First he hoed a small area until the dirt was broken up. Then he raked out the clumps of grass, pulling up those stubborn weeds. The fertilizer was lightly put on and worked into the ground with a hoe. Next, plastic stuff was placed all over the plot of land and stuck to the ground at intervals of 3 feet to keep the grass from growing and to allow the rain to drain through and bring needed moisture to the roots. Then holes were cut in the plastic stuff, not too far apart. Francois planted some flowers through the plastic stuff into the ground. Then over the plastic stuff and around the plants pebble rocks were placed to hold down the plastic and so the area would look neat. Francois made planting a garden look easy.

2. The following sentences lack clarity. Revise these sentences to make the meaning clearer.
   a. The speed limit is somewhere between 50 and 60 mph.
   b. The tickets are to be distributed sometime next week by the committee.
   c. In came my father to tell me the good news.
   d. Maintain good health by exercising regularly, eating a balanced diet, and for goodness sake, keep a positive attitude.

ACTIVE AND PASSIVE VOICE

Which of these sentences do you like better and why?

ACTIVE VOICE:	Maria hit the ball during Saturday's game.
PASSIVE VOICE:	The ball was hit during Saturday's game by Maria.

Most people prefer the first sentence because it is direct, short, and interesting. As a result, it is easier to read than the second sentence.

Look at the verbs in each sentence. The active voice sentence uses only one verb. The passive voice sentence uses two verbs: the verb *to be* + the past participle of another verb. (The verb *to be* includes *is, am, are, was, were, to be, been,* and *being.*) The past participle is simply the past tense form of the verb that uses a helping verb.

Look at the subject in each sentence. In the active voice sentence, the subject is the *doer* of the action. In other words, *Maria* performs the action: she hits the ball. In the passive voice sentence, the subject is being acted upon. In other words, the ball was acted upon (was hit) by Maria.

Use active voice when you want to emphasize an action. Because active voice sentences are more direct, you should write in active voice unless you have a very good reason for writing in passive voice. Sometimes there are good reasons to use passive voice.

1. If you do not know the doer of the action, passive voice gives you the opportunity to leave out the doer.

    Passive: The money was taken.

    Active: ? took the money.

2. Maybe you know who the doer is, but don't want to say. Sometimes passive voice can help you be diplomatic or polite.

    Passive: Your blueprints have been delayed.

    Active: We lost the blueprints.

    Passive: The vase was broken.

    Active: You broke the vase.

3. Scientific writing calls for an objective tone, which is hampered when the doer of the action is included in the sentence. Scientific writing tries to focus on the process, not the person.

    Passive: The fluid volume was increased 20% by adding sodium.

    Active: The fluid volume increased by 20% with the addition of solution.

4. Sometimes the receiver of the action is more important than the doer. You might want to emphasize the receiver by using passive voice. Ads, in particular, like to stress *you* as the receiver of services companies can offer.

> Passive: Richard Nixon was elected president for two terms.
>
> Active: The people of the United States elected Richard Nixon president for two terms.

> Passive: You are kept up-to-date with *Newsweek*.
>
> Active: *Newsweek* keeps you up to date.

Changing Voice: Passive to Active. Look for two-word passive voice verbs, the verb *to be* and the past participle. If you see that a report contains too many passive voice sentences, convert the passive verbs to one-word active verbs by 1) placing the doer as the subject of the sentence, 2) adding a doer that is not included in the sentence, or 3) turning the simple subject of the verb into a direct object.

> Passive: The car was repaired by the mechanic.
>
> Active: The mechanic repaired the car.

> Passive: The window was replaced last month.
>
> Active: Calvin replaced the window last month.

Changing Voice: Active to Passive. If your science report calls for more passive voice constructions, decide what process, material, or mechanism you want to emphasize and place that item in the subject position. Make sure your verb includes *to be* + the past participle.

Try changing the direct object of the verb into the simple subject of the passive voice verb.

> Active: The scientist added a cooling agent to the compound.
>
> Passive: A cooling agent was added to the compound.

> Passive: The window was replaced last month.
>
> Active: Calvin replaced the window last month.

The Inside Track: Apply What You Learned

1. Find the passive voice verbs in the following sentences. Then change these passive voice sentences to active voice:
   a. The accident report is submitted by the manufacturing engineer.
   b. My homework was lost on the computer.
   c. The key to my house has been lost.
   d. The Area VI Tennis Classic is being sponsored by the Alpha Deltas in May.

e. The blueberry bushes were ordered by my sister, who is landscaping the backyard.

f. According to our parents, my brother and I are needed to run errands for the family business this Saturday.

2. Locate the active voice verbs. Then change these active voice sentences into passive voice.

   a. John Hinkley shot President Reagan.

   b. The chemist introduced sulfuric acid to the mixture.

   c. Sally Malone, your teacher's aide, sent three difficult students to the office last week.

   d. An unknown person robbed Mr. Miller's convenient mart.

   e. Onyx Computer provides you with complete support.

   f. You waste fuel when you idle your car at stop signs.

3. Read the memo below. Consider the content and identify the audience. Decide which verbs should be active voice and which should be passive voice and revise accordingly.

   TO: Salvadore Alvarez, Public Relations Director

   FROM: Elenore Lucia, Crew Chief, Graphics

   DATE: 31 October 20—

   SUBJECT: Production Delay for Employee Apreciation Project

The artwork you requested for the Employee Appreciation display will not be ready for the 15 November 20— deadline. While the Graphics professionals usually are very aware of scheduling, this time my assistant, Frank Stankwych, overlooked two other major projects.

Despite our problems, some of your requests will be completed on schedule. The two lighted stars can be hung from the skylight. The posters covered with employees' photographs may be printed. In addition, Erin Taft and Vinnie Delgado will produce the traditional Employees of the Year Awards booklet. The booklet will be available to visitors and staff beginning 1 December.

GENDER-UNBIASED LANGUAGE

Technical writers should be sensitive to diversity in the workplace. One way to begin is to use gender-unbiased language.

1. Avoid biased language by choosing words that include both genders.

USE	RATHER THAN
representative	Congressman
firefighter	fireman
police officer	policeman
mail carrier	mailman or postman
chair/presiding officer	chairman
supervisor/manager	foreman
synthetic	manmade
polite	ladylike
doctor	woman doctor
nurse	male nurse
people/humanity/human beings	mankind

2. Avoid biased language by using pronoun references that include both genders.

The sentence below implies that all scientists are men:

> Each scientist files his laboratory's OSHA report after completing his quarterly review.

Two ways to solve this problem are 1) to reword the sentence to omit any reference to gender and 2) to include both genders:

    a. Each scientist files the laboratory OSHA report after completing the quarterly review.

    b. All scientists file their laboratories' OSHA reports after completing their quarterly review.

    c. Each scientist files his or her laboratory's OSHA report after completing the quarterly review. (Using *his* or *her* can be awkward if repeated in a number of sentences.)

3. Avoid biased language by referring to men and women in the same way when using courtesy titles in similar situations. The preferred title for women (unless you know the woman's preference) is *Ms.*

USE THIS	NOT THIS
David Griego and Erica Stokes	David Griego and Erica
Mr. Barnes and Ms. Carlisle	Peter Barnes and Ms. Carlisle
Jeff and Cara Peterson	Mr. and Mrs. Jeff Peterson
Carol and Anthony Russo	Carol Russo and her husband

4. Avoid biased language in letter salutations by including both sexes. Of course, you should use the receiver's name if at all possible. When you cannot determine the receiver's name, these options may be used:

    a. Use a job title.

       Dear Personnel Officer:

    b. Omit the salutation and complimentary close (simplified letter style).

    c. As a last choice, use either of the following:

       Dear Sir or Madam:

       Dear Madam or Sir: (alphabetical)

The Inside Track: Apply What You Learned

Revise the sentences below to eliminate biased language.

1. Each of the paratroopers was trained to his maximum ability.

2. Miss Maxine Falkner, Faustino Diaz, and Ronald Heinz are listed as having senior security clearance.

3. Jarrod should address his employment cover letter to "Dear Sir."

4. Any businessman needs to be aware of his educational options.

5. The nurse must record her observations in the patients' charts.

6. All mankind is responsible for making the earth a cleaner, safer place to live.

7. Mrs. Hillary Rodham Clinton, Attorney General Janet Reno, and Al Gore appeared in the photograph.

8. The foremen will file their reports with the CPD director each Friday.

9. The woman doctor should begin her letter to the Swiss hospital administrator with "Dear Sir" since she does not know the administrator.

10. Did you ever want to be a fireman or a policeman when you were young?

YOU ATTITUDE

With the exception of the science lab report, most technical writing should be reader-centered rather than writer-centered. A reader-centered approach, or *you* attitude, attempts to look at situations from the reader's perspective instead of the writer's perspective. The *you* attitude points out advantages to the reader and makes him or her more likely to accept what you say.

You will use the *you* attitude to persuade your audience to think or act in a certain way. For example, you might send an e-mail to your supervisor asking for time off, a letter to a newspaper editor opposing a proposed city curfew, or a letter to a dry-cleaning service department asking for a reduction in your bill because your clothes were not clean when you picked them up.

Notice the difference between the *I* or *we* attitude and the *you* attitude in the following examples. The *you* attitude sounds friendlier, more positive.

PARENT:

I or *we* attitude:

I don't want to see that basketball left outside again. The wind will blow it down the street, and it will be gone!

You attitude:

Remember to put away your basketball. If you leave it outside, the wind might blow it down the street and you might not be able to find it.

MANUFACTURED-HOME DEALER:

I or *we* attitude:

Do we, at Mountain View Homes, have deals! Our 14 x 70 single-wides have been marked down 20%. And our 14 x 80s can be purchased with a rebate of $1000!

You attitude:

You can find a real deal at Mountain View Homes. You can purchase our 14 x 70 single-wides at 20% off the regular price. And you can receive a rebate of $1000 on a brand new 14 x 80.

In the first example, the *you* attitude points out the advantages to a son or daughter of putting away a basketball. In the second example, the *you* attitude stresses how a customer can benefit from buying a home from Mountain View Homes. Not only is the *you* approach psychologically smart as a motivator, but it also makes a good sales pitch.

To use the *you* attitude, simply consider the situation from your reader's standpoint. What is the advantage to him or her? Then, where appropriate, add more *you*'s and *your*'s to your message and take out some of the *I*'s, *we*'s, or company names. Point out the benefit of your message to your reader.

1. Rewrite these sentences to reflect a stronger *you* attitude. Remember, you can't eliminate uses of *I, we,* and company names, but you can slant the writing to be more reader-centered. Add any information that may help the reader see the advantages to him or her.

   a. We will ship the rest of your order next week.

   b. Powell Insurance Company is reliable. We have been in business for more than 50 years at the same location.

   c. I want you to take the conversational Spanish classes for several reasons.

   d. Your overdue account must be paid within 30 days, or we will give you a poor credit rating and stop taking your orders.

   e. We do not have your order in stock. We will notify you when we do.

   f. I expect you to be home by midnight for several reasons.

   g. I don't think you should choose clothes that are difficult and time-consuming to take care of.

   h. We want all students to stay on the school grounds during lunch so they won't be late for class.

   i. We have marked down all furniture for our moving sale. We'd rather sell the furniture than move it. Everything must go!

   j. The university requires you to take 30 semester hours of general college courses.

2. Rewrite this garage sale announcement to reflect a stronger *you* attitude.

   Our Volunteer Club has many items for sale. Our members are selling tapes, CDs, and T-shirts we have never worn. One member is bringing boxes full of science fiction novels. We are selling game cartridges and earrings. The earrings are handcrafted by one of our members. We have a set of golf clubs, a black-and-white TV, and a chest of drawers. These items and many more can be seen at 2323 East Third Street on Saturday morning at 6 a.m. We hope to raise enough money to help victims of the recent floods in our area.

EFFECTIVE TRANSITIONS

Like any good writing, technical documents need logical connections between ideas. These connections make writing smooth and improve comprehension. Four techniques help a writer to achieve these logical relationships between ideas and between sentences and paragraphs:

- Repeated key words

- Pronouns

- Parallel structures

- Transitional terms

REPEATED KEY WORDS

Repeated key words often refer to the topic or the important information in a document. They remind readers of what is significant in the discussion or what the document is trying to achieve. For example, if you were writing about lumber cut for housing construction, you might begin with the word *lumber* and later repeat that word or use synonyms such as *boards, logs, planks,* or *timber.*

PRONOUNS

While repeating key words can improve coherence, using the same word over and over can become boring. So writers also use pronouns to tie ideas together. Read the partial instructions below to see how the use of pronouns connects ideas and improves coherence.

> When you're planning to paddle down a river, get an accurate, large-scale map and mark the rapids on it. Study it and keep it handy. Rapids are caused by a drop in the riverbed, so remember that you might not see them when you approach.

The pronoun *it* refers to *map,* and the pronoun *them* refers to *rapids.* The difference in the singular *it* (*map* is singular) and the plural *them* (*rapids* is plural) keeps readers from becoming confused.

PARALLEL STRUCTURES

Writers also use parallel structures to link content within and between sentences. Like parallel lines in math, parallel structures in writing mean grammatically similar words, phrases, and sentences, as in these examples.

> My favorite winter sports are ice fishing, skiing, snowboarding, and skating.
>
> NOT
>
> My favorite winter sports are ice fishing, skiing, snowboarding, and to skate.

> As a parent, I care about the safety of my children. As a police officer, I care about the rights of individuals. And as a citizen, I care about getting criminals off the streets.
>
> NOT
>
> As a parent, I care about the safety of my children. The rights of individuals is important to me in my role as a police officer. Because I am a concerned citizen, I want to get criminals off the streets.

The repeated grammatical structure helps to connect ideas.

TRANSITIONAL TERMS

Transitional terms (or transitions), the fourth technique for improving coherence, are words or phrases that highlight the relationships between ideas.

Below is a list of some transitional terms you might use. The note on the left indicates the relationship the term implies in its connection.

MEANING	TRANSITIONAL TERMS
Addition	also, in addition, moreover, furthermore, and, as well as, besides
Contrast	but, however, yet, nevertheless, on the contrary, on the other hand
Time	before, after, currently, afterward, during, later, now, recently, then, meanwhile, while, at the same time
Emphasis	in fact, of course, indeed, truly
Example	for instance, for example, to illustrate
Sequence	first, second, third, etc.; next; finally; last
Cause and effect	therefore, consequently, thus
Similarity	likewise, similarly, also, in the same way

Below is a paragraph showing how transitional terms can be used to improve coherence.

> This past summer I had guests from Sweden who told me about cooking in bed. At first, I thought my friend sat in bed while preparing vegetables. No, she told me that she literally cooks her food in bed while she goes to the beach. For example, she starts potatoes on the stove and, once the water is boiling, removes the pot from the stove, places it in the bed, and surrounds it with blankets. The potatoes are done when she returns a few hours later. However, I would be concerned about bacteria growing during this kind of low-temperature slow cooking.

The Inside Track: Apply What You Learned

1. Identify transitional elements in the following passages.

   a. A thunderstorm is a process. It begins with warm air rising. The storm then feeds on moisture and heat. As the rising air becomes cooler, water drops form from the condensing vapor. A picture of the air currents inside a thunderhead could look like a nest of writhing snakes.

   b. In 1940, Comity's hired its first female employee. In 1948, Comity's made that employee the company president.

   c. The PTO shaft was slightly bent in the crash. Consequently, I cannot operate the conveyor belt.

2. Revise the following sentences to create parallel structure.

   a. With Najik, enjoy scanning that is faster, works more precisely, and which can be more economical than ever before available.

   b. First is the group who reacts to the trend by selling every energy stock in the portfolio. As a result of the trend, the second group responds with a threat to sell every energy stock in the portfolio.

   c. First, select a single or double mat for the print, and then the picture will need a frame, and finally you must choose whether to use nonglare or plain glass.

   d. Security officers will be stationed in the following locations:

      - In the entrance foyer

      - The computing center

      - The president's office will be heavily guarded

      - Two officers will be on top of the manufacturing building.

   e. According to some users, the Turbo 040 is the best upgrade available; others say the best upgrade is the ChipStar.

3. Combine each of the following groups of short, choppy sentences into a single sentence by using transition strategies.

   a. The veterinarian prescribed an anesthetic. The anesthetic was for the dog. The pharmacy could not fill the prescription.

   b. Sound waves that hit a plain wall bounce back to distort the sound. Sonex-covered walls absorb the sound waves that hit the walls. Absorbing these waves enhances the sound.

   c. The problem with the collating machine is worn gears. The mirrors on the collating machine are scratched and are part of the problem. The collating machine's levers, which are bent, are a problem.

   d. To apply for the position, job candidates must fill out an application form. They must fill out the form completely. The candidates must submit a resume. They must supply a list of three references.

GLOSSARY

A

abstract a short, concise version of a longer piece of communication; includes only the most important general information

academic writing the expository and persuasive writing done in academic circles; examples include personal essays, research papers, analyses, and arguments

accommodate to adjust; to change circumstances so that others will be more comfortable or more at ease

active voice refers to a verb whose subject performs the action of the verb; when the subject of the sentence performs the action of the verb

adrenaline a stimulant, something that excites and creates extra energy

ambiguous more than one interpretation is possible; describes writing that means different things to different people

anecdote a short narrative

anticipate to guess or predict before actually reading a passage what kind of reasoning it might present

appendix usually the last element or special part of a formal report; a place to include documents, data, or graphics not necessary to the discussion in the report but perhaps helpful or interesting to the audience

appendixes the plural of *appendix;* usually the last elements or special parts of a report; places to include documents, data, or graphics not necessary to the discussion in the report but perhaps helpful or interesting to the audience

archives collections or repositories of documents

auditory relating to the sense of hearing or perceived through the sense of hearing

B

background knowledge knowledge and vocabulary already learned that a reader calls upon to better understand new information

bar graph a graph using a horizontal axis and a vertical axis to compare numerical data, drawn with heights or lengths of rectangular bars

block style the letter style that aligns the return address, dateline, and closing flush with the left margin

buffer something positive written to soften bad news to come

C

call outs the names of specific parts of a diagram, connected to the diagram or drawing with lines

cautions statements designed to keep a person from harming the mechanism he or she is working with

chart a drawing with boxes, words, and lines to show a process or an organizational structure

chronological resume a traditional resume that provides a history of employment and education in reverse chronological order

citations written indications of the sources for borrowed materials

close-ended questions questions that restrict the number of possible answers

collaborative writing writing with others in a group

conclusions the logical, inductive leaps made after considering all of the details of an experiment; what is learned from an experiment

concurrent testing determining the usefulness of a product or an activity by observing someone's performance while he or she is using the product or engaging in the activity

copyediting proofreading a document for correctness in spelling, grammar, and mechanics and publishing a document in the appropriate format

criteria the plural form of *criterion;* the factors on which a decision is made; things to consider when making a decision. *The criteria are cost and safety.*

criterion singular; a factor on which a decision is made; something to consider when making a decision. *The criterion is safety.*

culture the special beliefs, customs, or values that are specific to a particular group of people or a particular region

D

date line the feature of a press release that identifies the location of a story

deductive reasoning reasoning from the general to the particular

design elements considerations in writing a document that affect page layout; the way a document looks

diagram a line drawing

direct approach a presentation strategy in which you state the main idea first and then explain and support that idea with details

direct quotation the use of borrowed ideas, words, phrases, and sentences exactly as they appear in the original source

documentation a system of giving credit for borrowed ideas and words

double bar graph a graph using a horizontal axis and a vertical axis to compare pairs of numbers, drawn with heights or lengths of rectangular bars

double line graph a graph using a horizontal axis and a vertical axis to compare trends and show relationships between two sets of data, drawn with lines

draft an early version of a document that is subject to change

drafting the stage after planning when the writer actually writes a first, second, or third (or more) version of the document

E

electronic resume a resume that is posted on a web site or sent as part of an e-mail or as an attachment to an e-mail

embargo to prohibit or to request that a story not be published

ethics a system of moral standards and rules that guides human behavior

executive summary a short synopsis of what a proposal is about; written to meet the needs of a busy decision maker; located at the beginning of a formal proposal

experiments the controlled observations of natural phenomena

explanations information coming after a step and providing additional data to clarify the step

expository writing writing to explain or inform

expressive writing writing to express or portray personal observation or feeling

external audience a receiver outside the sender's organization; listeners outside an organization

F

feedback the verbal and nonverbal response to a communication process or product

field research research done in the field, especially through surveys and interviews

field test checking your instructions with a small sample of people to see whether the instructions are clear

fiscal year the operating or business year, a calendar that runs from July to June, rather than January to December

flowchart a drawing with lines and arrows to show a process or series of steps

follow-up letter a letter thanking a prospective employer for an interview

formal outline a listing of main ideas and subtopics arranged in a traditional format of Roman numerals, capital letters, lowercase letters, and numbers (I., A., 1., a.)

formal table numerical information set up in rows and columns and drawn with rules; used to present figures

format the details of a document's arrangement: the type of document, its length, the preferred style manual, and its organization; the layout of a publication; standard elements of a document's presentation

freewriting writing freely to discover an idea; can be open (no topic yet), focused (on a topic), or looping (stopping, summarizing, and continuing)

functional resume a nontraditional resume organized according to the most important function or skill for the job

G

glossary an alphabetical listing of terms accompanied by their definitions, located at the end of a proposal

goodwill the feeling of friendship; the value of doing things that create mutual admiration and respect

graphic organizers portray notes visually with a system of circles, rectangles, and connecting lines that show the relative importance of one piece of information to another

graphics information presented in a visual form, such as tables, graphs, and diagrams

groupthink the tendency of group members to conform to the wishes of the group without thinking through an issue individually

H

hook in a news story, an opening element whose purpose is to engage the reader, grab attention, and lead into the subject; attention-getters; words or sentences designed to engage the reader or to create interest in an idea

hypothesis a pattern to help organize knowledge and predict other events

I

imaginative writing writing such as novels, short stories, drama, and poetry whose situations grow out of fantasy or imagination; events and people are fictional although the themes may reveal universal truths

imperative mood the form of a verb that signals a command or instruction; the subject is "you" or understood "you"

incident reports reports that objectively relate the details of unusual events, such as accidents or equipment malfunctions

indirect approach a presentation strategy in which the main idea is not presented up front; you build evidence to convince the audience of your point

inductive reasoning reasoning from the particular to the general

inferences judgments about reading that the author does not make for the reader

informal outline a listing of main ideas and subtopics arranged in a less traditional format of single headings and indented notes

informal table a simple table with two or three items, drawn without rules and stubs

internal audience a receiver inside the sender's organization; listeners within an organization

J

jargon the highly specialized language of a discipline or technical field

K

keywords important words, especially nouns, in a scannable resume that match the employer's list of key qualifications

L

letter of application a letter accompanying a resume; highlights major qualifications for a job

letter of transmittal a letter formally or officially conveying a formal report from the writers to the external audience

limitations factors or situations that prevent problem solving

line graph a graph using a horizontal axis and a vertical axis to show a trend or relationship between numbers, drawn with lines

literary reading reading literature such as short stories, essays, poetry, and novels

M

margin notes notes made in the margins of text

Maslow's Hierarchy of Needs the division of human needs into basic needs (physiological, safety, and belonging) and higher-order needs (esteem and self-actualization)

mechanism description a description of a device; includes the purpose of the device and overall description, a description of parts, and the function of each part

media a system or means of mass communication

medium a means by which information is conveyed, such as a newspaper article, a television commercial, or a speech before a live audience

memo of transmittal a memorandum formally or officially conveying a formal report from the writers to the internal audience

memos/memorandums brief written internal communication

modified block style the letter style that begins the return address, dateline, and closing at the center of the page

multiple audience an audience that includes readers whose points of view differ

multiple bar graph a graph using horizontal and vertical axes to compare data, drawn with two or more bars for each measurement

multiple line graph a graph using more than one line to compare data

O

objectivity an attitude signifying that no personal bias or opinion has distorted or slanted a researcher's thinking

online instructions instructions using computer technology as the medium; some types include help menus, CD-ROMs, or web-based instructions

online resume a type of electronic resume posted on a web site

open-ended questions questions that encourage the respondent to provide any answer he or she likes; the questions give no suggested answers

organizational chart a drawing with boxes, words, and lines to show how an organization is structured

P

pace to read efficiently; to read at a rate that is slow enough to allow the mind to absorb information but fast enough to complete the reading assignment

pagination the assignment of sequential page numbers within a document

parallel structure repeating the same grammatical structure of a phrase or sentence

paraphrase presenting someone else's ideas in your own words, phrases, and sentence structure

passive voice the verb *to be* plus the participle of the main verb; used in scientific writing to focus on the process instead of the performer

periodic report a report, issued at timed intervals, informing the audience of the progress made on all of the projects of an organization during the reporting period

periodicals materials published at specified intervals of time, such as magazines, journals, newsletters, and newspapers

persuasive writing writing to convince others

pie graph a circular graph showing how parts relate to the whole; the whole equals 100 percent

plagiarism the act of using another person's words and/or ideas without properly documenting or giving credit

planning the first stage of the writing process during which a writer thinks of an idea and plans how to develop and research it

point-by-point organization a comparison/contrast structure that covers two or three items under one criterion

population the group from whom you want to gather data

prefatory material parts or elements of a report that come before the main text (introduction, body, and conclusion)

preview statements an overview of the order of ideas in a presentation

preview to look over a reading assignment before reading it; to determine the subject matter and questions you may have about the material before reading it

primary sources direct or firsthand reports of facts or observations, such as an eyewitness account or a diary

primary the reader(s) you are responsible to first; the reader(s) who asked for or authorized the document

priority order organized from most important to least important

professional journals magazines or other periodicals published by and/or written exclusively for a particular discipline, such as a journal written specifically by engineers for engineers or by physicians for physicians

progress report a report that tells the audience what work has been completed and what work remains on one particular project during the reporting period

proposals persuasive documents that offer a solution to an identified problem or need

PSA public service announcement; news published for the benefit of the public

public relations plans or actions taken by an individual or an organization to create a favorable relationship with the public

publishing sending a document to the person who requested it

purpose a specific end or outcome to be obtained; what you want your reader to do after reading your document

R

rank the relative importance of one criterion to another; usually ranked from most important to least important

receptive audience readers who are open to ideas or suggestions in a recommendation report

recommendation report a report that helps decision makers compose choices; after comparing and contrasting two or three choices to a common set of criteria, it recommends (strongly suggests) one choice over the other(s)

recursive a circular or back-and-forth motion; describes the movement of the writing process back and forth along predictable stages

reliable data provides results that can be duplicated under similar circumstances

reporting period the time span covered by a report

resignation letter a letter written to an employer or a supervisor stating the writer's intention to resign or leave the company

respondents people chosen to answer questions

results observable effects of an experiment

resume a one- or two-page summary of job qualifications; uses elements of page design to highlight the most impressive qualifications

retrospective testing checking the usefulness of a product or an activity after

someone has used the product or performed the activity

reverse chronological order organized backward through time

revising reading a document and making changes in content, organization, and word choice

RFP request for proposal, an advertisement seeking proposals to solve a problem or fill a need and often listing criteria for the solution

rhetorical question a question designed to provoke thought; a question for which the speaker expects no answer

role the function or job someone performs at work

S

sample a subgroup with the same characteristics as the entire population

sans serif type faces without cross strokes on the tops and bottoms of letters, such as Arial

scannable resumes resumes written to be scanned for keywords by an optical scanner

schematics drawings or diagrams

scientific method using inductive and deductive reasoning and a system of controls to objectively explore natural phenomena

scope the extent of treatment, activity, or influence; what is included and what is not included; what you examine in your efforts to solve a particular problem

second person use of "you" or an understood "you"

secondary audience the reader(s) you are responsible to after you have met the needs of the primary audience

secondary sources indirect or secondhand reports of information, such as the description of an event the writer or speaker did not witness

select audience a single person or group whose point of view is the same

serif type faces with cross strokes on the tops and bottoms of letters, such as Times New Roman

set of instructions a step-by-step list of actions necessary to complete a task

shaping a step early in the writing process during which a writer narrows a topic, determines a direction for a topic, generates subtopics, and organizes the subtopics

sociological influences social factors such as culture, family, and class that cause buyers to purchase certain goods and services

solicited letter a letter of application written for an advertised position

solicited proposal a proposal that is written in response to an RFP or upon the request of a supervisor or manager

solicited report a report in which readers ask for several alternatives

spatial order organized through space as in right to left, left to right, top to bottom, bottom to top, or east to west

stage fright anxiety or fear experienced when a person speaks to or performs for an audience

standard the limits to a criterion; further defines each criterion

step one action in a set of instructions

style the way an author uses words and sentences

subcriteria a smaller category of criteria that fall under a criterion, the larger category; helps to define the criterion

summarize to condense longer material, keeping essential or main ideas and omitting unnecessary parts, such as examples and illustrations

summary a condensed version of a piece of communication; includes general information and may include a few important details

T

technical communication communication done in the workplace; the subject is usually technical; the purpose and audience are specific; the approach is straightforward

technical reading reading science, business, or technology publications

technical vocabulary specialized words used in specific ways unique to a particular discipline

technical writing writing done in the workplace; the subject is usually technical, written carefully for a specific audience; the organization is predictable and apparent; the style is concise; the tone is objective and businesslike; special features include visual elements

tentative outline an informal, changeable plan for organizing topics and subtopics

testimonials personal stories or people's statements (often famous people) endorsing a product or service

text file an ASCII plain text file that can be opened by most word processing programs

tone emotional overtones; the way words make readers feel

trip reports reports that tell what was accomplished during a trip and what was learned from a trip

U

unreceptive audience readers who are not open to ideas or suggestions

unsolicited letter a letter of application written for an unadvertised position

unsolicited proposal a discovery proposal, one that is written because the writer discovered a problem or need and has a solution to offer

unsolicited report a report that has not been asked for; the audience is not expecting the recommendations

V

valid data provides an accurate measurement of what you intend to measure

verbal table information given in rows and columns; uses words instead of numbers

W

warnings statements designed to keep a person from being harmed

writing process the stages a writer goes through to write a document; includes planning (prewriting, shaping, researching), drafting and revising, and copyediting (proofreading and publishing)

INDEX

A

Abstract, 196–198
  defined, 192, 340
  for formal proposal, 348–349
Academic Universe, 53
Academic writing, 2, 15–16
Accommodate, 24, 28
Accuracy, 222
Active voice
  in composing instructions, 179–180
  defined, 170, 216
  vs. passive voice, 231–232
Address, inside, 123–124
Adrenaline, 268, 272
AltaVista, 54
Ambiguous, 2, 16
American Heritage Stedman's Medical Dictionary, The, 53
American Institute of Graphic Arts, The, 146
American Psychological Association (APA), 57–58
Anecdote, 268, 274
Anticipate, 356, 361
AOL Instant Messenger, 186
APA. *See* American Psychological Association
Appendix
  defined, 294, 318
  in formal proposal, 348, 351
  in recommendation report, 310–311
Archive, 46, 51
Asterisks, 246
Audience
  constructing graphics for, 154–165
  diversity and multicultural awareness, 312
  for e-mail, 114
  for employment communication, 242–243
  external, 106, 115
  for graphics, 148
  interests of, 30, 32
  internal, 106, 114
  for letters, 115
  meeting needs of, 27–36
  for memos/memorandums, 114–115
  for oral presentation, 272, 284
  and purpose, planning for, 24–45
  primary, 33
  and reader, 27
  receptive, 294, 302
  sales, 134–135
  secondary, 33
  select, 28–32
  unreceptive, 294, 302
  in workplace technical writing, 11–12
  See also Multiple audience
Auditory, 268, 284
Author credentials, 61–63

B

Background, cultural, 30
Background knowledge, 356, 362
Bad news statement, 130
Bar graph, 142, 157. *See also* Multiple bar graph
Biased language, 34
Bibliography
  defined, 58–59
  in formal proposals, 348, 351
  in reports, 336
Blackboard, 186
Block style, 106, 123, 125
Body, 123–124
  drafting, of informal proposal, 341–342
  of formal proposal, 348, 350
Boldface, 146, 246, 252
Brainstorming, 304–305
Brief correspondence. *See* Correspondence
BTW. *See* By the way
Buffer, 106, 130–132
Bullets, 146, 246
By the way (BTW), 117

C

Call out, 142, 164
Capitals, 146, 246, 252
Caption, 120
Career. *See* Technical writing in the workplace; Writing@Work
Catalog, library, 52
Cause/effect relationship, 368–369
Cause-to-effect order, 88
Cause-to-effect reasoning, 233
Cautions, 170, 175–176
CBE. *See* Council of Biology Editors

Chart, 142, 156
  constructing, 162–165
  decision, 147
Chicago Manual of Style, The, 58
Chronological order, 88, 238, 253
Chronological resumé, 238, 240, 249
Citation, 46, 60
Classifying, 88
Clip art, 12
Closed-ended question, 46, 70–71
Closing, 123–124
Code of ethics. *See* Ethics
Collaborative writing, 80
  advantages of, 97
  disadvantages of, 97–98
  organizing projects, 99–101
College of Wooster, 183
College View, 16
Colon, 257
Color, 12, 152–153
Column, 12
Comma, 257
Commercial organization (.com), 63
Common knowledge, 57
Communication, principles of effective, 112. *See also* Employment communication
Communication Dilemma, 13, 39
  breach of ethics, 208
  checking sources, 373
  disclosing information, 282
  documentation, 57
  external proposal, 347
  good stewardship, 115
  honesty on job application, 253
  job interview, 39
  meanings of colors, 152
  news releases, 223
  online instructions, 187
  recommendation reports, 301
  writing collaboratively, 100
Communication Update
  communication devices, 134
  desktop publishing software, 12
  diversity and multicultural audience awareness, 312
  electronic portfolio, 250
  formal proposal, 350
  free images from Internet, 153
  group presentation, 288
  groupware tool, 99

lab reports, 229
Microsoft Word, 350
mind-shaping software, 363
Online Computer Library
  Center, Inc. (OCLC), 53
resumés, 251
software and international
  languages, 29
trip report, 202
video teleconferencing, 181
World Cat, 53
Comparing and contrasting, 88
Comparison discussion, 309
Complaint letter, 132. *See also*
  Letters
Composing strategy, 342–345
Computerized catalog, 52
Computer media, 186
Computer software. *See* Software
Conclusion
  drafting, of informal proposal,
    342
  of formal proposal, 348, 350
Conclusion(s), 91, 216
  from lab reports, 229–230
  of oral presentation, 275
Concurrent testing, 170, 183–184
Contemporary Authors, 62
Contrast discussion, 309
Copyediting, 80, 83, 93–94
COPY NOTATION, 124
Correspondence, 106–141
Correspondence archives, 51
Council of Biology Editors (CBE),
  57–58
Credentials, author's, 61–63
Credibility, 223
Criteria, 294, 300
  devise, 304–305
  evaluating, 312–313
  for recommendation report, 311
  researching, 313
  setting, 311–312
Criterion, 294, 309–310
Cultural background, 30
Culture, 24

D

Data
  organizing, 88–89
  primary, 68–75
  secondary, 51–55
  valid, 46, 75
Database, web-based, 53
Date
  defined, 216, 227
  line for, 122–124
  style of, 122
  See also Publication date

DATE line, 122
Decimals, align, 150
Decision chart, 147
Deductive reasoning, 216, 230
Definitions, 176, 181–182. *See also*
  Glossary
Dependent variable, 158
Design, 164
Design element, 142, 146–147
Desktop publishing software, 12
Details, 182–183
Diagram
  constructing, 162–165
  defined, 142
  as design element, 147
Dictionary, 94
Direct approach, 268
Direct quotation, 46, 66–67
Discussion, 309
Document
  design and graphics of,
    142–169
  designing, 144–147
  planning purpose, scope, and
    medium, 37–41
Documentation, 46, 118
  defined, 56
  of secondary sources, 56–60
Double bar graph, 142, 158–159
Double line graph, 142, 160–161
Draft, 80, 90
Drafting, 80, 83, 90–91
Drawing, 164

E

EbscoHost, 53
Educational institution (.edu), 63
Educational references, 245
Electronic address. *See* Internet
  address
Electronic media, 147
Electronic resources, 53–55
Electronic resumé, 238, 250–252
Elsevier, 53
E-mail, 111–113, 252
  audience for, 114
  formatting, 119
  personal, 121
  prewriting, 117
  software for, 117, 119
E-mail resumé, 250–251
Embargo, 216, 227
Emoticon, 117
Emotion, 117
Employment communication,
  238–267
  audience for, 242–243
  getting started on, 244–245

Employment letter
  composing, 258–263
  request for interview, 259
  sentence structure, 260
  summary of qualifications, 259
ENCLOSURE NOTATION, 124
Encyclopedia, 53
Encyclopedia Britannica, 53
Encyclopedia Britannica web site,
  53
Encyclopedia.com, 94
*Encyclopedia of Educational
  Technology, The,* 53
*Encyclopedia of Space Science and
  Technology (2003),* 53
Esteem, 134
Ethical conduct, 17
Ethics, 2
  breach of, 208
  for technical communicators,
    18–19
  and technical writing, 17–19
  See also Focus on Ethics
Evaluating sources, 61–63
Examples, 91
Excite, 54
Executive summary
  defined, 318
  in proposal, 336, 348–349
  in report, 340
Experiment, 216, 229
Experimentation, 74–75
Explanation
  defined, 170
  in instructions, 175–176,
    181–182
  as part of message, 127
Expository writing, 2, 11
Expressive writing, 2, 11
External audience, 106, 115, 268,
  271
External proposal, 335–336

F

Fact, historical, 91
Feedback, 268, 284
Field research, 2, 294, 313
Field test, 170, 182–185
Figure, 151
Fiscal year, 192, 205
Flowchart
  constructing, 162–164
  defined, 142
  as part of prewriting, 174
Focused freewriting, 86
Focus on Ethics
  active *vs.* passive voice, 231
  code of ethics in workplace, 14
  copyright permission, 59

evaluate what you read, 360
factual errors in daily news stories, 360
fair representation, 304
honesty on resumé, 257
international businessperson, 275
personal e-mail, 121
problem-solving skills, 339
reports, 209
representing data accurately with no distortion, 159
pharmaceutical companies' responsibilities, 182
stereotypes in writing, 34
working collaboratively, 98
Follow-up letter, 242–243, 260–261
  defined, 238
  model of, 261
Font
  in electronic resumé, 252
  for formatting resumé, 246–247
  size, 12, 146
  style, 12
Footnotes, 155–156
Formal outline, 356, 363
Formal proposal, 335–336
  composing, 346–351
  parts of, 348–351
  prewriting, 347–348
Formal proposal model, 324–334
Formal table, 142, 155–156
Format, 24, 40, 106
Formatting, 119–126
  proposal, 337
  recommendation report, 306–310
Formatting graphics, 150–153
Formatting letter, 123–125
Formatting memo/ memorandum, 120–123
Formatting news release, 226–227
Formatting resumé, 246–247
For-profit organization (.com), 63
Freewriting, 80, 86
FROM line, 121–122
Functional resumé, 238, 241, 250

G

Gale Research, 53
General reference materials, 53
Glossary
  defined, 318
  in proposal, 336, 348, 350–351
  when to use, 181
Good news message, 126–129
Goodwill, 106, 111–112, 242
Goodwin, Doris Kearns, 56

Google, 54
Government organization (.gov), 63
Grammar, 93–94
Grammar checker, 94
Grant proposal, 335, 337
Graph
  construct, 157–162
  as special feature, 12
Graphic aids, 282, 288–289
  guidelines for choosing, 278
  guidelines for creating, 280–281
  types of, 279–280
Graphic organizer, 356, 364–365
Graphics, 142, 147, 153
  audience for, 148
  cluttered, 150–151
  constructing, for audience and purpose, 154–165
  formatting, 150–153
  free, from Internet, 153
  incorporate, in instructions, 177
  integrate, with text, 151–152
  Internet, 147
  learn to read, 370–371
  purpose and objectives for, 149
  sourcing, 152
  who reads, 148–149
Grolier Online Encyclopedia, 53
Group presentation
  answering questions, 289
  dividing topic, 287
  graphic aids and handouts, 288–289
  managing presentation, 289
  setting time limits, 287–288
  transitioning between speakers, 288
Group proposals, 336
Groupthink, 80, 98
Groupware tool, 99

H

HAND. *See* Have a nice day
Handouts, 288–289
Have a nice day (HAND), 117
Headings
  consideration for, 89
  as design element, 147
  in electronic resumé, 252
  in letter, 123
  in resumé, 247–249
Highlighters, 146
Historical facts, 91
Hook
  defined, 106, 216
  in news story, 223

in persuasive message, 133
in sales letter, 135–136
Horizontal axis, 157–159
HotBot, 54
Hotmail, 186
Humor, 113
Hypothesis, 216, 230

I

Idea, shaping, 87–89. *See also* Main idea
Illustrations, list of, 348–349, 351
Imaginative writing, 2, 16
Imperative mood, 170, 179
Incidental report, 192, 203–204
Independent variable, 158
Index, 54
Indirect approach, 268, 272
Inductive reasoning, 216, 230
Inference, 2
Inflections, for oral presentation, 284
Informal outline, 356, 363
Informal proposal, 335–336
  body of, 341–342
  composing, 340–345
  conclusion of, 341–342
  introduction for, 341
  model of, 320–323
  summary for, 341
Informal table, 142, 154–155
Information, organize, for news release, 224
Informative message, 126–129
Informative report. *See* Report
Inside address, 123–124
Instructions, 170–191
  audience for, 173–174
  composing, 179–185
  explanations, 181–182
  field test, 183–185
  formatting, 177–176
  getting started on, 173–174
  guidelines for writing steps, 179–180
  incorporate graphics in, 177
  organizing and formatting, 175–178
  precise details, 182–183
  prewriting, 174
  set of, 173
  steps for, 179–180
Intellectual property thief, 57
Interests, of audience, 30, 32
Internal approach, 268, 272
Internal audience, 106, 114, 271
Internal citation, 60
Internal proposal, 335–336
International date style, 122

Internet, 53–55
    free images from, 153
    search engines, 54–55
Internet address, 54, 63
Internet graphics, 147
Internet Technical Writing Course
    Guide, 305
Interview, 72–73, 75
Introduction
    drafting, 90–91
    of formal proposal, 348, 350
    of informal proposal, 341
    in instructions, 175–176
Italicizing, 246, 252
Italics, 146

J

Jargon, 2, 13, 24, 29
Journal. *See* Periodical
Journaling, 86–87

K

Key, 159
Keyword, 54–55, 238, 251
Keyword connectors, 55
Knowledge level, of audience, 29,
    32

L

Lab report, 216–217, 220
    composing, 230–233
    formatting and organizing,
    229–230
    graphics, 233
    results of, 228, 230
LAN. *See* Local area networks
Languages, international, 29
Left justification, 146–147
Letterhead, 12
Letter of application
    defined, 238
    employee communication,
    242–243
    model of, 260
    parts of, 258–260
Letter of transmittal, 318,
    348–349, 351
Letters, 110–113
    audience for, 115
    employment, 257–263
    follow-up, 238, 242–243,
    260–261
    formatting, 123–125
    parts of, 123–124, 258–260
    personal, 125
    prewriting, 118
    resignation, 238, 242–243,
    262–263
    scannable, 238

solicited, 238, 259
styles of, 125
of transmittal, 318, 348–349
unsolicited, 238, 259
See also Complaint letters;
    Sales letters
Lexis-Nexis, 53
Library catalog, 52
*Library of Congress Subject
    Headings, The,* 52
Library ThinkQuest, 30
Lighting, 285
Limitations, 318, 338
Line graph, 142, 159–160. *See
    also* Multiple line graph
Line graphics, 147
Link, 63
Lists, 257
Literary reading, 356, 359–360
Local area network (LAN), 54
Logo, 12
Looping, 86
Love and belonging, 134

M

Magazine. *See* Periodical
Main idea, 127
Main point, 196
Manual, 175
Mapping, 85–88
Margin notes, 356, 362
Maslow's Hierarchy of Needs,
    106, 134
Mechanism, 368–370
Mechanism description, 192,
    199–200
Media, 216
Medium, 24, 37, 39–41
Memo of transmittal, 318,
    348–349, 351
Memo/memorandum, 106, 109,
    111–113
    audience for, 114–115
    with bad message buffer, 130
    with direct approval, 127
    formatting, 120–123
    prewriting, 118
Memo template, 120
Merriam-Webster Online, 53, 94
Message
    bad news, 129–132
    compose, 126–137
    delivering, 286
    good news letter, 128
    indirect, 129
    informative and good news,
    126–129
    for oral presentation, 272

persuasive, 133–137
MetaCrawler, 54
Microsoft Outlook Express, 119
Microsoft Word, 120, 186, 350
Military (.mil), 63
Milli Vanilli, 56
Mind-shaping software, 363
Mirror, 284
MLA. *See* Modern Language
    Association
*MLA Handbook for Writers of
    Research Papers* style sheet, 40
Modern Language Association
    (MLA), 57–59
Modified block style, 106, 123, 125
Momma, 54
Monster.com, 249
Morse code, 28
Motivate, 133, 135–136
Multiple audience, 24, 28, 32–36
Multiple bar graph, 142, 158–159
Multiple line graph, 142, 160–161

N

National Park Service, 207
New releases, 221–227
Newsletter. *See* Periodical
Newspaper. *See* Periodical
News release, 216, 218–219
    accuracy, 222
    beginning story, 223–224
    composing, 222–226
    credibility, 223
    cutting by editor, 225
    formatting, 226–227
    organizing information, 224
    reporter's questions, 223–224
NewsWeek, 53
New York Times, The, 53
New York Times Index, 53
Nonleading questions, 69–70
Nonprofit organization (.org), 63
Notes
    for oral presentation, 276–279
    repeat, aloud, 366
    taking, 64–67, 174
    taking, on reading passage,
    362–363, 366
Numerical data, 372

O

Objectivity, 216, 229–230
Observation, 73–75
Occupational Outlook Handbook,
    249
OCLC. *See* Online Computer
    Library Center, Inc.
Online catalog, 52
Online Computer Library Center,

Inc., 53
Online instructions, 170, 186–187
Online resumé, 238, 250–252
Open-ended question, 46, 70–71
Open freewriting, 86
Open punctuation, 125
Oral presentation, 268–293
    audience, 272
    check room, 285–286
    conclusion, 275
    graphic aids, 279–281
    guidelines for, 274
    message delivery, 286
    organizing and composing,
    273–275
    personal appearance, 282
    planning, 271–272
    preparing for, 276–283
    presenting, 285–286
    rate, volume, and
    pronunciation, 283
    rehearsing, 283–284
    topic and message, 272
    using tape recorder, 283–284
    See also Group presentation
Organization
    of data, 88–89
    of instructions, 175–178
    in workplace technical writing,
    12
Organizational chart, 142,
    163–164
Organizational strategies, 253
Outline
    for oral presentation, 276–279
    of recommendation report,
    306–309
    for shaping idea, 88
    for taking notes, 363

P

Pace, 356, 372–373
Pagination, 318, 349, 351
Pagination cues, 227
Paper media, 147
Parallel structure, 238, 254
Paraphrase, 46, 65–66
Passive voice, 216, 231–232
Periodical, 46, 52–53
Periodic report, 192, 205, 209–211
Personal appearance, for oral
    presentation, 282
Personal essay excerpt, 6
Personality, of audience, 30–32
Personal letters, 125
Persuasive message, 133–137
Persuasive writing, 2, 294, 302
Photograph, 12, 164–165
Physiological needs, 134–135

Pictographs, 147
Pie graph, 142, 147, 161–162
Plagiarism, 46, 56–58
Planning, 80, 83
    choosing a topic, 85–87
    for oral presentation, 271–272
    proposal for, 335, 337
    shaping idea, 87–89
Point by point, 294, 309
Population, 46, 68
Positive close, 130
Positive statement, 130
PowerPoint, 278
Precision, 231–232
Prefatory material, 318, 351
Preparing, for oral presentation,
    276–283
Presentation. See Group
    presentation; Oral presentation
Presentation collaboration. See
    Group presentation
Presentation graphics software,
    276
Press release. See News release
Preview, 356, 362
Preview statement, 268, 273
Prewriting, 116, 174, 347–348
Prewriting e-mail, 117
Prewriting letter, 118
Prewriting memo, 118
Primary, 24
Primary audience, 33
Primary data, collecting, 68–75
Primary source, 46, 50
Print styles, 146
Priority order, 238, 253
Problem and solution, 88
Problem-solving strategy, 338–339
Process, 174, 368
Professional journal, 356, 359
Progress report, 211
    composing, 205–209
    defined, 192
    model of, 194–195
Pronunciation, for oral
    presentation, 283
Proofreading, 93. See also
    Copyediting
Proposal, 318–355
    composing strategies with
    model, 342–345
    defined, 318, 335–337
    external, 335–336
    formal, 335–336, 346–351
    formatting, 337
    getting started on, 338–339
    for grant, 335, 337
    group, 336
    informal, 335–336, 341

internal, 335–336
    model of formal, 324–334
    model of informal, 320–323
    planning, 335, 337
    request for, 318
    research, 335, 337
    sales, 335, 337
    solicited, 318, 335–336
    unsolicited, 318, 335–336
ProQuest, 53
PSA. See Public service
    announcement
Publication date, 61
Public relations, 216, 221
Public service announcement
    (PSA), 216
Publishing, 80, 83, 93–95
Punctuation
    in resumé, 257
    styles of, 125
Purpose, 37–38
    constructing graphics for,
    154–165
    defined, 24
    plan for audience and, 24–45

Q

Qualifications, summary of, 259
Questioning, 87
Questions, 366
    answer, during group
    presentation, 289
    copyediting, for analysis, 93
    in survey, 69–71
    See also Interview
Quotation, 91. See also Direct
    quotation

R

Ragged-right edges, 146–147
Rank, 294
Rate, for oral presentation, 283
Reading, 87–88
Reasoning, line of, 368–370
Receptive audience, 294, 302
Recommendation report, 294–317
    appendices, 310–311
    brainstorm solution, 304
    comparison/contrast
    discussion, 309–310
    composing, 311–313
    defined, 300–302
    define problem, 303
    devise criteria, 304–305
    evaluate criteria, 312–313
    format and organize, 306–310
    get started on, 303–305
    model of, 296–299
    outline for, 306–309

research criteria, 313
    set criteria, 311–312
Recursive, 80, 84
Reference, 245. *See also* General
    reference materials; SUBJECT
    line
Reference initials, 123–124
Regarding. *See* SUBJECT line
Rehearsing, for oral presentation,
    283–284
Reliable data, 46, 75
Report, 182–215
    abstract, 192, 196–198
    incidental, 192, 203–204
    mechanism description, 192,
    199–200
    periodic, 192, 205–211
    progress, 192, 205–209
    solicited, 294, 301, 303, 305
    summary, 192, 196–198
    trip, 192, 201–202
    unsolicited, 294, 301, 303, 305
    See also Recommendation
    report
Report archives, 51
Reporter's questions, 223–224
Reporting period, 192
Request for proposal (RFP), 318,
    336, 338
Research paper excerpt, 5
Research proposal, 335, 337
Resignation letter
    audience for, 242–243
    contents of, 262
    defined, 238
    sample of, 263
Resources
    electronic, 53–55
    general reference materials, 53
Respondents, 46, 68–69
Results, 216
Results, lab, 228, 230
Resumé, 242–243
    chronological, 238, 240, 249
    composing, 254–257
    electronic, 238, 250–252
    e-mail, 250–251
    formatting, 246–247
    functional, 238, 241, 250
    headings for, 247–249
    online, 238, 250–252
    organizing, 247–249
    punctuation, 257
    scannable, 238, 250–252,
    256–257
    word choice, 254–256
Retrospective testing, 170, 183–185
Reverse chronological order, 238,
    253

Revising, 80, 83, 90–92
RFP. *See* Request for proposal
Rhetorical question, 268, 274
Roget's Thesaurus, 94
Role
    of audience, 29–30, 32
    defined, 24

S

Safety needs, 134
Sales letter, 134–138
    example of, 137
    organizing and composing,
    135–137
Sales proposal, 335, 337
Salutation, 123–124
Sample, 46, 68–69
Sans serif, 146–147, 268, 281
Scannable resumé
    defined, 238, 250–252
    keywords for, 256–257
Schematics, 147, 362, 3356
Science lab report. *See* Lab report
Scientific method, 216, 229
Scope
    defined, 24, 318
    of proposal, 338
    of writing, 37–39
Scott Foresman Handbook Online
    Research Guide Overview, 305
Search engine, 54
Seating, 285
Secondary audience, 24, 33
Secondary data, finding, 51–55
Secondary source
    defined, 46, 50
    documenting, 56–60
Second person, 170, 179
See the Sites
    American Institute of Graphic
    Arts, The, 146
    Chicago Manual of Style, The,
    58
    College of Wooster, 183
    College View web site, 16
    Cyborlink, 30
    document design, 146
    group proposals, 336
    Internet Technical Writing
    Course Guide, 305
    learn to build web sites, 146
    Library ThinkQuest, 30
    Merriam-Webster online
    dictionary, 94
    Modern Language Association
    (MLA)
    Monster.com, 249
    National Park Service, 207
    Occupational Outlook

    Handbook, 249
    Scott Foresman Handbook
    Online Research Guide
    Overview, 305
    Society for Technical
    Communication web site, 16
    take notes on downloaded
    articles, 371
    University of Wisconsin-Eau-
    Claire, 183
    U.S. Department of Labor, 249
    U.S. Food and Drug
    Administration, 227
    Virginia Tech Writing
    Guidelines for Engineering and
    Science Students, 207
    writing center web sites, 227
    writing processes, 117
Select audience, 24, 28
    cultural background of, 30, 32
    interests of, 30, 32
    knowledge level of, 29
    meeting needs of, 29–32
    personality of, 30–32
    role of, 29–30, 32
Self-actualization, 134
Self-assessment, 244
Sell, 133, 135–136
Semicolons, 257
Serif, 268
Set of instructions, 170, 173
Shaping, 80
Sidebar, 12
Siebel Systems, Inc., 357
Signature, 123–124
SIRS, 53
Society for Technical
    Communicators (STC), 16, 18
Sociological influences, 106,
    134–135
Software, 276
    desktop publishing software, 12
    e-mail, 117, 119
    and international language, 29
    mind-shaping, 363
    presentation graphics, 276
    programs for international
    languages, 29
    word processing, 120
Solicited letter, 238, 259
Solicited proposal, 318, 335–336
Solicited report, 294, 301, 303,
    305
Sources, 155–156
    evaluating, 61–63
    for graphics, 152
    note taking from, 64–67
Spatial order, 88, 192, 199
Special features, in workplace

technical writing, 12–13
Spell checker, 94
Spelling, 93
"Spiders," 54
Stage fright, 268, 271–272
Standard, 294, 312
Statistical Abstract of the United States, 91
Statistics, 91
Steps
  defined, 170
  guidelines for writing, 179–180
  for instructions, 179–180
Stereotypes, 34
Stop and Think
  audience expectations of graphics, 149
  audience for e-mails, memorandums, and letters, 115
  brainstorming, 305
  charts and diagrams, 165
  citing sources, 60
  collecting primary data, 75
  copyediting, 95
  define secondary sources, 55
  delivering negative information, 137
  direct quotation, 67
  drafting and revising, 92
  e-mail privacy and security issues in prewriting, 118
  employment communications, 243
  evaluation sources, 63
  executive summary or abstract of formal proposal, 351
  eye contact in oral presentation, 286
  freewriting and shaping, 89
  goodwill, 113
  graphic aid, 282
  group presentation, 289
  heading of recommendation reports, 310
  instructions, 174, 185
  letter of application, 263
  mechanism description, 200
  model proposals, 337
  multiple audiences, 36
  news releases, 227
  oral presentation audience, 272
  order of names, 125
  organizing instructions, 178
  passive voice, 233
  practice organization, 275
  problem solving, 339
  progress and periodic reports, 211
  purpose, scope, and medium of document, 41
  reading strategies, 373
  recommendation reports, 302, 313
  recursive nature, 84
  references, 245
  rehearsal for oral presentation, 284
  reporter's questions, 204
  resumé, 253, 257
  sections of proposal, 345
  solicited and unsolicited recommendation reports, 305
  strategies for online instructions, 187
  summaries and abstracts, 198
  summarizing, 101
  technical reading vs. literary reading, 360
  technical writing compared to academic and imaginative writing, 16
  trip report, 202
Style, 2, 13
Style manual, 40
Subcriteria, 294
Subject, 11
Subjective knowledge, 230
SUBJECT line, 117, 122, 124
Subtopic, 91
Summarize, 46, 65
Summary
  defined, 192, 196–198
  drafting, 341
  See also Abstract; Executive summary
Summary of qualifications, 259
Surveys, 75, 184–185
  population, 68
  preparing, 69
  questions, 69–71
  respondents, 68–69
  sample, 68–69

T

Table, 12, 147
  constructing, 154–157
  formal, 155–156
  informal, 154–155
  verbal, 151–152, 156–157
Table of contents, 348–349, 351
Tape recorder, 283–284
Technical communication, 2, 7
Technical communicator, ethics for, 18–19
Technical reading, 356–377
  anticipate line of reasoning, 368–370
  learn to read graphics, 370–371
  versus literary reading, 359–360
  model for, 358
  pace yourself, 372–373
  pay attention to numerical data, 372
  previewing material, 361–362
  read more in technical subject, 373
  repeat more difficult notes aloud, 366
  strategies for reading technical passages, 361–373
  take notes on reading passage, 362–366
  understand vocabulary, 366–367
Technical research, 46–79
Technical vocabulary, 356
Technical writing
  and academic writing, 15–16
  characteristics of, 11–14
  compared to other writing, 15–16
  defined, 2–23
  ethics and, 17–19
  and imaginative writing, 16
  process for, 83–84
  in workplace, 8–10
Technical writing excerpt, 4
Temperature, 285
Template, memo, 120
Tentative outline, 80, 88
Testimonials, 91, 106, 136
Text, 146, 151–152
Text file, 238, 251–252
Thank-you letter. *See* Follow-up letter
Thesaurus, 94
Time limits for group in presentation, 287–288
  for oral presentation, 284
Title, 152
Title page, 348–349, 351
TO line, 120–121
Tone, 2, 14
  creating suitable, 112–113
  in workplace technical writing, 14
Topic, choosing, 85–87
Traditional style dates, 122
Transmittal, letter or memo of, 318, 348–349, 351
Trip report, 192, 201–202

U

Underline, 146, 246, 252
University of Wisconsin, 183
Unreceptive audience, 294, 302
Unsolicited letter, 238, 259

Unsolicited proposal, 318, 336
Unsolicited report, 294, 301, 303, 305
U.S. Department of Labor, 249
U.S. Food and Drug Administration, 227

V

Valid data, 46, 75
Variable, independent and dependent, 158
Verbal table
  defined, 142, 156–157
  for integrating graphics with text, 151–152
Vertical axis, 157–159
Video camera, 284
Virginia Tech Writing Guidelines for Engineering and Science Students, 207
Vocabulary
  as part of writing style, 13
  technical, 366–367
  for technical writing, 356
  See also Jargon
Volume, for oral presentation, 283

W

Wall Street Journal Index, 53
Warm Up
  analyzing audience for proposal, 338
  attitudes toward reading graphics, 154
  audience effect on what someone says and does, 37
  benefits of planning, 85
  benefits of writing collaboratively, 96
  characteristics of good writing, 15
  composing informal proposal, 340
  computer media, 186
  consequences of misleading statements, 17
  consequences of sending misdirected messages, 114
  criteria, 311
  defining problem in recommendation reports, 303
  differences in writing environments, 11
  documentation, 56
  document design, 145
  elements of formal proposal, 346
  employment communication, 242, 244
  errors, 93
  evaluating sources, 61
  experience with research, 49
  formatting, 119
  formatting instructions, 175
  graphics, 148
  group presentation, 287
  how audience might effect language, 27
  importance of written communication, 111
  incidental report, 203
  instructions, 173
  lab reports, 228
  mechanism description, 199
  message, 126
  news releases, 221
  note taking, 64
  organizing and composing oral presentation, 273
  possible topics for proposals, 335
  prewriting and planning, 116
  progress reports, 205
  public speaking, 271, 285
  recommendation reports, 300, 306
  rehearsing for presentation, 283
  research types, 68
  resumés, 254
  summary, 196
  talk about what you read, 361
  technical reading, 359
  technical writing profession, 7
  trip reports, 201
  using notes or outlines for presentations, 276
  what you already know about research, 51
  writing process, 83, 90
Warnings, 170, 175–176
Web. *See* Internet
Web address. *See* Internet address
Web-based database, 53
WebCT, 186
Webster's Dictionary, 53
White space, 146–147
Who's Who in America, 62
Who's Who in Science, 62
Who's Who in Small Business and Entrepreneurship Worldwide, 62
Word choice, in resumé, 254–256
Word processing software, 120
Work habits, 101
Workplace
  characteristics of technical writing in, 11–14
  ethics in, 14, 17
  researching in, 49–50
Work references, 245
Works cited. *See* Bibliography
World Book Encyclopedia, 53
World Cat, 53
World Wide Web. *See* Internet
Write-To-Learn
  audience and purpose, 24
  correspondence, 106
  document design and graphics, 142
  employment communication, 238
  informative reports, 192
  instructions, 170
  news releases and lab reports, 216
  oral presentations, 268
  proposals, 318
  recommendation reports, 294
  technical reading, 356–377
  technical research, 46
  technical writing, 2
  writing process, 80
Writing bibliography model, 48
Writing collaboratively, 96–101. *See also* Group presentation; Collaborative writing
Writing process, 80–105
  choosing topic, 85–87
  copyediting and publishing, 93–95
  defined, 80
  drafting and revising, 90–92
  planning, 85–89
  shaping idea, 87–89
  writing collaboratively, 96–101
Writing@Work
  audience and purpose, 25
  e-mail communications, 107
  employment communications, 239
  introduction to technical writing profession, 3
  lab reports, 217
  oral presentations, 269
  peer editing, 81
  persuasive writing, 319
  recommendation report, 295
  reports, 193
  research, 47
  self-promotional tools, 143
  step-by-step instructions, 357
  technical writing skills, 171

Y

Yahoo, 54, 186